THE SALOME ENSEMBLE

| THE |
SALOME ENSEMBLE

Rose Pastor Stokes, Anzia Yezierska, Sonya Levien, and Jetta Goudal

| Alan Robert Ginsberg |

Syracuse University Press

For a listing of books published and distributed by Syracuse University Press, visit www.SyracuseUniversityPress.syr.edu.

ISBN: 978-0-8156-3442-3 (cloth)   978-0-8156-1065-6 (paperback)
978-0-8156-5365-3 (e-book)

Library of Congress Cataloging-in-Publication Data
Names: Ginsberg, Alan Robert, author.
Title: The Salome Ensemble : Rose Pastor Stokes, Anzia Yezierska, Sonya Levien, and Jetta Goudal / Alan Robert Ginsberg.
Description: First Edition. | Syracuse, New York : Syracuse University Press, 2016. | Includes bibliographical references and index.
Identifiers: LCCN 2015047512| ISBN 9780815634423 (cloth : alk. paper) | ISBN 9780815610656 (pbk. : alk. paper) | ISBN 9780815653653 (e-book)
Subjects: LCSH: Arts, American—New York (State)—New York—20th century. | Stokes, Rose Pastor, 1879–1933. | Yezierska, Anzia, 1880?–1970. | Levien, Sonya, 1888?–1960. | Goudal, Jetta, 1891–1985. | Jewish women artists—New York (State)—New York. | Women immigrants—New York (State)—New York. | New York (N.Y.)—Intellectual life—20th century. | New York (N.Y.)—Social conditions—20th century.
Classification: LCC NX511.N4 G56 2016 | DDC 709.747/0904–dc23 LC record available at http://lccn.loc.gov/2015047512

Manufactured in the United States of America

To June and Ian

Contents

Illustrations

Preface

In the following investigation a preponderance of the evidence leads to the Salome Ensemble. This was a quartet of Jewish women who immigrated to the United States around the beginning of the twentieth century. They left clues in published and unpublished work, contracts, correspondence, commentary, and court transcripts that draw widening circles embracing these women individually, in groups, and in the encompassing society. These cultural artifacts enable a micro-historical approach to women's history and immigration history. Rose Pastor Stokes, Anzia Yezierska, Sonya Levien, and Jetta Goudal began with four classic markers of low status: They were poor, Jewish, female, immigrants. They ascended socially and professionally, propelled by strong will, talent, and hard work, and became agents of change. These women arrogated power by controlling their social visibility in private and public spaces. They were a disorderly collection, informal, impermanent, and loosely bound by common purposes, empathy, and willful affiliation. They cooperated deliberately and effectively, inside and outside of formal associations, clubs, and institutions. Sometimes they were unconsciously influenced by each other. Together they created *Salome of the Tenements*, a popular novel and a Hollywood movie, which reflected, clarified, and guided their lived experiences. Each built an independent career and engaged in political and artistic expression at a time when they were denied many formal legal rights. They loved but refused to be subordinated to men. They chose to become Americans in the process of determining what that meant. By challenging the status quo they helped advance the rights of women, workers, immigrants, and other disadvantaged people. Of course they were not perfect. The women of the Salome Ensemble possessed many virtues, but they also were deeply flawed, as we all are, and their flaws are as instructive as their virtues. Their achievements proclaim the content of their characters and the contexts of their lives.

Rose Pastor Stokes, Anzia Yezierska, Sonya Levien, and Jetta Goudal have long attracted the attention of literary scholars and political, cultural, and film historians. Yet their friendships and works with each other have been little noted, despite the fact that the intersections of their lives had great significance to them, and more to teach modern readers than their individual affairs and artistic efforts considered separately. Their convergences disclose valuable insights about building identity, solidarity, and social change.

Until now, nothing has been written about what these women did for each other and meant to each other. Until now, nothing has been written about how these women befriended each other, how they collaborated professionally, and all that they accomplished together. Until now, nothing has been written chronicling how this small group of women blended their life experiences into a novel and translated that novel into a movie, contributing, learning, and benefiting each in her own way. Until now, their coalition as an ensemble has not been recognized and explored.

The failure to address these crucial connections is an omission that precludes full knowledge and appreciation of these women and their history. That omission creates the need to relate this previously untold story that cries out to be told. This book aims to rectify that failure, redress that omission, and fulfill that need. Upon close examination, the story of the Salome Ensemble reveals antecedents of contemporary gender, class, and ethno-racial issues with which we still grapple today. These women left a lasting legacy that continues to benefit even those who have never heard their names.

Acknowledgments

One of the satisfactions of completing this book is the opportunity to thank those who composed the wonderful support system that helped make it possible. My studies at Columbia University introduced me to many brilliant professors who became advisors, mentors, and friends. Learning with them was a privilege, a pleasure, and an invaluable education. Foremost among these are Andrew Delbanco, Ross Posnock, and Casey Blake, who provided patient counsel, comment, and criticism while sharing their vast knowledge of intellectual history and literature, and the precious resource of time from their busy schedules. They emphasized the connection of literary to historical and philosophical writing, posed challenging and provocative questions, and directed me to a profusion of important sources of information. These three professors offered guidance, instruction, wisdom, and unflagging support.

I benefited from the resources of many great institutions. The story of the Salome Ensemble was revealed in the Manuscripts Section, the Moving Image Section, and the Motion Picture, Broadcasting and Recorded Sound Section of the Library of Congress; the general collections of the New York Public Library, the Dorot Jewish Division and the Dewitt Wallace Periodical Room of the New York Public Library, and the New York Public Library for the Performing Arts; the Manuscripts and Archives Division of the Yale University Library; the Huntington Library, Art Collections and Botanical Gardens; the Howard Gotlieb Archival Research Center of the Boston University Library; the U.S. National Archives and Records Administration; the National Film Information Service; the Tamiment Library and Robert F. Wagner Labor Archives at the New York University Library; the Margaret Herrick Library of the Academy of Motion

Picture Arts and Sciences; the George Eastman House; the Louis B. Mayer Library at the American Film Institute; the Butler Library at Columbia University and the Rare Books Section of the Butler Library; the California State Archives of the Office of the Secretary of State; the National Center for Jewish Film at the Brandeis University Library; the Women's Film Preservation Fund; the Anthology Film Archives; the Museum of the Moving Image; the NYC Department of Buildings; the New York County Archives and the Business Section of the New York County Archives of the New York County Clerk; the Corsa Collection of the New York Historical Society; the YIVO Library at the Center for Jewish History; the Office for Metropolitan History in New York City; the New York State Archives Partnership Trust; Paramount Pictures Corporation; and Viacom, Inc. This narrative also is informed by the burgeoning literature and commentary about the individual women of the Salome Ensemble and their work.

I am grateful to so many people who provided insight, advice, inspiration, and encouragement throughout this project. I wish to thank Andrew Erdman; John Fabian Witt; Werner Sollors; Matthew Frye Jacobson; Jonathan Sarna; William Schwartz; Andrew Dolkart; Zoran Sinobad; Sebastian Nelson at the California State Archives of the Office of the Secretary of State; Kristine Krueger at the Margaret Herrick Library of the Academy of Motion Picture Arts and Sciences; Sarah S. (Sue) Hodson at the Huntington Library; Judy Schiff and Claryn Spies at the Manuscripts and Archives division of Yale University Library; Alex Rankin at the Howard Gotlieb Center at Boston University; Larry McCallister at Paramount Pictures; Joshua Brown at CUNY; Zachary Loeb at the YIVO Library at the Center for Jewish History; Seangill Peter Bae at Columbia University Libraries; Jay Troger; Anthony Slide; Kevin Brownlow; Erik Brouwer; Do Groen; Sharon Pucker Rivo; Suzanne Wasserman; Jannette Pinson at the Museum of the Moving Image; and Kate Donovan at the Tamiment Library. My appreciation goes also to Deanna McCay and the Syracuse University Press. Thanks to copy editor Jill Root for her patience, insight, rigor, and attention to important detail. Special thanks to Sasha for constancy, cheerful enthusiasm, and empathy.

My desire to produce this work was inspired by the stories of my family members including my grandparents Louis and Sally Ginsberg and

Harry and Bessie Trachtenbroit. Grandma Bessie continued to tell her own stories for one hundred years, and she was among the many teenage immigrant Jewish girls who went to the movies in 1925 in New York City to see *Salome of the Tenements*. My determination was enabled by my father, Irwin Ginsberg, who told me I could do anything I set my mind to, and my mother, Sheila Ginsberg, who still tells me so. I also thank those who are my purpose and motivation, who bring me the most love and joy in all things, and who endured and encouraged the long effort to complete this book: my wife, June, and my son, Ian.

Introduction

The central goal of this book is to find and apprehend the Salome Ensemble. The unifying strategy is to explore what these individuals gave and received from each other, and what they gave and received from *Salome of the Tenements*,[1] a shape-shifting, genre-crossing work that speaks with the heteroglossia of their combined voices. The guiding premise is that this exploration provides pleasure, provokes interest, produces knowledge, and prompts insight. I have deployed various investigative searchlights to support the premise, pursue the strategy, and achieve the goal. If directed with true aim, my thesis is that these searchlights do more than illuminate the Salome Ensemble; they also reveal and clarify details of American culture of the early twentieth century, particularly how certain immigrants found and founded America, and built American selves. Examining these individual lives alongside related works of literature and film is a way to acquire and comprehend otherwise inaccessible knowledge, to expose and observe the force of ideas passing between people in pursuit of personal and social change.

This method places the subjects in historical context even while connecting them to the present. That context includes such cultural movements and moments as the Progressive Era, World War I, women's suffrage, feminism, mass immigration, urbanization, industrialization, and the labor movement. Thoughtful discussion of these compels consideration of gender, ethnicity, social class, and race. The choice to focus on works of imaginative expression as resources and reflections of these particular contributors highlights the aesthetic nature of immigrant assimilation and female performativity. It requires a close reading of the novel *Salome of the Tenements* and the movie adaptation, in tandem with the individual life histories and interactions of the women of the Salome Ensemble. Questions of aesthetics, judgments about what is beautiful or ugly, and ethics, judgments about what is good or bad, are integral to this study. It is, then, about both time-bound and timeless themes.

This work engages in a historicism that straddles traditional modes of literary and historical analysis. The narrative is something of an intermarriage of historical and literary inquiry. As such, it is bound to navigate, negotiate, and honor the customs and pieties of a hybrid scholarly genealogy. That should not be so controversial, although the merits of such an approach have been debated. Richard Rorty argues that literature, and particularly the novel as a form, wields more power than philosophy or history to advance social progress, moral imagination, empathy, and acceptance of human difference.[2] While acknowledging the power of the novel, historian Inga Clendinnen counters persuasively that history, the record of "past actuality," offers resources that even great novels lack, necessary for "sharpening the moral vision by way of an exercised imagination."[3] History, she avers, imposes greater moral obligations on the reader than fiction does, and the alert, active reader feels and learns from this obligation.[4]

I choose to agree with both sides of this argument and to privilege history and literature equally as sources of cultural transmission to be mined for truths made richer by comparison and combination. Ronald Hoffman applauds the power of histories written "from a biographical perspective informed by anthropology, psychology, literary analysis, and material culture."[5] Jessica Lang argues that a "disconcertingly entrenched barrier . . . too often, and at great expense, separates literary and historical analysis," which prevents access to knowledge available to those who "bridge these two modes of inquiry."[6] For Lang, close reading is a "unifying act" of both disciplines. "This idea of dwelling on text . . . goes to the heart of both literary and historical values."[7] Simon Schama commends "the free companionship between literature and history," and suggests that "the truths likely to be yielded by" great historical writing "will always be closer to those disclosed in great novels or poems than the abstract general laws sought by social scientists."[8]

Rose Pastor Stokes, Anzia Yezierska, Sonya Levien, and Jetta Goudal individually require and repay passionate attention. Together, they impart depth and wisdom about each other and their historical moment. Cumulatively their stories create a Rashomon Effect in which overlapping narratives from different points of view limn the collaborators in high relief. They are, as Lytton Strachey said of the biographical subjects of his 1918 *Eminent Victorians*, "too important to be treated as mere symptoms of the past."[9] Nevertheless, they are excellent exemplars of a particular past, the period in early twentieth-century America in which they struggled to create identities and achieve social change. Their life stories and their shifting web of connectivity shed light upon their past and inspire fascination. Their transitive discourse produced the popular novel and Hollywood movie called *Salome of the Tenements*, which entailed the integration of lived experiences in a collaborative effort of artistic and personal creation.

Rose Pastor Stokes was the role model for the fictional *Salome of the Tenements*. Anzia Yezierska wrote the novel. Sonya Levien wrote the screenplay, and actress Jetta Goudal portrayed her on the silver screen. The protagonist of the novel and the film was an amalgamation of her four creators, and, like them, a remarkable combination of Salome and Cinderella.

During the same years that the Salome Ensemble worked together, Albert Einstein propagated the theory that knowledge of certain phenomena can only be obtained by observing them as groups, which he called "ideal ensembles."[10] In Einstein's ensemble theory, they never fuse and always retain their individual distinct particularities. Special, complete knowledge of them is attainable only by understanding their characteristics both as a group and as individuals. They become entangled and affect each other in ways that make it impossible to perceive their actions as other than connected, but their separate identities never are effaced. The women of the Salome Ensemble and the fictional character they created never fused and always retained their separate identities. They became entangled and affected each other in ways that make special, complete knowledge of their actions attainable only by observing their characteristics both as a group and as individuals. Einstein's ensembles were composed of the individual particles that combine to form the substance of the universe. The ensemble theory of this book derives from the individual participants who combine to form the substance of society.

The Salome Ensemble is profitably compared and contrasted with *The Metaphysical Club* of philosophical pragmatists illuminated by Louis Menand,[11] the idea of *Imagined Communities* described by Benedict Anderson,[12] and the *Beloved Community* of Young American Intellectuals who were their contemporaries.[13] These women inhabited what Edmund Burke called a little platoon of society,[14] and were instrumental players in the symphony of cultural pluralism in which, Horace Kallen noted, "the playing is the writing."[15] Together they improvised a harmony that resonated with readers and movie audiences.

These women transgressed the limitations of totalizing, fixed identity-thinking to construct solidarity from willful affiliation, as described by David Hollinger.[16] They moved beyond ethnicity to make connections based on consent, not descent, a transition elucidated by Werner Sollors.[17] They engaged with larger communities of discourse in cultural production in the manner explained by Robert Wuthnow.[18] A systems theorist would note that these women served as ecological resources for each other, as collaborators and inspirations, and also by dint of their association with other groups and institutions such as settlement houses, newspapers, magazines, movie studios, labor unions, political parties, government agencies, and state and federal courts.

The adventures of the Salome Ensemble began decades before their four-year joint project to launch the book and the movie, and continued for many years thereafter. The roots of their alliance reach back to European Jewish enclaves in the last decades of the nineteenth century. Three came from the Russian Pale and one from Amsterdam. They conceived and pursued their own versions of the American dream. All four of these ambitious immigrants separated from their Orthodox Jewish upbringings to enter romantic relationships and marriages with prominent Gentile American men. But their connections to their religious roots were never completely severed. Through their own talent and hard work they became wealthy and famous before 1922 when the novel was published by Boni and Liveright publishers and remained so long after 1925 when the film

Salome of the Tenements was released by Paramount Pictures.[19] Nevertheless, in subsequent decades their names have faded from popular memory.

The lives of these individuals expose the broad contours of the social and cultural landscape in which they lived. To study them, particularly as immigrants and as women, is to fulfill historian Ronald Hoffman's prescription to "concentrate on individual life experiences and how they could be probed for deeper meaning."[20] The full measure of their value derives not from their uniqueness but rather from their exemplariness.[21] They demonstrate, as Jill Lepore has written, how individual lives can serve "as an allegory for broader issues affecting the culture as a whole," and the power of "solving small mysteries about a person's life as a means to exploring the culture."[22]

In books about Theodore Roosevelt, Woodrow Wilson, John Dewey, Cecil B. DeMille, and other "great white men" of their time, Rose Pastor Stokes, Anzia Yezierska, Sonya Levien, and Jetta Goudal might make cameo appearances. In this book the great men are deliberately cast in minor roles while the exemplary women strut and fret their hours upon the stage. By placing them front and center, by refusing to allow these women to fade behind the bold print of palimpsests of the supposedly great and mighty, we discover and recover knowledge about the unfolding of particular lives and cultural issues. That is a production of knowledge relevant and resonant then and now.

Anzia Yezierska had a year-long romantic interlude with the married public intellectual John Dewey that affected both of them for the rest of their lives. I examine that relationship and draw new conclusions about it in the context of Dewey's philosophical pragmatism. I also explore various literary sources of inspiration upon which Yezierska drew, including Tolstoy's *Anna Karenina*, Edith Wharton's *The House of Mirth*, and George Eliot's *Daniel Deronda*.

Sonya Levien married her boss, Carl Hovey, the editor-in-chief of the *Metropolitan* magazine, after her former lover, Sinclair Lewis, married someone else. Levien also earned the avuncular affection of Theodore Roosevelt and the abiding friendship of John Reed. Once ensconced in Malibu as a screenwriter, Levien hosted weekly luncheon salons for the Hollywood elite, serving buffet fare that reflected the cultural melding of

New England Anglo-Saxon Protestant and Russian Jewish immigrant that characterized her own marriage: hot buttered crumpets and tea alongside pickled herring with sour cream and onions, and chopped liver on black bread. She won an Academy Award for Best Screenplay in 1955 for a film called *Interrupted Melody*.

Rose Pastor Stokes was a journalist, poet, playwright, and political agitator who campaigned tirelessly for suffrage, women's and workers' rights, racial equality, and access to birth control. Her uncompromising socialism and communism eventually alienated and estranged her from former admirers. Woodrow Wilson invited her to dine with him at the White House four months before his Justice Department indicted her on federal criminal charges. She was convicted under the Espionage Act of 1917 for writing a letter to the editor of a newspaper. Pastor Stokes married a Gentile millionaire scion of a blue-blood New England dynasty, then divorced him after twenty years and at age forty-seven married a twenty-nine-year-old, poor, Jewish, socialist scholar.

Jetta Goudal was born and raised in Amsterdam. Right after World War I she came to the United States and became an actress. Once, when she was romantically linked to Rudolph Valentino, the actor's wife had Goudal fired from a major Hollywood film in which she was to star with him, causing a tabloid scandal. Jetta Goudal affectionately called her boss Cecil B. DeMille "Papa." She later successfully sued Papa for damages when he broke her movie contract, raising a greater uproar in the press than her Valentino affair. She won the case but derailed her career. That marked the third, but not the last, time in a decade that Goudal had the audacity to sue a movie mogul, establishing lasting judicial precedents and strengthening legal rights of all actors along the way. Goudal remained an incorrigible narcissist, but her unrestrained pursuit of self-interest led down an unlikely path to championing women's and worker's rights, in courts of law and labor union advocacy.

Rose Pastor Stokes rescued Sonya Levien from sweatshop drudgery by hiring her as a secretary. Pastor Stokes actively worked to launch both Yezierska's and Levien's careers, and encouraged them to help each other. When Levien became a prominent magazine editor, Pastor Stokes sent her Anzia Yezierska's short stories to publish. Levien published many of

Yezierska's stories in the *Metropolitan* magazine over a period of years. This support was pivotal to Yezierska's career as a writer. Then Levien got a big break in the movie business when Paramount Pictures tapped her to write the screenplay for Yezierska's first novel, *Salome of the Tenements*. That job served as a springboard for Sonya Levien's fifty-year career as a screenwriter. Jetta Goudal portrayed the main character on film and found in Sonya Levien a sympathetic collaborator willing to listen to the temperamental actress's questions and suggestions, and work with her to fine-tune scenes. Levien apparently was the only screenwriter to win the respect and trust of the irascible Goudal.

Their individual friendships and intermittent professional collaborations had enduring importance to these four women, and their influences on each other remained indelible. Together they transformed direct experience into literature and literature into motion pictures. They provided each other emotional support, useful advice and information, connection to a professional and social network, and career promotion.

The first chapter discusses the historical and cultural context in which the women of the Salome Ensemble connected, and introduces recurrent themes of the narrative. It explores the methods, motivations, and resources upon which these women drew to build personal identities. Chapters 2 through 5 present overlapping biographical sketches. Each derives from the perspective of one of the women of the Salome Ensemble, with attention focused on their connections and their collaboration on *Salome of the Tenements*.

Chapter 6 springs from a close reading of the novel *Salome of the Tenements* and describes the literary, cultural, and personal influences that informed it. *Salome of the Tenements*, having descended into obscurity from the nineteen-thirties through the seventies, in the decades since has been rediscovered and keeps gaining new readers. This discussion delves into the reasons for this growing attention and popularity, including those aspects of the work from which much pleasure is derived, its literary merits and flaws.

Chapter 7 describes the aesthetic challenges, opportunities, compromises, and transformations presented by the translation of the novel from literature to film, the profound changes that different media imposed on the telling of the story, the impact of collaboration on authorship and authority, and what is lost and found in translation.

Chapter 8 expands on the historical, social, and cultural milieu in which the women of the Salome Ensemble worked. I draw conclusions about how the process of collaboration in the production and reproduction of *Salome of the Tenements* reflected and affected the contributors, how the work reflected and affected the social context in which it was created, and some striking connections between the history of the Salome Ensemble and the modern American scene.

Salome of the Tenements was a communal project of pragmatic truth-testing and a social enterprise of defining and designing American selves. It is time to recall the Salome Ensemble for an encore and reveal their compelling stories for twenty-first-century readers who continue to benefit from their artistic, cultural, legal, and political achievements.

THE SALOME ENSEMBLE

| 1 |

Character Building

Salome of the Tenements is the story of a poor, struggling, female reporter for a Jewish newspaper on the Lower East Side of New York City in the nineteen-twenties. The intrepid but highly emotional journalist is assigned to interview a millionaire philanthropist from a patrician Protestant family. The young woman pursues the man by dressing, decorating her room, and behaving in ways calculated to win his approval. They reach across differences in social class and ethnic-religious background, and fall in love. Afterward, harsh reality intrudes upon sentimental romance.

By crafting a persona to achieve her goals, this young woman recapitulates a process of self-creation to which readers and movie audiences could relate. The ethical and aesthetic considerations and consequences of her actions were issues confronted by Rose Pastor Stokes, Anzia Yezierska, Sonya Levien, and Jetta Goudal, the four creators who built the character.

The claim that four Jewish women immigrants produced a novel and a movie requires explanation and evidence. It raises questions about authorship and authority. The answers begin with their identities. The women of the Salome Ensemble were born into European Jewish enclaves where, if they had stayed, their identities would have been received, ascribed, and fixed, not achieved, chosen, and fluid. Spouses, social status, religious practices, and living places all would have been selected for them. Instead, in the America they entered, they learned that identities are multiple, plural, and elective, like careers, spouses, and homes. In their new country, it soon became evident that even identities that are received, such as family or religion, must be voluntarily accepted or rejected, and therefore chosen.[1]

Rose Pastor Stokes, Anzia Yezierska, Sonya Levien, and Jetta Goudal embraced the right to choose how to live their lives. This complex chore of choosing is encompassed in the concept of subjectivity, becoming a social person, exerting control even while admitting outside influences.[2] It is, therefore, simultaneously personal and communal. The process of crafting identity occurs at an intersection of autonomy and community, a nexus between the individual and the group. *Salome of the Tenements* provided such a nexus and served as an instrument with which the contributors imagined identities and fashioned subjectivities. The story follows the central female character's formation and expression of an individual female self. The women who crafted her employed her as a resource for enacting their own subjectivities. The work appeared and reappeared in different forms and formats, revised, edited, and rewritten. The creators, the character, and the work itself are best understood as resisting finality.

Kathy Peiss writes, "It was in leisure that women played with identity, trying on new images and roles, appropriating the cultural forms around them."[3] It was not only in leisure. Creative work also could and did provide similar opportunities for self-invention. In *Salome of the Tenements*, Pastor Stokes, Yezierska, Levien, and Goudal created an intersubjective space in which to rehearse social skills and behaviors, test attitudes, try on types and levels of visibility, and fashion selves. The main character of the story became an imaginary surrogate available for them to experiment with varieties of personal and social comportment and presentation. As they each contributed parts of themselves to the character and the narrative, they also were collaborating in the processes of self-definition. Their experiences are illustrative of the concept of "personality integration," defined as "the coordination of various aspects of an individual's personality with each other and with the social environment."[4] Ross Posnock uses the phrase "uncoerced intersubjectivity" to describe such deliberate encounters with others, and mimesis, imitation, or emulation of their differences.[5]

Rose Pastor Stokes, Anzia Yezierska, Sonya Levien, and Jetta Goudal approached and reacted differently to similar challenges of self-creation, and they infused those differences into the heroine of *Salome of the Tenements*. Personal temperaments and external circumstances compelled these women to make choices, but not the same choices. Many of their choices were influenced by and represented in the making of *Salome of the Tenements*.

Rose Pastor Stokes was, in 1905, a reporter for a Jewish newspaper on the Lower East Side of New York City. She did interview James Graham Phelps Stokes, a wealthy, patrician, Protestant philanthropist and scion of an aristocratic New England family. They fell in love and married. Afterward, various harsh realities intruded on their happiness. While these details mirror the outlines of the story of Sonya Vrunsky and John Manning in *Salome of the Tenements*, the similarities between the Stokes couple and their fictional counterparts mostly end there.

Pastor Stokes was a committed socialist and internationalist. After World War I she became an ardent communist. Her husband's political views were more moderate, and a rift widened between them until it could no longer be repaired. The Stokes marriage deteriorated slowly over twenty years largely because of the political differences between the spouses. There is no reflection of this aspect of the Stokes marriage in the fictional couple of *Salome of the Tenements*.

Instead the romance in the novel evinces striking similarities to the real-life passionate relationship that author Anzia Yezierska had with public intellectual John Dewey, and this correspondence was no accident. The spouses in the movie more closely reenact the marriage of Sonya Levien and Carl Hovey than that of Rose Pastor and Graham Stokes. Anzia Yezierska had been married and divorced by the time she wrote the novel, and the marriage in the book ends in divorce. Sonya Levien remained happily married, and when she wrote the screenplay, she altered the story to save the main character's marriage.

The exhortation to active self-creation in America was consistent with philosophical, intellectual, cultural, and political movements of the era. At the time the Salome Ensemble came together, philosophers including Charles Pierce, William James, Oliver Wendell Holmes Jr., and John Dewey promulgated, promoted, and practiced radical empiricism and philosophical pragmatism in efforts to seek and to create truth.[6] Progressives, social democrats, cultural critics, and intellectuals such as Walter Lippman, Waldo Frank, Randolph Bourne, Van Wyck Brooks, and Lewis Mumford augmented philosophical pragmatism with an added emphasis on aesthetic creativity as a source of values to transcend self-interest, hedonism, fear, and the will to power.[7] The women of the Salome Ensemble became personally acquainted with these men. They knew them, admired them, challenged and emulated them.

Each detail of character development and every plot turn in the *Salome of the Tenements* book and the movie yield insight into the historical era and the lived experiences of the creators. Focus on their social position as immigrants and women sheds clarity on their personal and artistic character building. They navigated an uncertain space between Cinderella and Salome in the quest for status and questioning of authority.

Exiles and Intruders

All four women of the Salome Ensemble were European immigrants to America. The act of immigrating compels the building of a new personal character, self-creation, translation, and transformation. The very first thing immigrants arriving in America are asked to do is identify themselves. This was the deceptively simple request made of the millions who entered at the advent of the twentieth century, stepping off boats in New York Harbor, before 1892 at Castle Island like Rose Pastor Stokes and Anzia Yezierska, and after 1892 at Ellis Island like Sonya Levien and Jetta Goudal. It became clear to these modern pilgrims that the requirement to self-identify carried with it an opportunity to actively build new characters, to attempt to become who they wanted to be. This point of entry was for these four Jewish women the start of a liberating process of self-definition, free of many of the externally imposed restrictions they had been born into. There was a dizzying freedom invited with this opportunity to hitch to a desirable future and slip the anchor of an escapable past.

They were compelled to decide whether to keep their "real" names or fabricate new ones, and what other information to provide, withhold, or reinvent about their personal histories. These decisions were made by the immigrants themselves. Recent scholarship exposes the popular misconception that it was immigration officers who changed immigrant surnames. Dara Horn disputes this "perennial myth," noting that ships' manifests, passports, and other travel documents precluded deliberate or accidental alteration of names by officials. It was the immigrants who decided, and Horn notes that "many immigrants chose new names for themselves in America . . . But that was after they left Ellis Island."[8]

After leaving Castle Island or Ellis Island, these immigrants had to communicate their choices to listeners from whom they were separated by language and culture. They saw what could be lost in translation and what could be found. So much challenge, opportunity, and power were conferred with the implicit authorization to become self-made women. After crossing out of the lands of their origins to arrive at the destination of their dreams, the women of the Salome Ensemble endeavored to reconcile the America they imagined with the America and the Americans they observed. Their American dream confronted their America seen, in a very real instance of ideas facing the test of experience. They had to conceive, articulate, and perform the new selves they wished to inhabit.

It is natural to think of the arrival of immigrants in a new country as the beginning of their stories. But every immigrant is an exile who has ended a chapter in order to begin anew, a point emphasized by historian Matthew Frye Jacobson. Diasporic Jews in particular have been perceived, by themselves and others, as perpetual exiles.[9] One consequence of such exile is recollection of the life and the place left behind, colored by nostalgia, revulsion, relief, regret, and inevitable revision. Jacobson cites Marcus Klein's observation that "[e]very body wants a ghetto to look back to."[10] Remembrances become tempered by serial revisions like rewrites of previous endings. In this way, immigrant beginnings create new endings that accumulate to fashion a usable past. The ghetto the mind looks back to is a product of shifting memory influenced by new experience supported by the legacy of past actuality. It provides a springboard from which to launch new identities. A great example is the fictional Anatevka, the *shtetle* that emerged from the mind of Sholem Aleichem.

Pastor Stokes, Yezierska, Levien, and Goudal were forced to choose how to assimilate, how to cope and thrive in unfamiliar circumstances, how much of the Orthodox Judaism of their personal histories to retain, how much of the margin of difference that distinguished them from other Americans to hold onto and how much to relinquish. They had to observe and decipher Americans and choose what to emulate and what to reject. For a time these four women coalesced around the project of making *Salome of the Tenements*. They found each other and chose to willfully affiliate in what amounted to a solidarity ensemble.[11]

Immigrants are not only exiles. They also are intruders. They pierce the boundaries of the receiving society and disrupt the status quo by their very presence. Whether they are welcomed or shunned, their outsider status is conveyed in the gaze of natives. This status hinders efforts to emotionally integrate present circumstances and imagined past. Looking ahead instead, they confront the new facts of their otherness in terms of language, ethnicity, culture, and customs.

In America, Pastor Stokes, Yezierska, Levien, and Goudal found themselves romantically and intellectually attracted to people whose backgrounds were vastly different from their own, particularly men of wealth and prominence from established Protestant families. Like the fictional character they constructed, they were caught between the longing to belong, to conform, to gain acceptance, and the longing to hold on to past affiliations and the individual differences that set them apart. Such circumstances can drive people to seek voluntary bonds of empathy and the solidarity of willed affiliation. Such conditions stir strong emotions. Stimulated in part by observations of immigrant behavior and relations with Americans by birth, empathy discourse in psychology and philosophy burgeoned at the time of the Salome Ensemble.[12]

In fact, empathy discourse is an apt description of the project of collaborative character building that produced *Salome of the Tenements*. Empathy posits identification and assimilation that efface boundaries. It is a means of gaining access to the interiority of others, beginning and ending in experience. The emotional experience of another provokes the receptive observer to interpretation and introspection, leading to vicarious experience. This kind of "empathetic border crossing,"[13] which allows the assimilation of another's experience, is analogous to the assimilation of immigrants into American society. Art can spark empathetic receptivity, assimilation, and vicarious experience. Lionel Trilling wrote that art "promotes the social sharing of highly valued emotional experiences."[14] Ann Mikkelsen refers to "assimilative empathy" of "immigrant and native alike," which occurred in the first decades of the twentieth century, infusing not only relationships between people, but also people experiencing art, "aesthetic empathy," and even people relating to consumer goods, Walter Benjamin's idea of "empathy with the commodity."[15]

The Yiddish word for empathy or compassion is *rachmones.* Rose, Anzia, Sonya, and Jetta demonstrated rachmones for one another. They formed bonds that began before and endured long after their work on the novel and the movie. Empathy, or rachmones, denotes stronger connections than "pity" or "sympathy." Pity and sympathy imply a level of detachment that can devolve into condescension and disrespect. The force of empathy creates a shared space, a field of intersubjectivity, where emotional knowledge is produced. The bonds of empathy and the field of intersubjectivity are adduced here to affirm, as Louis Agosta writes, that "[n]ot only does the individual belong to the community but the community is an aspect of, is functionally represented within, the individual."[16] Anzia Yezierska's erstwhile paramour John Dewey argued that freedom and individualism could be realized only in the context of community.[17] The connected lives of the women of the Salome Ensemble disclose the struggle of intelligent, creative people in early twentieth-century urban America to reconcile their desires for autonomy and solidarity as they came to inhabit an "intersubjective community."[18] Empathy facilitates the transformation of exiles and intruders into insiders and intimates.

American Institutions

Although personal desires and external influences stimulate the construction of character, the process also requires a combination of resources, experience, skill, and teamwork. In America the Salome Ensemble found many resources for fashioning social selves. The rise of mass media provided newspapers, novels, stage plays, and motion pictures, all cultural forms of imagining that grew ubiquitous and powerful in the first half of the twentieth century. The act of writing for various media served multiple purposes. It was an instrument with which to change society. It was a means to make money. It was therapy. It was an activity through which to make professional, personal, and even romantic connections. Her writing as a reporter is what introduces the protagonist of *Salome of the Tenements* to her American dream man.

Mass media, courts of law, labor unions, corporations, settlement houses, universities, and other American institutions supported immigrant efforts to acclimatize and assimilate. Settlement houses were social welfare institutions, often funded by private philanthropies. Each had its own mission statement and each provided services designed to achieve its goals. Social workers and affluent volunteers taught English, cooking, domestic science, and other classes. "These institutions were generally modeled on the pattern of Jane Addams's Chicago Hull House. Affluent do-gooders and social workers lived in the settlement houses and tried to 'uplift' downtrodden slum dwellers."[19] Addams had modeled Hull House on the original settlement house called Toynbee Hall in London. The settlements often served as popular recreation spots for the young and single. They varied in their methods of providing services to immigrants and attempting to promote assimilation into American society. In a few cases the programs included Christian proselytizing to young Jewish immigrants.

The main characters in *Salome of the Tenements* meet at a settlement house. Rose Pastor Stokes and James Graham Phelps Stokes met and worked together at the University Settlement, and Rose also worked at the Educational Alliance, a settlement house located on East Broadway. Like other settlement houses, the Educational Alliance pursued a particular type of education. "Its function was really to Americanize the immigrant, to remold the young immigrant as an American citizen," notes Mary Dearborn.[20] This aspect of settlement houses as facilitators of the assimilationist, "hundred percent Americanism" goals of some Progressives concerned Pastor Stokes, and caused some pushback among the young women who were subjected to this generally gentle indoctrination in return for the childcare, lending library, recreational, counseling, and other services they provided. Anzia Yezierska was among the young immigrants who bridled at what they perceived as demeaning condescension and misguided coercive instrumentalism tied to the social uplift promised by the settlements. Jetta Goudal spent her first several years in New York City living in the Martha Washington Hotel for Women, a private, for-profit institution financed by many of the same benefactors who supported the settlement houses, an example of philanthropic capitalism.

Law, Liberty, Rights, and Responsibilities

The American legal system was particularly empowering for those attempting to construct and enact independent personal identities in the first decades of the twentieth century. Central plot points in *Salome of the Tenements* involve the legality of a predatory lending agreement, the prosecution of corrupt landlords and loan sharks, and divorce laws. For the Salome Ensemble and their contemporaries, a belief in the rule of law as the basis of American nationhood fostered confidence that order could be found amid the chaos of urban modernity. The idioms of visual imagery and law fostered the evolution in America of Benedict Anderson's concept of a new "imagined community."[21] Richard Hofstadter states that Americans find "the solution to everything in laws."[22]

President Theodore Roosevelt, who became a close friend and colleague of Sonya Levien, applauded the importance of the 1904 Supreme Court decision in the Northern Securities antitrust case as affirmation of the preeminence of law in the United States. The case stood for "the fact that the most powerful men in this country were held to accountability before the law."[23] Early twentieth-century Americans were thus reassured by President Roosevelt that bankers and corporate titans answered to government institutions of law, not the other way around. Early twenty-first-century Americans long for similar reassurance, which appears not to be forthcoming. Hofstadter states that "[i]ndustrial society was to be humanized through law," and that "[t]he insistence that the power of law be brought to bear against such gratuitous suffering is among our finest inheritances from the Progressive movement."[24] "'In America the law is king,'"[25] Thomas Paine proclaimed in 1776. To legal historian Robert Ferguson, Paine was a "prophet of the revolution," who recognized that the rule of law is central to "the conceptualization of American life."[26] E. J. Hobsbawm defines "a *populus* or people . . . by the will to obey a common law."[27] The longing to rely on the rule of law as a modality for pursuing order out of chaos was expressed in American popular culture, especially early motion pictures. Historian Robert Wiebe identifies the "search for order" as one of the most powerful forces driving change in America between 1877 and 1920.[28]

In the course of their own search for order, the women of the Salome Ensemble discovered that American law was profoundly different from the regimes of the Russian czars and the tenets of Orthodox Judaism that had governed their pasts. They found the differences empowering and

liberating. Legal scholar Robert Cover compares and contrasts the foundational myths that underlie liberal Western legal culture and the Judaic
legal culture that prevailed in the birthplaces of Pastor Stokes, Yezierska,
Levien, and Goudal. These different myths give rise to different conceptions of the individual as an independent self and as a member of society.
Cover explains that Western post-Enlightenment legal theory, and particularly American legal theory, proceeds from the word *rights* and the
concepts to which that word refers. These ideas emerge from the founding myth of the social contract, which holds that individuals consensually
enter an agreement in which they surrender certain rights in return for
collective security. Other rights are retained or inalienable. Cover demonstrates that in Judaism, the key word is *mitzvah*, which means command-
ment or obligation to do what is morally righteous. Commandments or
obligations emerge from a very different myth, in which individuals do
not consent to enter a social contract but instead the community is divinely
chosen and the obligations are compulsory, not voluntary.

The different starting points of rights and obligations lead to different
and sometimes contradictory outcomes. "The jurisprudence of rights,"
Cover argues, has been more effective than that of obligations in limiting "the most far-reaching claims of the State" and has been deployed
effectively "in countering organic statist claims."[29] Each of the women of
the Salome Ensemble learned to rely on the power of American jurisprudence based on rights to contend with government force. For example,
the following chapter investigates how Rose Pastor Stokes learned to
navigate the court system in a harrowing but ultimately successful effort
to extricate herself when the federal government of the United States
threatened her with ten years in a penitentiary for exercising her right to
express political beliefs. Cover further contends, "The jurisprudence of
rights has proved singularly weak in providing for the material guarantees of life and dignity flowing from the community to the individual,"
which a system based upon moral obligations is better equipped to fulfill.[30] Pastor Stokes, Yezierska, Levien, and Goudal retained the cultural
memory of ethical imperatives from the reasoning of Orthodox Judaism. They demonstrated this memory by their participation in collective
and individual actions to promote the welfare of the downtrodden and

dispossessed and by reaching back to help others after achieving their own successes.

The women of the Salome Ensemble, along with millions of other Jewish immigrants to America, were confronted with the challenge to resolve conflicting implications of these different philosophical foundations of community and society. They carried assumptions about righteous obligation from their Orthodox Jewish backgrounds into an American landscape constructed on rights theories. This challenge was further complicated by the rise of laissez faire industrial capitalism and the counterforce of socialism, which offered contradictory interpretations of rights and added the concept of "entitlements." In America these immigrants could celebrate legal and social institutions that provided some restraint upon power and assigned to them theoretical entitlements to minimal humane requirements for living. Nevertheless, Cover states, "In Jewish law, an entitlement without an obligation is a sad, almost pathetic thing," and acting to fulfill moral obligation "is the closest thing there is to a Jewish definition of completion as a person within the community."[31]

Legal contracts presented additional practical challenges for these women trying to define autonomy and affiliation, rights and responsibilities. Anzia Yezierska used the street smarts she developed selling and buying from pushcarts to shrewdly negotiate book contracts with publishers. Yet she experienced strong resistance to entering any employment contract. She could sell her wares, but not bind herself as an employee. To Yezierska there was a crucial difference between selling her labor and selling the product of her labor. She saw employment contracts as instruments of constraint, not consent. "[Y]ou know my awful aversion for signing any contracts that would bind me in any way," she wrote to one publisher.[32] In Anzia's view, an employment contract entailed surrendering autonomy for the illusion of security. She viewed a marriage contract as analogous, for a woman. This struck her as volunteering to be held behind the bars of a gilded cage—a fool's bargain.

Sonya Levien was a lawyer, and she had no such anxieties about contracts for employment or otherwise. Levien was confident in her ability to understand and negotiate favorable terms, and she also understood that contracts can be amended or terminated. Jetta Goudal grew up in

Amsterdam where she observed her father conducting business as a diamond merchant. Consequently contracts did not intimidate her. In fact, more than the other women of the Salome Ensemble, Goudal perceived contracts not only as necessary instruments for conducting business, but also as potential weapons to be deployed in disputes. As her career progressed Jetta became an adept and confident movie contract negotiator, and she fired lawsuits at employers who failed to live up to her agreements.

Fashion Agency

Fashion is another vital and highly valued resource for building character. The women of the Salome Ensemble were concerned with fashion in every sense of the word. To fashion, meaning to design, build, and create, describes their production of stories for print, stage, and screen. It also applies to their composition of fictional characters and enactment of their own personalities in the lifelong process of fashioning selves. These activities involved the autonomous and group production of knowledge to guide decision and action. Fashion as used to describe clothing is central to the performance of identity, and was a consuming passion for Rose Pastor Stokes, Anzia Yezierska, Sonya Levien, and Jetta Goudal. Clothing confers the power to conceal and to reveal, as when Salome removes her veils. Fashion also refers to what is current and relevant in a given social context and historical moment. The latest fashion refers to a consensus about what is fleetingly, temporarily popular and attractive. To be in or out of fashion is to assimilate or to retain a margin of difference with the dominant culture. Fashion describes the distinct, personal style of an individual, or a style that is socially sanctioned, accepted, and practiced by many. Visual fashion transcends language, providing a means of nonverbal communication that conveys information about wealth, status, sexual allure, beauty, formality, festivity, propriety, prurience, deviance, or depravity. The harmonious combination of separate elements that complement each other is called a fashion ensemble. The important meanings and messages of clothing and fashion, and also the significance of how clothing is produced and procured, are explored in the unfolding story of the Salome Ensemble.

Female Visibility

Fashion and clothing are components of a larger dialectic of female visibility as an instrument of power and agency. Elective or volitional female visibility is and has been a focus of perennially fierce emotions and combustible disputes in societies past and present. The women of the Salome Ensemble discovered that the ability to control female social visibility is a skill that is necessary and useful to the successful building of character. The strategies of female visibility pursued by these women and their contemporaries contradicted traditional notions of public and private spheres. Scholars Alison Easton, R. J. Ellis, Janet Floyd, and Lindsey Traub note that the dichotomizing categories of public and private spheres "certainly did not constitute the norm for most women" who experienced "critical change in the cultural visibility of women" in the late nineteenth century and the Progressive Era, "whether it was a visibility attained by them, granted to them, or contested by them."[33]

The main character in *Salome of the Tenements* exerts great effort to compose her appearance for her wealthy American suitor. She faces the challenge many American women confronted in the early twentieth century as the imagined boundaries between public and private spheres were progressively effaced. A delicate balance was sought, between the image of Salome's lewd dance and Cinderella's demure appearance at Prince Charming's ball. It is worth noticing that Salome's veils selectively conceal and Cinderella's glass slippers selectively reveal. Tolstoy's Anna Karenina, Edith Wharton's Lily Bart in *The House of Mirth*, and George Eliot's Gwendolyn Harleth and Mirah Lapidoth in *Daniel Deronda* are some of the many fictional characters who confront this challenge of female visibility and power, appearances, disappearances, and defiant reappearances.

Rose Pastor Stokes, Anzia Yezierska, Sonya Levien, and Jetta Goudal exercised control over their personal, professional, and social visibility, choosing when to appear and when to disappear in public and private spaces, literally and metaphorically. They controlled their visibility as an assertion and an instrument of self-agency, self-ownership, and personhood. The rise of mass culture in the early twentieth century was accompanied by the increasing use of female spectacle for various purposes.

Control of one's visibility conferred social, political, economic, and sexual power.

Cultural historian Susan Glenn notes that the complex term "New Woman" was used at the turn of the twentieth century variously to refer to women who "experimented with new forms of public behavior," to "assertive women who defied traditional expectations," and as a "symbol of women's longing for personhood."[34] A "highly visible group of unorthodox females," using theatrical performance of female spectacle, as singers, dancers, and comediennes, became "resources for female activists who engaged in various forms of political agitation in the first decade of the twentieth century," and "believed that it was necessary for women to organize together in order to attain equality with men."[35]

Among the most influential role models of the Salome Ensemble was the internationally famous Sarah Bernhardt, a French actress with Dutch Jewish roots who cultivated the subversive art of what Glenn refers to as *Female Spectacle*.[36] Bernhardt inspired young women by her example to seize the power of female self-display. Glenn places Sarah Bernhardt at the vanguard of "a modern culture of spectacle." She calls Bernhardt "a cultural provocateur" whose "methods of self-display set the standard to which . . . especially other female performers, would aspire," and a "progenitor" of "female self-promotion" in a stark reversal of a Victorian genteel tradition that had defined "womanliness" as "selfless devotion to others" (11–12). For Jewish immigrants, the concepts of "genteel" and "Gentile" were intertwined. "The Bernhardt Effect," Glenn explains, is displayed by an "egotistical female artist who not only promotes her plays but actively constructs, exhibits, and advertises her own curious and flamboyant personality" (29).

"Sarah Bernhardt and the idea of Salome were closely linked in the popular imagination," Glenn writes (98). Oscar Wilde wanted Bernhardt to play the heroine of his *Salome* play. Sander Gilman writes that "Sarah Bernhardt's association with the Salome tradition created a public scandal," when, "[i]n June of 1892 Bernhardt had begun rehearsals for Oscar Wilde's drama at the Palace Theater in London. Within the month, the examiner of plays for the Lord Chamberlain denied his approval for its performance, since it represented biblical figures on the stage. . . . And for a moment, this British theatrical scandal linked the figures of Salome and Sarah Bernhardt."[37] Although she never performed the role, Glenn writes that "Bernhardt's name remained firmly implanted" in the public consciousness of the image of Salome,[38] and Gilman adds of *"La Divine Sarah"* that "she truly seemed to be the role's ideal embodiment."[39]

Vanishing women, invisibility, disappearance, and vanishing subjects at first appear to be antithetical to the phenomenon of female spectacle and assertive visibility. But these concepts join in the dialectic of visibility that provides insight into the Salome Ensemble. In *Vanishing Women*,[40] literary and film historian Karen Beckman identifies "vanishing *as* spectacle," in nineteenth-century theatrical magic and early film.[41] A woman who disappears can be understood to boldly refuse to appear, to retain agency over her visibility and power as female spectacle. Conversely, a woman who chooses to display herself, electing to deploy her power as female spectacle, can be understood to demonstrate her refusal to disappear. "Disappearance," notes Beckman, "offers a strategy of defiant resistance to the problematic paradigms of female visibility."[42] There remains an ambivalent, unsettling aspect of disappearance in the ever-present threat of reappearance. The enormously popular magic acts in late Victorian British and American theaters contained many variations on the "Vanishing Lady." These involved various levels of implied violence of enclosing the lady in a box, sticking swords and knives into the box, sawing the box in half, and other illusions. The emotional tension raised by these illusions was released with the reappearance of the lady, unharmed. The manner of the reveal conveyed different levels of agency in the lady or the male magician. The lady might reappear seated comfortably in the theater audience, or she might simply emerge from the reassembled box. She occasionally reappeared as a disembodied voice. When the illusion was transferred to early motion pictures, the lady frequently refused to reappear, and played various tricks on the hapless magician. It became a depiction of subversive female power.

Embracing the Pejorative

The women of the Salome Ensemble drew inspiration and ideas for building character from various female paragons, role models, heroines and antiheroes, femmes fatales, seductresses, sirens, and vamps. Salome, the craven seducer and destroyer of men, is only one of the female power icons in history, scripture, and literature appropriated by the Salome Ensemble and their contemporaries. By embracing both the estimable and pejorative characteristics, and reinterpreting and repurposing the power of Salome, Hawthorne's Hester Prynne, the biblical queens Esther and Vashti, Cinderella, and others, they contributed to the creation of New Womanhood and modern feminism.

The New Testament Salome's mother, Herodias, divorces her first husband, who is Salome's father and King Antipas's brother. Then she marries her ex-brother-in-law, King Antipas. The king has divorced his first wife to marry his brother's ex-wife, Herodias. In modern parlance, this family has issues. King Antipas then asks Salome to "dance," a euphemism for stripping. She demurs, affirming self-agency and defiantly refusing to obey and expose herself. She will not appear upon command and she will not reveal her nakedness. Rather, she will choose and control her degree of visibility. Her power to defy the king is enabled by his salacious attraction to her, and by her problematic relationship as both his stepdaughter and niece. Shakespeare's Hamlet is something of a male mirror image, as the king's stepson and nephew. Salome's mother remains only peripherally visible in most versions of the story, although the mother is depicted as the instigator in some tellings.

Jokkanen expresses disapproval of the marriage of Herodias and Antipas. Stirred in part by his criticism of her mother and stepfather, Salome is attracted to Jokkanen, John the Baptist, but he refuses her, thwarting her power, insulting her self-esteem. Now enraged, she decides to deploy the power she previously withheld. For Hamlet, the play is the thing; for Salome it is the dance. She performs the dance of the seven veils in return for the king's promise to grant her any request. The assertive use of female visibility empowers Salome to force the king to bring her the head of John the Baptist.

There is a strange but remarkable echo in Salome's behavior of the earlier biblical story of King Solomon, who suggests cutting a baby in half and giving one half to each of two women who claim to be the mother. The real mother renounces her claim rather than see her child harmed, thus revealing the truth to the king, who returns the unharmed child to the rightful parent. The real mother will not destroy the object of her love. She will sacrifice her own needs for the well-being of her child. Salome, whose name is the feminine form of Salomon, does not relent when confronted with the homicidal cutting of the object of her love. Salome's love of self surpasses her love of another.

The name Salome, like the name Salomon, derives from the root word *shalom*, which means "peace." Yet Salome is the opposite of peace; she is neither passive nor pacifying. Salome is an agitator, an irritant, a fighter, a symbol and source of force, frenzy, and power. She commands attention and response. She demonstrates the ability first to conceal herself and then to make a spectacle of herself. She defiantly vanishes, and defiantly reappears. Men cannot control her.

This ungovernable quality abets the appropriation and repurposing of Salome, the dangerous, murderous, insane, irresistible beauty, to emphasize her enormous power. The search for female power captivates imaginations and fuels fascination with the Salome story. The contradictions between willful visibility and invisibility are elemental sources of Salome's power, and are resources for examining the Salome Ensemble.

Nathaniel Hawthorne's heroine Hester Prynne allows herself to be displayed as a female spectacle, with a scarlet *A* emblazoned on her chest intended to proclaim her sin. She is forced to appear, but Hester manages to retain personal agency. She is a foreign immigrant to New England, and she submits to the authority of local law. Nevertheless, Hester Prynne defiantly refuses to inhabit the role of depraved fornicatress to which authority attempts to reduce her. Through her bearing and demeanor she shows moral strength and subverts her punishment. She surrenders but never gives herself away.

Unlike Salome, Hester won't dance. She stands still, calm, imperturbable. Her spectators are struck silent, captivated by her self-possession. Her power is magnified not only by what she reveals, but also by what she conceals. She does not relinquish or reveal her particular, individual, "inmost Me."[43] She does not identify the father of her child, but protects him, shields him from harm, and accepts public censure while allowing him to remain invisible in plain sight. The onlookers do not know

Dimmesdale's identity, but they witness Hester's refusal to expose him. Aware of the immensity of the burden Hester chooses to bear by maintaining that defiant refusal, they and we infer her enormous strength of will. Hester resists the coercive power of the state, vanquishes opprobrium, and wins approbation.

Hester's protection of Dimmesdale is the antithesis of Salome's murder of Saint John. Standing upon the scaffold before the public, she displays self-assurance, devotion to her child, and even her handiwork as a seamstress. She is not defeated by the slut-shaming ritual imposed on her by law. Hester's retention of dignity through sheer force of will denies her spectators the cathartic release of schadenfreude, refashioning the audience reaction into admiration.

Werner Sollors highlights Hester's subversion of authority, strength of will, and insistence upon exercising volition:

> [W]hat is Nathanial Hawthorne's *Scarlet Letter* (1850) but the story of Hester Prynne, a woman who was separated from Chillingworth, the old-world embodiment with whom she had been connected in a marriage that was not based on love and that remained associated with paternal authority? Separated from the old world by the "road" which took her to America, a road she can visualize again from the scaffold, she takes up with Dimmesdale, the living spirit of the new world, love, and a higher law; and their consent relationship had a "consecration of its own."[44]

Salome and Hester Prynne fascinate their audiences by taking ownership of their transgressive behavior. Self-controlled visibility enables them to transform social powerlessness into a source of power. Hester uses her power to protect the lives of her ecclesiastical lover and her child. Her self-sacrifice saves others and saves herself. She achieves peace of mind and long life. Hester Prynne endures. She does not disappear.

In the New Testament, Salome disappears. However, the ancient historian Josephus writes that after the death of Jokannen, the historical figure Salome married twice and bore three sons.[45] Moreover the Salome character in popular culture does not vanish; she defiantly reappears as a symbol of power. She is scary, intimidating, repugnant, and strong enough to repel predators.

Susan Glenn describes the seemingly endless variations of the image of Salome that were portrayed on vaudeville stages and movie screens during the first two decades of the twentieth century, a phenomenon that contemporaries labeled "Salomania."[46] The modern performers relished the opportunity to play a female character with irresistible power to seduce, dominate, and conquer men. Of course the performers shared with their audiences the knowledge that they were acting; that is, pretending. Everyone knew that the actress remained in control, retained agency even as she performed the role of a character spinning out of control. These actresses and dancers took a female symbol of dangerous and ultimately self-destructive force, and recreated her as a power icon. Mesmerized audiences were drawn into a sort of solidarity with the performers. While the biblical character evoked revulsion, the Salome players were rather admired, desired, and a little feared, like Hester Prynne.

There are important connections to be made between Salome, Hawthorne's Hester Prynne, and the scriptural Queen Esther. In the Book of Esther, the Persian king hosts a great royal festival. Following months of celebration, the king convenes a smaller party of important men who continue the feast and drunken revelry. Queen Vashti hosts a similar celebration for noble women. The king commands his beautiful Queen Vashti to appear and dance for the party of drunken men, meaning to strip, to be fully visible, to display her naked beauty as a possession of the king, to reinforce his subjects' envy and respect. But Vashti refuses to appear, refuses to obey, and defies the king's will while retaining self-proprietorship and control of her visibility. She, not the king, is her own master. Embarrassed before his subjects and infuriated, the king banishes (vanishes) Vashti, causing her to disappear. It is not completely clear whether Vashti is exiled or killed. Afterward, the king feels remorse; his self-defeating action has not made Vashti accede to his demands, but simply made her permanently invisible. He punishes her, but cannot force her to obey. After he fails to make her appear he can never make her reappear.

A new queen is sought to console the despondent king. Esther, a poor, virtuous orphan, a Jewish stranger in a strange land, rises from poverty and wins the heart of the king. After a "beauty contest" search, Esther "appears" and is chosen to replace Vashti. To compete in this beauty contest, Esther spends a year having clothing made for her, and having her hair, face, and body decorated, accessorized, embellished, and adorned with frankincense and myrrh, cosmetics and jewelry. Still, she is described as modest, guileless, and possessed of the beauty of simplicity. Despite the fact that Esther starts out with natural beauty and alluring charm, her appearance is enhanced to make her worthy of the king, with enhancements somewhat contradictorily labeled wholesome and simple. Esther consents to obey the king and to appear upon his command. But there is a remnant of female agency retained in the royal need to receive Esther's consent, which is a legacy of Vashti's refusal. Also, Esther does hide a part of her that is not visible, her Jewishness. Thus, from the start Esther is active, not passive, and she exercises volition in a space bequeathed to her by Vashti. Esther does not reveal her inmost Me.

Years later, Queen Esther appears unbidden at the king's chambers to plead with him to overrule the viceroy Haman and save the Jews of Persia. She risks her life by exercising agency, making herself visible as an act of her own will rather than obedience to the king. Esther's choice is the opposite of Vashti's refusal to appear at the king's command, the action that caused Vashti's downfall. Instead of punishing Esther for audacity, the king welcomes her assertive appearance, and grants her request to rescue her people. She does not request Haman's head on a platter, but she does cause him to be sent to the gallows.

Salome's ferocious self-love causes the heinous murder of her putative lover and leaves her as an object of derision and revulsion. Yet her power cannot be denied. Hester Prynne shields her lover and her child, quietly bears enormous burdens, and wins respect and admiration. The Jewish Queen Esther intermarries with a powerful, wealthy Gentile king, remains loyal to her husband, protects her uncle, saves the Persian Jewish community, and defeats the villain who had threatened them all. Esther retains agency even as she defers to the king. She keeps her Jewish identity even while assimilating into the dominant secular culture.

Many other women who figured in history, literature, and legend influenced Rose Pastor Stokes, Anzia Yezierska, Sonya Levien, and Jetta

Goudal. Among them was Sarah Bernhardt, who could inhabit disparate roles from Salome to Hamlet. Sonya Levien was compared to a Circassian dancer.[47] When she became a union activist Jetta Goudal was called a Joan of Arc,[48] and Rose Pastor Stokes had "eyes that reputedly shone with the intensity of a Joan of Arc."[49] Amazed at her rejection of his lucrative contract offer, film mogul William Fox asked Anzia Yezierska, "Who do you think you are? Joan of Arc, waiting for the voices?"[50]

The characteristic that most emphatically connects the Salome Ensemble with these real and imagined women is female agency. They had free will and they exercised volition. With varying degrees of success these iconic women retained autonomy while engaging with community. They pursued the status of personhood and encountered the allure of difference. They derived power from deliberate female spectacle; elective, volitional visibility; willful self-display; disappearance and defiant reappearance. All were outcasts, outsiders, others, and foreigners who longed to belong and longed to be loved. They questioned authority and quested for the status of personhood.

There is one more female icon who demands inclusion in this narrative, a counterintuitive one. Cinderella seems an unlikely choice at first. After all, the poor, guileless Cinderella, buffeted by evil stepsisters and stepmother on one side and a magic fairy godmother on the other, the girl who must be saved by Prince Charming in order to live happily ever after, does not appear to exude female power and agency. And yet, consider. Cinderella calculatedly changes her clothing and appearance to display virtue and beauty, hiding or veiling her poverty and low social status. She starts out as an orphan and outcast. She controls her visibility, appears unbidden and unexpected by the prince, on her own initiative, albeit with the help of sympathizers. With cunning disguise and seductive dance she wins the heart of the prince. She selectively conceals and reveals in order to magnify her female power, not completely unlike Salome and her seven veils. Cinderella willfully appears and then disappears from the prince's view. And she gets her man.

All the women of the Salome Ensemble were occasionally identified as Cinderella in the press and private correspondence. The following chapters show how female power icons connect with *Salome of the Tenements* and its creators. Some of these connections comfortably affirm cherished expectations. Others, like a sympathetic Salome and a subversive Cinderella, challenge what feel like timeless verities. Real lives are filled with such contradictions, as those explored in coming chapters attest.

|2|

Rose Pastor Stokes Was beyond the Pale

Imagine a grey, windy day in the tiny village of Augustowo in the Russian Pale of Settlement in 1877. A group of Jewish peasants dressed in their ragged best clothing are gathered in a small *shul*. A bearded rabbi stands at the front where four young men prepare to lift a *chuppa*, a wedding canopy fashioned from a prayer shawl, on wooden poles. The groom stands, signs of nervousness and annoyance alternating in his facial expressions. This *khossen*, this groom, is a widower with a son. The little boy, two years old, wanders among the grownups, increasingly impatient. The groom and the rabbi look out a side window, searching the distance, and then at the bride's mother and father, who smile apologetically. The bride's parents also gaze outward, toward a little house across a small, bare field. Worry informs the mother's face, while the father grows angry. The bride, the *kallah*, is not there. The bride's mother and father shrug their weary shoulders and leave the synagogue. They walk silently across the way to their little house. The others watch them through the window.

Mother and father enter the house to find a young girl weeping, still in her coarse, everyday work clothes, her wedding dress lying on the bed beside her. The father begins to shout, the daughter to shriek and cry, the mother to try to quiet them both while gathering up the dress and pushing it on the girl. A few minutes later the girl is wearing the dress and still weeping. The parents hold their daughter, each taking one arm. They lift her up and half-carry, half-drag the sobbing girl across the barren hillside to the shul and the waiting wedding party.

The Jewish girl was Hindl Lewin, and she was punished for transgressive, dangerous behavior in the eyes of her family and community. Hindl had the chutzpah, the audacity, to try to choose her own husband.

1. Rose Pastor Stokes at her desk, 1906. Yale University Library, Manuscripts and Archives, Rose Pastor Stokes Papers, MS 573, microfilm.

She fell in love with a Polish man who was not Jewish, and told her parents that she wanted to marry him. This rebellious flouting of paternal authority entailed potentially dire consequences for the couple and their families. At this time and place, unfortunate experience taught that love and intermarriage between Jew and Gentile would invite ostracism from the Jewish community and violence from anti-Semitic neighbors and government authorities.

These events took place a world away and a dozen years after the end of the American Civil War. In Russia, only four years later the assassination of Russian Czar Alexander II was followed by an eruption of anti-Jewish violence, pogroms, and new discriminatory legislation. Hindl's attempt to choose was more than audacious within the context. It was nothing less than a private revolution, a flouting of community norms, defiance of civil and religious authorities, and an attempt to take power from the father to whom tradition granted the prerogative to select a husband for his daughter. It also was a reckless risk to her physical safety and the safety of others. And so Hindl was forced to marry Jacob Wieslander, the Jewish widower with the two-year-old son, who was chosen by her father.[1] The parentally approved wedding took place very much against the bride's will. The bonds of matrimony were imposed on her like chains.

The unhappily married couple had a daughter they named Rose Harriet. Before the girl turned three, however, Jacob Wieslander abandoned his family and fled to America, leaving behind even his young son from his prior marriage. The boy was placed with relatives of his father. Cut loose, mother Hindl and daughter Rose seized the degree of freedom created by their abandonment and soon were in motion. For Rose these events launched a lifelong trajectory beyond the Pale, from Russia to London, to Cleveland, New York City, and beyond. They joined millions like them in waves of immigration and urbanization that swelled American cities between 1880 and 1920. Hindl, who changed her name to Anna, was emancipated, but Rose never forgot the legacy of ethnic separation, forced marriage, patriarchic oppression, travails of poverty, and trauma of paternal desertion. Repression, coercion, and persecution contributed to a predilection in Rose to defiance, insurrection, and liberation.

The Russian "Pale of Settlement" was a bounded area of Russia and Poland within which Jews were legally required to live from 1791 to 1917. The boundaries of the Russian Pale were the first of many invisible barriers that Rose would cross during her lifetime. Russian Jews generally were permitted to commute outside the Pale during the day to work, but were legally bound by curfews to return to the restricted areas at night. These were not the borders of a nation-state, but rather legal barricades that enforced ethnic, religious, and what was perceived as racial separatism.

According to the *Oxford English Dictionary,* the word *pale* is derived from the name for pointed wooden stakes used to make protective fences around military forts, also called "paling" or "palisades." It also applied to sharp wooden stakes used as weapons with which to "impale" enemies. Usage of the word evolved to mean the area within a boundary or fence, or an area subject to particular legal jurisdiction. There was an Irish Pale between the late twelfth and the sixteenth centuries, and a Pale in Calais in northern France from the mid-fourteenth to the mid-sixteenth centuries, both being areas under English jurisdiction. The phrase "beyond the pale," to mean outside permitted boundaries, physical, behavioral, or metaphorical, derives from the same word.

Rose's life was defined by repeatedly venturing beyond the pale. She moved with her mother to London, where she was registered in school as Rose Rosenthal, taking as a surname the married name of one of her mother's sisters. Rose and Anna were living in London in 1886 when the Russian anarchist Prince Peter Kropotkin arrived there and became "highly regarded in the Russian Jewish community in the East End."[2] Rose was only seven years old when Kropotkin went to London, too young for politics, but her mother, aunts, and uncles were part of that Russian Jewish East End community attracted to the anarchist aristocrat.

In London, Anna met and married Israel Pastor, a Jewish well-meaning ne'er-do-well who never could surmount the obstacles of poverty and ethnic discrimination. Expenses rose with the arrival of a new son. They later moved to America, traveling in steerage. Israel Pastor went first to work to earn enough money to bring his family. At the age of ten, Rose Pastor and her mother and half-brother entered the United States through Castle Garden, in 1890, two years before the opening of Ellis Island as an immigrant processing station. The Pastors did not stay in New York, but moved immediately to Cleveland, where Israel Pastor had found employment. Anna had five more children with Pastor. His employment was not steady. He descended into depression and alcoholism, and eventually abandoned the family. By time she was a teenager, Rose Pastor had seen her mother twice deserted by husbands. Twice Rose had been abandoned by fathers.

Rose remained devoted to her mother and half-siblings, and took on the role of family caretaker and breadwinner, or "bread giver," to use Anzia Yezierska's phrase.[3] At the age of eleven Rose went to work rolling cigars by hand in a factory in Cleveland, a job that she continued for several different employers during the next twelve years.[4] Some of these jobs were in large factories and others were in small, home-based operations called "buckeyes."

Sweatshop Scholar

During these years Rose Pastor read the few books that were available to her, including Charles Lamb's *Tales from Shakespeare*,[5] and wrote poems

and stories when she could. Work conditions in these sweatshops generally were poor, hours were long, and the pay was meager. Cigar-factory
co-workers introduced Rose to socialism, an ideology that appealed to her
and that her bosses considered subversive. In 1901, at the age of twenty-
one, she learned how to operate a new "high-tech" cigar-making machine,
which earned her a coveted job promotion and a jump in pay to fifteen
dollars a week. She had been paid only six dollars a week for rolling cigars
by hand.

But her hard-earned advancement was short-lived. One day a senior
executive opened her desk drawer and found a book, *Collectivism and
Industrial Revolution* by Belgian socialist Emile Vandervelde and published
by a socialist cooperative run by Charles Kerr.[6] The presence of this borrowed book cost Rose Pastor her job promotion. She was demoted back to
the ranks of the workers who rolled cigars by hand, struggling once again
to eke out six dollars a week.

During her sweatshop years, Rose read copies of the *Jewish Daily
News* (*Yiddishes Tageblatt*), published in New York City, which neighbors
and co-workers shared with her. She responded to the editors' requests
for letters from working girls describing their lives. A letter she wrote
in 1901 appeared in the paper, and the editors invited Rose to contribute
regularly, pieces that would "talk to girls."[7] Rose Pastor wrote under the
pen name Zelda. She corresponded with her editor A. H. Fromenson, who
traveled to visit her in Cleveland. Rose's biographers Arthur and Pearl
Zipser write that after this meeting the correspondence with Fromenson
"took on a more ardent tone and there was talk of marriage."[8]

In 1902 she informed the editors that she could no longer contribute,
because she had become president of a Cleveland Zionist organization,
Bnai Zion. She dreamed of a socialist Jewish nation that would join an
international socialist movement. After receiving a barrage of letters from
disappointed readers about the discontinuation of "Zelda's" advice column, and enthusiastic lobbying from Fromenson, the *Jewish Daily News*
offered Rose Pastor a job in New York writing for the paper at fifteen dollars a week. She moved to New York and took the job, later sending money
for her mother and siblings to join her. Upon arrival at her new office, she
learned from female co-workers that her supposed fiancé Fromenson was

a womanizer, and was apparently engaged to at least one other young woman. Poor young Rose was heartbroken. Sadder but wiser, she became friends with another young woman contributor to the *Jewish Daily News*, Miriam Shomer, who provided a shoulder to cry on. Work, friendship, and the excitement of New York City helped Rose mend her broken heart and move on. Miriam Shomer introduced Rose Pastor to many of her friends, including a young cooking teacher who went by the name Hattie Mayer and later became known as the novelist Anzia Yezierska.

The founder and owner of the *Jewish Daily News* was Kasriel Sarasohn, another Russian Jewish immigrant. Historian Tony Michels notes that "Socialists detested Sarasohn, as he did them."[9] "[T]he *Tageblat* [*Jewish Daily News*] was a private business, not the voice of a social movement. The *Tageblat* belonged to the Sarasohn family, whereas socialist newspapers

2. Rose Pastor Stokes. George Grantham Bain Collection, Library of Congress.

were owned by democratically run publishing associations representing popular organizations."[10] The newspaper's hostility to socialism and socialists must have caused discomfort for Rose, who harbored socialist views when she began working for the *Jewish Daily News*, views that ripened into a full-fledged belief and devotion to socialist ideals. "The *Tageblat* promoted religious Orthodoxy yet advocated a selective approach to Americanization. It denounced socialists for dividing the Jewish people, but expressed concern for the plight of 'honest' workers."[11]

Rose Pastor was a multitasker. She did volunteer work at settlement houses and wrote and spoke at public gatherings about politics, women's suffrage, family planning, workers' rights, and socialism. As a reporter she interviewed Lillian Wald, head of the Henry Street Settlement, and many other prominent personalities on New York's Lower East Side.[12] In one article Rose warned of the "Christianizing influence" she detected at the Jacob Riis Settlement.[13] While writing for the newspaper, Rose Pastor frequented another settlement, the Educational Alliance, which was founded by Louis Marshall, Joseph Schiff, Isidore Strauss, and other wealthy German Jewish philanthropists. In the summer of 1903 she served as a counselor for a group of teenage girls from the Jewish Educational Alliance and the University Settlement. The arrangement was supposed to end when autumn leaves turned, but the girls, especially Sonya Levien, protested and convinced Rose to stay with them. Rose Pastor also became a playwright and a translator of Yiddish poetry. One of Rose's plays, *The Woman Who Wouldn't*, was published as a book by G. P. Putnam's Sons in 1916.[14]

In 1903 the newspaper assigned her to interview James Graham Phelps Stokes at the University Settlement near the corner of Eldridge and Rivington Streets. Rose was greatly impressed with this patrician, noble fellow, who, while controlling railroad, mining, and real estate interests, was an active philanthropist and spent time as well as money working to improve the lot of the poor. He was a scion of "one of the oldest and most socially secure families in the land, listed in Ward McAllister's register as one of the coveted Four Hundred," and had graduated Yale College and Columbia Medical School.[15] The profile she wrote about Graham for the newspaper betrays her immediate attraction to the man.

One glance at his face and you know Mr. Stokes loves humanity for its own sake and as he speaks with the sincerity which is the keynote of his character, you feel how the whole heart and soul of the man is filled with "weltshmerz"; you feel that, metaphorically speaking, he "has sown his black young curls with the bleaching cares of half a million men already."

Mr. Stokes is very tall, and, I believe, six foot of the most thorough democracy. A thoroughbred gentleman, a scholar and a son of a millionaire, he is a man of the common people, even as Lincoln was. He is a plain man and makes one feel perfectly at ease with him. Nor does he possess that one great fault that men of "his kind" generally possess—the pride of humility. He does not flaunt his democracy in one's face, but when his democracy is mentioned to him, he appears as glad as a child who is told by an appreciative parent, "you have been a good boy to-day."

Rose Harriet Pastor[16]

This is heady stuff for a self-educated twenty-four-year-old woman of the tenements to write about a wealthy, prominent, handsome bachelor. Her characterization of him as filled with "weltshmerz" must have warmed his patrician heart, but the line about having "sown his black curls with the bleaching cares of half a million men already" was not only flattering, it was erudite. It is a quote from an Elizabeth Barrett Browning epic poem or novel-in-verse published in 1856, called *Aurora Leigh*. The line is uttered by a young aspiring poetess to describe her cousin and would-be suitor who is devoted to social work. Rose Pastor also compared Graham Stokes to Abraham Lincoln. She envisioned him as an icon of American rectitude and perhaps her personal great emancipator.

If Rose was smitten, so was Graham. To Stokes, Rose was a beautiful, exotic other to whom he attributed alluring and ennobling traits not possessed by those in his wealthy set. And she was intelligent. And she admired him. James Graham Phelps Stokes was entranced by Rose Harriet Pastor. They fell in love with idealized perceptions of each other.

The poor, immigrant Jewish girl married the wealthy son of a prominent Episcopalian New England family with roots stretching back to Colonial America. Their lavish wedding in June 1905 was a tabloid sensation, with headlines declaiming the marriage of "Rose of the Ghetto"

3. Rose Pastor Stokes and James Graham Phelps Stokes wedding photo, June 1905. Yale University Library, Manuscripts and Archives, Rose Pastor Stokes Papers, MS 573, microfilm.

to a "Millionaire Socialist." Newspapers feasted on the most spectacular New York City society page wedding since Eleanor and Franklin Delano Roosevelt were wed three months earlier on St. Patrick's Day. Rose vowed to love and honor her husband, but she refused to utter the word *obey*. Anzia Yezierska and Sonya Levien mingled with the diverse crowd of high society types and Lower East Siders who attended the wedding of their friend and role model.[17] When the married couple returned from an extended European honeymoon, Rose hired Sonya Levien to work as Graham Stokes's secretary.

Crusading Couple

A month before Rose and Graham were married, a letter inviting interested persons to join in forming the Intercollegiate Socialist Society was signed by Graham Stokes, Thomas Wentworth Higginson, Charlotte Perkins Gilman, Clarence Darrow, William English Walling, Jack London, Upton Sinclair, and others. Rose and Graham joined the Socialist Party of America and the Intercollegiate Socialist Society, of which Graham served as president from 1907 through 1918.

Propelled by his money and influence and her indefatigable commitment, power at the podium, and attractive presence, Rose and Graham Stokes became activists in the socialist, labor, suffrage, and civil rights movements. Graham was briefly involved with the Municipal Ownership League, an insurgent political party started by William Randolph Hearst. Among other issues, it advocated public ownership of utilities. Her work as a crusading journalist and settlement worker was consistent with Rose's growing interest in the kind of participatory democracy and pragmatist conversion of experience to action espoused by John Dewey and Jane Addams. Rose increasingly devoted herself to political activism. She was convinced of the worldwide need for socialism, skeptical of the less radical social democratic and Progressive reform movements, and hostile to liberal laissez faire capitalism. Her ties to Judaism and Jewish community were somewhat attenuated, but her faith in international socialism grew.

Through her richer and poorer years Rose demonstrated steadfast commitment to helping working people. She chose the title *I Belong to the Working Class* for the unfinished autobiography she worked on during the year before she died in June 1933. She spoke inspiringly at public rallies in support of the more than twenty thousand New York City women who participated in a 1909 shirtwaist-makers' strike. This strike involved some cooperation between the Socialist Party, the International Ladies Garment Workers Union, and the Women's Trade Union League. She played a similar role in a 1912 hotel workers' strike in New York City led by the International Hotel Workers' Union with the backing of the Industrial Workers of the World (IWW), also known as the Wobblies.[18] Famed anarchist Emma Goldman was one of the organizers of the IWW.

For several years, Pastor Stokes had a strong alliance with Emma Goldman, principally based on their shared commitment to women's rights to birth control. Alexander Berkman, another political anarchist who also was Emma Goldman's lover, sent a handwritten note to Rose on January 20, 1913, inviting her to speak at an "affair" to celebrate the eighth anniversary of Goldman's magazine *Mother Earth*. He appealed to Pastor Stokes, "We should very much like to have you say a few words as you are our comrade in spirit," and noted that her friend Anna Strunsky also was invited.[19]

Pastor Stokes galvanized crowds at rallies in support of Margaret Sanger, Ida Rauh, and Emma Goldman when they faced arrest and imprisonment for disseminating birth control information. On April 19, 1916, Rose spoke at a "Birth Control" dinner at the Hotel Brevoort in Manhattan, which was organized in support of Goldman. The following day, Goldman was arraigned in criminal court "on the charge of dispensing information about birth control," the *New York Evening Sun* reported.[20] Goldman served two weeks in a prison workhouse for violating the Comstock Act, section 1142 of the New York State Penal Code. When Goldman was released on May 5, Rose Pastor Stokes was again among the public speakers at a rally for her, this time at Carnegie Hall. Rose's speech electrified the audience, and when it was over she handed out printed instructions on birth control methods, in violation of the law, but no police were present to interfere.

Mother Earth reported that Pastor Stokes said,

> I have broken the law over and over, because I believe that since science has shown the way, the mothers of the world should have the power and the right to control birth—to have as many or as few children as the conditions of their health or their particular material environment, coupled with a right standard of living, shall dictate. . . .
>
> I do not, of course, want to go to jail, and, again, I am not bidding for arrest. I wish to save all that, naturally. But I am not afraid. . . .

Therefore, be the penalty what it may, I here frankly offer to give out
these slips with the forbidden information to those needy wives and mothers who will frankly come and take them, as soon as the speaking is over.[21]

Inspired by the 1913 Patterson, New Jersey, silk workers' strike, Rose
wrote a poem, "Paterson," which appeared in the *Hoboken Socialist*.[22] Rose
contributed short stories, articles, and poetry to a variety of magazines
and journals including *Masses* and *Socialist Woman*, and remained an avid
writer of letters to the editors of newspapers.[23] Margaret C. Jones notes
that Rose Pastor Stokes was "one of the few *Masses* poets with firsthand
experience of factory work."[24] The multitalented Pastor Stokes also displayed her drawings in art galleries and shows, and sold some to private
buyers and popular magazines.

Rose translated and published the Yiddish poetry of Morris Rosenfeld, known as one of the "sweatshop poets." Rosenfeld was dismissed
from his job at the *Yiddishes Tageblatt* in 1921 by the paper's owner, Kasriel Sarasohn. This was the employer for whom Rose worked when she
first moved to New York. Before immigrating to the United States, Rosenfeld spent time in Amsterdam as a diamond cutter, where he might have
encountered Jetta Goudal's father, Moises Goudeket, who was an Amsterdam diamond merchant.

During her early years in New York, Rose's political activism extended
beyond socialism into issues of feminism. She worked, demonstrated,
wrote, and spoke extensively on behalf of women's suffrage, sexual liberation, equal legal rights for men and women, racial equality, and empowerment of women in business and the arts, in addition to birth control and
family planning.[25] She inspired young women factory workers, telling
them, "I want you to be working *girls* not working *machines*. I want you
all to be working, thinking women, not mere automatons!"[26] Rose Pastor
Stokes was concerned with the rights of personhood for all women and
workers, rights she believed that socialism would guarantee. As early as
1916 she told the audience at an Emma Goldman rally, "My chief interest is
not birth control but Socialist Propaganda."[27] In later years her activism on
behalf of feminism subsided as her focus on socialism and communism
grew more intense.

4. Rose Pastor Stokes. George Grantham Bain Collection, Library of Congress.

Early in their marriage, Rose Pastor Stokes and James Graham Phelps Stokes lived in a modest flat on the top floor of a building at the corner of Norfolk and Grand Streets on the Lower East Side. Later they split their time between a luxury townhouse they acquired on Grove Street in Greenwich Village and their own private fantasy island. Caritas Island was a two-acre island in Long Island Sound near Stamford, Connecticut. Graham had inherited the property and, after the marriage, built a house on it. Fellow socialists William English Walling and his wife, Anna Strunsky, and LeRoy Scott and his wife, Miriam Finn (née Selechnyck) Scott, lived in cottages on Caritas Island near Rose and Graham. Each of these three couples was composed of a wealthy WASP husband married to a Russian Jewish woman immigrant.

Graham and Rose Pastor Stokes presided over an active intellectual salon at their island retreat. For a decade, Caritas Island served as a meeting place and refuge for "a wide range of reformers, socialists,

politicians, propagandists, writers, artists, labor leaders, social workers, journalists and lawyers."[28] Caritas was part think tank, part artists' colony, part luxury retreat for a set notable for its diversity. Maxim
Gorky visited Caritas in 1906 and caused a minor scandal when the
press reported that he was accompanied by a woman who was not his
wife. Friends like Sonya Levien and Anzia Yezierska also were treated
to visits to Caritas.

Rose was a physically beautiful, engaging young woman who projected kindness, intelligence, sincerity, and seriousness. Friends and
acquaintances found her exceptionally attractive, possessed of a magnetic
aura and winning personality. Her many attributes, especially when experienced in the context of the lush surroundings of Caritas Island and the
edifying conversations of the brilliant guests, led many visitors to develop
romantic affection for their hostess. The Zipser biography of Rose affirms
that "[s]ome men, some women, some husbands and wives together were
smitten."[29] Anne Traubel, the wife of essayist, poet, magazine publisher,
and author Horace Traubel, "had a brief but ardent crush on Rose."[30] "I
touched you this summer and found you in divine ways never to lose
you," Anne wrote in a letter in which she proclaimed her love to Rose late
in 1909.[31] Rose had many such admirers.

Many years later, after their marriage dissolved, Graham would claim
that he had only reluctantly acquiesced in the entertaining at Caritas. In
1925 he wrote to Rose, "you have brought nothing but shame to me in
the use you have made at the cottage [as] a place of recreation for ingrate
enemies of America such as you had there before."[32]

On November 9, 1909, Rose told a reporter for the *New York Evening
World* that the world was ripe for a socialist rebellion, "the rebellion that
will be fought with the ballot if possible—as it is our right that it should
be—but with the bullet if necessary."[33] The language was echoed by Mal-
colm X in the 1960s concerning the civil rights movement. But Rose's statement should not be misread. She was calling for a worldwide socialist
revolution, which would be violent in some places. This does not neces-
sarily imply that she expected violence in the United States, where democracy encompassed in the availability of the ballot would make violence
unnecessary. Still, she remained committed to public, communal action,

and civil disobedience. Her positive feelings about American democracy would remain in tension with her belief in the depredations caused by capitalism. This tension would leave Rose ever oscillating, plagued by ambivalent feelings and conflicting loyalties.

Patriots and Profiteers

President Woodrow Wilson ran for re-election in 1916 while World War I raged in Europe. Wilson pledged to keep America out of the war, but it was a pledge he would not keep. To court Progressive and socialist-leaning voters during the election year, he promoted legislation designed to appeal to them. A national child labor law was passed in 1916, as well as a worker's compensation plan for federal employees and the establishment of an eight-hour workday for railroad workers. From the outbreak of combat in Europe in August 1914, two months after the assassination of Archduke Ferdinand, until the American Declaration of War in April 1917, American involvement in the war was fiercely debated. In 1915 and 1916 Wilson called for a "preparedness" campaign of "armed neutrality," and in late 1916 a policy of intervening diplomatically for "peace without victory." Following his second presidential election victory, Wilson took a more aggressive stance. Some Progressives, including the editors of the influential *New Republic* magazine, who had mustered only perfunctory support for the president and remained wary of joining the battle in Europe, changed their view at the beginning of 1917 and called on Woodrow Wilson to declare war.

Of the many provocations that sparked American anger, German submarine warfare was the most inflammatory. More than 250 Americans were killed on Allied ships sunk by Germany from 1914 through 1917, generating tremendous emotional impact on the American home front. The sinking of the British ship *Lusitania* in May 1915, in which more than 125 Americans lost their lives, provoked a furious protest from President Wilson that resulted in a temporary pause in these German attacks. But, in its urgency to prevent goods and services from reaching Britain, Germany soon resumed submarine torpedo warfare to sink growing numbers of nonmilitary ships from America and other nations. This was among the intolerable offenses cited by President Wilson in his April 2,

1917, congressional address calling for a declaration of war, in which he argued that "[t]he world must be made safe for democracy."

Historian David M. Kennedy emphasizes the influence of domestic political issues on President Wilson's decision to enter the war. "Deep social fissures had been opened by the enormous concentration of private capital and economic power in 'trusts,' by the effort of Progressive reformers to bring the corporations under public control, by labor disturbances, and by the arrival in America of over twelve million immigrants since the turn of the century."[34] Eric Rauchway notes the impact on the prewar political environment of the fact that almost 15 percent of Americans were foreign-born and one-third were either foreign-born or had at least one foreign-born parent according to the 1910 census.[35] Kennedy adds, "Of those 32 million persons from families with close foreign ties, more than ten million derived from the Central Powers."[36] In this context, xenophobia and openness to ideas about socializing the risks of industrial capitalism were ascendant in America.

The provocative effects of these conditions were magnified as they were incorporated into long-standing debates over defining characteristics of the American nation. In the United States, self-consciously conceived in law and aspirational language establishing "We, the people," social upheaval often has been met with attempts to limit those included in what Benedict Anderson calls the "imagined community."[37] This national identity crisis is further complicated by conflicting American conceptions of civic nationalism, founded upon law and citizenship, versus ethnic or racial nationalism. The resulting questions about inclusion and exclusion, and categories of us versus them, were emergent in the political and social climate in which Rose Pastor Stokes entered the fray.

Bull or Bully

Theodore Roosevelt, the U.S. president at the time of the Stokes's wedding, articulated changing attitudes, ideas, and definitions of "Americanism." In the 1890s, historian Gary Gerstle explains, Theodore Roosevelt promulgated the myth that the so-called "American race" had descended directly from Scotch Irish backwoodsmen "who bravely ventured forth into the trans-Appalachian wilderness to battle the Indians and clear the land."[38] By 1908, having served as governor of New York and president of the United States, Roosevelt's views on the subject had evolved. That year Roosevelt enthusiastically embraced the message of Irving Zangwill's play *The Melting Pot*.[39] The protagonist, David, is a Russian Jew who flees to New York after his family is killed in the 1903 Kishinev pogrom. His hard work and talent lead him to become a proud American, achieving financial success and marriage to a Gentile girl.[40] The implication was plainly that foreigners could become American through effort, talent, and pursuit of virtuous goals. This idealization of assimilation carried enormous cultural weight. It would be contested by many, including Horace Kallen, who published *Democracy Versus the Melting Pot* in the *Nation* in 1915,[41] and Randolph Bourne, who in 1916 argued in favor of a "Trans-National America."[42] In 1924 Kallen coined the term "cultural pluralism."

Like Zangwill, Rose Pastor Stokes drew her own lessons from the anti-Semitic violence of Kishinev. She wrote an editorial in *Jewish Daily News*, called "Kishineffing It," in which she argued that this ethnic violence in Russia obligated American Jews to protest both anti-Semitism and racist violence directed at African Americans. "Jew-baiting and Negro-lynching," she stated, "are two blunders well worth being freed from; Kishineffing outside of the land of Kishineff is a greater blot upon civilization than in that 'hell's kitchen,' Russia."[43] Zangwill's play focuses on the necessity for the ethnic other to "melt" or eliminate difference to become a worthy member of society. Rose's emphasis was on the imperative of the community to open itself to acceptance of difference and ethnic otherness.

In April 1917, following President Wilson's war announcement, the Socialist Party voted to oppose the United States' entry into the war, and Rose and Graham Stokes resigned from the Party. The couple came out publicly in support of Wilson and the Allies. Rose was inspired by the idea of making the world safe for democracy, not capitalism, and she began to respond with her typical activist enthusiasm.

The *New York Times* published Rose's letter of resignation from the Women's Peace Party in March 1917. The letter clarified her positions opposing capitalism, supporting democracy, rejecting the pacifist label, and insisting that she was not a patriot. "I love peace, but I am not a pacifist," she wrote. "I would serve my country, but I am not a patriot. . . . I seek for this country, as for the world, the highest good; and I consider it essential to support peace, or conflict, as seems best for the world's progress toward unity."[44] Pointedly, Rose proclaimed her own willingness to serve her country, even in the military if necessary. "If the United States enters the war, I shall regard it as the perfectly natural result of causes long inherent and deeply rooted in the worldwide competitive system. . . . I would serve if called upon, and I would recognize myself to be fighting or serving, not for national glory or for those petty 'spheres of influence' which our loudest voiced patriots would perhaps be definitely seeking through the war, but as an infinitesimal part of a great instrument, in use since the beginning of history, for the perfecting of human unity and human freedom."[45]

If she remained a staunch internationalist and cosmopolitan, Rose appeared to be moving toward what John Fabian Witt and Bonnie Honig describe as "rooted cosmopolitanism," defined by Witt as "one that combines local attachments with the universal principles of impartiality,"[46] and by Honig as "rooted not . . . in a national ideal but rather in a democratic ideal, one that seeks out friends and partners even (or especially) among strangers and foreigners."[47] After World War II, Joseph Stalin used the term "rootless cosmopolitans" derisively to refer to Jewish intellectuals and others whom he considered pro-Western and antipatriotic.

After more than twenty-five years in the United States, Rose Pastor Stokes had planted some roots. She could not help developing some respect and fondness for America, where she rose from poverty to wealth and influence and enjoyed many, but not all, of the benefits of democracy. American women had not yet won the right to vote. Of course Rose also retained her roots in Russian Jewish culture, a tradition in which individuals are commanded, obligated, to "*tikkun olam*," repair the world, and to help fellow human beings whenever they are able. With Europe embroiled in World War I, Rose hoped that America could be a force for repairing a world in dire need of such help.

Ambivalent American

During this period, Rose Pastor Stokes came as close as she ever would to American patriotism, although she was vexed, ambivalent, and uncomfortable with such a concept. On November 1, 1917, the *New York Times* printed a letter from Rose Pastor Stokes in which she asked citizens to support the troops by donating money to an organization called "The War Camp Community Recreation Fund," which provided "recreation of every wholesome kind the community has to offer" outside military training camps across the country. It was akin to bringing settlement houses to the soldiers, a kind of precursor to the United Service Organizations (USO). "While our soldiers and sailors are helping to make the world safe for democracy and for us," she wrote, "let us help to make the world safe for the soldier and the sailor."[48] Also in November 1917, Rose published a piece called "A Confession" in *Century* magazine in which she proclaimed her support for the American war effort and for President Wilson:

> America as I now conceive her, stands among the free nations of the world, eager to follow where Liberty beckons, eager to fight for a newer, better world, burning to strike a blow at Injustice and Oppression wherever these may rear their heads, whether they appear in the guise of German autocracy abroad or special privilege at home . . .
>
> No narrow nationalism could have moved me one inch from my old position. It was only when our President, and the American people behind, stood where the Socialist Party of this country should have stood that I became an American.[49]

Although she believed her position was consistent with her desire for a worldwide, internationalist, socialist transformation, Rose did revere democracy, and was as outraged as most Americans by German autocracy and brutal submarine warfare. According to historians Herbert Shapiro and David L. Sterling, who edited Rose's unfinished autobiography, "Earlier she had viewed nationalism as contradictory to internationalism," but her feelings changed for a brief time after she heard President Wilson's inspiring pledge to make the world safe for democracy. "Internationalism had made a nationalist of her when President Wilson" uttered those words.[50]

That same month, President Wilson's daughter Margaret invited Rose to have dinner with her and the president at the White House to help drum up support for the war effort, an invitation she declined.

While seeking an international workers' revolution, many socialists believed that the government of Imperial Germany and the czarist regime of Russia had to be overthrown to make way for a new world socialism. In the United States, it was more complicated. Before World War I many socialists favored democracy as a vehicle with which socialist reform could be accomplished. Like Rose, they resolutely opposed liberal, laissez faire capitalism. Social Democrats and Progressives joined in debating the need for social reform in the United States, while accepting various aspects of free-market economics.

Forty years later Milton Friedman argued that "a society which is socialist cannot also be democratic, in the sense of guaranteeing individual freedom."[51] Friedman made his argument in a post–New Deal United States that had become a hybrid capitalist society with important socialist components such as unemployment insurance and Social Security, neither of which undermined democracy or individual freedom. Friedman was one of the most ardent, eloquent promoters of free markets. However, notwithstanding the persuasiveness of his reasoning, the optimal balance of public and private influence in an economy appears to be contingent upon prevailing conditions and imperatives, and, therefore, ever in flux. The Progressive Era reformers confronted this same debate while pursuing their goals for economic and social change. Many, like Graham Stokes, believed that some mix of private property, regulated free markets, and public ownership of utilities could improve the human condition over time.

After Germany sank the *Lusitania* in 1915, a surge of American nationalist fervor was a predictable result. American socialists could indulge this feeling while urging socialist elements in Germany to overthrow their militant government. When Germany invaded Belgium in August 1914, Emile Vandervelde, the first member of the Belgian Labor Party to hold a position as a government minister, was part of the Belgian commission that protested to President Wilson about German aggression. Emile Vandervelde was the author of *Collectivism and Industrial Revolution*, the book that was found in Rose's desk at the cigar factory in Ohio in 1901, causing her to lose her job. In September 1914 Rose Pastor Stokes met with Vandervelde and his wife in New York. Rose was a member of the committee of the Intercollegiate Socialist Society that welcomed Madame Vandervelde upon her arrival in New York Harbor on the RMS *Cedric*, a White Star Line sister ship of the *Titanic*.[52]

Utopian Dreams, Dystopian Realities

As the United States entered the war, socialists, including Rose Pastor Stokes, continued hoping for an international workers movement that would replace capitalism with socialism. The overthrow of the czarist regime in Russia in February 1917 was followed by the chaos and upheaval of the provisional government, which was in turn supplanted by the November 1917 Bolshevik accession. These events provoked starry-eyed optimism, fueling what turned out to be futile and naïve hope for the realization of utopian socialist dreams. Even President Wilson, in his April 2, 1917, call for American entry into the war, averred that "Russia was known by those who knew it best to have been always in fact democratic at heart."[53] It would quickly become a democratic heart broken. Within a year, Russia would instead become known by those who knew it best for deserting the Allies and signing the humiliating, ill-fated Treaty of Brest-Litovsk with Germany, for perpetrating the Jacobin atrocities of the Red Terror, and for descending into a civil war characterized by violence and starvation on an unprecedented scale. All this pain and suffering would only lead Russia to the threshold of Stalinism. Political activists like Rose Pastor Stokes and anarchist Emma Goldman, and journalists like John Reed and their Progressive cohort, would never recover from the disappointment and disillusion of the aftermath of the Russian Revolution. Dystopian realities crushed their utopian dreams. John Reed, who worked closely with Sonya Levien at the *Metropolitan* magazine before World War I and published *Ten Days That Shook the World* in 1919, died in October 1920 in Moscow.[54] Emma Goldman recoiled from the Bolsheviks after witnessing the horrors of the Russian civil war. She left Russia in 1921, and wrote a series of newspaper articles that later were published as the books *My Disillusionment in Russia* (1923) and *My Further Disillusionment in Russia* (1924).[55] But Rose never gave up. She publicly broke with Emma Goldman and several other former comrades and colleagues who distanced themselves from the Russians. Rose Pastor Stokes persisted in supporting socialism, communism, and the Soviet regime until her untimely death in 1933.

President Wilson pursued his own utopian dreams, including that of a League of Nations that would prevent future wars by creating international legal institutions and international laws. It would be a worldwide imagined community of nations. Ironically, his was a different take on the "internationalism" propounded by communists and socialists, including Rose Pastor Stokes. But the president's dreams also would be defeated or deferred. Internationalists throughout history have tended to underestimate the power of nationalisms. The trauma of the First World War did not align the ideologies of disparate nations sufficiently to persuade them to meaningfully surrender sovereign authority to international laws or institutions. The promulgation of international laws and institutions continued, and continues today of necessity, albeit with inconsistent results. But in 1918 the people of the world, and even the people of the United States, did not share Woodrow Wilson's vision of a global imagined community. A lack of international consensus on the meaning of even basic concepts of democracy, liberty, nationalism, industrial economics, class, and race combined with the cacophony of U.S. domestic politics to thwart Wilson's efforts. Many socialists in the United States maintained, and certainly Rose Pastor Stokes was convinced in 1918, that the combination of socialism and democracy was necessary and inevitable. They did not yet foresee the Great Depression or the Second World War. Neither could they presage the coming century-long ideological battle in which socialism and capitalism would compete and crash into each other until in practice the lines between them began to blur. Even defining and maintaining the principles of democracy were not simple. For the Soviet socialists, the ideal of a "dictatorship of the proletariat" turned into a tyrannical dictatorship over the proletariat, and democratic hopes were dashed by totalitarian Bolshevism and Stalinism. For President Wilson and the American Progressives, some democratic first principles were sacrificed as they grappled with wartime exigencies. The strength of American law and institutions provided instruments for the restoration and revitalization of those principles of civil liberties after the war, but not before some American citizens were unjustly forced to suffer significantly.

In 1902 Woodrow Wilson had offered his thoughts on the importance of government transparency and freedom of speech for democracy in an essay called "The Ideals of America."

> No man can deem himself free from whom the government hides its action, or who is forbidden to speak his mind about affairs, as if government were a private thing which concerned the governors alone. Whatever the power of government, if it is just, there may be publicity of governmental action and freedom of opinion; and public opinion gathers head effectively only by concerted public agitation. . . . the right to know and the right to speak out . . . [56]

In his April 2, 1917, call for a declaration of war, the president criticized the "autocratic" German government for creating an atmosphere "where no one has the right to ask questions."[57] But President Wilson was not consistent in his support of the freedom to dissent, and he apparently saw no contradiction of democratic values in his pursuit of a wartime censorship program and efforts to root out subversives. In that same speech the president asserted, "If there should be disloyalty, it will be dealt with with a firm hand of stern repression."[58]

In May Jane Addams addressed the City Club in Chicago, voicing her hopes that the United States would remain "tolerant to pacifists in time of war" and that "fellow-citizens, however divided in opinion, will be able to discuss those aspects of patriotism which endure through all vicissitudes."[59] Rose Pastor Stokes had made clear that she was not a pacifist. She believed that a war to make the world safe for democracy could be justified. But she came to believe that the United States was not in fact fighting to make the world safe for democracy. The way she saw it, the fighting was intended to make the world safe for capitalism and profiteering, goals she could neither justify nor support.

At the president's urging, the Espionage Act of 1917 was passed on June 15. Rose Pastor Stokes, Eugene V. Debs, and a host of others who insisted on their right to question authority and criticize the government would be arrested, indicted, and in many cases imprisoned under this statute. The Espionage Act provided for fines of up to $10,000 and prison sentences of up to twenty years for anyone found to "interfere with the operation and success of the military."[60]

The impact of the Espionage Act was soon felt in the academic world. In June 1917, the same month that the Espionage Act was passed, Columbia University President Nicholas Murray Butler announced that "he was now imposing a ban on the expression of disloyal views on campus," by which he meant that Columbia would no longer tolerate expressions of opposition to American intervention in the war.[61] In August Columbia University psychology professor James Mckeen Cattell was fired for expressing his opposition to the draft in a letter to three congressmen. In October Henry Wadsworth Longfellow Dana, grandson of the poet Longfellow, was fired from Columbia's English department for his anti-draft sentiments. A third Columbia professor, historian Charles Beard, resigned in protest.

From Invited to Indicted, and Friendly Enemies

By the end of 1917, Rose Pastor Stokes recanted her support for President Wilson and the American war effort. The Bolshevik Revolution inspired her, and she had never wavered from her ideological commitment to socialism. She felt uneasy about the politics of the individuals who applauded her initial pro-war stand. In her autobiography, Rose asserts that soon after leaving the Socialist Party and offering support to the president and the war effort, she was plagued with self-doubt. These misgivings were inflamed by the fulsome approbation she received from "motley political elements" of which Pastor Stokes was either skeptical or scornful.[62] She would not repose with the strange bedfellows of political expedience. In November she declined the invitation to dine with the president at the White House, and four months later she was indicted under the Espionage Act.

Graham Stokes joined with others like him who had resigned from the Socialist Party to try to form a new socialist party called the National Party that would vow to "put America first." Rose called it "a labor party with labor left out,"[63] and declined to join. This new party never got off the ground. She soon decided to return to the Socialist Party and to oppose American participation in the war. "It was a war for markets," she wrote, "yet I began to see it as a war for democracy. It was a war of European and American Capitalism for control of oil in the East. I came to see it distortedly as something beside—as a war of liberation—a war that would precipitate the Social Revolution!"[64] Rose followed in the well-worn footsteps of those who first voted for the war before voting against it.

Graham and Rose reached a political impasse at this time, which also marked an irrevocable split in their marriage. They spent less and less time together, their marital status increasingly ambiguous. Anzia Yezierska was privy to her friend's circumstances, and had experienced her own ambiguous marital status more than once. Yezierska's protagonist in *Salome of the Tenements*, incorporating elements of Pastor Stokes's and Yezierska's personal histories, ends up at the end of the novel in the midst of an uncertain marital predicament, not quite divorced from one husband, but engaged to a new fiancé. Rose Pastor Stokes and James Graham Phelps Stokes remained married for several more years before divorcing in 1925, becoming what Rose called "friendly enemies,"[65] as he aligned politically with Social Democratic and Progressive reformers and she steadfastly held on to international socialism and communism. At the time of their divorce, Rose wrote to Graham, "In the very nature of our respective backgrounds, it was inevitable that you should place yourself on the side of capitalism, I, on the side of the workers."[66] Graham insisted that personal, not political differences had ended the marriage, writing to Rose, "'Political differences' have little if anything to do with our trouble, Girlie." The problem is "your wholly selfish determination to disregard my feelings in our home."[67] Notwithstanding their different perceptions of the way their relationship devolved, Rose and Graham arrived at the sad realization that, as Keren McGinity observes, "Intermarriage, like all marriage, is a relationship of power."[68]

After twenty years of marriage Graham sued Rose for divorce for adultery, citing an affair she had after they had separated. Less than five months later he married a woman from a wealthy family in the same upper-class social set into which he was born.[69]

You Ought to Be in Pictures

The American government war publicity machine was reluctant to give up on Rose in 1917. The president and many supporters were gratified when Rose, a well-known leftist with a favorable public image, at first spoke out approvingly of their efforts. The president's Division of Films of the Committee of Public Information offered to make Rose Pastor Stokes a movie star. On October 31, 1917, Louis W. Mack, director of the Division of Films, wrote to Pastor Stokes:

> The Division of Films, Committee on Public Information is building an immigrant film at the present time.
>
> We are going to show scenes of people who have been born in alien countries, who have become American citizens, and achieved places of worth and prominence. There will be two women in the picture.
>
> We would like to have you enact one of the parts.[70]

Pastor Stokes declined Mack's offer, but she did try to star in at least one other movie. Rose wrote a screenplay titled *Shall the Parents Decide?* in 1917 with French filmmaker Alice Guy-Blaché for a film intended to promote propaganda of a different kind than the war fervor of the Committee on Public Information.[71] This was to be about birth control. Guy-Blaché was known as the first female movie director. Following two decades producing and directing silent films in France, she moved to the United States in 1907 and continued her prolific and successful career. In her autobiography Pastor Stokes recalls being offered "the leading role" in the film, which she joked would be called "The Least-Loved Rich Woman in the World."[72] Rose writes that silent film star Clara Kimball Young's manager, Lewis J. Selznick, arranged a screen test, "made a reel of me, declared me a Sara Bernhardt and offered me a contract."[73] In the end, production funding could not be obtained because the film was considered too controversial. Cinema historian Martin F. Norden links the film's failure to materialize to the advent of a "new conservatism" that coincided with "the United States hurtling toward direct military involvement in the Great War."[74] The same political pressures created Rose's chance to star in a pro-war propaganda film and prevented her from starring in a pro-birth control propaganda film. Neither film was made.

Espionage

In January 1918, just two months before the federal indictment of Rose Pastor Stokes, she was asked by L. Ames Brown, the director of the federal government's Division of Publicity of the Committee on Public Information, if she would contribute something in writing to be used for the pro-war propaganda campaign. Even after she declined his offer, citing her "convictions regarding imperialism and freedom of speech," Brown wrote again that he was "most emphatically unwilling to give up a hope of getting a contribution to our war propaganda from you."[75] He was unwilling, but he remained unable. His hopes for Rose would go unfulfilled. The federal government tried to use its sovereign power to pressure Rose to display obedience. The ancient Persian king had tried to pressure his Queen Vashti into such a performance. But Vashti would not dance, and neither would Rose. Pastor Stokes proved to be as defiant as her Persian predecessor. And just as Vashti's disobedience was followed by banishment, the federal government tried to banish Rose Pastor Stokes to prison.

Rose rejoined the Socialist Party of America and resumed support of the Intercollegiate Socialist Society. She remained somewhat inscrutable, sharply criticizing President Wilson and the justifications and goals of the American war effort, while maintaining "her belief that, now that the battle had been joined, Germany must be defeated."[76] Rose's difficulty in reconciling her political positions recalls Randolph Bourne's description of "irreconcilables," in his essay "The War and the Intellectuals," which was published in June 1917 in *The Seven Arts*. The Espionage Act was passed that month and Rose's difficulties were ramping up. Bourne called for a mobilization of "irreconcilable radicals," intellectuals who would refuse to support the war effort. "The 'irreconcilable' need not be disloyal," Bourne wrote. "He need not even be 'impossiblist.' His apathy toward war should take the form of a heightened energy and enthusiasm for the education, the art, the interpretation that make for life in the midst of the world of death."[77] Bourne hoped that irreconcilables would join in challenging the popular support for the war. The term "irreconcilables" would later be applied to others, including Idaho Senator William Edgar Borah, a Republican who questioned the Wilson administration's war spending and disapproved of details of the Treaty of Versailles. Borah had a long adulterous affair with Theodore Roosevelt's daughter Alice. They had an out-of-wedlock child together.

David Kennedy writes, "The Socialist Party was among the first groups to feel the whip of official wrath" of the Espionage Act.[78] On July 17, 1917, just a month after the act became law, Kate Richards O'Hare was arrested after giving a speech in Bowman, North Dakota, titled "Socialism and the War."[79] O'Hare was an editor of *National Ripsaw*, a St. Louis–based socialist journal. She was sentenced to five years in prison, and served in Missouri State Prison from April 15, 1919, after the Armistice but before the Treaty of Versailles, until May 29, 1920, when President Wilson commuted her sentence to time served. President Calvin Coolidge later pardoned O'Hare.

After rejoining the Socialist Party in February 1918 and renouncing her fleeting support for the Wilson administration's war effort, Rose Pastor Stokes returned to the political speaking circuit on a barnstorming tour that took her through several states. Graham Phelps Stokes stayed home. On March 17, 1918, Rose was the keynote speaker at the Hotel Baltimore at the state dinner of the Woman's Dining Club in Kansas City, Missouri. No transcript or recording was made of her remarks, but press reports highlighted her criticism of businessmen who exploited the war effort for personal profit.[80] She scoffed at the noble justifications for the war expressed by President Wilson. The *Kansas City Post* reported that "Mrs. Stokes said if this country had gone to war in the cause of democracy it would have entered when Belgium was ravished or when the *Lusitania* was sunk."[81] This criticism of President Wilson's timing in entering the war echoes that of Randolph Bourne, who in an August 1917 essay called "The Collapse of American Strategy" also pointed to several provocative events that might have justified U.S. military involvement between 1914 and 1917. "The President convicts himself of criminal negligence in not urging us into the war at that time," wrote Bourne.[82]

Acutely aware, as always, of the power of the press, Rose believed that an article in the *Kansas City Star* distorted the meaning of her speech to the Women's Dining Club. Seventeen years earlier she had written a letter to the editor of a newspaper, *Yiddishes Tageblatt*, which had changed her life by rescuing her from the sweatshops and bringing her from Cleveland to New York City. She now wrote a letter to the editor of the *Kansas City Star* that also would profoundly affect her life, this time in a negative way. That letter read,

> To the Star: I see that it is, after all, necessary to send a statement for publication over my own signature, and I trust that you will give it space in your columns.
>
> A headline in this evening's issue of the Star reads: "Mrs. Stokes for Government and Against War at the Same Time." I am not for the government. In the interview that follows I am quoted as having said, "I believe the Government of the United States should have the unqualified support of every citizen in its war aims."
>
> I made no such statement, and I believe no such thing. *No government which is for the profiteers can also be for the people, and I am for the people, while the government is for the profiteers.* (Emphasis added)
>
> I expect my working class point of view to receive no sympathy from your paper, but I do expect that the traditional courtesy of publication by newspapers of a signed statement of correction, which even our most Bourbon papers grant, will be extended to this statement by yours
>
> Yours truly,
Rose Pastor Stokes[83]

The federal government of the United States would attempt to pin this letter on Rose as a badge of dishonor in an attempt to shame her into remorse and obedience. But Rose responded willfully in the proud, subversive tradition of Hester Prynne. She displayed the letter defiantly, refused to repent, and spurned the coercive force of the ruling authority. Four days later, on March 23, 1918, Rose Pastor Stokes was arrested by U.S. Marshall William A. Shelton in the lobby of the Horton Hotel in Willow Springs, Missouri. She had spoken before an audience the night before at the Opera House in Willow Springs. The criminal charges were not based on the contents of her speech but rather on her letter to the editor of the *Kansas City Star*. Rose was charged with violating three provisions of the Espionage Act:

UNITED STATES ESPIONAGE ACT OF 1917

Whoever, *when the United States is at war,* shall

willfully make or convey false reports or false statements with intent to interfere with the operation or success of the military or naval forces of the United States or to promote the success of its enemies

and whoever, *when the United States is at war,* shall

willfully cause or attempt to cause insubordination, disloyalty, mutiny, or refusal of duty, in the military or naval forces of the United States,

or shall

willfully obstruct the recruiting or enlistment service of the United States, to the injury of the service or of the United States,

shall be punished by a fine of not more than $10,000 or imprisonment for not more than twenty years, or both.[84] (Emphasis added).

In jail in Missouri, far from home, Rose Pastor Stokes sought help from her husband. Their marriage was troubled, and this incident did not help. A series of telegrams between Rose and Graham immediately following her arrest illustrate the tension between them.

"Don't arouse people against cause of social democracy," Graham admonished Rose in his first wire. "Awful reports in papers here. Graham."

It was not lost on Rose that her husband's first concern was for the cause of social democracy, not his wife's well-being. Both spouses understood his pointed reference here to his new political bent toward pro-American, moderate social democracy as opposed to the radical, revolutionary socialism and communism with which Rose became more and more closely aligned.

"Your message misdirected dear; send it to jingo capitalist press. Am under arrest," was Rose's terse reply.

"Dreadfully, dreadfully sorry," a chastened Graham answered. "Advise where I can find you. Much love, Graham." He would find her at the U.S. marshal's office in Kansas City.[85]

Graham Stokes arranged for $10,000 bail for Rose, and hired attorneys to defend her. Her trial began on May 20, 1918. The political divide separating Rose and Graham widened as time passed. Their disagreements about U.S. entry into World War I combat, exacerbated by her very public arrest, trial, and conviction, magnified the rift that led to their divorce. They remained married throughout the criminal proceedings, however, and he paid her legal expenses.

Trial and Tribulation

The trial of Rose Pastor Stokes was significant in several ways. First, it was a criminal case based on a statute so new that courts were in the early stages of interpreting and applying it. The law's requirement of proof of criminal intent on the part of the accused posed particular challenges.

Second, the timing of the statute's passage during war and the consequent challenge to interpret and apply legal rules designed specifically to address wartime conditions increased the urgency with which the outcome of this case was anticipated by government officials, the press, and concerned citizens of all political persuasions. Observers feared either that the war effort might be hindered or that war hysteria might be inflamed, whether Rose Pastor Stokes was acquitted or convicted. What seemed to be at stake was nothing less than the fate of the nation's military men on the foreign battlefield and the cherished freedoms for which they were fighting.

Third, this statute was a direct challenge to the Constitution's First Amendment insistence that "Congress shall make no law . . . abridging the freedom of speech, or of the press." This challenge required a reckoning with the civil liberties essential to American democracy. These rights were trumpeted to distinguish the United States from the Imperial German Republic, and to justify America's military entry into the war. A series of cases brought under the Espionage Act, its amendments, and the subsequent Sedition Act of 1918 challenged the federal judiciary to define the parameters of the First Amendment. Federal justices were called upon to articulate the legal, philosophical, and practical protections and limits of freedom of speech. Oliver Wendell Holmes Jr. and Learned Hand were prominent among the justices whose opinions on these matters were respected as dispositive.

Fourth, the trial itself was tainted by procedural errors, including misleading judicial instructions to the jury, and the admittance into evidence of statements that were irrelevant to the case but intended to inflame prejudice against Rose.

Rose's criminal defense attorneys were Seymour Stedman of Chicago and Harry Sullivan of Kansas City. Stedman was a prominent civil rights lawyer from an Anglo-Saxon family with roots reaching back to the American Revolution. Stedman later served as chief defense counsel in the trial of Eugene V. Debs, and ran as the vice presidential candidate of the Socialist Party of America in 1920, on the ticket with Debs as candidate for president. The prosecutors were U.S. District Attorney Frances M. Wilson, who had been appointed by President Wilson (no relation) in 1917, and Elmer B. Silvers. U.S. District Judge Arba S. Van Valkenburgh presided. Van Valkenburgh had been nominated to the bench of the U.S. District Court for the Western District of Missouri in 1910 by President William Howard Taft.

The statement in Rose's letter to the *Kansas City Star* that "no government that was for the profiteers could be for the people" formed the basis of the criminal charges. This statement, the prosecution insisted, was a deliberate action intended to influence young men to decline to enlist in the military, to cause soldiers and sailors to refuse to perform their duties, thereby assisting the enemy and hindering the U.S. war effort. For this criminal act, the prosecutors asked that Rose be sent to federal prison for (1) ten years for the interference with enlistment, (2) ten years for encouraging insubordination and desertion among the troops, and (3) ten years for working to help the enemy to defeat the United States in the war.

The defense presented evidence that Pastor Stokes harbored only positive sentiments toward the American military. It pointed out that Rose's husband was a sergeant in the Ninth Coast Artillery of the New York National Guard, and that two of her brothers were in the U.S. military, one in the army and one in the navy. Like many Americans in wars throughout the country's history, she supported the troops but opposed the war.

Rose encountered a public as hostile as Jane Fonda later faced after visiting the Viet Cong. An all-white Midwestern male jury in Missouri in 1918 sat in judgment of Rose Pastor Stokes, a Russian Jewish radical leftist

East Coast immigrant woman who arrived in the United States poor, married the wealthy Graham Stokes, lived in luxury in Greenwich Village, and traveled the country fighting for leftist political causes, and now was protesting the war effort. Press coverage depicted Pastor Stokes as an ungrateful, disobedient wife leading her wealthy, uxorious husband astray.[86]

There was also a serious issue of political poor timing working against Rose Pastor Stokes. She had taken a public stance in favor of international socialism and the Bolshevik regime that had acceded to power in Russia in November 1917. The Bolsheviks and Germany had signed the Treaty of Brest-Litovsk in March 1918, just two months before Rose Pastor Stokes's trial commenced. That treaty declared peace between Russia and the Central Powers, and Russia's exit from World War I, in effect a Bolshevik abandonment of America and the Western Allies while empowering the German enemies. This action expanded American wartime anti-German sentiment to include Russia. Rose Pastor Stokes had never supported the German government of Kaiser Wilhelm II. She had, in fact, publicly called for a socialist people's revolution to overthrow the Kaiser. But her pro-Bolshevik stance was used by the prosecutors to tar her as pro-German and anti-American.

The prosecution made much of Rose's Jewish immigrant background, referring to her in its closing statement as a "foreign woman," and "the most vicious German propagandist in the United States of America."[87] Rose Pastor Stokes was thirty-eight years old and a U.S. citizen at the time she was indicted. She had spent twenty-seven of her thirty-eight years in the United States, but she was excoriated as a "foreigner" during her trial by the prosecutor and the press. President Wilson and federal Committee on Public Information officials George Creel, L. Ames Brown, and Louis W. Mack had hoped to portray Rose as a patriotic American cheerleader in their pro-war propaganda campaign. Now the prosecution was eager to banish Rose as a foreign enemy.

I Love All Countries

Political scientist Bonnie Honig describes this phenomenon as the "undecidability of foreignness—the depiction of foreigners as good and bad for the nation."[88] Patriotism and nationalism were emotionally evocative issues underlying the criminal charges. At the trial, the prosecutor asked Rose, "Do you believe in patriotism?" She answered, "I love all countries."[89] But this space of ambivalence and ambiguity provided no refuge for Rose, or for other socialists, leftists, and radicals after America entered the war. As historian Christine Stansell explains, "Ambiguity—a fuzziness about where one thing left off and another began—was one of [the leftists'] most valuable political resources, allowing them to create otherwise incomprehensible analogies and identifications. The drawing of lines between 'them' and 'us'—most especially between 'America' and 'us'—was not a familiar political skill. Drawing lines would become more of a habit after the Manichean dichotomies of Communism had infiltrated the political culture, but in 1917 it was a skill of the right, not the left."[90] Rose's habit was to cross forbidden lines, not to respect them. She served as a symbolic receptor to which different constituencies could transmit various concerns about class, race, gender, and nationalism. That she was an immigrant who abjured patriotism, a spouse in intermarriage, and a campaigner for birth control and against the war effort made her a powerful lightning rod for many kinds of prejudice.

To her friend the novelist Anzia Yezierska, Rose Pastor Stokes was a new kind of Salome, a dangerous, subversive, defiant, and inspiring woman who wielded feminine power to impose her will and achieve her goals. The men who ran publicity for President Wilson's government propaganda machine hoped that Rose could be depicted as a biblical Ruth, that is, a virtuous foreigner whose "immigration re-performs the social contract," as Bonnie Honig explains, and shores up "by way of explicit consent" the receiving nation's self-image as "legitimate" and "choiceworthy."[91] What the Creel Commission was after, but Rose would not provide, was reinforcement of "[t]he myth of an immigrant America [as] a national narrative of choiceworthiness."[92] George Creel had been a newspaper writer and publisher and a social reformer before being tapped by Woodrow Wilson to head the Committee on Public Information. Creel also had been a colleague of Sonya Levien when they both worked at The People's Institute and the inaptly named National Board of Censorship, which actually worked to fight censorship and protect free speech in motion pictures.

To Rose Pastor Stokes's young protégé, Sonya Levien, the indictment and conviction of her mentor harkened back to her father's indictment and conviction in Russia some three decades earlier. Levien's father, Julius, had been banished to Siberia for distributing political pamphlets deemed seditious. Now the friend in whose house she had lived, who had given her a job that provided not only money but education and access, was facing the possibility of a ten-year sentence in federal prison, all because she had written a letter to the editor of a newspaper expressing her political opinions. Sonya Levien would carry these lessons about the danger of political speech for the rest of her life.

Rose Pastor Stokes's trial became a cause célèbre, covered closely in the press, and monitored by those in the highest positions of political power. The emotional drama of the trial reflected the war frenzy that concurrently swept the nation. The prosecution used questionable tactics to intimidate the defendant and influence the jury. For example, thirty-five witnesses were subpoenaed, but only twenty were called to testify. The rest apparently were brought in merely to intimidate by their presence. These included a prominent army recruiter and administrative officers from Camp Funston, a central Kansas military facility where the press reported that the federal government sent conscientious objectors who were beaten by guards, held under cold showers, and marched at bayonet point.

A series of prosecution witnesses testified about Rose's speech at the Woman's Dining Club, not the letter to the *Kansas City Star* on which the criminal charges were based. The judge admitted testimony that Rose said that the United States was not in the war to make the world safe for democracy, but rather "to save the loans extended to the Allies by J. P. Morgan."[93] Witnesses testified that during the speech Rose said she was sorry that she had written a patriotic poem after being inspired by young American soldiers marching on Fifth Avenue in New York City. The poem, called "America," contained the lines

Wearing the uniform of world democracy!
That is why I love you.
That is why I am ready to give my all to you.
Oh, my America.[94]

The judge admitted the poem into evidence to illustrate that Rose had renounced it. Thus the judge allowed the prosecution to offer Rose's words of ambiguous patriotism as proof of her "espionage." Legal scholar and Harvard Law School professor Zechariah Chafee Jr. wrote in 1919, "although Mrs. Stokes was indicted only for writing a letter, the judge admitted her speeches to show her intent, and then denounced the opinions expressed in those speeches in the strongest language to the jury as destructive of the nation's welfare, so that she may very well have been convicted for the speeches and not for the letter."[95] Judge Van Valkenburgh did not prohibit District Attorney Wilson from witheringly referring to defense attorney Stedman as "a socialist lawyer." The judge sustained an objection when the district attorney (D.A.) suggested a negative inference could be drawn from the fact that the defendant's husband had not testified. Forced to acknowledge the venerable rule that one cannot be compelled to testify against one's spouse, the D.A. apologized, but the jury had heard the remark.

The defense brought character witnesses, including Florence Kelley, to testify to Rose's devotion to social work and public service. Kelley was a noted political and social reformer, who had joined with Graham Stokes and others in 1909 to found the National Association for the Advancement of Colored People (NAACP).

Rose testified in her own defense, describing her background working in sweatshops and her lifelong concern for the plight of poor working people. She introduced statistics illustrating the massive increase in wartime profits by many American corporations, from a report of the War Finance Committee. She read excerpts from Woodrow Wilson's 1913 book *The New Freedom*, in which he warned against business interests subverting the power of the federal government. In that book Wilson had deplored "the control of the government exercised by Big Business." He invoked the power of selective visibility used by corporations, stating, "An invisible empire has been set up above the forms of democracy," by "bosses and their employers."[96] Before the war this would not have qualified as a radical statement, nor perhaps would Rose's letter to the *Kansas City Star*. In 1911, in *Other People's Money and How the Bankers Use It*, Louis Brandeis had inveighed passionately against "the suppression of industrial liberty, indeed of manhood itself," caused by the "banker-barons" of the "Money Trust," and demanding public disclosure of "concentration of capital" that threatened "the New Freedom." "Publicity," Brandeis wrote, "is justly commended as a remedy for social and industrial diseases. Sunlight is said to be the best of disinfectants; electric light the most efficient policeman."[97]

But the United States was now engaged in war. Woodrow Wilson was no longer a state governor or a university president; he was a wartime president, a commander in chief. Many private citizens and government officials reacted in wartime with reflexive aversion to airing any criticism of the American democracy or its forms of industrial capitalism until its enemies were vanquished. Some perceived this attitude as patriotism, to others it was war fever. Unfortunately for Rose, the sentiment was a palpable presence in the courtroom, and the prosecution made the most of it. In his closing argument, the district attorney called her, with onomatopoeic exuberance, "a frenzied fanatic upon Socialism."[98]

Justice Van Valkenburgh's instructions to the jury were particularly prejudicial. The justice told the jury that the *Kansas City Star* newspaper in which Rose's letter was published had a wide circulation and was read by members of the armed forces, young men of enlistment age, and their wives, sisters, mothers, fathers, brothers, sweethearts, and friends. Given that her words reached all of these readers, the judge asked the jury, how "could they fail to . . . interfere with the operation and success of the military?"[99]

The judge's instructions to the jury also focused on Rose's use of the word *government* in her letter, in which she wrote that "the government is for the profiteers." Justice Van Valkenburgh instructed the jury to interpret Rose's statements as renunciations of the United States of America's form of government. To the prosecution and the trial judge, it was clear that Rose was a foreign enemy. Apparently the jury agreed. A guilty verdict was returned three days after the defense rested.

On May 31, the day before Van Valkenburgh announced Rose's sentence, U.S. Senator William E. Borah, Republican of Idaho, spoke in the Senate about the case. He said that the conviction "was due partly to the fact that she stated that no government that is for the profiteers can also be for the people," and he agreed that "[n]othing is truer than that statement." He added, "I am for the people where the Government is for the profiteers."[100] On June 1, 1918, one week after the guilty verdict, Rose Pastor Stokes was sentenced to three concurrent ten-year sentences in a federal penitentiary. She filed a motion requesting a new trial, but it was denied.

On June 14, 1918, in a letter to Attorney General Thomas Gregory, President Wilson wrote that the verdict was "very just."[101] The president suggested indicting the *Kansas City Star* for printing Rose's letter, but this idea was rejected. Seven months later Alfred Bettman, assistant to the attorney general, wrote, "The [Rose Pastor Stokes] ten year sentence was . . . ridiculously excessive."[102]

On June 16, Rose Pastor Stokes's friend Eugene V. Debs spoke in Canton, Ohio, before a crowd of 1,200 people. In his speech, he defended Rose, stating, "Rose Pastor Stokes! And when I mention her name I take off my hat. Here we have another heroic and inspiring comrade. . . . She said nothing more than I have said here this afternoon. . . . I want to admit without reservation that if Rose Pastor Stokes is guilty of crime, so am I. . . . And if she ought to be sent to the penitentiary for ten years, so ought I without a doubt."[103] And so he was, without a doubt. Debs was charged under the Espionage Act with intentionally obstructing military recruitment, found guilty in September 1918, and sentenced to ten years in prison. Debs ran his 1920 presidential campaign from federal prison in Atlanta, Georgia. He was pardoned by President Warren G. Harding in 1921.

The criminal convictions of Kate O'Hare and Rose Pastor Stokes motivated Eugene V. Debs to pursue the public antiwar campaign that resulted in his own arrest, conviction, and imprisonment. In his autobiography, the legendary attorney Clarence Darrow asserted that the conviction of Rose Pastor Stokes incited Debs. Darrow wrote of Debs, "I have always felt that he would have gone through the period without accident except that Rose Pastor Stokes was indicted for opposing the war. The case was ridiculous and flimsy, but the judge and jury were deeply prejudiced, as all of them were through that period, and Mrs. Stokes was convicted. Mr. Debs immediately protested in the strong and vigorous language that he knew how to use. But Mrs. Stokes did not go to prison; a higher court reversed the case, and she was never tried again."[104]

A *New York Times* editorial suggested that Rose's conviction would serve as an important lesson to others of her "clan" that they ought to confine "their anti-American utterances to New York, where juries are more amiable, and that in future, when they go West, they will modulate their voices." It went on to insist that Rose did not deserve to be labeled a martyr. Because she initially supported the war effort and then opposed it, "she is proof instead of that weakness of soul which cannot stand out against . . . unpopularity among her old companions,"[105] the antiwar socialists. But Rose had willingly and courageously sacrificed her popularity, and insisted on acting on her beliefs throughout her life, regardless of personal consequences. This was a quality Rose had in common with Jane Addams, who was excoriated in the press for her pacifist views. Rose's changing positions, especially on the war intervention, simply demonstrate her human limitations, her fallibility, and her struggle for clarity.

Rose Pastor Stokes appealed her guilty verdict and promptly resumed her work as a political agitator. On May 12, 1919, her appeal came before the U.S. Circuit Court of Appeals, Eighth Circuit, in St. Louis, Missouri. By that time, of course, the Armistice had been reached and the Treaty of Versailles had been signed. An unknown aspiring actress named Julie Goudeket fled Europe and arrived in New York soon after the war, and changed her name to Jetta Goudal. Six years later Jetta starred as a fictionalized version of Rose Pastor Stokes in the film *Salome of the Tenements*.

Pastor Stokes's argument on appeal was that she had criticized the Wilson administration specifically, not America generally. She had not opposed the principles and institutions that compose the government of the United States. She declared that she was acting in the Jeffersonian tradition of patriotic dissent. The question concerned the intent of the accused and the meaning of the word *government* in her letter to the *Kansas City Star*. The appeals court decision noted that Rose's letter was written and published "at a time when this nation was, and for nearly a year had been, at war," and "The imperative demands" created by the war "compelled the payment of high prices for the necessary materials and services to prosecute the war, until the air was filled with rumors of extraordinary profits."[106]

If her intent in her letter to the *Kansas City Star* was to criticize the policies of the Wilson administration, she could be a patriot. She could be understood as passionately advocating policies she believed to be in the best interests of the country. However, if she had been advocating the overthrow of the government of the United States, she could be deemed a foreign agent to be reviled and jailed as a spy.

Reviewing the record, the appeals court decided that the facts presented could only support the conclusion that Rose was criticizing the Wilson administration, not the Declaration of Independence, the Constitution, the Stars and Stripes, and the American democratic way of life. The trial court justice's instructions had improperly prejudiced the jury, which constituted reversible error. Still, the appeals court asserted that a legitimate question remained for the jury, concerning whether Rose either intended to hinder recruitment by the U.S. military or to aid and abet its enemies. The appeals court was somewhat deferential to trial court justice Van Valkenburgh, confirming for example that Rose's letter contained a deliberately false statement, because President Wilson had clearly announced the government's war aims, and supporting profiteers was not one of them. On March 9, 1920, the Circuit Court of Appeals vacated the trial court verdict and remanded the case to the lower court for a new trial. Federal prosecutors took no action to initiate a new trial.

Freedom of Speech

In a case of this nature in the twenty-first century, the defense would likely focus on the freedom of speech guarantees of the First Amendment. But federal case law surrounding the scope of the First Amendment had not yet clarified the limits and the liberties that twenty-first-century U.S. citizens take for granted. In 1918, when the Pastor Stokes trial occurred, the American Civil Liberties Union did not yet exist. In 1919, following the war, the predecessor National Civil Liberties Bureau, which had advocated for internationally recognized civil rights, was reorganized by Crystal Eastman, Helen Keller, and others into the American Civil Liberties Union, after which its agenda was reoriented to promote civil rights under domestic American law. This change was motivated in part to redress the very restrictions on civil liberties that were imposed on Rose Pastor Stokes and others during the war by the Wilson administration. However, at the time of Pastor Stokes's federal prosecution, the American legal language and judicial precedents regarding freedom of speech rights were not yet sufficiently developed to provide resources for her defense. For Rose Pastor Stokes, the controversy was about obligations as well as rights. The way she perceived it, she had been forbidden to fulfill her moral obligation to publicly voice her understanding of the truth.

Other criminal cases under the Espionage Act reached the U.S. Supreme Court beginning in 1919, providing opportunities for spirited debate on the correct interpretation and enforcement of the statute, and its permissibility under the Constitution. Jurists Learned Hand and Oliver Wendell Holmes Jr., and Harvard professor Zechariah Chafee Jr., were among the most influential legal thinkers who debated and defined the parameters of this statute, and specifically its relationship to the First Amendment.

In a 1919 Supreme Court opinion in the case of *Schenk v. United States*,[107] Justice Holmes affirmed the lower court judgment that Schenk's distribution to draftees of leaflets opposing conscription violated the Espionage Act. But in this opinion, Holmes offered the contextual interpretation of protected speech that became a standard against which to judge future cases: "the character of every act depends upon the circumstances in which it is done. . . . The most stringent protection of free speech would not protect a man in falsely shouting fire in a theatre and causing a panic. . . . The question in every case is whether the words used are used in such circumstances and are of such a nature as to create a clear and present danger that they will bring about the substantive evils that Congress has a right to prevent."[108] In a dissenting opinion in the case of *Abrams v. United States*,[109] Justice Holmes approached the argument from the other side, explaining the social interest in protecting freedom of speech. He wrote that "the ultimate good desired is better reached by free trade in ideas—that the best test of truth is the power of thought to get itself accepted in the competition of the market."[110] This language was an iteration of the philosophical pragmatism that Holmes had discussed decades earlier with The Metaphysical Club, whose members included William James and Charles Pierce. John Dewey was greatly influenced by philosophical pragmatism.

Zechariah Chafee Jr. elaborated on the social interest in preserving freedom of speech in a 1919 *Harvard Law Review* article. "The First Amendment protects two kinds of interests in free speech," he wrote. The interest of individuals is "the need of many men to express their opinions on matters vital to them if life is to be worth living." The second kind of interest in free speech, according to Chafee, is itself divided into "two very important social interests," the first being the interest "in public safety" and the second being the public interest "in the search for truth."[111] But the Circuit Court of Appeals, Eighth Circuit reversal of Rose Pastor Stokes's guilty verdict was not based upon such lofty legal principals; it limited its focus to her intended meaning of the word *government*.[112] In 1921, under the Warren G. Harding administration, the government finally dropped the espionage case against Rose Pastor Stokes. She never had to serve her prison sentence.

Communism

In September 1919, while awaiting decision on her appeal, Rose helped found the Communist Party of America, along with others including John Reed, Claude McKay, Michael Gold, and Robert Minor. This was the advent of the Red Scare during which thousands were arrested, deported, and imprisoned in Palmer Raids ordered by U.S. Attorney General A. Mitchell Palmer and other anticommunist law enforcement actions at the state and federal levels. Rose was among those arrested at an illegal, underground meeting of the Communist Party of America in Bridgman, Michigan, in 1922. The meeting was raided after a confidential informant, code-named "Special Agent K-97," alerted federal officials. Once again Rose Pastor Stokes was threatened with federal indictment and sentence to a penitentiary. Although some participants in the Bridgman underground meeting, such as William Z. Foster and C. E. Ruthenberg, were put on trial, charges against others including Rose Pastor Stokes apparently were dismissed.[113]

Undaunted by her Bridgman, Michigan, arrest, Rose traveled to Moscow in 1922, where she served on the Negro Commission to the Fourth Congress of the Communist International (Comintern), at which she chose to be called Sasha or Comrade Sasha. Otto Huiswood and the poet Claude

5. Rose Pastor Stokes dressed for the Russian winter during the Fourth Comintern, 1922. Yale University Library, Manuscripts and Archives, Rose Pastor Stokes Papers, MS 573, microfilm.

McKay were Rose's colleagues on the Negro Commission at the Fourth Comintern.[114] As historian Mari Jo Buhle notes, after World War I Bolshevism became a consuming passion for Rose Pastor Stokes. Buhle writes,

> Stokes had little compunction about attacking any semblance of gender solidarity within the Communist movement. In a 1922 interview she affirmed her indifference to the "purely feminist," and lavished praise instead upon female proletarians who united with "strength and courage in the battle for workers' control of America." She later advised the Comintern to sponsor "Committees of Women" but solely

as mechanisms to spread propaganda among working-class women. She denied flatly that there was a "separate woman's problem."[115]

Buhle perhaps overstates the case that Rose had no interest in feminist concerns. Her longtime commitments to dissemination of birth control information, gender equality in marriage and divorce, women's suffrage, and participation in women's organizations such as the Heterodoxy Club suggest that Rose Pastor Stokes was hardly indifferent to purely feminist issues, notwithstanding her strong commitment to socialism and communism. Still, class politics did appear to dominate her attention toward the end of Rose's life.

During Thanksgiving week of 1922, while Pastor Stokes was in Moscow, Samuel Goldwyn released the film version of Anzia Yezierska's *Hungry Hearts*, and Boni and Liveright publishers released *Salome of the Tenements*, Yezierska's novel inspired by and based on the life of Rose Pastor Stokes. Rose divorced Graham Stokes in 1925, the year the *Salome of the Tenements* film was released.

In November 1925, Emma Goldman sent a letter to Sonya Levien. Goldman was living in London, having left Russia in despair over the violence, curtailment of civil rights, and other depredations of the Russian civil war. Ideologically, Goldman had been a political anarchist as opposed to Rose Pastor Stokes's commitment to socialism and communism. Still, Pastor Stokes and Goldman had considered themselves comrades and proponents of the Russian Revolution. However, when Goldman renounced Bolshevism and Pastor Stokes persevered in supporting the cause, the result was a rancorous breach between the two women. In her letter to Levien, Goldman excoriated Rose Pastor Stokes as a "bitter enemy," a "blind fanatic," and a "bigot."[116] Even so, Emma Goldman did not fail to express some empathy and female solidarity with Rose relating to the breakup of the Stokes marriage:

> However, that need not lead you to believe that I am not feeling with Rose Pastor Stokes in her domestic tragedy. I must say the separation did not come as a surprise to me. I often wondered how Rose could live side by side with Stokes who was such a lifeless and bloodless creature. But

then, she will probably suffer less since her separation than if she had continued to live a life which gave her nothing but pain. I am glad that she had the courage to go and live her own life in her own way.[117]

As her marriage to Graham was ending in 1925, Rose had a brief affair with Irving Grossman, whose family owned resorts near Albany, New York, and Lakewood, New Jersey. Grossman was married and his wife, Sarah, was pregnant, but he eventually left Rose and divorced Sarah for yet another young woman whom he later married.[118] Although they had separated, Graham Stokes discovered the affair and used it as grounds to divorce Rose for adultery. Adultery was one of the few legally acceptable grounds for divorce in New York State at that time. Irreconcilable differences or political disagreements were not considered in divorce courts.[119] To obtain the divorce that both spouses wanted, Rose Pastor Stokes had to subject herself to public humiliation in court, bearing the label of adulteress as defiantly as Hester Prynne.

She wrote about her frustration at this injustice in the laws of divorce:

The mantle of shame appears to fall upon the defendant in our case. It should be placed upon the shoulders of the State of New York where it properly belongs. There is due to any state no small measure of disgrace to any state whose laws will not permit one to get a divorce unless one is willing to be made a subject for scandal. . . .

The real scandal (the wife who gives herself to the husband without love—the husband who gives himself to the wife without love)—the real breach is given a veneer of sanctity by the church and covered with a cloak of decency by the law.[120]

In 1927, at the age of forty-seven, Rose Pastor Stokes married a twenty-nine-year-old penniless Jewish, communist, Greenwich Village teacher named Issac "Jerome" Romain or Romaine, also known as V. J. Jerome or Victor Jeremy Jerome. Romaine had a young son from a previous marriage, evoking a strange echo of the marriage of Rose's parents in Augustowo fifty years earlier. But her mother had been forced into that marriage; Rose had developed too strong a will to ever succumb to matrimonial coercion. She retained the power to make such decisions. Rose had chosen Stokes to be her first husband, and later she had decided to divorce him. She chose Romaine to be her second husband.

The Way She Was

Rose Pastor Stokes played many public roles, including cosmopolitan, internationalist, socialist, socialite, suffragist, labor leader, activist, journalist, poet, playwright, author, indicted criminal, immigrant, mentor, and role model. She also served as inspiration for the protagonist of the novel and then movie *Salome of the Tenements*. She intervened in some of the stormiest debates about American law and nationhood before, during, and after World War I. Her political oscillation made her available as a symbol of virtuous or threatening foreignness at the center of confrontations between patriots and cosmopolitans that ended up in the federal courts. As the tectonic plates of national and world politics shifted beneath her, Rose Pastor Stokes fell into a dangerous space outside of politically correct comfort zones. She never completely extricated herself.

Rose Pastor Stokes did not live long enough to experience the moral clarity that most Americans attained after witnessing Stalinism, Nazism, fascism, World War II, and the Holocaust. Breast cancer required her to undergo a mastectomy in 1930, but the cancer recurred and traveled to her lungs.[121] She resorted to various new, unproven treatments, including extract of mistletoe, which was supposed to adjust the pH level of her blood. Rose traveled to Frankfurt in 1930 and 1933, desperately seeking experimental techniques of radiation treatment for terminal cancer. It was all in vain. She remained a political activist until her death in 1933 of lung cancer, possibly contracted as a result of her years laboring in cigar factories. She had never smoked.

Rose Pastor Stokes died in Germany only months before Hitler came to power.[122] She died too soon to witness the social safety net created by the New Deal under President Franklin Roosevelt, who was elected just a few months before Rose died. Had she lived longer, perhaps the ambivalence and oscillation that characterized her struggle to respond to the events and challenges of the Progressive Era, the Russian Revolution, and the Great Depression would not have hindered her after the Moscow Show Trials of 1936 through 1938, the Hitler–Stalin Pact of 1939, and the 1941 bombing of Pearl Harbor. Franklin D. Roosevelt's New Deal social and economic policies surely were more closely aligned with Rose's ideals than were Woodrow Wilson's tepid concessions to the Progressives and his odious infringements of civil rights. At the time of her death, she was writing an autobiography, which was published unfinished, posthumously.

One can imagine Rose Pastor Stokes during the 1940s becoming a more mainstream political activist, like the fictional Jewish activist Katie Morosky portrayed by Barbara Streisand, whose heart is broken by Hubbell Gardner, the handsome Gentile screenwriter played by Robert Redford in the 1973 film *The Way We Were*. But Rose's life was cut short, and she remained an unrepentant, intransigent communist to the end. Rose Pastor Stokes was caught in what John Fabian Witt has called the "collision between the obligations of loyalty exacted by the nation-state on the one hand and internationalist ideals of cosmopolitan citizenship on the other."[123] Unwilling to submit to the prevailing "us or them" choices, she remained ever beyond the pale.

| 3 |

Anzia Yezierska Was between the Lines

Anzia Yezierska's origins remain obscure. She was born around 1880 in what is now Poland. Her self-promoted legend holds that the exact date of her birth was forgotten. With no birth certificate or written record, she chose to celebrate her birthday in October and adjusted her age whenever it seemed expedient.[1] Anzia was the seventh of Pearl (Shana Perl) and Bernard (Baruch) Yeziersky's ten children,[2] nine of whom survived to adulthood. It is also difficult to pinpoint her birthplace with certainty. It might have been the village of Plock, sometimes recorded as Plotsk, or Plock, or Plinsk. Historian Bettina Berch adduces persuasive evidence that it actually was a different shtetle called Maly Plock, around 125 miles away from Plock.[3] Adding to the confusion, some 500 miles east of those villages there was yet another shtetle called Polotsk, also sometimes transliterated as Plotsk, which was the childhood home of Mary Antin, immigrant author of *The Promised Land*.[4]

In Yezierska's memories her early childhood was spent in a cold outpost of mud-floor huts. It was one of hundreds if not thousands of such hamlets scattered throughout the Russian Pale in which Jews were permitted to eke out a meager existence, apprehensively clinging to family and tradition, fearful of pogroms, Cossacks, and forced conscription in the czar's army. Eventually Anzia and her family became exiles, forced to leave their precarious living place and immigrate to America. These uncertain origins inculcated in Anzia an affinity for ambiguity, ambivalence, and oscillation from which she drew a kind of strength. She was animated by a volatile mix of strong will and insecurity.

If a father's absence wounded Rose Pastor Stokes, it was a father's powerful presence that scarred Anzia Yezierska. Bernard Yeziersky presided

6. Anzia Yezierska soon after the birth of her daughter. From the Anzia Yezierska Collection, Howard Gotlieb Archival Research Center, Boston University.

over his wife and children with implacable paternal authority, a restrictive patriarch mandating gender-specific roles and obligations from which Anzia recoiled and rebelled. Yezierska's father was a *melamed*, a Hebrew scholar and teacher, a learned man whose family worked to support his studies. Men who chose such lives in Eastern European Jewish communities often were simultaneously revered as holy men and disdained as ineffectual dreamers. When they moved to the United States the disdain increasingly outweighed the reverence. Anzia's mother was the breadwinner, or bread giver, who supported the family. Bernard cloaked commandments to his family in the robes of divine authority. He was infuriated by Anzia's refusal to surrender her lofty ambitions, to relent and embrace the role of obedient daughter. He never approved of her moving into a flat of her own while unmarried, of her career as a writer, of her divorces, of what he considered her inappropriate life. Anzia's eventual achievement of fame, artistic approbation, and financial success did not temper his derision, which left her distraught. Moreover, her father's lifelong devotion to the spiritual and disdain for the practical instilled in Yezierska a frustrating dualism with which she endlessly struggled.

Yezierska's troubled relationship with her parents worried and in-spired her. As she navigated the challenging transitions from old to new country and teenager to adult, her parents represented a past that she could neither escape nor recapture. She felt pity and revulsion for her mother's self-sacrifice. She revered and feared her father, and never broke free of her unfulfilled psychic need for his approval. She explores the im-pact of these emotions repeatedly in her fiction.

Yezierska's fiction also contains shifting memories of her little child-hood shtetle. Her depictions of her "ghetto to look back to"[5] evoke images of Vitebsk, birthplace of Marc Chagall (née Moishe Segal) and the fictional Anatevka, home of *Tevya, The Milkman* in the stories of Sholem Aleichem (née Solomon Naumovich Rabinovich). *Music*, Chagall's famous paint-ing of a fiddler on the roof of a shtetle house, was inspired by a Sholem Aleichem story called *Stempenyu: A Jewish Romance*.[6] In an interesting cir-cularity, this same Chagall painting inspired the title *Fiddler on the Roof* for the musical play and film adaptations of Sholem Aleichem's *Tevya* stories.[7]

Stempenyu: A Jewish Romance is based on the true story of a violinist or fiddler, an itinerant klezmer musician as famous in his milieu as a mod-ern-day rock star. He falls in love with a girl from a small village where his band performs, resulting in a kind of nineteenth-century precursor to *Bye Bye Birdie*.[8] But in this story both the rock star and the bobbysoxer hap-pen to be married to others. The would-be seduction fails and they return to their spouses, the sanctity of marriage preserved.

Anzia Yezierska was a real-life shtetle girl who dreamt of a hand-some Stempenyu, a poet who would sweep her off her feet and save her from poverty and loneliness. Yezierska's fantasy poet as the perfect male lover suggests a secular reimagining of her father the Talmudic scholar. In her idealized version, the man is above base material and crass com-mercial concerns, freed from such banalities by the fame and fortune generated by his art. His wife does not have to support him; she lives in luxury and basks in reflected glory. She is his muse, receiving his adoring gaze and rewarding him with inspiration. He remains devoted to art and beauty, immersed not in words of scripture like her father but in sublime words of love. Yezierska fell secretly in love at sixteen with a poet who had been seeing her older sister Annie. When Annie rejected him, Anzia proclaimed her feelings. The man only laughed, but her attraction to poets and musicians survived,[9] and Yezierska incorporated this incident into a scene in her 1925 novel *Bread Givers*.[10]

As an adult Yezierska zealously pursued an education in history, philosophy, poetry, and literature. She hoped this secular knowledge would, as Carol Schoen notes, "provide the necessary background that could link her with the native born [Americans], and it would serve as a substitute for the sacred [Jewish] texts which she, as a woman, was forbidden to study."[11] The imaginary American poet would provide Yezierska the love and approval she could not win from her father. While her father revered only the divine, the dream poet revered only Anzia.

Escaping oppression and religious persecution in Eastern Europe, the Yezierskys entered a different kind of Pale in the Lower East Side of New York, where boundaries were drawn not by law, but by poverty, ethnicity, and social class. The family entered the United States through Castle Garden in Battery Park at the southern tip of Manhattan around 1890, a few years before the opening of Ellis Island in New York Harbor as an immigrant processing station. One of her older brothers preceded the family to America and changed his name to Max Mayer. Anzia took the name Hattie Mayer but later reclaimed her Russian Jewish "real" name.[12] Bernard Yezkiersky remained a Hebrew scholar and teacher, and his wife, Pearl, earned money by peddling from a pushcart. As they grew old enough the children were put to work to help support the family.

Anzia was ten or eleven years old when she arrived in New York. The experiences of her first American decade crushed her childish great expectations. The squalor of tenement life was overwhelming. She had known poverty and hunger as a child in Russia, but nothing like this. New York subjected her family of eleven to unbearable overcrowding in small apartments in dark, filthy, airless buildings. In later years Yezierska filled stories and novels with these painful remembrances. Among the most frequent themes in her fiction are the hunger, dirt, and darkness of the tenements. Light, food, clean clothes, and airy surroundings are the most coveted desires of her characters. Nevertheless, when these material needs are met, the characters face, as Anzia did, spiritual crises.

Yezierska and her family lived in the tenement conditions of the 1890s that reformers and muckrakers such as Lawrence Veiller and Jacob Riis described and photographed. The buildings were designed to comply with the meager regulations of the Tenement House Act of 1867 and the Tenement House Act of 1879, the latter known as the "Old Law." Old Law tenement apartments typically contained windows in kitchens and outer rooms, and windowless inner rooms and bedrooms. Water was provided from common faucets either for each floor or sometimes only on the ground floor for an entire building containing eight flats and forty or fifty people. Outhouses were in alleys behind the buildings, and sanitary conditions abysmal. It was not until the Tenement House Act of 1901, the "New Law," that the most egregious of these conditions were addressed, and even the new regulations required only tiny airshafts to provide a modicum of light and ventilation to inner rooms.[13] Irving Howe notes that during the last quarter of the nineteenth century, in the Lower East Side Yiddish press, "The word *finsternish*, darkness, recurs again and again, as the one note Yiddish readers could be expected immediately to recognize—their lives are overcome by *finsternish* and it is to escape *finsternish* that men must learn to act."[14]

Yezierska rejected all forms of female subordination. She was dissatisfied with the female role models available to her. Her mother seemed to slave in thankless drudgery, trapped within the limits of the tenements and the prescripts of Orthodox Judaism. Anzia's sisters married and proceeded to live lives of wifely servitude like their mother. Yezierska bridled at the restrictions and responsibilities imposed on her at home with her family. In her teens she worked as a housekeeper, sewing machine operator, laundress, waitress, and cook. The menial positions she endured left her physically exhausted and spiritually degraded. She could not reconcile herself to work in a sweatshop or as a domestic servant.

These factors fueled Yezierska's determination to achieve self-proprietorship, ownership of herself and her labor. Although she could not always maintain mastery over her emotions, Anzia would never willingly cede control of her destiny to any other master. She perceived poverty, family, and ethnicity as the bars of a cage in which she could never achieve the full status of personhood, and never fully become an American, whatever that word might mean. She strove to escape from squalor and constraint. Her fictional *Salome of the Tenements* cries out, "I was trapped by poverty in a prison of ugliness—dirt—soul-wasting."[15]

At around the age of seventeen in 1897, Yezierska took the emotionally wrenching step of moving out of her parents' apartment, bursting through a literal and figurative closed door. She vanished, hoping to reappear in a new and better place. For a young, unmarried woman to move out on her own was contrary to Yezierska's family and Jewish cultural tradition. Although it was increasingly common at the turn of the twentieth century, it remained something of a scandal, a *shahnda*, a source of shame, raising questions about the stability of her family and her own morality. Historian Kathy Peiss writes that "living alone spelled immorality among many immigrants."[16] Yezierska sublet a series of rooms in tenement flats, supporting herself with what meager pay she could earn as a waitress, a housemaid, a garment industry sweatshop worker. As if anticipating Virginia Woolf's 1929 essay *A Room of One's Own*,[17] Anzia perceived clearly that she needed money and a room of her own before she could achieve real independence.

Dramatically bursting through doors became a recurring theme for Yezierska. At several important moments in her life, she barged in or stormed out through closed doors in paroxysms of emotion, either to flee perceived bonds of confinement or to pursue imagined opportunity. These were instances of willful, assertive appearance and disappearance, deliberate display, concealment, and deployment of female spectacle. Yezierska tried to exercise control of her visibility to accrue and exert power. Sometimes the magic worked, and sometimes it did not.

In Thomas Pynchon's 1990 novel *Vineland*, the protagonist Zoyd Wheeler "transfenestrates" once a year. He crashes through windows (defenestration suggests going out of open windows while transfenestration requires the breaking of glass) in order to retain the official designation of insanity that entitles him to monthly government disability checks.[18] For Anzia, no broken glass was necessary, although broken promises and personal relationships did result. She did not use windows but doors as portals through which to make dramatic entrances and exits and break through barriers.

In 1899 or 1900, around the age of twenty, she moved into the Clara de Hirsch Home for working girls. Yezierska impressed Sarah Ollesheimer, wife of banker Henry Ollesheimer, and some other wealthy patrons of the Clara de Hirsch Home. They voted to pay Anzia's tuition to Teachers College at Columbia University. Until she could satisfy Columbia's preadmission requirements she attended night school at the New York City Normal College, working at low-paying, menial jobs, often putting in ten-hour days before classes. She continued to work as she progressed through Columbia. Yezierska graduated with credentials as a teacher of domestic science in 1904, the year that philosopher-educator John Dewey joined the Columbia faculty. But she did not meet Dewey until 1917.

While matriculating at Columbia, Yezierska attended classes, parties, and social activities at the Jewish Educational Alliance, a settlement house. She met Rose Pastor Stokes at another settlement house, the University Settlement. Rose was only a year or two older than Anzia, but by the time they met in 1902 or 1903, Rose was a twenty-four-year-old reporter for the *Yiddishes Tageblatt*, also working as a counselor for girls at the settlement, while the approximately twenty-three-year-old Anzia was still struggling to finish her last year at Columbia Teachers College in between menial jobs. Sonya Levien was then a fifteen-year-old girl in a group at the University Settlement for which Rose was a summer counselor. The three girlfriends' lives changed when Yezierska and Levien watched Rose Pastor marry Graham Stokes and catapult to great wealth and social status in 1905.[19]

Yezierska craved a liberal arts education, but she was pushed by her wealthy benefactresses to acquire a diploma in teaching domestic science. John Dewey propounded the idea that education "is a process of living and not a preparation for future living."[20] This was easier to express in the abstract than in a syllabus or lesson plan. In practice it amounted to an attempt to apply the radical empiricism and philosophical pragmatism Dewey shared with Charles Pierce, Oliver Wendell Holmes Jr., and William James. Jackson Lears writes that these methods of thinking held, among other things, "that ideas be evaluated with respect to their actual consequences in everyday life."[21] This kind of logical positivism had offshoots and influences in politics, law, and even quantum mechanics.

Dewey and his wife, Alice, built the experimental Laboratory School at the University of Chicago where students "learned by doing."[22] The intuitive logic of the education as life theory did not prevent missteps or unintended consequences in its implementation. Anzia Yezierska was a poignant example. She wanted an education in the humanities, not a trade school diploma, and although her training enabled her to obtain remunerative employment, she felt coerced into becoming a cooking teacher. This left her frustrated, resentful, and longing for a different career path.

The wealthy Mrs. Ollesheimer had chosen the practical training program for Anzia with benevolent if condescending intentions. But Yezierska was willful, rebellious, and temperamentally resistant to obedience to rules. Although she was grateful, she also rejected the idea that philanthropy authorized a donor to dictate the behavior of the recipient. She was enraged that acceptance of charitable assistance required her to surrender self-agency. In keeping with her Eastern European Jewish background, Yezierska perceived charity as a mutual exchange between donor and recipient. An exchange, not a gift. The donor ought to be grateful to the recipient for providing the opportunity to fulfill a moral obligation. In 1927 she published a novel titled *Arrogant Beggar*, a cunning reference to her conflicted feelings about being a charity recipient.[23]

Yezierska often found herself in need of help, yet she detested feeling like a supplicant. One aspect of this conflict emerged from the collision of concepts of rights and obligations that confronted her as an inheritor of Orthodox Jewish social traditions and an adopter of the American version of Western Enlightenment rights theories. In the shtetle she had left behind as a child, charitable giving was considered an obligation of those who could afford to give. The recipient of largesse under such a system theoretically would not suffer the stigma and shame borne by a person in the same predicament in a society like the one she encountered in America, which lauds giving but acknowledges no special obligation to give. For the novel *Arrogant Beggar* Anzia chose a quotation from Ralph Waldo Emerson as an epigraph:

> We do not quite forgive a giver. The hand that feeds us is in some danger of being bitten. We can receive anything from love, for that is a way

of receiving it from ourselves; but not from anyone who assumes to bestow. . . . We ask the whole. Nothing less will content us. We arraign society, if it do not give us besides earth, and fire, and water, opportunity, love, reverence, and objects of veneration.[24]

Katherine Stubbs comments that "Emerson's statement goes beyond the simple observation that receiving largess threatens the self-reliance of the recipient. Emerson argues that it is a human tendency to feel entitled to receive from society intellectual, psychological, and spiritual sustenance. But while Emerson's use of the pronoun 'we' suggests that this sense of entitlement is universal, it is crucial to understand that Yezierska's concept of entitlement may well have been very different from accepted American precepts regarding charity."[25]

The Orthodox Jewish tradition that informed the childhood experiences of the women of the Salome Ensemble affirms that the "wealthy were under obligation to help" the poor.[26] In December 1924 Sonya Levien wrote, "It is the *duty* of a Jew to give charity."[27] Yezierska's central character in *Salome of the Tenements* insists that "it's the duty from every good Jew to help an orphan get herself a husband."[28] She argues that this duty requires her miserly landlord to paint her tenement flat so that she can meet potential suitors there. The concept of an arrogant beggar is loaded with the contradictions between Eastern European Jewish and American culture.[29]

Yezierska's defensive obstinacy in response to criticism, and her continued ambivalence about cooking, hindered her attempts to find a full-time teaching position. She disdained the exaltation of cooking as domestic science. Anzia never saw herself as a scientist; she perceived herself as an artist. She despised what she felt was a deceptive label for the kind of mundane drudgery she had endured as a domestic servant. In Yezierska's estimation she was compelled to teach girls how to be good wives or kitchen maids, not cordon bleu chefs.

The practical consequences of applying John Dewey's philosophical pragmatism to education were deeply unsatisfying to Anzia, because the methodology forced her to learn from the kinds of experience selected and mandated by experts and philanthropists. This amounted to social engineering, and Anzia was an unwilling subject. Jackson Lears acknowledges that pragmatism "was the most influential philosophical consequence of the quest for immediate experience."[30] Nevertheless, he writes, "The long-term results were anticlimactic. Among Dewey's epigones, pragmatism never entirely escaped the utilitarian cast of mind; the pragmatic criterion of truth became 'what works' and education for living became vocational training."[31] This kind of vocational training was particularly disappointing for those, like Anzia Yezierska, who felt that they had been forced into the wrong vocation. It was not what John Dewey had intended. In fact he made clear that he disagreed with reformers and proponents of scientific management who wanted to separate academic from industrial education, precisely the problem that Anzia Yezierska had faced. Dewey wrote that "[t]he kind of vocational education in which I am interested is not one which will 'adapt' workers to the existing industrial regime; I am not sufficiently in love with the regime for that."[32]

After graduating from Columbia Teachers College, Yezierska worked as an itinerant substitute cooking teacher in New York City for several years, unable and perhaps disinclined to secure a permanent teaching position. She expressed ambivalence with behavior that oscillated between defiance and self-sabotage. Supervisors told Anzia that her appearance was too unkempt for a teacher, but she rejected their grooming tips. She was a beautiful young woman with blue eyes, red hair and lovely complexion who wore her hair long and wild, and she disdained the new popular taste for rouged cheekbones and Cupid-bow lipstick. Her clothing was tattered because she could not afford new clothes. This was particularly galling to Anzia, because she was captivated by fashion and the transformative power of clothing.

She decided to become an actress, and won a scholarship in 1907 to the American Academy of Dramatic Arts, where she studied for a year. Cecil B. DeMille also was a student there. Yezierska was almost thirty by then, and after a brief flirtation she never pursued this career path. Nevertheless, at the Academy she formed some lasting friendships, including one with Irma Lerner. Lerner became a reporter for *Variety*. Fifteen years later, Yezierska modeled the character Gittel in *Salome of the Tenements* on Lerner, and Anzia arranged for Lerner to be cast as Gittel in the

Salome movie. The training as an actress proved valuable, demonstrating for Yezierska how certain Americans viewed themselves and others. It helped her understand what Catherine Rottenberg calls "performative" aspects of American-ness, social class, ethnicity.[33] It also clarified common signifiers of foreignness in American literature and film, including flamboyant modes of dress and speech, and agitated behaviors that Sianne Ngai refers to as "animatedness."[34]

After acting school, Yezierska moved into a dormitory at the Rand School at 112 East 19th Street. The Rand School, founded in 1906 by Carrie Rand, was a "socialist institution—the Forward called it the socialist yeshiva," writes Mary Dearborn.[35] John Dewey, Scott Nearing, Charlotte Perkins Gilman, and Charles Beard were among the many Rand School teachers and lecturers. The Rand School and Columbia University were social and physical spaces in which Yezierska and Dewey traveled in near proximity, but they apparently never directly encountered each other in these early years. Years later when the Rand School closed, its vast library

7. Anzia Yezierska in a Red Cross volunteer uniform. From the Anzia Yezierska Collection, Howard Gotlieb Archival Research Center, Boston University.

ended up at New York University where it remains today as part of the Tamiment Library.

An inspiration to write awakened slowly in Anzia Yezierska. She often visited one of her sisters, Annie, who lived in a squalid tenement flat with her husband and growing brood of children. Annie regaled Anzia with stories about her family and neighbors, and narrated them using an exaggerated version of the Russian Yiddish accent of their immigrant *lanzmen* (old country compatriots). Anzia and Annie embellished these anecdotes for amusing and dramatic effect, and Anzia began to write them down. These notes formed the basis of her first story, "The Free Vacation House," first written around 1909, shortly after she left the Academy of Dramatic Arts. The story was rejected by all the publications to which she submitted it, but Anzia persisted. In response to the rejections, Yezierska rewrote, reedited, and resubmitted the story, only to have it rejected again.

Exercising Her Prerogative

Early in 1910, when she was about thirty years old, Yezierska went to a party hosted by a friend, a Miss Kalisher, where she met Arnold Levitas, a courtly thirty-one-year-old German Jewish printer and proofreader. Arnold wrote to thank Miss Kalisher for the party and asked her "to kindly remember me to Miss Mayer [Anzia]."[36] Soon Anzia and Arnold began an intense affair, complete with passionate letters professing their love and longing to be together, and many rides on the Long Island Railroad, shuttling between her Manhattan residence at the Rand School and Northport, Long Island, where he worked for a printing company. Arnold introduced Anzia to his family and a group of his German Jewish best friends, among them a successful lawyer named Jacob Gordon. Yezierska and Levitas's visits and letters continued with increasing frequency and ardor from March through the beginning of November 1910.

On November 2, she signed a letter to Arnold, "Lovingly yours, Anzia."[37] Within days she revealed that she had been seeing Jacob Gordon while Arnold was busy in Northport. Although he was shocked and wounded, Levitas offered Anzia time to decide between the two men. A week later she wrote to Arnold, "You know how I have struggled to be true to myself and to both you and Gordon—but I have come at last into the light! Yesterday, Nov. 9th Gordon and I were married by Mayor Gaynor at City Hall," and closed with the signature, "Anzia Mayer Gordon."[38]

The drama did not end there. Yezierska left Gordon after their wedding night. On November 21, just twelve days after the wedding, she wrote to Arnold Levitas, "I have left Gordon for you."[39] Declaring that the marriage was never consummated, Gordon filed for annulment a few months later. In what became her first experience with personal publicity, Yezierska spoke with newspaper reporters, and the following May "a flurry of articles appeared in the *New York American*,[40] and the Hearst wire service,"[41] highlighting Anzia's explanations of her ideas about marriage without sex. She claimed she was surprised that Gordon expected sex to be a part of the marriage. She said she sought with Gordon an "ideal state of perfected friendship," a "spiritual relationship" and "mental companionship."[42] It is impossible to confirm the veracity of these statements, or whether there was in fact any sexual relationship between Anzia Yezierska and Jacob Gordon, who had been seeing each other for months before the wedding. In 1910 and 1911, a declaration that the marriage was not consummated would have been required by a court to grant an annulment, something both Gordon and Yezierska wanted. Moreover, Arnold Levitas's willingness immediately to accept Anzia's return to him almost certainly was facilitated by Gordon and Yezierska's insistence that they did not have sex.

Yezierska was not naïve about sex. Sexuality was taught to girls in the settlement houses she frequented. In fact her close friend Rose Pastor Stokes often lectured and handed out written materials about birth control and sex education. Yezierska read the 1911 English translation of the book *Love and Marriage* by Swedish reformer Ellen Key, which included an introduction by Havelock Ellis.[43] She liked *Love and Marriage* enough to recommend it and send a copy to a friend and former classmate from the American Academy of Dramatic Arts. The book included information on the "New Woman" and modern ideas concerning "sexual morality, free love, marriage, and divorce."[44] Key argued that women should actively seek fulfilling love and sexual relationships, and that women were justified in ending any marriage that did not satisfy them sexually. Yezierska also was "entranced," writes Mary Dearborn, by the fiction of Olive

Schreiner, which contained frank depictions of sexuality and discussions of gender roles and race relations.[45]

Yezierska's marriage to Jacob Gordon was annulled by May 1911, about six months after the wedding. She married Arnold Levitas in July. The marriage to Levitas was consecrated with a religious ceremony but no civil marriage license, and therefore was not recognized in civil law. She became pregnant by September, and took maternity leave from teaching. Within a few months she decided that the New York City winter would be too dreary to face, and she and Arnold should move to California. Her sister Fannie lived with her husband and children in Long Beach, south of Los Angeles. Anzia went to stay with Fannie early in her pregnancy, to enjoy the health benefits of the warm weather, to become familiar with California, and to look for places to live and work. The plan was for Arnold to follow later. She discovered during a side trip to San Francisco to visit an artist friend that she liked San Francisco, Oakland, and Berkeley far more than Los Angeles, but she returned to her sister for the rest of her pregnancy. Because Arnold was reasonably secure in his job, Yezierska's sister advised him to stay employed in New York rather than move to California and risk financial insecurity just when they were about to become parents. They took Fanny's advice, and Arnold remained in New York, while Anzia stayed in Long Beach and gave birth to a daughter, Louise, on May 29, 1912. Two months later, she and the baby took a train back to New York.

Anzia lived the domestic life of wife and mother for the next two years. She depended on her husband for money, and was responsible for cooking, cleaning, and childcare. Yezierska despaired to find herself in the very role she had seen her mother and sisters fall into, the role she had renounced years earlier when she fled her parents' home. Despite her strenuous efforts to achieve education and independence, she seemed repeatedly to fall back into what she perceived as forms of traditional female subordination, as a cook, waitress, cleaning woman, domestic servant, and now housewife and stay-at-home mother. She longed for something she could not define. These were years of discontent with married life and contemplation of what kind of future might fulfill her sense of longing. During her pregnancy she had returned to the idea of writing fiction. She kept revising and resubmitting for publication the story she wrote in 1909, "The Free Vacation House," but magazine editors kept rejecting it. After Louise was born and they returned to New York, Yezierska resumed her writing.

Her friend Rose Pastor Stokes was increasingly active as a playwright, translator of Yiddish poetry, and political agitator, a leader in the areas of labor rights, women's suffrage, reproductive and contraceptive rights, and international socialism. Pastor Stokes became a celebrity, and an inspiration to Yezierska and a generation of young women. Sonya Levien became a secretary to Rose and James Graham Phelps Stokes and enrolled in law school at New York University. Levien soon entered the glamorous world of popular magazine writing and editing, encouraged and assisted by the social network and resources provided by Rose Pastor Stokes. Anzia looked to Rose and the young friend she referred to as "Miss Levine," as role models and emblems of the kinds of success that could be hers.[46]

Yezierska wanted to burst out of her emotionally constricting domestic life. While she was away from him in California, Yezierska had written love letters to her husband, and perceived him from a distance as a sensitive poet. As long as he was out of sight, she could create a fantasy vision of Levitas. But the quotidian challenges of living together dispelled her illusions. She hated housekeeping. She also was determined not to succumb to the self-abnegating demands of married life that consumed her mother and sisters. Fifteen years earlier, Anzia had burst out the door of her parents' apartment to disappear and escape the stultifying atmosphere. Now she longed for another escape.

When baby Louise turned two, Yezierska hired a nanny and returned to work as a cooking teacher. This provided her some independence from Levitas, some money of her own, and a taste of freedom. Still, she remained unhappy and unfulfilled in the marriage.

And then something momentous happened for Anzia Yezierska. After six years of rejections and rewrites, "The Free Vacation House" was finally accepted for publication in 1915 in a magazine called the *Forum*. At the age of thirty-five Yezierska published her first literary work. This was two years before she met John Dewey.

Yezierska reacted with her customary impetuous exuberance. She had crossed the country to California twice before, once as a single girl and again during her pregnancy. Both times she stayed with her doting sister Fannie in Long Beach. She now wrote to tell Fannie the good news about getting her story published. Fannie replied with congratulations and informed her that she was ill and wishing for Anzia's company. Inspired by her literary arrival and her sister's request, Yezierska abruptly left Arnold and three-year-old Louise with barely a word of explanation and boarded a train for California. One day she simply walked out of the apartment and vanished. Her first two letters to Levitas were marked "Return to Sender" because, having recently moved to the Bronx, she wrote the wrong address on them. With the error corrected, she sent more letters, "How are you and the baby?" But she didn't stop or return home; she pressed on to California, visiting Fannie in Long Beach, and traveling on to San Francisco to see her bohemian intellectual friends.

Yezierska returned to the Bronx two months later, to baby Louise and husband Arnold. There she stayed for nine more months, quarreling endlessly with Arnold over money, housekeeping, motherhood, and marriage. In March 1916 Yezierska moved into a rented room with her daughter, not far from Levitas's apartment. She asked her friend Rose Pastor Stokes for help getting more work published. Pastor Stokes sent Yezierska's stories to Sonya Levien, who had become the fiction editor at the *Metropolitan* magazine, and to other contacts in the publishing world.

Then Anzia disappeared again, this time with Louise. In April 1916, barely one month after moving out, Yezierska took her four-year-old daughter and lit out for the territory without telling Arnold. "My life is one endless running away from the things that drag me down," Sonya Vrunsky explains in *Salome of the Tenements*.[47] Anzia and Louise, mother and daughter, traveled cross-country by train as they had done when the baby was a newborn, this time from New York back to California to stay with Fannie. Yezierska figured she and Louise would move to San Francisco where she'd look for a job. She did not communicate with Arnold for two and a half months. Arnold Levitas frantically and futilely recruited the help of the police as he searched in vain for his vanished wife and daughter.

After visiting her sister in Long Beach, Anzia took Louise to San Francisco, staying for a while with a friend, Miss Pollak. She began a love affair with Hugo Seelig, a poet she had met in New York. But this lasted only four months. In September, Yezierska wrote to Rose Pastor Stokes, "I am so dead. The man I loved died and with him went all the life out of me."[48] Seelig was very much alive, but he had stopped seeing Anzia.

Yezierska took a job at a settlement house in San Francisco. She was required to live there and board young Louise elsewhere. Miss Pollack was disturbed by this arrangement; she grew concerned about the child's well-being and contacted the Women's Protective Bureau of Oakland to investigate. Here was a strong arm of the coercive ruling authority brought in to interfere with Anzia's relationship with her baby, triggering instinctive fear of state power. Yezierska was not entirely sure of her legal rights.

The Women's Protective Bureau communicated with Yezierska and Levitas about baby Louise. The Bureau's involvement agitated both parents, stoking their fears and anger. At one point the Bureau sent Arnold a telegram expressing concern that Anzia was planning "to place the child with some people who are at present mixed up indirectly with the bomb throwing episode in San Francisco."[49]

A bomb had disrupted a San Francisco parade in support of President Wilson's "preparedness" and "armed neutrality" policies. "Nine spectators were killed, many others injured. News reports ascribed the act to anarchists who opposed U.S. entry into World War I. Tom Mooney, a leader of the International Workers of the World (IWW) and his assistant, Warren K. Billings, were arrested."[50] The trial of Billings and Mooney became an international cause célèbre as persuasive evidence emerged that the two men had been framed. Nevertheless, they were convicted. Mooney was sentenced to death and Billings to life in prison. Emma Goldman and Alexander Berkman "led a campaign to commute labor militant Tom Mooney's death sentence."[51] This campaign attracted support from John Dewey, Sinclair Lewis, Eugene V. Debs, Lincoln Steffens, Crystal Eastman, Theodore Dreiser, Upton Sinclair, Carl Sandburg, and many others. A letter-writing campaign "magnetized national interest and helped expose what turned out to be perjured and shameless collusion of the authorities."[52] Mooney's sentence was commuted to life in prison, and both men served twenty-two years before being released in 1938.

But Anzia Yezierska was more dilettante than militant. The incendiary and apparently absurd insinuation that she was connected with anarchist terrorists caused Yezierska's brothers and sisters to get involved after Arnold Levitas frantically telegraphed his in-laws for help. They spoke with Anzia, and confirmed that Louise was safe. In the biography of her mother penned by the grownup Louise, she notes that Yezierska "was politically always a bystander, agreeing with the arguments, but too absorbed in her own fierce struggle to participate in a movement."[53]

In December 1916, out of money, broken-hearted from the breakup with Hugo Seelig, consumed with guilt over her inability to care adequately for her daughter, yet adamant to pursue her writing, Yezierska capitulated and agreed to surrender Louise into Arnold's custody. "I have decided to tear my heart out of my body," she wrote to Rose Pastor Stokes; "I have decided to send Tynkabel [Louise] back to her father for a few years until I get back on my feet."[54] One of Anzia's brothers agreed to travel with Louise. The little girl crossed the country in the protective care of her uncle and went to live with her father and paternal grandmother in New York. Yezierska remained in California, writing, for ten more months.

Anzia wrote to Rose Pastor Stokes, imploring her to visit young Louise at Levitas's apartment and to speak kindly to the child about her mother. Yezierska kept writing stories and asking Pastor Stokes to help get them published. She wrote candidly to "Dear Rose":

> I am presuming on your friendship in asking you this favor. Will you read over the enclosed 4 stories & will you take them to the editor of Everybody's & then to Miss Levine of the Metropolitan?
>
> I am sending them to you because you were the one who first gave me the idea that inspired me to write them. I'm enclosing the letter from Everybody's, so you can remind the editor that he was interested in my former stories.

Need I tell you what a tremendous help it is to have you interest the
editor in the stories?—it is like helping the dumb to become articulate—
the self-bound to become socially free.

Affectionately yours

Hattie[55]

Yezierska returned to New York in November and spent Thanksgiving with Rose. "Through Thanksgiving Day of 1917, when Anzia was
herself despairing, she had listened to Rose's recital of how that much-
envied marriage [to Graham Stokes] had fallen apart."[56] Both women were
approaching the end of their marriages. Both were facing professional
and personal challenges. Rose and Anzia were confidantes supporting
each other through hard times.

Winter of Their Discontent

Woodrow Wilson brought the United States into World War I combat in
April 1917, and Rose and Graham Stokes quit the antiwar Socialist Party
in support of the president's decision. Sonya Levien married Carl Hovey
in October. Rose asked citizens to support American troops in a November 1, 1917, letter in the *New York Times*,[57] and proclaimed her support for
the president's war effort in *A Confession* in the November issue of *Century*
magazine.[58] Following the overthrow of the czar in February and months
of chaotic ineptitude as the Russian provisional government attempted
unsuccessfully to form a democracy, in November the Bolsheviks acceded
to power in Moscow while Pastor Stokes and Yezierska condoled in New
York. That same month Rose changed her mind about the war and declined
to dine with the president at the White House.

Anzia Yezierska bore witness to her friend's troubles. She offered empathy and a shoulder to cry on. But Yezierska was primarily self-involved, and
she had her own problems. She was desperately trying to pursue her writing career. Rose was a steadfast and stalwart friend to Anzia. Even while
Rose Pastor Stokes confronted daunting marital, legal, and political problems, she continued to play a central role in launching Yezierska's career,
providing inspiration and advice, and submitting Anzia's stories to publications that previously had published Rose's work and with which she had

connections and acquaintances. Sonya Levien proved to be the most important of these connections. Their shared affection for Rose and the active
encouragement of their mutual friend fostered Yezierska and Levien's professional collaboration. During the second Wilson administration, Levien
was a literary editor at the *Metropolitan* magazine,[59] and she bought and
published Yezierska's stories, including "Where Lovers Dream" in 1918.

Louise Levitas Henriksen writes, "Sonya Levien, the sympathetic editor" of the *Metropolitan*, "virtually started Anzia's career by buying *Where
Lovers Dream*."[60] By publishing her stories in the *Metropolitan*, Levien gave
Anzia a byline and a paycheck, and much more. She placed Yezierska in
a literary cohort of the highest status, transforming her from a complete
unknown into a member of a pantheon of the famous who shared repeated
pride of place in the *Metropolitan*'s hallowed pages. These included F. Scott
Fitzgerald, John Reed, Sir Arthur Conan Doyle, Joseph Conrad, Rudyard
Kipling, Theodore Dreiser, Maxim Gorky, Noel Coward, Carl Sandburg,
P. G. Wodehouse, Rudolph Valentino, and many others. In the March 1918
issue of the *Metropolitan*, Anzia's name and her story appeared along with
those of Theodore Roosevelt, Booth Tarkington, and Sinclair Lewis. March
1918 also was the month of Rose Pastor Stokes's arrest under the Espionage
Act. Anzia's success as a writer began to rise just as her friend Rose was
feeling the weight of criminal indictment and the collapse of her marriage.
Sonya Levien continued to publish Yezierska's stories. In the February 1921
issue of the *Metropolitan*, Anzia's story "My Own People" appeared alongside pieces by F. Scott Fitzgerald and Herbert Hoover.

After Yezierska's writing career took off and her marriage to Arnold
Levitas ended, she believed that Arnold hated her. However, according to
their daughter, long after their love and marriage ended and he remar-
ried, and for the rest of his life, Arnold Levitas saved all of Yezierska's
letters along with the two letters he wrote beginning and ending their
time together.[61] Arnold and Anzia remained civil to each other and shared
custody of Louise as she grew up.

Dear John

In December 1917, just weeks after returning to New York from San Francisco and catching up over Thanksgiving week with Rose Pastor Stokes,

Yezierska burst through another closed door. She pushed unannounced into the office of Columbia University professor John Dewey and asked for help getting a full-time teaching job. She also gave him some of her stories to read. Dewey was a lecturer at the Rand School at which Anzia had been living, and she might have heard him speak there. The fifty-eight-year-old Dewey was intrigued by Anzia, who was then around thirty-eight. These two apparently recognized in each other a sorrow and longing with which they were separately familiar. That recognition led to empathy despite their very different backgrounds and circumstances.

Dewey had written about his difficulty in trying to gracefully accept the loss of youth and the challenges of growing older, lamenting in a poem that he showed to no one, "The loins of fire and head of grey."[62] He was devastated by the deaths of his two sons and the terrible impact these losses had on his wife. Dewey was in the public spotlight, caught in the intellectual great debate over World War I. He was excoriated by his former admirer and acolyte Randolph Bourne in essays such as "The War and the Intellectuals"[63] and "Twilight of the Idols."[64] Bourne died in 1918 in the catastrophic Spanish Flu epidemic that took millions of lives.

Dewey was one of the most prominent public intellectuals who supported President Wilson and the war effort, along with Walter Lippman, Herbert Croly, and Walter Weyl who wrote for the *New Republic.* Casey Blake writes that "Dewey insisted that intellectuals take hold of the 'social possibilities of war' and shape them in accordance with social-democratic values."[65] This turned out to be naïve idealism. To Bourne, the embrace of "war technique"[66] was as heinous as it was futile. "War," Bourne wrote in the same essay, "determines its own end." Moreover, "Idealism should be kept for what is ideal." Yezierska engaged in a romantic and intellectual relationship with John Dewey while maintaining her close friendship with Rose Pastor Stokes. During the same months of 1918, Dewey was harshly criticized for publicly supporting the American war effort and Pastor Stokes was tried and convicted for publicly opposing it. Stuck in the middle and far more concerned with her own personal goals, Yezierska provided empathy, comfort, encouragement, and support to both John Dewey and Rose Pastor Stokes.

8. Anzia Yezierska at her typewriter. From the Anzia Yezierska Collection, Howard Gotlieb Archival Research Center, Boston University.

By the time she met John Dewey, Anzia Yezierska had survived two failed marriages, the loss of custody of her daughter, vexing estrangement from her parents and her ethnic roots, a chaotic and stressful career path, and the lack of either a stable living place or financial security. She could barely manage to earn enough money to make ends meet. And yet she remained on fire. She strove, she aspired, she longed for life, and she threw herself into new challenges, risks, strenuous action, and edifying experience. To John Dewey she was exotic, young, physically alluring, different. To Yezierska, Dewey was a heroic American intellectual, a man whose admiration was more important and meaningful to her than romantic love or sexual desire. She could idealize their relationship as a kind of courtly love. He was an American icon and a secular intellectual. And secretly he wrote poetry, something he revealed to Anzia and to almost no one else, not even his wife. Here was the composer of love poems she had dreamed of all of her life, her Stempenyu.

John Dewey's affection signified to Anzia his acceptance of her as worthy of membership within the American people. Dewey held a key to Yezierska's sense of self similar to that which F. Scott Fitzgerald's Daisy Buchanan held for Jay Gatsby. This was the comforting illusion that the status-secure insider possesses power to confer American identity upon the arriviste, providing validation and legitimacy. As Gatsby built an ill-gotten American fortune to prove his worthiness to Daisy, so Anzia built an American literary career to prove her worthiness to Dewey. Status envy and the quest for upward mobility were among many themes implicated in Gatsby's desire for Daisy and Yezierska's desire for Dewey.

Dewey read Yezierska's stories and observed her teaching a cooking class. He told her to quit teaching and concentrate on writing. He bought her a typewriter, the first she ever had, and arranged permission for her to audit one of his seminars in social and political philosophy at Columbia, in the School of Arts and Sciences, not the Teachers College to which she had previously been consigned against her will.

The typewriter was a magical gift. It was a luxury she could not afford to buy herself, an instrument with great practical utility for her, and a confirmation that John Dewey was really seeing and paying passionate attention to Anzia. To Yezierska, this was not American-style charity redolent of coercion of the kind she received at the Clara de Hirsch Home. This act of giving was therapeutic, emotionally uplifting, spiritually affirming for John Dewey. That made it a beautiful exchange in which both parties benefited. Later he gave her a job as a translator on a research study he was conducting on the social life of the Philadelphia Polish community. Anzia and John fell in love.

An important motif in Yezierska's fiction is that longing and desire are never sated, but linger as driving forces that propel action. Her creative use of emotional friction and irreconcilability is subtly consistent with literary modernism, and with Dewey's philosophical pragmatism. The embrace of indeterminacy did not come easily to John Dewey. He traveled a learning curve or arc of experience as his philosophy evolved. In 1882, at the age of twenty-three, he entered graduate school at Johns Hopkins University. There he studied philosophy with George S. Morris and psychology with G. Stanley Hall.[67] Dewey embraced the promise of "higher unities and synthetic resolutions" of Morris's neo-Hegelianism.[68] These unities and resolutions appeared to hold the potential to heal what Dewey would later describe in *From Absolutism to Experimentalism* (1930) as "an inward laceration" of alienation and "isolation of self from the world, of soul from body, of nature from God."[69] Robert B. Westbrook explains that when the philosopher "abandoned absolute idealism for an original and compelling pragmatic naturalism in the 1890s, Dewey remained infected with what he lightly characterized to William James as the 'Hegelian bacillus of reconciliation.'"[70] He yearned for certainty in a world that did not provide it. And so he tried to force it. This bacillus infected Dewey's pragmatism with a strain of instrumentalism that threatened to reduce its practical application to what Casey Blake has called "synthesis through coercion."[71] That is why Anzia Yezierska felt like a square peg forced into a round hole when her rich patronesses agreed to pay her tuition as long as she enrolled in a vocational training program in domestic science at Columbia Teachers College.

The idea of resolving contradictions and unifying opposites tantalized John Dewey and Anzia Yezierska. They thought of each other as their own antitheses, as the poles of a compelling dualism. Convinced as they were that opposites attract, this became their self-fulfilling prophecy. Yezierska would revisit this idea in *Salome of the Tenements* and other works of fiction. Mary Dearborn argues that "Yezierska erred in setting the two cultures in a dichotomy so absolute that its only resolution could come in absolute union. In Dewey, she met a man who bought in as fully as she to such a dichotomy, a man so repulsed by dualisms that he saw them everywhere he turned."[72]

The timing was perfect. They met at the moment in their lives when each of them was most vulnerable, in need of validation, and yet determined to surmount their problems. John Dewey and Anzia Yezierska were sad and tense and needy. Their empathetic recognition and receptivity to each other opened floodgates of emotion and desire. In 1906, in *Beliefs and Existence*, Dewey wrote, "To be a man, is to be thinking desire."[73] A dozen years later, in the poem "Two Weeks," he wrote to Yezierska of the desire she had reawakened in him. He was overwhelmed by passion "that surges / From my cold heart to my clear head."[74]

Yezierska was fascinated by Dewey's opposition of the cold heart and the clear head. She appropriated and repurposed his words in *Salome of the Tenements* by having her protagonist lament, "I haven't the sense to get cold in the heart and clear in the head like the American-born women of ice."[75]

Dewey and Yezierska's relationship recalls that of Lambert Strether and Maria Gostrey in Henry James's 1903 novel *The Ambassadors*.[76] Like Strether, whose wife and son died, the deaths of Dewey's two sons plunged him into depression and spiritual dormancy. Strether's identity was shattered by "the two deaths, that of his wife and that, ten years later, of his boy," which resulted in a "period of conscious detachment occupying the centre of his life."[77] Strether, understandably, never recovered from his losses, and neither did Dewey. As Gostrey did for Strether, Yezierska acted as a guide and an inspiration for Dewey, a sympathetic member of the fellowship of those who suffer from what seems like divine indifference to life's vicissitudes.

In *Red Ribbon on a White Horse*, Anzia reminisces about her time with Dewey. "We dined often on the East Side. At first, I had been embarrassed about showing him the dirty streets, the haggling and bargaining, and the smells from the alleys of the ghetto where I lived. But what I had thought coarse and commonplace was to him exotic. My Old World was so fresh and new to him it became fresh and new to me."[78] She recalls, "He asked me to take him to an East Side restaurant and we went to Yoneh Shimmels."[79] Yoneh Shimmels is a knish bakery on Houston Street that remains open to this day. In the same manner, Maria Gostrey helps Lambert Strether discover Paris. Gostrey, like Yezierska, was a younger woman who reawakened an older man's desire to "[l]ive all you can; it's a mistake not to."[80]

Both the Henry James novel and the Dewey-Yezierska affair were moved by the tremendous force of a woman who remains offstage, invisible. In *The Ambassadors* Mrs. Newsome never appears directly, but she exercises enormous influence over the rest of the characters and the sequence of events.[81] She is Strether's fiancée, employer, and benefactor, a peculiar combination of roles. Mrs. Newsome's invisibility or absence from the center of the novel's action serves to magnify her immense power.

In Dewey's case, the offstage presence was his wife, Alice, with whom he had shared thirty-two years of marriage, a collaborative career, the joy of having six children together, and the unbearable anguish of losing two sons. Alice had descended into her own somnambulistic depression. She was a phantom presence to Anzia Yezierska, but she was a real and integral part of Dewey's life past, present, and future. Westbrook suggests that

Dearborn and others have failed "to see the moral and emotional weight of Alice's claim on Dewey, and the deep ties of obligation that bound him to her despite the difficulties of their marriage."[82]

It is worth noting that Westbrook emphasizes the power of "obligation" over the weaker force of a "right" or "entitlement" that either Dewey or Yezierska might have had to "freedom" and "the pursuit of happiness." Yezierska must have recognized this primal imperative of spousal obligation, despite her own two failed marriages. Dewey might have sought the vivifying shock of experience with Anzia, but it is not likely he ever harbored a serious intention to abandon his wife and family. Perhaps when it became clear that there would be no sexual consummation, or perhaps after one occurred, Dewey ended the affair and returned to his wife. Strether defies Mrs. Newsome even as he rejects a relationship with Maria Gostrey. Dewey's behavior was a betrayal of his wife, but in the end he rejected a relationship with Yezierska and returned to Alice.

The breakup was abrupt and painful. When confronted with the real possibility of being together, apparently Yezierska hesitated, and the affair ended. In *Red Ribbon on a White Horse*, she describes an encounter "at the pier under the Williamsburg Bridge."

> For a long moment we stood silent. Then I was in his arms and he was kissing me. His hand touched my breast. The natural delight of his touch was checked by a wild alarm that stiffened me with fear. . . . His overwhelming nearness, the tense body closing in on me was pushing us apart instead of fusing us. . . .
>
> Sensing my unyielding body, he released me.
>
> At the door I was torn between asking him up to my room and the fear that if I gave myself to him I'd hate him. And if I didn't, I'd lose him. He settled it by kissing me good night and walking away.
>
> The moment he turned the corner I wanted to run after him and beg him to come home with me. But instead I stumbled slowly back to my room.[83]

The occurrence at the Williamsburg Bridge contained an echo of her first marriage, when on her wedding night she claimed to have balked and refused a sexual relationship. As her husband Jacob Gordon had done seven years earlier, John Dewey reacted by ending the relationship. The description of the scene at the bridge also reflects Anzia's indulgence in romantic fantasy. In the dense tenement living conditions of her adolescence, couples pursued intimacy despite the lack of privacy, and she remembered witnessing them in hallways, stairwells, and rooftops on hot summer nights.

Near the beginning of *Salome of the Tenements*, when the protagonist is planning her first lunch date with millionaire John Manning, she encounters a group of poor children on the streets of the Lower East Side dancing to the music of "a hand-organ" playing "the latest popular air." "Sing it, sing it," she calls to the children. "Don't stop at dancing." She dances with the children as they sing the words of the chorus: "Just a little love, a little kiss, I will give you all my life for this."[84] The song, "A Little Love, A Little Kiss," was introduced in the United States in 1912. Operatic tenor Mario Lanza recorded it on a best-selling album in 1951. The English lyrics to which Yezierska referred were:

> When the phantom night of summer covers
> Field and city with a veil of blue
> All the lanes are full of straying lovers
> Murmuring the words I say to you
>
> Just a little love, a little kiss
> Just another tour of a world of bliss
> Eyes that tremble like the stars above me
> And the little word that says, you love me
>
> Just a little love, a little kiss
> I would give you all my life for this
> As I hold you fast, and bend above you
> And I hear you whispering, I love you.[85]

These lyrics poignantly illuminate Yezierska's psyche. In the song two lovers embrace and kiss outdoors on a summer night. This describes an imagined romantic rapture version of the traumatic rupture of Dewey and Yezierska's love affair at the Williamsburg Bridge. It is a chaste fantasy that could not be reconciled with the sexual reality that would have been consummated in a hotel room or in Anzia's flat. Louise Henriksen argues that Yezierska was conflicted because she "desired the consummation" that she simultaneously found "unthinkable."[86]

Several observers have judged the romance of John Dewey and Anzia Yezierska a failure. A debate has arisen about whether the blame for this failure can be placed on Dewey or Yezierska, or shared equally between them. To Mary Dearborn, it is clear that the affair ended because "Dewey treated Yezierska very shabbily" and "finally it was Dewey's failure."[87] Henriksen suggests that Anzia indulged in the performance of a fantasy with Dewey that could not be sustained, "that Anzia had been playing a role,"[88] and that Dewey figured out that "Anzia could not love him."[89] Robert Westbrook agrees that "Anzia had been playing a role," and "was at least as responsible as Dewey for its collapse."[90] Carol Schoen suspects that the breakup "may have been due to the different roles each had assigned to the other, he seeing her as a passionate woman, she visualizing him as a hero."[91] Yezierska wavered in her many fictional depictions of the affair, often presenting the female character as regretting her own hesitation to pursue the romance, but just as often emphasizing the male character's cruel coldness. In *Red Ribbon on a White Horse*, the Dewey character curtly dismisses her with "You're an emotional, hysterical girl, and you have exaggerated my friendly interest."[92]

It is my argument that Yezierska and Dewey's relationship was a pragmatic success. It provided great benefits and inspiration to action during the months of the romance, and for many years thereafter. Dewey felt invigorated, energized by the attentions of a beautiful, exotic young woman. Anzia's confidence was boosted by the admiration bestowed upon her by a man she viewed as a paragon of native-born American-ness, a brilliant, respected academic who was secretly, as only she knew, an anguished, passionate poet. This romance could hardly have been better timed or crafted to fulfill the needs of these two lovers. Moreover, it ended in an extremely beneficial manner, leaving each of them with renewed determination and with no wounds from which they could not heal. Quite the contrary, both Dewey and Yezierska went on productively with their lives. For Anzia, the end of the Dewey affair marked the beginning of her soaring literary success.

Dewey acquired new motivation, energy, and mental clarity. After ending the romance with Anzia, he shook off debilitating depression, confronted the shortcomings in his philosophy that were cast in high relief by the Wilson administration's curtailment of civil rights during the World War, and integrated the bitter criticism directed at him by Randolph Bourne and the other Young American Intellectuals. He returned to his wife apparently without the remorse and recrimination that might have accompanied sexual infidelity or a more prolonged affair. Dewey moved with Alice to Japan and China for three years, seeking and accepting the benefits of new experience and difference, in pragmatist fashion. Anzia and John each moved on to the next chapters of their professional lives, and to fulfilling, active engagement in family and personal relationships. They left each other not damaged, but rather somewhat repaired.

There is no way to prove or disprove Yezierska's assertion that their sexual longing for each other was left unquenched. It is clear from the writing of both Dewey and Yezierska that their relationship seethed with emotional and sexual desire. Yezierska was a notoriously unreliable reporter of facts, known to reshape events from her own and others' experiences for literary effect, and in the many fictional versions she wrote about her affair with Dewey, some renditions depict a sexual denouement and others do not. Whatever the physical expression, their affair was deeply affecting for each of them, and the residual passion of these ex-lovers smoldered for years after they parted.

Emotional energy generated by unsated appetence fueled their creative output, as evidenced by much of Yezierska's published fiction and Dewey's philosophical writing, particularly his poetry, which remained a secret until years after his death. Carol Schoen asserts that "the one year of close association" with Dewey "provided Yezierska with the courage and inspiration to follow her dream of becoming an author, and brought her increased creativity and success."[93] One need not downplay the trauma of the experience with Dewey in order to acknowledge, as Anne C. Rose writes of Anzia Yezierska, that "[t]he affair was painful, but no less a cherished part of herself."[94]

Yezierska shattered some of Dewey's most limiting misconceptions. She confronted him as a flesh and blood incarnation of the imagined poor, immigrant, uneducated masses in need of his concepts of education for life and social engineering. Anzia demonstrated that she was no mere lump of clay awaiting the shaping efforts of a benign sculptor, but a passionate human being with needs and flaws and beauty and talent, capable of influencing as well as being influenced by Dewey. She was no stereotypically exotic, erotically free primitive, but an admiring, intelligent, hesitant young woman whose sexual anxiety or ambivalence toward a famous, married, older man should not have been surprising. Yezierska's refusal to surrender self-agency and her failure to perform or respond predictably according to his preconceived assumptions apparently provided Dewey with a revelatory experience akin to that described by Henry James in the Ellis Island section of *The American Scene*. Anzia Yezierska embodied for Dewey what James called "the inconceivable alien," to whom "we, not they, must make the surrender."[95] Anzia Yezierska woke John Dewey up and helped him clear his mind.

Shortly after the affair, Yezierska wrote, "I don't belong to those who have a place in this world. I belong to the outcast, the beggar, the mad, the lost."[96] This self-characterization as an outsider or other became a central theme of her fiction. Rose Pastor Stokes titled her autobiography *I Belong to*

9. A pensive Anzia Yezierska. From the Anzia Yezierska Collection, Howard Gotlieb Archival Research Center, Boston University.

the Working Class.[97] But Anzia Yezierska did not belong, really, to the working class or any other class. This was not because no one would have her, but rather because she refused, despite the pain of alienation, to belong even to those who would accept her. She would not submit to the reductionist identity logic of fixed affiliation and pigeonhole categorization. She channeled her emotions into her writing. Her art flowed from a broken heart and a romantic bent.

Longing and Belonging

Historian Jackson Lears writes that "[a]ll history is the history of longing."[98] Lears argues that much of American history is comprehensible as emerging from a longing for rebirth and regeneration. But there are many forms of longing, and Anzia Yezierska's life and work are illustrative of a longing for solidarity, a longing to belong that, like the search for conversion experience or rebirth, also is a force frequently encountered in American history. Yezierska articulated this desire repeatedly in her writing. Yet when opportunity for personal or group connection presented itself, she steadfastly, paradoxically refused to belong. In her actions and her fiction she continually broke away from personal commitments and affiliations.

These ambivalences complicated and compromised Yezierska's ideas about self-definition and immigrant assimilation. She deliberately distanced herself while desperately seeking connection. Yezierska often wrote about her desire to transform herself into an American, but she and her protagonists retained, as Lori Harrison-Kahan writes, "ambivalences about assimilation."[99] Carol Schoen adds that Anzia was "torn between her love for her heritage and her resentment at its demands; she would always feel the pull to become part of American life, yet rail at its materialism and hypocrisy; she would always demand her right to be whatever she wanted to be, yet suffer from loneliness when she cut herself off from others."[100]

Groucho Marx joked, "I don't care to belong to any club that will have me as a member."[101] Although she often complained of feeling rejected, lonely, and homeless, Yezierska refused to be a member of any club, whether or not it would have her, with the exception of ad hoc, informal, temporary affiliations such as the Salome Ensemble. Her daughter called

Anzia "[a] rebel against every established order" who wrote about a feeling of "homelessness," a "feeling of not belonging" similar to the "alienation" explored in the literature of the Lost Generation writers and Young American critics, intellectuals, and philosophers who were Yezierska's contemporaries.[102]

In fact, Yezierska fled the responsibilities of personal relationships while nevertheless pressing others for emotional or professional support and assistance. In her neediness Yezierska appeared to respect no one else's personal boundaries. Throughout her life she latched onto friends, mentors, relatives, and others whom she believed could help advance her career. She perceived these people as her saviors, but in fact she endeavored to conscript them as (revered) servants. She elevated one after another admired friend to the imagined pedestal of hero-worship, only to be disappointed when they rejected her or revealed feet of clay.

The worthiness she attributed to her literary goals allowed her to feel authorized to pressure others to help her. Alice Kessler-Harris writes that "[e]veryone admired her and no one could bear to be with her for very long."[103] Yezierska used her calling as an artist as an excuse to justify her solipsism. She often wrote about feeling guilty, but these feelings rarely caused her to compromise for the sake of another. She displayed manipulative guilelessness, childishly assuming that those around her would always assign their highest priority to helping Anzia. She was not malicious, but rather self-obsessed and self-protective.

The quest for solidarity, for belonging to something greater than one's self, remains a time-honored theme in American literature. Andrew Delbanco writes that the pursuit of "the indispensable feeling that the world does not end at the borders of the self" provides hope against melancholy, and is constitutive of what he calls "the real American Dream."[104] In Thomas Pynchon's novel *Against the Day*, Dahlia Rideout is a young American woman who spends her late-nineteenth-century childhood moving from town to town, crossing and recrossing the country with her stepfather, an itinerant photographer. As an adult she travels the world and finds herself "almost surrendering to the impossibility of ever belonging,"[105] almost, but not quite, surrendering because she cannot completely escape the longing to belong. And so it was with Anzia Yezierska. Vivian Gornick describes

Yezierska as "a misfit all her life. Throughout the years she saw herself standing on the street with her nose pressed against the bakery window: hungry and shut out. No matter what happened, she felt marginal. Not belonging became her identity, and then her subject."[106] It was a subject that Yezierska mined for value throughout her literary career.

In the fall of 1918, after Dewey broke off their relationship, Yezierska enrolled in a creative writing class at Columbia and wrote a story called "Soap and Water and the Immigrant." She sold that story to Herbert Croly at the *New Republic* in 1919,[107] apparently with some help from Dewey, who had been a *New Republic* editor and contributor. Yezierska's "The Fat of the Land" was published in the August 1919 issue of *Century*, and it was named the best short story of 1919 by Edward J. O'Brien in his *Best Short Stories of 1919*.[108] That same year Yezierska sold "The Miracle" to Sonya Levien at the *Metropolitan*. "The Miracle" contained the first of many fictionalized versions of Yezierska's relationship with John Dewey. Jo Ann Boydston notes that "The Miracle" "marks the beginning of her use of the Dewey *persona* and life in her writings—a practice she repeated often, gradually adding and embroidering details about him, about herself, and about their relationship."[109] In 1989 Norma Rosen wrote a novel based on the Yezierska-Dewey liaison, essentially recapitulating Anzia's efforts to draw value from that material.[110] Yezierska was more successful.

While Anzia Yezierska gained career momentum as a fiction writer for popular magazines, Sonya Levien began to break into the movie business. In 1919 Levien received her first on-screen credit as writer of the original story for the film *Who Will Marry Me*, produced by a studio called Bluebird Photoplays. Jetta Goudal was in New York City doing office work in 1919 and 1920, aspiring to a theatrical career. Rose Pastor Stokes was awaiting the decision on appeal of her espionage conviction. In September 1919 Pastor Stokes was one of the founders of the Communist Party of America, along with John Reed, Claude McKay, Michael Gold, and Robert Minor.

Houghton Mifflin published Yezierska's short-story collection *Hungry Hearts* in October 1920. (John Reed died that month in Moscow.) The book received a few laudatory reviews but it garnered little attention and meager sales. Rose Pastor Stokes was recuperating from illness or simply taking time away from her husband, staying in North Carolina with her friend the novelist Olive Dargan, who published under the pseudonym Fielding Burke.[111] By early December Anzia was frustrated to find herself a published author who remained financially insecure. The happy holiday shoppers in midtown Manhattan maddened her with their indifference to her plight. "If I could only throw a bomb right there in the middle of Fifth Avenue and shatter into a thousand bits all this heartlessness of buying!"[112] Yezierska was no anarchist; this was just a childish rant.

Eschewing real bombs, Yezierska set off the fireworks of female spectacle by bursting through another closed door, this time into the office of Dr. Frank Crane. Crane was a Protestant minister and a newspaper columnist syndicated throughout the United States by Hearst newspapers. She marched in on him unannounced, prepared to deliver one of her patent emotional outbursts. But Frank Crane was not John Dewey. Finding Crane to be a pale, fragile man who regarded this intruder silently, Anzia could do no more than apologize, hand him a copy of *Hungry Hearts*, and leave.[113]

Dr. Frank Crane fell in love with Yezierska's book much as John Dewey had fallen in love with Anzia. Crane devoted a column to praising *Hungry Hearts*, telling America that Yezierska had "dipped her pen in her heart" to write her short stories.[114] He called her "[a]n undying flame."[115] His article attracted new attention to Anzia, helping to boost sales of *Hungry Hearts* and generate growing demand for her stories and articles in literary and popular magazines. For the first time in her life Anzia could just about support herself with the money she earned from writing.

Yezierska fled the Russian shtetle of her childhood, wrenched herself out of her parents' tenement flat, and endured years of menial work in restaurants, private homes, and sweatshops. She earned a wide-ranging education at Columbia Teachers College, the Academy of Dramatic Arts, and the stacks of the New York Public Library. She spent a decade as an itinerant substitute cooking teacher, came through two failed marriages, single motherhood, and a traumatic romantic affair with one of the most prominent public intellectuals in the nation. And then at the age of thirty-eight Anzia Yezierska became an "overnight success." Her short stories began to sell regularly in magazines such as *Century, Metropolitan, Harper's, Nation, New Republic,* and *Good Housekeeping.*

Finding and Founding

In Yezierska's story "How I Found America" from her *Hungry Hearts* collection, a teacher reads to the female protagonist the following passage from a book called *Our America* by Waldo Frank.[116] "We can go forth all to seek America. And in the seeking we create her. In the quality of our search shall be the nature of the America that we create."[117] Yezierska took delight in Frank's insight. In her title "How I Found America," the word *found* contains the dual meanings of "discover" and "establish." Yezierska proclaims herself both a finder and a founder of America.

Yezierska's attraction to Waldo Frank was another point of connection with John Dewey. Frank was linked to Dewey in several ways. A novelist, journalist, historian, and literary and social critic, Waldo Frank was one of a group of Young American critics of the 1910s, 1920s, and 1930s, which, in addition to Frank, included Randolph Bourne, Van Wyck Brooks, and Lewis Mumford. They and their cohort cultivated what historian Casey Blake calls an "aesthetic or subjectivist version of pragmatism, which supplemented Dewey's theory of a democratic culture of experience with an artisanal critique of the separation of art and labor." They encountered this critique in the work of English radicals such as John Ruskin and William Morris, but it also "had significant parallels in the American Transcendentalism of Ralph Waldo Emerson, Henry Thoreau, and Walt Whitman."[118] Blake affirms that "the connection between the Young Americans' work and that of John Dewey provides some important lessons. Bourne, Brooks, Frank, and Mumford may have savaged Dewey and 'pragmatic liberals' time and time again after 1917, but they were far more indebted to Deweyan pragmatism than they cared to admit."[119]

This strain of intellectual thought had obvious appeal to Anzia Yezierska after her affair with John Dewey. Here was a group of former protégées and students of Dewey's who were native-born Americans in possession of education and rhetorical tools necessary to subject the master's work to criticism that he could not ignore. They privileged art, literature, and creative thinking as resources for the formation of values to augment pragmatistic technique and guard against its devolution into coercive instrumentalism. This was an effective challenge to the combined exaltation of scientific method and derogation of idealism in Dewey's work, a challenge that supported an inference that Dewey sacrificed values to technique. Frank, Bourne, and Brooks offered a credible critique of John Dewey, the man who broke Anzia's heart, based on an argument that he had stumbled into an error in philosophical thinking that appeared to rationalize and justify the dehumanizing consequences of war and industrial capitalism. Moreover, their prescription for emending that error was imaginative thinking, aesthetic creativity, and reverence for the power of art and literature. How could Yezierska resist?

In 1916 Waldo Frank married Margaret Naumburg, a former graduate student of Dewey's and Barnard College roommate of Evelyn Dewey, John Dewey's daughter. Naumburg started the first Montessori School in the United States, and founded the progressive Walden School. She "counted Walter Lippmann as 'one of her closest men friends.'"[120] Waldo Frank was one of the very few people with whom John Dewey ever discussed his poetry. This occurred while Frank was editor of the *Seven Arts* magazine in 1916 and 1917, shortly before Dewey met Yezierska. Jo Ann Boydston's introduction to *The Poems of John Dewey* quotes Frank referring to Dewey's poetry on two occasions. First, in 1926 in the *New Yorker*, Frank described Dewey as "a Christian and a poet," noting that "[h]is poems are unpublished; yet his driest work is builded on a mystic faith. . . . If he had revolted deeply from the world, he would have been a lyric poet. . . . If he had been able to find his beauty today in today's world, he would have been a great religious poet."[121] Also, in his *Memoirs*, published in 1973, Frank stated that Dewey "confided; yes, he wrote poetry of a sort. Oh, no! it was not to be seen."[122]

In 1921 Samuel Goldwyn bought the film rights to *Hungry Hearts* from Yezierska for ten thousand dollars, which represented a vast fortune to her. Goldwyn brought the struggling young writer out of the finsternish darkness of New York and into the sunshine and limelight of the movie business. Yezierska arrived in Hollywood after traveling first class by train from New York, courtesy of the studio. She was startled to find herself followed by press and paparazzi, and showered with attention by the Hollywood publicity machine. All of this had been arranged by Goldwyn's marketing department. Yezierska wrote about how excited and overwhelmed she felt, as she exuberantly anticipated being initiated "into the sacred circle."[123] At first she lived in a hotel suite paid for by the company and worked in the Goldwyn offices at the studio back lot. Before long she moved in with her sister and pocketed the studio's housing expense reimbursement money during preproduction and the beginning of filming of *Hungry Hearts*. There is a street named Manning Avenue that winds from Westwood to Culver City, which might have provided Yezierska with the name John Manning for the wealthy husband in *Salome of the Tenements*.

After a few months of trying to work with Anzia, Abraham Lehr, head of production at Goldwyn wrote, "Don't want Yezierska as aside from her being a hindrance to [the director, E. Mason Hopper] she will make impossible a sane shooting schedule."[124] Her written suggestions about the film's screenplay contained enough material to fill eight or ten movies. At the same time, Yezierska found that she couldn't write new stories while in Hollywood. She could not cope with the luxuries; the private office, the full-time secretary, the hotel living, the steady salary, the company of "eminent authors" made her uneasy.[125] She felt conflicted, ashamed to live so comfortably while remembering how others still suffered.

Yezierska had watched Rose Pastor Stokes struggle to adjust to life with the wealth of James Graham Phelps Stokes. Pastor Stokes expressed unease with the advantages conferred by her husband's capitalist fortune. She insisted that she belonged to the working class. She endorsed and promoted international socialism as a solution to the problems of the poor and oppressed. Yezierska believed that her writing was an instrument with which to express the suffering of the poor and oppressed, and a means of assisting them. Living in a Hollywood hotel with a steady salary and perks felt to her like selling out, breaching faith with her cohort of leftists, artists, and poor working immigrants. She sympathized with the plight of her secretary, who was paid only twenty-five dollars a week and had to spend most of it on clothing to maintain a worthy appearance for the company. Yezierska imagined her father's voice admonishing her, "Can fire and water be together? Neither can godliness and ease."[126] She could not ignore the inexorable emotional tug of New York City and her Lower East Side roots. While *Hungry Hearts* was still being filmed, Yezierska left Goldwyn and returned to New York. She quit California discouraged, disillusioned, confused, and conflicted, and later wrote about these experiences in an essay called "This Is What $10,000 Did to Me."[127]

Three and a half years after they had last spoken with each other, Anzia Yezierska telephoned John Dewey, who had recently returned from Asia. Filming of *Hungry Hearts* was completed and Goldwyn Studios, which would later morph into MGM, was holding private screenings in New York. She invited him to one of the screenings, to show him what she had accomplished since they parted. Dewey declined. He asked Anzia to return the letters he had sent her. Yezierska declined.

Contract Claustrophobia

There are contracts to sell services or labor, and contracts to sell goods, the fruits of labor. Yezierska felt strongly about the difference between signing a contract to sell a finished article, book, or story, and signing a contract obligating her to work on writing projects assigned by a boss. She struggled to articulate the difference that she intuitively perceived. Yezierska would gladly work for herself and only then sell what she wrote. She had been a menial servant for bosses and masters, and once she broke free she assiduously avoided such arrangements. After she left Goldwyn, movie producer William Fox offered Yezierska a lucrative three-year contract to write stories that his company would adapt for motion pictures. The money and stability were compelling to Anzia, who had known poverty and uncertainty. Nevertheless, she refused to sign the contract. Writing was Yezierska's emancipation. She could not bear to transform her labor of love into wage slavery. As long as she remained free of any employment contract Yezierska could perceive herself as an artist and entrepreneur, not an employee. When Fox asked her why she would not sign the contract he offered, she replied enigmatically, "The trouble with a contract is that it's a contract."[128]

The ambivalent attitude to contracts, the law, and authority in general was consistent with Yezierska's background. In her childhood memories of Russia, the law represented barriers, limits like the invisible boundaries of the Pale and the frightening edicts of the czar enforced by Cossacks. In America the civil divorce law imposed a time-consuming and unpleasant process to attain an annulment of her first marriage. She refused to get a marriage license with Arnold Levitas, consecrating their union with only a religious ceremony, perhaps thinking this would prevent legal entanglements in her personal life. If so, her plans were thwarted, because when she surrendered custody of her daughter to Levitas, she had to permit him to legally adopt Louise in order to confer legitimacy on her. Laws gave landlords the power to evict poor tenants. Religious laws adhered to by her father offered no acceptable role or refuge for women of Anzia's disposition.

When Anzia Yezierska left Hollywood in 1921 and reappeared in New York, she sacrificed security for self-ownership. This was an act of great courage and determination. In light of this courageous act, it makes sense that the project Yezierska took up next was *Salome of the Tenements*, the story of a young woman who rejects the unearned luxury of her husband's wealth and chooses to become self-sufficient through hard work. It is the story of a woman who sacrificed security for self-ownership. Yezierska's role model Rose Pastor Stokes did the same thing.

Asserting self-proprietorship required these women to reject the oppressive patriarchal authority of bosses, fathers, husbands, laws, and traditions. In Yezierska's world, law and authority were feared as instruments of power that demand surrender and impose harsh punishment. In *Salome of the Tenements*, an extortionate loan contract enshrined in a purportedly enforceable legal document from a ruthless pawnbroker leads the protagonist to humiliation and the breakup of her marriage. One must hide, flee, evade, or as a last resort confront such authority.

In New York she resumed her writing. Upon completing a story, article, or novel, Yezierska avidly entered the fray of the literary marketplace and fought for favorable terms on publishing contracts. Anzia Yezierska was not a lawyer like her friend Sonya Levien, but with her own livelihood at stake she was highly motivated and no shrinking violet. Anzia was an aggressive self-advocate. She had learned techniques of bargaining from experience selling and buying from pushcarts in street markets, *hondling*, negotiating, and arguing with vendors of herring and apples and household goods years earlier on the Lower East Side. Yezierska applied the same skills to pressure publishers for advances, royalties, and commitments to spend lavishly to advertise and publicize her work. She possessed the sophisticated acumen needed to understand and fine tune details of publishing agreements, to deftly negotiate every aspect of her intellectual property. She studied each clause to determine how it affected her rights and the obligations of the publisher. Sometimes Yezierska convinced astonished publishers to modify what they considered standard clauses in their contracts, to reserve her rights or provide more favorable outcomes for her. She would not allow others to push her around or take advantage of her.

One example of her perseverance is preserved in letters from 1920 through 1922 between Yezierska and Ferris Greenslet, the genteel Brahmin senior editor of the Houghton Mifflin publishing company in Boston. Greenslet was Yezierska's first book publisher. He was familiar with several of her short stories from magazines. During their first meeting, when Greenslet suggested that she write a novel, Anzia pushed him to agree instead to publish a collection of her short stories. He told her that short story collections did not sell as well as novels. Yezierska responded with a modest proposal, a marketing idea she was certain would boost sales: Mr. Greenslet should invite Herbert Hoover to write a preface for her book. Hoover had run the relief effort under President Wilson to feed millions of starving Belgians, Russians, Germans, and others after World War I. He became secretary of commerce under President Warren G. Harding before ascending to the presidency himself in 1929. Yezierska also asked for a $1,200 advance against royalties to support her as she wrote new stories to add to the book. Greenslet politely declined to contact Hoover or pay an advance, but he agreed to publish *Hungry Hearts*.

When Greenslet sent Yezierska a draft contract, she replied in a note, "I cannot sign clause three of the agreement."[129] She proceeded to negotiate clause by clause for better terms. "As to the dramatic rights & rights of translation—those ought to be subject to agreement, not 'equally divided'"(140). The most significant of the contractual terms on which Yezierska clashed with Greenslet were those covering film rights. "The best publishing houses such as McMillans (*sic*) do not request their authors to give up any motion picture rights," she lectured the publisher, displaying some chutzpah (140). Greenslet coldly answered that he was "sorry that you don't consider us one of the best publishing houses," but he agreed to allow her to retain film, dramatic, and international rights (132). These would prove lucrative for Yezierska.

Why did Yezierska imagine that a movie company might purchase film rights to her stories? Part of the answer lies in the power she drew from the Salome Ensemble. Yezierska knew that Sonya Levien had sold stories and screenplays for Hollywood films and that Rose Pastor Stokes had co-written a screenplay and agreed to star in a movie extolling birth control, although that film was never produced.[130] Yezierska had followed Rose Pastor Stokes and Sonya Levien into the world of magazine publishing. She believed that she could follow her friends into writing for the movies.

Her badgering of Greenslet did not stop there. Two years later, in July 1922, Yezierska wrote him again. She had read in a trade newsletter that *Hungry Hearts* was to be published in England. "I am surprised that I have not been notified. Will you kindly let me know how it has been arranged, royalties, etc."[131] Yezierska's aggressiveness with Greenslet might have influenced his decision not to publish her novel, *Salome of the Tenements*. In the novel, the main character's resemblance to the author's character did not escape his notice. Declining on behalf of Houghton Mifflin to publish *Salome of the Tenements*, Greenslet wrote to Yezierska that "the book is not an entire success."[132] The protagonist Sonya Vrunsky, he opined, "is so unattractive, not to say repellent, that it seems to us likely to handicap the success of the book."[133]

He apparently was exhausted and offended by this woman he perceived as an ingenuous irritant. It is fair to say that Greenslet simply found Anzia personally annoying. She was too challenging for him, never acquiescent. For Anzia, who had experienced a passionate and ultimately painful affair with John Dewey just a few years earlier, cold dismissal by the austere Greenslet must have resonated with a familiar pang. Dewey had ended the affair and moved to Asia for three years, in effect making Yezierska disappear from his life and vanishing from hers. Now, three years later, Greenslet was reenacting Dewey's dismissal, in effect telling Anzia to disappear.

Nervous Narcissist

She was resilient. As she had done after the breakup with Dewey, Anzia found another suitor, in this case a new publisher. And, again as she had done after the breakup with Dewey, she achieved greater success than she ever had before. The film version of *Hungry Hearts* was released on Thanksgiving in November 1922. It was a much happier Thanksgiving than the somber one she had spent with Rose Pastor Stokes in 1917. In an early example of tie-in publicity, the innovative firm Boni and Liveright timed the release of the novel *Salome of the Tenements* to coincide with the *Hungry Hearts* film release.[134] Boni and Liveright was formed by Horace Liveright and Charles Boni in 1917, and during the subsequent dozen years the firm published the works of John Reed, Djuna Barnes, Sigmund Freud, Upton Sinclair, Ezra Pound, Theodore Dreiser, T. S. Eliot, and a host of other great writers, many of whom could not attract the interest of staid, conservative publishers such as Houghton Mifflin. Yezierska was about forty-three years old when *Salome of the Tenements* was published.

She sold the *Salome of the Tenements* film rights to Famous Players–Lasky Paramount Pictures for $15,000. The film was released in 1925, the same year that Yezierska published a new novel, *Bread Givers*. Publisher Bernarr Macfadden paid her another $5,000 for reprint rights to serialize *Salome of the Tenements* in six installments in the magazine *Beautiful Womanhood*. She was happy to sell the serial rights, but Anzia turned down Macfadden's offer of another $100 a week to write a monthly column and act as a consultant to the editing staff.[135] Once again she refused to be tied to an executory contract requiring her to provide personal services, to perform on command. *Salome of the Tenements* sold well and royalties plus revenues from ancillary rights established some financial security for Anzia Yezierska.

Responding to critics who were repelled by the protagonist of *Salome of the Tenements*, Anzia wrote, "People in the Ghetto are high-strung . . . what seems hysterical or overemotional to Anglo-Saxons in them is a natural state."[136] Emotional intensity, anxiety, fear, frustration, and defensive aggressiveness recurred so endlessly in Yezierska's writing and her personal interactions that friends became concerned for her well-being and exasperated by her unrelenting dysphoria and self-pity. Will Rogers befriended Anzia during her brief stay in Hollywood. She relates in *Red Ribbon on a White Horse* a conversation in which Rogers admonished her for her endless expressions of angst.

"Must you fiddle the same tune forever? Suppose you give us another number,"[137] Rogers said. But Anzia could not stop fiddling precariously on the roof of the little house in the shtetle in her mind.

She asked Rogers, "Have you ever wanted what you couldn't be, or what you couldn't do?"

Rogers replied, "Gal! You're like a punch-drunk prizefighter, striking an opponent no longer there. You've won your fight and you don't know it."[138]

Salome of the Tenements provided Anzia Yezierska further entrée into a New York–based literary and social scene. She became acquainted with such luminaries as Sherwood Anderson, Sinclair Lewis, Willa Cather, and F. Scott Fitzgerald. In 1923 she traveled to London and Paris and met with George Bernard Shaw, Israel Zangwill, H. G. Wells, John Galsworthy, Joseph Conrad, and Gertrude Stein. Anzia begged the writers she met to share the secrets of their literary success.

Returning from Europe by ship, she booked herself into steerage, desiring to reconnect with the experiences of traveling as a poor immigrant that she had known as a child. What she discovered was that "[y]ou can't be an immigrant twice!"[139] She had hated the squalor of steerage as a poor child and thirty-two years later as an affluent adult she found it intolerable. She had romanticized her past, forgetting that she had not chosen steerage. She had been forced into steerage by the poverty she had now escaped. Repulsed by the appalling accommodations, she moved to a second-class cabin after one night. Yezierska was confronted with the fact that time, life in America, education, and money had changed her. She remained sympathetic to the plight of those poor passengers whom she now understood did not want to remain in squalor any more than she did. Yezierska's new, evolving self was inconsistent with the memory of who she had been, but she was uncomfortable in the past and the present.

Yezierska pursued a friendship and love affair with Clifford Smyth. He was the chief editor of the *New York Times Book Review* and in 1922 he became editor of the *Literary Digest International Book Review*. Like John Dewey, Smyth was an older, intellectual scion of an aristocratic Anglo-Saxon family with Puritan roots that predated the American Revolution. She was about forty-two and he was fifty-seven, married with grown children. Smyth encouraged Yezierska, edited some of her manuscripts, and helped her get some stories published. She dedicated the novel *Bread Givers*, published in 1925, to Smyth.

Yezierska published a collection of short stories called *Children of Loneliness* in 1923, and a novel, *Arrogant Beggar*, in 1927, both of which were modestly successful. But her fame and the approbation of readers and critics started to wane. She spent one year from summer 1928 to early autumn 1929 at the University of Wisconsin, on a Zona Gale Fellowship, which gave her free access to university classes while all her expenses were paid. In 1921 novelist and playwright Zona Gale became the first woman to win the Pulitzer Prize for Drama, for the dramatization of her novel *Miss Lulu Betts*. Gale became another in a series of friends whom Yezierska idolized and forced herself upon. Aware of her tendency to wear out her welcome and exhaust her friends' patience, before traveling to Wisconsin she wrote to ask "Zona—dearest friend" to please remain understanding "in spite of the unreasonable things I may do and say."[140]

Anzia Yezierska published seven books of fiction in her lifetime, two of which were made into Hollywood films, many short stories and magazine articles, and more than fifty reviews in the *New York Times Book Review*. But her career path was bumpy. Yezierska lost most of her savings in the stock market crash of 1929. She published another novel, *All I Could Never Be*, in 1932.

By 1932 Rose Pastor Stokes was fighting the terminal cancer that would take her life the following year, and trying to finish and publish her memoirs. That autumn Yezierska lived in Arlington, Vermont. She wrote to Rose, offering moral support and inviting her ailing friend to visit her to rest and recuperate. Their correspondence indicates that the rivalry between Rose Pastor Stokes and Emma Goldman, which started when Goldman renounced the Bolsheviks after the Russian civil war, continued to the end of Pastor Stokes's life. Anzia wrote to Dear Rose:

> When you spoke to me—you felt you ought to get at least as good an advance as Emma Goldman. As a matter of fact the publishers lost heavily on Emma's book. In fact publishing is in such a bad state that Putnam has practically withdrawn from the company & taken a job in the story dept of the Paramount movies. His name is still with the firm—but he is practically out of it. But if you know what you want with your book— you have something to hold on to—& you can find a publisher in spite of the depression & you do not have to wait till the book is finished. If you feel you must have a change to go on with the book I'd love to have you come out here for a little visit. If you have no car you can hitch-hike down here & the quiet in this place will do you a world of good. A few days or a week of this might just be the [inspiration] you need to complete the book. I'm working on a play now and I'm so taken up with this that I have no time to think of this last one just published. Once a book is out of my hands—I let fate take of it take its course (*sic*) & forget about it & go on with the new thing before me. Do let me know if you feel like coming. If you think I can be of any use in any way with the mss. let me know. I'm going to N.Y. Sunday but will be back in a few days & any note will be sent on to me.
>
> Yours, Anzia[141]

During the Great Depression Yezierska went to work for the Federal Writers Project of the Works Progress Administration (WPA). She had spent long years in arduous toil in poverty and obscurity, followed by sudden, disorienting success and fame, and then just-as-sudden marginalization and rejection. After her third novel *All I Could Never Be* in 1932, she was unable to get any book published for years. With unflagging tenacity, she refused to give up writing. Like Dostoevsky's protagonist in *Notes from Underground*, even when "confronted with the impossible," she was "not going to be reconciled to it."[142] She labored on as an invisible woman, stubbornly writing her notes from underground, eventually reascending upon the literary stage in 1950 with the release of the semiautobiographical novel *Red Ribbon on a White Horse* after an eighteen-year professional interregnum. Her experiences working with the WPA served as the basis for a section of *Red Ribbon on a White Horse*, which was published when she was about seventy years old.

Although she found the WPA frustrating and degrading, she needed the money. Also, it provided her the opportunity to commiserate with a group of struggling writers, some of whom would never achieve publishing success, others whose fortunes had risen and fallen as Anzia's had done, and still others who were diamonds in the rough, young writers who would later produce masterpieces and achieve the recognition they deserved. Among her WPA friends was Richard Wright, who would write the novel *Native Son* and his autobiography, *Black Boy*.

Yezierska's life and her writing reflected a commitment to what literary scholar Ross Posnock calls "the politics of nonidentity," a form of defiant individualism characterized by "deliberately eluding identification and direct affiliation."[143] She would not be pinned down. Anzia engaged in a never-finished process of becoming, of ever-not-quite arriving. She tapped into the power of contradictions. This was not a mode of living geared to the attainment of emotional quietude. Anzia Yezierska attained not conventional peace of mind but the satisfaction that accompanies the embrace of experience, difference, knowledge, and artistic expression. She was attracted to what W. E. B Du Bois called "a certain tingling challenge of risk."[144] Yet she was a nervous narcissist. She continued to perceive herself as a Russian Jewish immigrant long after she became an American. However, she also insisted that she was an American while continuing to portray herself in her writing as a newly arrived Jewish immigrant. Louise Levitas Henriksen noted that her parents were "both assimilated Jews," and that neither her mother, Anzia Yezierska, nor her father, Arnold Levitas, "had ever introduced their daughter to Judaism."[145]

Anzia Yezierska exerted great effort struggling with dualisms, including conflicting imperatives of body and mind, the material and the spiritual, the desire for love and the need for freedom. This was a woman who never appeared settled, and never appeared comfortable with her circumstances. She thrived as an artist on the tension arising from these binary oppositions. Historian Alice Kessler-Harris writes, "She never did reconcile the dichotomies in her life."[146] Ann Shapiro observes that Anzia Yezierska was, in a way, caught between the lines, remaining "forever poised between the world of the East Side Jew and that of the American intellectual, unable to find a home in either."[147] Yezierska's female protagonists always change, but they never fully assimilate. John Dewey famously wrote that for hyphenated Americans, the hyphen should attach, not separate.[148] Anzia Yezierska's heroines evolve, not into hyphenated Americans but rather into something new: creolized immigrants or American hybrids.

Gay Wilentz writes of Anzia Yezierska that "throughout her life and in her fictional and autobiographical writings, she was always committed to radical change—particularly on a personal level."[149] Blanche Gelfant argues that Yezierska's central themes of hunger, identity, America, and storytelling "do not admit of finality. They allow for no end point, no fixed site, or position, or state of being."[150] This, Gelfant suggests, is why Yezierska "felt impelled to tell the story of these women—of her self— again and again, the same story of a transformation never complete or satisfactory, of an Americanization never free of self-betrayal, of a hunger never satisfied."[151]

In her fiction, Yezierska uses dialect, and Yiddish cadences, grammar, and pronunciations, juxtaposed against the English of native speakers to build bridges between immigrant and American readers. Her nonfiction essays and many articles for the *New York Times Book Review* demonstrate Yezierska's command of Standard English. She was deliberate in her bending, breaking, and reshaping language to evoke the ambiguity, alienation, hybridity, and effort it cost her characters to express themselves. Yezierska's language was purposefully constructed and deployed to tempt and challenge her readers. Her narrators and her characters draw the reader in emotionally as they struggle, endlessly unable to fashion the sublime sentences to which they aspire. Part of Yezierska's message is contained in her depiction of the immigrant's inability to accurately and beautifully express herself in English, and the yearning of her characters to do so. The author's yearning also is conveyed in the frustrating reach that never quite grasps the stylistically beautiful expression, yet somehow communicates the experiences, emotions, thoughts, and personalities of her characters.

10. Anzia Yezierska on a park bench. From the Anzia Yezierska Collection, Howard Gotlieb Archival Research Center, Boston University.

In Norma Rosen's novelized reimagining of the love affair of Dewey and Yezierska, the fictional Anzia says, "I'm between Scylla and Charybdis." Rosen's narrator adds that these "were for all she knew two avenues in Minsk."[152] The real Yezierska, an autodidact who earned a college and postgraduate education, no doubt understood quite well the meaning of Scylla and Charybdis. Nevertheless, Rosen's joke sounds like one Anzia would have put in the voice of one of her own fictional characters. Yezierska's occasional fictitious depiction or pretense of guileless ignorance notwithstanding, she possessed keen intelligence and deep knowledge of a wide variety of subjects.

Anzia Yezierska was a voracious reader of poetry, literature, history, and philosophy. "As an educated woman who read widely, she knew the works of such major American figures as Emerson, Whitman, and James," notes Carol Schoen.[153] Her lifelong enchantment with poets and poetry makes it safe to assume she was familiar with the works of Homer and Ovid, and that she encountered the colloquial use of "between Scylla and

Charybdis" to signify a dilemma, similar to the phrase "between a rock and a hard place." Yezierska was well acquainted with unsolvable dilemmas, situations in which only unsatisfying alternatives appeared. She generated energy and art and emotional distress from the tension emanating from such circumstances.

Just a handful of pictures of Anzia Yezierska survive, taken at various times in her long life. These pictures present her in the full flower of youth with a coy Giaconda smile on her lips and a mischievous light in her eyes, and then at other stages of adulthood, maturity, and old age. There is strength in her appearance, and a hint of self-satisfaction. There also is a shadow of doubt and insecurity. But the photos and drawings viewed separately or together do not capture the woman. The complete Anzia Yezierska, the fiery, irreconcilable writer, could never be taken by a photograph. Too many aspects of her personality could not be fixed, could not be made visible that way. No photograph could reveal Yezierska's penchant for bursting through shut doors in search of opportunities or to flee constricting bonds. No photograph could convey her love of music, including classical, jazz, and popular music of her day. Yezierska's fiction contains clues and revelations for the attentive reader, including references to the joy she found in music and in poetry. Her daughter wrote, "It's hard to find Anzia's real face (or her emotion-charged, explosive personality) in the slick pictures and accounts of her life."[154] Yezierska was better able to express herself as an artist with words than through visual modes of film or photography. The best way to develop a true picture that exposes Anzia Yezierska's spirit is to read *Salome of the Tenements* and her other writing, and to find the author between the lines.

|4|
Sonya Levien Was behind the Scenes

Sara Opeskin never forgot the painful price her father paid for questioning authority. She was born in December 1888 in Panimunik, a village with fewer than fifty homes in the Russian Pale of Settlement, the bounded area of Russia, Poland, and the Ukraine in which Jews were confined by law from 1791 to 1917. Sara was the first of five children of Julius and Fanny Opeskin, the big sister of four younger brothers.

After the assassination of Czar Alexander II in 1881, the Russian government cracked down on dissidents, increased the violent enforcement of the limits of the Pale, and passed the draconian May Laws of 1882, which placed more onerous restrictions on Jews. These conditions forced Russian Jews into increasingly defensive enclavism and foreclosed opportunities to assimilate into the wider society.[1] They also encouraged widespread emigration to the United States, other Western countries, and such far-flung refuges as Bombay and Shanghai, where Sephardic Jewish families had established strongholds. In the United States, their release from the oppression of the Pale fueled the enthusiasm with which many Russian Jewish immigrants embraced Americanization and assimilation.

Before his daughter's second birthday, Julius Opeskin was arrested as a radical dissident and sentenced to hard labor in Siberia. He was an admirer of the anarchist Prince Peter Kropotkin, and he had worked for a publisher of clandestine political pamphlets. Julius was banished from his shtetle and sent east to a harsh wilderness on the Russian steppes. During frozen Siberian winters while her father labored in mines, Sara huddled with her mother, her baby brother, and her paternal grandfather. Anzia Yezierska was thinking of people like Julius Opeskin when she penned

11. Sonya Levien in hat
and shawl. Sonya Lev-
ien Papers, Huntington
Library, San Marino,
California.

the protagonist's lamentation for Russian Jews "stifled in Siberian pris-
ons" in the novel *Salome of the Tenements*.[2]

Grandfather Opeskin was a rabbi and a schoolteacher, a highly educated Orthodox Jew. Unlike most Eastern European Orthodox Jews of the
late nineteenth century, he also possessed a modern, secular education.
He taught Sara to read Hebrew scriptures, knowledge that would tradi-
tionally have been imparted only to boys. He also taught her Russian,
German, French, and Latin. The family members spoke together infor-
mally in Yiddish. This grandfather counted a priest in the Greek Orthodox Church among his close friends. The secular and religious knowledge
she received from her grandfather served Sara throughout her life. In
America, she had to drop out of school after eighth grade to work and
help support her family, but her early home schooling whetted an appetite
for learning that later drove her to pursue higher education.

Julius Opeskin toiled for two years in Siberia before he escaped. A German engineer named Levien helped him flee to the United States in 1891. Julius had no choice but to leave his family behind and raise money to send for them later. In America, he adopted the engineer's surname and became Julius Levien. He found solidarity among anarchist sympathizers in New York, both Jewish and Gentile, admirers of Prince Kropotkin, members of labor unions, the Jewish labor organization called the Workman's Circle or Arbeter Ring, and clubs and associations with which he shared political views. But these groups functioned for him primarily as community organizations, providing opportunities to socialize with socialists. Either chastened by his time in Siberia or mellowed by his experiences in the United States and the struggle to reunite his family, Julius no longer actively participated in radical politics.

In 1896, when Sara was eight years old, Julius had finally saved enough money to bring his family to New York.[3] They all left the Opeskin name behind and became Leviens. Sara became Sonya. The Leviens lived in cramped, squalid tenement apartments. As a teenager, Sonya worked in sweatshops, including several years in a factory making feather dusters. Like her father, Sonya relieved the drudgery of these jobs by pursuing social, cultural, and community activities. She was something of a joiner with a talent for charming those in authority. She spent time at the Educational Alliance and the University Settlement, where she met Rose Pastor Stokes and Anzia Yezierska.

Anarchism, Socialism, Capitalism

In America, millions of Eastern European Jewish immigrants were encouraged to assimilate by learning and adopting the language, behavior, and customs of the native-born. In striking contrast to Russia, in America they found opportunities to work and live among non-Jews and to practice Judaism in peace. They became active participants in what historian Daniel Rodgers calls "the transnational reach of social politics," in which "the Atlantic functioned for its newcomers less as a barrier than as a connective lifeline."[4] These immigrants relayed information about what they encountered in America back to friends and relatives who remained in the old countries through letters, telegrams, postcards, pamphlets, newspapers, books, and sometimes telephone calls. A small number traveled back and forth between Europe and the United States and shared their information face to face. As a consequence, their new behaviors and adaptations to life in the United States generated a transatlantic counterforce that echoed in the countries they left behind.

Many Eastern European Jewish socialists brought their politics with them when they immigrated to the United States at the end of the nineteenth century. But political influence moved between Europe and America in both directions, and not only among Jews.[5] "Between 1870 and 1920," writes James T. Kloppenberg, "two generations of American and European thinkers created a transatlantic community of discourse in philosophy and political theory."[6] The New York City junction of that community of discourse was the origination point for many transformative ideas and practices. In one important example, "New Yorkers played a pivotal role in the emergence of the Jewish labor movement in Russia," writes Tony Michels, because "[c]ontrary to an old misperception, eastern European Jews did not import a preexisting socialist tradition to the United States."[7] Instead, anarchist and socialist literature often was sent east by socialists in New York, initially non-Jewish, German immigrants, where it reached some Jews like Julius Opeskin in Russia.[8] "For a while," during the Progressive Era, writes Jackson Lears, "socialism was as American as cherry pie."[9] The German immigrant roots of socialism in America fueled anti-socialist sentiment in the United States during World War I. Socialist opponents of American involvement in the war were suspected of being pro-German. Rose Pastor Stokes was among those who faced such accusations.[10]

The appeal of political anarchism and socialism to Russian Jews in the late nineteenth century is not difficult to comprehend. David Hollinger writes, "A history of forced and invidious separation made many Jews enthusiastic about the idea of a universalist, socialist state."[11] The hope was that such a state would be democratic and that all would be able to participate. Still, some were wary from the outset about exchanging the coercive power of the czar for the centralized power of a socialist state, even with the theoretical protection of democratic institutions, which never materialized in what became the Soviet Union. Political anarchism proffered the utopian vision of a society with no dangerous concentration of power. For those used to living conditions in which the state is unstable, violent, repressive, and anti-Semitic, an ideology that calls for the decentralization, reduction, or elimination of state power has obvious appeal. Kropotkin's emphasis on mutual aid, and political anarchist goals of workers' compensation and death benefit insurance, municipal ownership of utilities, and labor ownership of factories resonated with Jews who were unable to avail themselves of the protective power of the state or the rule of law. The authority of Jewish law had been maintained for centuries without the coercive power of a state. As a result, access to civil or social justice was not perceived by these Jews as requiring the existence of a national government; in fact, state governments created obstacles to the pursuit of legal justice. Sonya Levien's earliest lesson in politics was that the government could take fathers away from little girls.

In 1901 at the age of thirteen, Sonya Levien committed an archetypical act of capitalism. She borrowed thirty-six dollars to pay tuition for a course in stenography. She took a loan, originated a debt by enlisting a lender's confidence in her creditworthy character and future success. The ability to inspire that trust was one of very few resources available to Levien, her only bankable asset. She had no other collateral. In 1925, the year the film *Salome of the Tenements* came out, Levien recalled that "a member of the school board loaned me $36, which permitted me to study stenography, and that was my entering wedge into the literary field. It took me four years to pay that debt."[12]

Although much attention has justly been directed at Yezierska's inspiration by Pastor Stokes for the main character in *Salome of the Tenements*, less noted are the deliberate, unmistakable similarities the protagonist bears to Sonya Levien. Yezierska patterned the relationship between the characters Sonya Vrunsky and John Manning on the marriage of Rose Pastor and Graham Stokes and the author's own romantic affair with John Dewey. But there also are striking references to the marriage of Sonya Levien and Carl Hovey. The character is named Sonya Vrunsky. Both Sonyas, Levien and Vrunsky, married their patrician Anglo-Saxon bosses.

When she wrote the screen adaptation of the novel, Levien altered the character in ways that heightened the resemblance.

Using the narrator's voice in the novel, Yezierska acclaims "Sonya Levien, a plain stenographer," who became "one of the biggest editors."[13] In addition to sharing the name Sonya, Yezierska's protagonist and Levien both were Jewish denizens of the Lower East Side who worked in sweatshops, learned to be stenographers, graduated to careers in journalism, and became secretaries to wealthy Gentile philanthropists who married poor Jewish immigrants. Yezierska's Sonya Vrunsky tells of her past experience as a sweatshop worker who had worked hard to become "a stenographer in a beautiful office,"[14] which led her into journalism. Anzia had witnessed young Sonya Levien's start as a stenographer and her professional rise into journalism through hard work, talent, and the assistance of friends like Rose Pastor Stokes. Yezierska venerated Pastor Stokes and Levien.

Like Levien, the character in the novel launches her upward mobility by borrowing money. However, in the novel the lender is a miserly pawnbroker, not the kind of friendly school board member who helped Levien. Sonya Levien's endearing personality inspired a lender's confidence, which she justified by repaying the loan. The less endearing heroine in the novel is compelled to be clever to conjure loan collateral. Yezierska's Salome enlists a loan shark in a form of project financing, in which the money is used to fund the borrower's pursuit of marriage to a millionaire. So tangible do her great expectations seem that the cynical usurer risks his capital with no more collateral than her promise to pay after she captures her conjugal prey. When payment comes due, she defaults and the lender resorts to blackmail and extortion.

Friends and Allies

In the summer of 1903, groups of teenage girls from the Jewish Educational Alliance and the University Settlement on the Lower East Side joined together to form a club. The counselors who led them during the fall and winter months left for the summer and newspaper reporter Rose Pastor was recruited to be their summer counselor. Rose recalled, "We talked, read books and papers, and discussed individual and home problems. At times, I spoke to them about Socialism."[15] In July, Rose Pastor met her future husband James Graham Phelps Stokes. At the end of the summer the other counselors returned and Rose planned to leave. But the girls had fallen in love with Rose and did not want to let her go. Rose was touched by the entreaties of the young women. "They would waylay me as I came from the office and hammer away at my resistance. Sonya Levien . . . of the blue eyes and black hair, and the smile as kind as my grandfather's cried real tears as we stood on the curb debating the matter. I finally relented and offered a compromise; I would visit the club provided the leader raised no objection."[16]

Two years later Rose Pastor Stokes hired Sonya Levien to be Graham Stokes's secretary. This was 1905, the year of the Stokes wedding and the same year that Sonya became a naturalized U.S. citizen. "Through an East Side settlement I met Rose Pastor Stokes who got me the position of secretary to her husband. Mr. Stokes was away a great deal and I took advantage of his wonderful library to prepare for my regents examinations."[17]

Sonya Levien was seventeen years old when she became a secretary for Graham Stokes. In addition to their library, Sonya's position in the Stokes household gave her entree into the worlds of leftist New York high society, intellectual salons, international socialism, women's suffrage, birth control, magazine writing and playwriting, and labor union organizing. Pastor Stokes introduced Levien to Yezierska, to the members of the Heterodoxy Club of women intellectuals, to the writers and editors of the *Masses*, and many others. The Stokes's lavish wedding, celebrating this marriage across ethnic, religious, and social class lines, was a media spectacle, and it made a lasting impression on Yezierska and Levien, both of whom attended.[18] These young women witnessed their close friend and fellow Jewish immigrant emerge from poverty and enter high society through intermarriage with a fabulously wealthy Anglo-Saxon Protestant from a venerable New England family. The Stokes wedding demonstrated that the Cinderella fantasy depicted in stories and films was not just possible but real and right before their eyes.

Sonya Levien earned a New York State Regents high school equivalency certificate in 1906 and then attended New York University Law School from 1906 to 1909. She applied for admission to the New York State

Bar Association in September 1909. Rose's husband, Graham, wrote a letter of recommendation to the New York State Bar supporting Sonya's application for admission. He called Levien "a young lady of excellent character" who had been "a member of my household for a number of years."[19] Levien became a New York lawyer just twenty-three years after Katherine Stoneman, the first woman admitted to practice law in New York State in 1886.

Levien was one of the earliest female graduates of New York University Law School, along with the feminist journalist Crystal Eastman, who enrolled in the law school in 1905. To put their achievement in perspective, in 1910 there were only 133 women lawyers in New York State and only 588 women lawyers in the entire United States, including Crystal Eastman and Sonya Levien. "A career in the law was a bold decision for a woman in 1904 and 1905," writes legal historian John Fabian Witt. "Of all the major American professions, law was probably the most unwelcoming to women."[20]

But law was just a stepping-stone in Sonya Levien's career path. While still in law school, perhaps inspired by Rose Pastor Stokes's success as a journalist, Levien contributed some short humor pieces to *Life* magazine. "[B]efore long I was making $30 a week from them," she recalls. "That steered me into magazine work."[21] Soon after graduating from law school Levien decided not to practice law.

Keeping Company

She was attracted to writers, writing, and public service. In 1908 Sonya Levien met writer Sinclair Lewis. "As the saying goes, 'we kept company' for several years. . . . Yes, we talked of marriage—seriously."[22] Reformer Mary Simkovitch wrote in 1917, "Sometimes a passion for the theater will lead a girl to go with a man with whom she is unwilling to keep company and yet who expects his payment."[23] The preferred currency for such payment was understood to be some level of sexual contact. Yet in 1924 Sonya Levien wrote, "I've been a whole-hearted anarchist, a socialist and a suffragist, and I remember once making a most eloquent speech about the higher idealism of free love. But I've always felt—and practiced—that to spoon in the dark with a fellow one is not engaged to constituted a sin."[24] Of course she was a wife and the mother of a son and a daughter by the time she wrote that. Whether or not Sonya Levien and Sinclair Lewis ever spooned in the dark during the several years they kept company and talked seriously of marriage remains a matter of incorroborable conjecture. Sinclair Lewis was known to keep company with many attractive young ladies in those years.

Sinclair Lewis spent a month in 1906 in New Jersey at Upton Sinclair's Helicon Hall utopian community. "Prof. John Dewey, of Columbia" was among the official managers of Helicon Hall.[25] Other Helicon visitors included Charlotte Perkins Gilman, William James, and George Bernard Shaw. Upton Sinclair was active in the Intercollegiate Socialist Society with Rose Pastor and James Graham Phelps Stokes. In February 1914 Charlotte Perkins Gilman and Rose Pastor Stokes spoke on a panel on the topic of "The Wages of Shame vs. The Shame of Wages," hosted by the Twilight Club.[26]

Sonya Levien was twenty when she met Sinclair Lewis, and he was twenty-three. Lewis was working on his first novels, *Hike and the Aeroplane* and *Mr. Wrenn, Gentle Man*. *Hike* was published in 1912, followed by *Mr. Wrenn* in 1914. *Hike and the Aeroplane* was written for young male readers, a boys' adventure story that begins at a prep school. *Hike* is an unabashed celebration of American values, capitalism, and pre–World War I naiveté reflecting the moment of the Taft presidency. This book contains little of the incisive social criticism that characterizes Lewis's later works.

The story is about a teenage football star and his good-natured side-kick at a military high school in Northern California, possibly modeled on the San Mateo Military Academy, which Lincoln Steffens had attended. The boys ride horses through mountain passes overlooking the Pacific Ocean, and fly a whiz-bang newly designed "aeroplane" from the California shack in which an eccentric mechanic has built it with his own hands, all the way to Washington, DC. As the boys complete one of the first-ever cross-country flights, they land periodically to refuel at an automobile gas station or to save a damsel in distress fleeing from armed desperadoes. They arrive in Washington just in time to present the new technological marvel to the most senior five-star generals of the U.S. army, who gratefully jump at the opportunity to pay one million dollars to buy a fleet of the new planes. The military advantages afforded to America by the acquisition of these planes will allow the United States to patrol trouble spots around the world in order to prevent war! The boy heroes manage to use the plane to help some good guys prevail over a group of Mexican revolutionary banditos in Baja before returning to the high school campus to win the big, final football game of the season. Hike, of course, is the nickname of the quarterback.[27]

The episode about the Mexican revolutionaries in Baja would have particularly appealed to Sonya Levien. It appears to be based on the real-life story of the Magón brothers, Mexican revolutionaries who worked with the International Workers of the World and launched an ill-fated series of attacks from revolutionary communes in Baja in 1911. One of the brothers, Ricardo Flores Magón, was influenced by the writings of Peter Kropotkin, the Russian anarchist who was admired by Sonya Levien's father. Kropotkin had moved to London when Rose Pastor lived there as a child. Ricardo Magón was convicted in 1918 under the Espionage Act of 1917 in one of the same series of prosecutions that captured Eugene V. Debs and Rose Pastor Stokes.[28] Magón was sentenced to twenty years in federal prison.

From 1907 through 1911, Levien worked as a secretary to Samuel Merwyn. Merwyn was a novelist and an editor of the magazine *Success*, which was purchased in 1911 by the *National Post*. She moved to Boston for several months in 1911 to work as managing editor and business manager of the *Woman's Journal*, a publication affiliated with the National American Woman Suffrage Association. She left the *Woman's Journal* early in 1912 after only about six months, following differences of opinion with *Journal* owner Alice Stone Blackwell and her associate Agnes E. Ryan.[29]

While still living in Boston in 1912, Sonya Levien sent a short story to Carl Hovey, editor-in-chief of the *Metropolitan* magazine. Hovey replied that he liked the story but he believed it was too long. He asked her to consider cutting it in half. Carl Hovey had been a protégé of Professor Charles Townsend Copeland at Harvard, and had worked for Lincoln Steffens at the *New York Commercial Advertiser* alongside Hutchins Hapgood and Abraham Cahan. Hovey also had written biographies of Stonewall Jackson, published in 1900, and J. P. Morgan, published in 1911.[30] Levien wrote back to Hovey, thanked him for reading her story, and explained saucily that another literary magazine, *Ainslee's*, had accepted it despite its excessive length. By the end of 1912 Sonya moved back to New York from Boston and was hired by Carl Hovey as an editor at the *Metropolitan*.[31]

Multitasking Metropolitan

Sonya Levien often worked on many different projects simultaneously. While at the *Metropolitan*, she worked on the National Board of Censorship of Motion Pictures, as educational secretary and head of the Education Department, and at The People's Institute in 1913 and 1914. In October 1913 she published a commentary, *New York City's Motion Picture Law*, in *American City* magazine.[32] The People's Institute was founded in 1897 by Charles Sprague Smith, a Columbia University professor of modern languages and foreign literature. Graham and Rose Pastor Stokes introduced Sonya Levien to Sprague Smith and the People's Institute. Rose first met Sprague Smith in 1903 while on vacation at an Adirondack camp with Graham Stokes, who had secretly become her fiancé. Years later, Rose recalled chatting and playing chess with Sprague Smith at the camp.[33] Graham Stokes and his family supported and served on the Board of Directors of the People's Institute.[34]

The People's Institute was a community organization that assisted immigrants and Americans of all ethnicities in the ways of civic engagement through education and exchange of ideas. It shared some of the goals and methods of the settlement houses. In 1909 the People's Institute became a sponsor of the newly formed National Board of Censorship of Motion Pictures, which soon changed its name to the National Board of Review of Motion Pictures to eliminate the word *censorship*. New York City Mayor George B. McClellan Jr. ordered the closing of the city's nickelodeons on Christmas Eve of 1908, declaring that movies had a degrading impact on community morality. He also complained of fire hazards related to the use of highly flammable nitrate celluloid film stock.

Film producers and distributors responded predictably to defend their product. Movies, they contended, were in fact wholesome entertainment, and also a means of promoting healthy civic engagement in a virtual public square. To assuage the concerns of elected and self-appointed protectors of public safety and morality, or at least to circumvent them, a group of movie producers joined with the People's Institute to form the National Board. The National Board's "close affiliation with The People's Institute from 1909 to 1915 was informed by a set of assumptions about the social usefulness of moving pictures that set it apart from many of the ideas dominating American reform," writes Nancy J. Rosenbloom. Moreover the Board and the Institute "opposed growing pressures for legalized censorship."[35] The National Board, composed of Sonya Levien, John Collier, Frederic Howe, and Charles Sprague Smith, "recognized that *moving pictures had the potential to create empathy* among different people, to sustain neighborhood sociability, and to contribute to the general education of society" (emphasis added).[36]

The Board was also closely affiliated with Thomas Edison's Motion Picture Patents Company. Sonya Levien, who was by then a licensed attorney, worked with the National Board and the People's Institute to promote regulations to improve safety conditions in movie theaters by providing sufficient lighting and ventilation. She drafted a pamphlet called "Suggestions for a Model Ordinance for Regulating Motion Picture Theaters."[37] Levien's "model ordinance introduced the idea that the motion picture theatre should be a form of public service, licensed by the community for public welfare," and that movies should be perceived as "a form of journalism, of editorial discussion, and of platform discussion." It went on to assert that "[t]he motion picture may within a few years become the most important vehicle of free public discussion in America." Sonya Levien had "no desire to suppress the power of motion pictures."[38] She left the National Board and the People's Institute to focus on careers in magazine journalism and movie screenwriting. In 1916 Wilton Barrett held the position vacated by Levien on the National Board. Film historian Martin Norden writes that Rose Pastor Stokes "was among the two hundred-odd people who agreed to examine films on behalf of the National Board of Review of Motion Pictures" when Barrett was "in charge of coordinating the reviewers." Barrett arranged to introduce Rose to Alice Guy Blaché in 1916 so the two women could collaborate on the ill-fated birth control film *Shall the Parents Decide?*[39]

Like many individuals and the editorial staffs of many publications, the *Metropolitan* struggled to clarify its political views as the advent of World War I approached. In April 1912 the editors of the *Metropolitan* endorsed Theodore Roosevelt's "New Nationalism" campaign for president.[40] It was a time of competing definitions of American nationalism and progressivism. Roosevelt's vision of American character was based on the fortitude and rectitude he believed resulted from exposure to the American physical and social environment. He believed that Americanism entailed traits that could be acquired by some "assimilable" immigrant groups by living in the United States, engaging in worthy personal conduct, and intermarriage with native-born Americans. Once acquired, Roosevelt held that those traits could be inherited by future generations. Although not broadly inclusive, this civic pathway to Americanism implied that many, but not all, foreign immigrants could assimilate in the metaphorical melting pot and become American.

By June 1912 the editors of the *Metropolitan* wavered, still professing admiration for Roosevelt, but not endorsing him for president. The magazine's editorial stance recommitted to a combination of democracy and socialism, including "a thorough readjustment of the rewards of labor, so that all men may have a chance of real life and liberty."[41] The Socialist Party candidate, Eugene V. Debs, came in fourth in the popular vote, behind Taft, Roosevelt, and the victorious Woodrow Wilson.

In January 1914 Carl Hovey engaged in an epistolary exchange with the *New York Times* reminiscent of William Dean Howells's *A Hazard of New Fortunes*. It started with a press announcement that the Ford Motor Company would allocate ten million dollars of its profits to pay bonuses to its workers. Ford's announcement was aimed at generating goodwill while arguing that its factory workers fared better under capitalism than they would under socialism. Ford also doubled its workers' minimum pay to five dollars a day. In a subsequent editorial, the *Metropolitan* responded that it would not pay such bonuses to its own employees because it could not afford to. Writing in the *New York Times*, Ford's treasurer James Couzens then accused the managers of the *Metropolitan* of making poor excuses "for not practicing what [they] preached."[42] Couzens held this up as proof positive that capitalism is superior to socialism at providing for workers. Demonstrably, he wrote, labor was better paid by the Ford Motor Company, a staunch advocate of free market capitalism, than the socialist-leaning magazine the *Metropolitan*. Hovey bristled, responding that the *Metropolitan* magazine was a business with "a socialist ideal," which would share its bounty with employees if it could generate sufficient profits. The *Metropolitan* applauded the Ford Motor Company for profit-sharing with workers in keeping with socialist ideals. It is easy to imagine Henry Ford clenching his teeth in irate umbrage at this backhanded compliment. In the meantime, the *Metropolitan* would attempt to make its "business as successful as possible while doing everything" possible "for the workers under an admittedly imperfect system."[43]

Little Miss Anarchist

Sonya Levien worked at the *Metropolitan* with some of the most talented writers, philosophers, and politicians of the day, including thinkers who spanned the political spectrum, from John Reed to Theodore Roosevelt. Reed wrote the firsthand account of the Russian Bolshevik Revolution, *Ten Days that Shook the World*; had a love affair with Mabel Dodge; and married the feminist writer Louise Bryant.[44] Roosevelt affectionately called Levien "little miss anarchist." She edited and published the work of George Bernard Shaw, F. Scott Fitzgerald, Herbert Hoover, Sir Arthur Conan Doyle, Joseph Conrad, Rudyard Kipling, Theodore Dreiser, Maxim Gorky, Noel Coward, Carl Sandburg, P. G. Wodehouse, Anzia Yezierska, and many others. F. Scott and Zelda Fitzgerald became friendly over the years with Carl Hovey and Sonya Levien. The couples occasionally socialized together, and exchanged letters about personal and business matters.[45] Fitzgerald occasionally asked Carl and Sonya for editorial feedback on his works in progress.[46] Levien's work at the magazine also afforded her many opportunities to write and publish her own work.

In 1914 feminist and suffragist militarism broke out in England and Sonya Levien wanted to be there to report on the historic events. "The Metropolitan Magazine sent me over to study the situation and to buy stories from English authors. . . . I saw Shaw, Zangwill, Havelock Ellis and

May Sinclair and bought their stories. Being a graduate lawyer, I was able to draw up the contracts."[47] Women were not permitted to practice law in England until four years later, in 1918. After she returned from England, Sonya was promoted to the position of fiction editor of the *Metropolitan*.

A profile in a Hollywood newspaper in 1921 noted that "Miss Levien numbers her stay in England among her happiest memories, for there she was with her dearest friend, the Princess Saska, and her voice is soft as she speaks of her father's great love for Prince Kropotkin."[48] The Princess Saska was Alexandra Kropotkin, daughter of the anarchist prince. Alexandra Kropotkin moved to the United States and made a career in journalism, writing about cooking, home economics, marriage, personal finance, and other topics intended to appeal primarily to a female readership. From the late 1920s through the early 1940s, the princess wrote a column called "To the Ladies" for *Liberty* magazine. Beneath the byline "Princess Alexandra Kropotkin," she was described as a "Linguist, Traveler, Lecturer and Fashion Authority."[49]

In her autobiography, *Intimate Memories*, Mabel Dodge Luhan writes of the "intelligent face" of Carl Hovey, who brought Sonya Levien to salon evenings Dodge hosted while living in New York City: "Sonya Levien, a beautiful girl of Russian parentage, was Hovey's secretary and I always felt her judgment and her strength were a strong element in the office . . . *running things behind the scenes* in New York. Sonya had that most enduring quality: worthy weight and substance, character in short. I adored it" (emphasis added).[50] The ability to run things behind the scenes remained Levien's enduring strength.

Levien wrote a piece for the May 1915 issue of the *Metropolitan* celebrating Theodore Roosevelt's contributions since joining the magazine's staff after he lost the 1912 presidential election to Woodrow Wilson. The presence of the former president added excitement to what had already been an exciting place to work. One day, she wrote, Roosevelt kept Crown Prince Wilhelm of Germany and Mexican Revolutionary General Pancho Villa waiting in an anteroom for hours, while he sat debating politics with Carl Hovey and John Reed. Roosevelt and Reed hated each other. Sonya entered Hovey's office to have some copy approved for the magazine:

I find the room is filled with men lost in hot discussion. I hear the Colonel's voice saying, "I can forgive most purple passions, but *never* conscious, and planned brutality. Villa is a murderer, a bigamist!"

John Reed, who is disagreeing with everything and everybody, speaks up in a very superior tone of voice. "But Colonel," he replies, with assumed nonchalance, "*I* believe in bigamy."

We all turn to Mr. Roosevelt to see how he takes that staggerer, but that gentleman has already risen from his seat, and with a pleased gleam in his face thrust his hand out to John Reed in a congratulatory manner. "I am glad, John Reed," I hear him say, "to find you believe in SOMETHING. It is very necessary for a young man to believe in something."[51]

In 1918 Sonya wrote "Milk," an essay about visiting "from house to house with Col. Roosevelt" on New York's Lower East Side "in an effort to do something for the starving babies in these days of stress" when husbands and fathers were fighting overseas in World War I. In this essay she describes her own experiences growing up in poverty on the Lower East Side and the difficulty she had felt trying to reconcile the squalor of her circumstances with any positive images of the United States. Levien and her companions in penury "were no patriots," she writes. "Patriotism is a love and passion for one's country awakened by one's communal life."[52] Her childhood in America did not inspire such feelings.

"To us patriotism meant loyalty to ward-healers, to a nation controlled by capitalists, a nation that sanctioned the despoliation of its working classes. I was brought up on Karl Marx and enumerable red pamphlets bound in paraffin paper, and my suspicious mind saw the ravages of Capitalism all around me."[53] Her father had been banished to Siberia for helping to publish those red pamphlets bound in paraffin paper. In Russia, "The very solidarity of our hunger proved our spiritual salvation."

When she moved to America, "I had an inheritance of physical vitality and cultural background which gave me great advantage over the others."[54] She drew from a reserve of strength, family closeness, religious and secular education. These were her personal assets and attributes.

As her circumstances improved, her love of America blossomed. Growing up, Sonya Levien found that "[t]he study of American history brought with it the realization that it was an untainted story of a struggle for freedom, untainted as histories go. It obviously suffers from the mistakes of greed and youth, yet, with all that, this country affords opportunities for equality and democracy as no other nation in the world." Eventually, "Patriotism took sprout and grew."[55]

Still, even after she made a lot of money, Levien continued to question the shortcomings of industrial capitalism. "While I am not a Bolshevik," she told a reporter, "yet I frankly say there is no denial of some of the things accomplished by them. My father, on the contrary, is bitterly anti-Bolshevik, his radicalism is of another kind."[56] His kind of radicalism was political anarchism of the Kropotkin strain.

Levien's sympathies for the poor working class were not diminished by her own success. She argued that it is illogical to expect people who live without adequate food and shelter to develop a love of their country. "We would enlist the patriotism of the immigrants and at the same time strain their virtues beyond endurance."[57]

"A man cannot live like a pig and vote like a man," wrote Jacob Riis.[58] Sonya Levien communicated this concern to Theodore Roosevelt. She told the former president "about the vast throngs of people who drag themselves every morning at seven to the factories, work at some trifling job for eight, ten hours, day in, day out, year after year, without respite, without hope of ultimate release except through death. The unpleasant memory of my own similar beginnings keeps ever alive for me the sordidness of such an existence."[59]

She lamented Roosevelt's resistance to these entreaties. "My deep resentment against an industrial order that extorts so usurious a toll from its masses did not meet with the sympathy I had expected."[60] Roosevelt played the role of Charles Dickens's *Bleak House* character Mrs. Pardiggle, to Sonya Levien's Esther Summerson, although the ex-president was not wholly without empathy for the plight of the poor.[61]

"[T]here can be few people in the country more ignorant" than Theodore Roosevelt, said Rose Pastor Stokes.[62] Ten years earlier, as Levien well knew, Pastor Stokes told the *New York Times* that Roosevelt's "trust busting" and "trust curbing" ultimately would fail to repair flaws in the capitalist system that relegated working people to poverty and suffering. Rose believed that only a socialist economy, in which laborers owned the means of industrial production, could relieve the misery of the working poor.[63]

Roosevelt told Levien that "radicals laid too much stress upon the drudgery of the laborer's work." He contended that "very often it was a spiritual sluggishness and a consequent failure to discover the human aspects of one's job" that reduces it to drudgery. He acknowledged the need to redress the poor conditions, excessive hours, and low pay that too many workers endured. Nevertheless, he maintained "that ultimately any man's success or failure depended upon the man's own character."[64]

Roosevelt saw Levien as a shining example of one who did not succumb, but instead through fortitude and talent had transcended her poor origins. His point of view was that the worthy members of the lower classes could succeed. Levien's success was proof that it could be done. Theodore Roosevelt insisted that immigrants could transform themselves into Americans, and the poor could lift themselves out of poverty through hard work and virtuous conduct. He believed that individual effort and attitude were the most important factors.

A profile in the *American Hebrew* notes that the former president asked her to lead him through the Lower East Side "to investigate the difficulty the poorer sections were having in obtaining milk for children. Col. Roosevelt . . . asked Miss Levien to undertake the leadership for him and his group because she was familiar with that part of the city."[65] The neighborhood tour was part of a long-established pattern for Theodore Roosevelt. "Some of the most widely publicized acts by Commissioner Roosevelt," Aviva Taubenfeld writes, "were his legendary nighttime rambles through the seamier areas of New York City guided by [Jacob] Riis,"[66] almost twenty years before exploring the Lower East Side with Sonya Levien. Although the former president of the board of New York City Police Commissioners and governor of the State of New York was intimately familiar with the poor sections of the city, he always brought along a guide, and since she liked to take charge Roosevelt gladly deferred to Sonya Levien's natural talent for quiet leadership.

In an effort to clarify a vision of "composite" Americanism, Taubenfeld notes, "Roosevelt promoted the work of a select group of ethnic authors writing about the immigrant."[67] In addition to the Dutch immigrant Riis,

Roosevelt cultivated friendships with British Jewish playwright Israel Zangwill and Irish American satirist Finley Peter Dunne, and praised the work of Elizabeth Stern, daughter of Jewish immigrants, who wrote *My Mother and I*. Stern's ethnic origins were later questioned. At the *Metropolitan*, Sonya Levien copy-edited Roosevelt's articles and the two developed abiding mutual admiration and respect.

Sonya Levien guided Theodore Roosevelt through the Lower East Side in 1918, the same year that Anzia Yezierska guided John Dewey through those same streets. The odd couples walked the same neighborhoods. Had these two prominent American-born Anglo-Saxon Protestant men and their two Russian Jewish immigrant women companions bumped into each other on the streets of the Lower East Side, it would have been a happy reunion. Dewey had supported Roosevelt in 1912 and both men believed strongly in the importance of public education. Levien published Yezierska's story "Where Lovers Dream" in the March 1918 issue of the *Metropolitan*, an issue in which Theodore Roosevelt's byline also appeared. Dewey and Roosevelt both supported Woodrow Wilson's decision to enter America into World War I combat. Dewey and Yezierska's walking tour was a private search for knowledge and the romance of the unfamiliar, but Levien and Roosevelt were on a public mission to assist the city's poor.

Roosevelt and Levien each wrote articles for the *Metropolitan* about their excursion. The *American Hebrew* magazine reported that these articles achieved "direct results," in the form of "an increase in the number of milk stations on the East Side and a decided improvement in conditions there."[68] When Roosevelt died, Sonya lauded him in an encomium, "The Great Friend," published in *Woman's Home Companion* in October 1919.[69]

Antagonism at First Sight

In 1914 Sinclair Lewis married Grace Livingston Hegger. Sonya Levien married her boss, Carl Hovey, in 1917. "During those years," she said, "I had been thrown only with men whom it would have been difficult for me to marry because of the conflict between the Jews and Gentiles, though after all I did marry a man who comes from New England stock."[70] Anzia Yezierska suggested that mutual attraction between Jewish immigrants and American WASPs was the inevitable result of their ethnic differences. Levien described her initial reaction to meeting Carl Hovey as "antagonism at first sight."[71] For Jewish women and Gentile men, Yezierska believed that "the very nature of their antagonism willed them together," writes Mary Dearborn, despite or because "immigrant and native-born America were fundamentally at odds."[72] In "Mostly About Myself," a story from the collection *Children of Loneliness*, Anzia writes that "[s]ometimes a man and a woman are so different that they hate each other on sight." But once they get to know each other, "the very difference that drew them apart pulls them closer together than those born alike. Perhaps that accounts for the devouring affinity between my [Jewish] race and the Anglo-Saxon race."[73]

Novelty captivates and opposites attract. Racial and ethnic otherness often heightens the allure of forbidden fruit. But the differences need not be only racial or ethnic. Social class differences also stimulate romantic attraction. Catherine Rottenberg argues that in the novel *Salome of the Tenements* the attraction of the poor, aspiring Jewish immigrant female to the wealthy, American Anglo-Saxon Protestant male arises more from divergent social class status than race or ethnic difference. Because class in America has been defined as fluid rather than fixed in "the powerful myths of the American Dream," Rottenberg asserts that concentrating on class rather than race creates the "possibility of upward mobility." This suggests that, from the perspective of the poor Jewish immigrant, attraction to the wealthy Gentile emanates from a quest for social status rather than erotic attraction to a racially exotic other.[74] It is about much more than money. It involves longing to belong, the desire of the outsider for insider status, acceptance, and validation. This desire is magnified by the irresistible thrill of transgressing forbidden lines, asserting personal choice, and flouting parental will.[75] Sonya Levien told an interviewer,

> My husband and I have never had any race feeling between us, because we have known we were pulling for the same ideals, but my family objected. When they found that he wasn't going to beat me the way the Christians had the Jews in Russia, however, they gave their consent. Now they feel that I did quite well in getting someone who is head of

such a harmonious household. Neither of us is orthodox so our two children are being brought up to choose their religion. They were baptized
by my people just to please my mother and father, as it didn't make any
difference to my husband or me.[76]

(According to traditional Jewish practice, children inherit their mother's
religion.)

Before Sonya Levien's parents consented to her marriage to Carl
Hovey, her father, Julius, made two requests. First, that the children be
declared Jewish, which Sonya refers to above as being "baptized by my
people." This amounts to having a son circumcised in keeping with
religious ritual, and for a daughter, a ritual baby-naming. Julius's second request was that Carl Hovey be circumcised. Confronted with this
request, Carl explained to Sonya's four younger brothers that he already
was circumcised. When they told their father, Julius insisted the brothers go back and verify the fact with their own eyes. Once this was done,
the marriage was approved.[77] Levien and Hovey married on October 11,
1917. They remained married for thirty-nine years until Carl Hovey died
in 1956. They had a son, Serge, and a daughter, Tamara. Hovey also had
two children from a previous marriage, who lived with the newlyweds in
their home on East 92nd Street in New York.[78]

Busy Season

The autumn of 1917 was hectic for all the women of the Salome Ensemble.
On Sonya Levien's October wedding day, Anzia Yezierska was on her way
back to New York from San Francisco, where she had been living alone
and writing for more than a year. That month's issue of *Seven Arts* magazine contained Randolph Bourne's essay "Twilight of the Idols," in which
he forcefully criticized John Dewey, Walter Lippman, Herbert Croly, and
other Progressive thinkers affiliated with the *New Republic*, for implicitly
condoning human suffering by their support of "war technique." Jetta
Goudal remained in Amsterdam, trapped in the vortex of World War I.
Because the Netherlands officially maintained neutrality, combat remained
beyond that country's borders. But the economic hardships caused by the
war were severe, and the basic institutions of civic life were damaged. Sick,

wounded, and starving refugees poured into Holland from battlegrounds in other nations, straining resources and adding to the suffering. Jetta, still known as Julie Goudeket in those days, did volunteer work that exposed her to the traumatic impact of the war, and her sheltered childhood as the daughter of a diamond merchant gave way to harsh realities.

Rose Pastor Stokes did not attend Sonya Levien's wedding. Pastor Stokes was at a particularly difficult period in her life. Her health and her personal life were unraveling, and she was buffeted between political choices regarding American participation in World War I. Rose was on an exhausting barnstorming tour giving political speeches while her husband stayed home in New York. On November 2, 1917, British Foreign Secretary Arthur James Balfour issued his declaration in a letter to the Jewish Lord Rothschild publicly heralding British support for a Jewish homeland in the Levant. Pastor Stokes hoped it would be a socialist Jewish homeland. This was the month the Bolsheviks acceded to power in Russia. Growing political differences contributed to the slow, inexorable collapse of Rose's marriage to Graham Stokes. Her handwritten note of regret to "Dearest Sonya" on November 11, 1917, said,

> I have thought of you almost constantly—with a sort of passionate wish for your happiness . . . I wish I knew how to tell you what you have meant to me—you seem a *part* of my life—as indeed you *must know*. You were bound up with so much of it.
>
> I *grieved* when the Western trip was so prolonged that I couldn't hope to be one of your little wedding party. . . .
>
> God bless and keep you, little friend—you, and the good man you love.
>
> Ever faithfully your friend,
> Rose Pastor Stokes[79]

Within weeks, Rose Pastor Stokes declined a dinner invitation to the White House, recanted her support for President Wilson and the American war effort, and turned down an offer to star in a pro-war propaganda film. After snubbing Woodrow Wilson, Rose spent Thanksgiving in New York commiserating with Anzia Yezierska. Newlyweds Sonya Levien and Carl Hovey were on their honeymoon. In December 1917 Yezierska pushed her way into John Dewey's office at Columbia University to intro-duce herself and plead for career help. The Armistice took effect one year to the day after Rose's letter to Sonya Levien, finally freeing Jetta Goudal to flee to America.

Ever a multitasker like her mentor Rose Pastor Stokes, Sonya Levien began writing and sending stories to movie producers while she worked at the *Metropolitan*. After many rejection letters, she sold some stories to filmmakers beginning in 1918. In 1919 Levien earned her first on-screen credit for the film *Who Will Marry Me*, for adapting the scenario from a short story she had written. This was her first experience of converting literature to film. The convoluted plot bears the unmistakable influence of Rose Pastor Stokes. A poor young Lower East Side girl named Rosie runs away to a settlement house to escape an unwanted marriage arranged by her mother. There she meets a wealthy man who has been on a drink-ing binge since being dumped by a chorus girl. He marries Rosie, but wakes up sober and remorseful. He has a snobbish aunt who disdains Rosie. Rosie loves the wealthy husband, but decides to flee this class con-flict and return to her mother. The chorus girl has by this time married a mean husband, and now regretful, she visits the wealthy man she had dumped, only to find that he now is married to Rosie. The mean, jealous husband arrives and attacks the wealthy guy. The chorus girl shoots and kills her mean husband. In order to chivalrously protect the chorus girl, the wealthy guy takes the blame and resigns himself to life in prison. But Rosie shows up at the trial to testify (falsely) that she had encouraged advances from the mean guy, inciting the wealthy guy to shoot him in a jealous rage. Justifiable homicide? Sonya Levien's legal reasoning here is technical and not obvious. In any case, the wealthy guy goes free, and now full of gratitude, he realizes how great Rosie is and genuinely falls in love with her. They live happily ever after.[80] This film is an early example of the frequent use of the names "Rose" and "Sonya" for fictional charac-ters created by Levien and Anzia Yezierska, and the frequently employed trope of the poor, virtuous ghetto girl marrying a millionaire. Levien's second credit was for a Universal Pictures release called *Cheated Love*, which "tells the story of Sonya, a Jewish immigrant who is loved by a settlement worker but is in love with a doctor."[81]

In December 1919 Sonya Levien, pregnant with her first child, wrote a letter to Rose Pastor Stokes mostly filled with domestic gossip. Levien had been living in "the country," meaning Connecticut, at one of the homes she owned with husband Carl while their town house in Manhattan was refurbished. Rose was appealing her conviction under the Espionage Act. The appeal had been filed in March 1919 and this was the tense waiting period before the court decision reversing the conviction was issued in March 1920. Rose was routinely excoriated in the press. One journalist writing to another, Sonya reassured Rose that she knew the negative press was "outrageously inaccurate." She wrote to "Dearest Rose,"

> I ran away and have been living in the country so as to be free from the worries of plumbers, carpenters, and painters who are trying to make habitable a little house that we have bought on ninety-second street. Also I am expecting a baby in about two months and have had to keep

12. Sonya Levien the screenwriter at her desk with typewriter. Sonya Levien Papers, Huntington Library, San Marino, California.

quiet on that account, too, though I have been going on with my work at the office regularly. . . .

Of course I don't believe the press; they have become so outrageously inaccurate and biased that I can hardly bear to read any of them. And the docility and faith of the reading public seem to be imbecile.

After my little spree at the hospital is over, I am going to force myself upon you if only for a short hello.[82]

Skepticism of the popular press was a familiar topic of discussion between Pastor Stokes and Levien. "I see," wrote Rose to Sonya in 1910, "that the press can misrepresent favorably as well as unfavorably to one. I suppose it's anything to make a sensation and boom circulation."[83]

13. Sonya Levien visiting Rose Pastor Stokes and James Graham Phelps Stokes at Caritas Island. Yale University Library, Manuscripts and Archives, Rose Pastor Stokes Papers, MS 573, microfilm.

Confident Contractor

Sonya Levien continued selling screenplays to Hollywood. Famous Players–Lasky, which had merged with Paramount Pictures, bought her stories "The Heart of Youth" and "Baby Doll" from Levien, for $2,500 and $3,000 respectively. "Baby Doll," filmed and released under the title *The Top of New York*, was about the hardships endured by poor people forced out of the Sutton Place neighborhood of New York by gentrification. The film studio liked her writing enough to offer her a full-time job in 1921, around the time the Harding administration finally dropped the espionage case against Rose Pastor Stokes.

On October 5, 1921, two months before she left for Hollywood, Levien typed a letter to Pastor Stokes on *Metropolitan* letterhead. Although the paper was embossed with "SONYA LEVIEN, Editorial" at the top left corner, the signature read "Sonya Levien Hovey." The letter began, "If you happen to be in New York City next Sunday, do come up to my tea party." The Hoveys were hosting a party for the Irish players from the Abbey Theater in Dublin, and Sonya added, "there will be quite a list of people there whom you know." She graciously recalled the Stokes estate on Caritas Island, adding, "Carl and I can't forget the charming visit we had with you and that adorable bit of paradise you live on."[84]

Sonya Levien later told *Success* (the magazine she had worked for years earlier with Samuel Merwyn), "I had an offer from Famous Players–Lasky to sign a contract. . . . It was to begin with $24,000 a year, and to increase at the rate of $5,000 a year for five years. I could not resist it."[85] Who could blame her? This is the 2015 equivalent of a starting salary of $319,000 with annual raises of $66,000 guaranteed to more than double the salary in five years.[86] "I was filled with delight and thoughts of a low-hung, deep-cushioned racy-looking roadster."[87] Upon her arrival in Hollywood in December 1921 under contract as a scriptwriter, Sonya Levien was described in a newspaper article as "one of the best beloved figures among struggling authors."[88] Struggling author Anzia Yezierska would have agreed.

Yezierska had declined offers from Samuel Goldwyn and Twentieth Century Fox to sign contracts like the one Sonya Levien accepted.

Yezierska left Hollywood in April 1921, eight months before Levien arrived.[89] Yezierska went east and Levien went west, following fateful decisions that set them on different lifelong paths. They had divergent interpretations of what it means to enter contracts, arising from their very different temperaments and the tension between the desire for affiliation and the desire for autonomy. This is a salient example of the individuals of the Salome Ensemble demonstrating distinct reactions to very similar situations. It also shows the roots of some of the differences between the novel and the film versions of *Salome of the Tenements.*

Yezierska feared that an employment contract was tantamount to indentured servitude. She had no trouble negotiating and signing contracts to sell a short story, essay, or novel that she had written. This type of contract involved a single, discrete transaction, leaving her free to do as she pleased afterward. But she had worked in sweatshops where the effect of an employment contract was to limit workers' rights and expand those of the employers. Those contracts treated employers as masters and employees as servants, a conceit at which Anzia bristled. Marriages involved different kinds of problematic contracts, and Yezierska had experienced the unpleasant consequences and legal complications of extricating herself from such entanglements.

Unlike Anzia Yezierska, Sonya Levien was comfortable entering a contract while retaining personal autonomy. Levien perceived a legal contract as a form of willful affiliation that could be exited at will.[90] She had a lawyer's knowledge and experience negotiating contracts to buy and sell stories, to embody employment and compensation agreements, and for various other purposes. As far back as 1914 Levien had drawn up contracts to purchase stories she bought in London about the militant suffragist movement for the *Metropolitan.* She saw contracts as tools for building consensual, not coercive relationships. Sonya Levien could focus without fear on the benefits that such affiliations could provide.

In 1922, while Levien worked in Hollywood, Yezierska lived in New York and wrote *Salome of the Tenements.* In an interview that August, Yezierska expressed admiration and gratitude that Sonya Levien had published her short stories in the *Metropolitan* magazine, helping her to "emerge from obscurity."[91] Tired of traveling back and forth cross-country, missing her husband and infant son, Sonya Levien broke her Famous Players–Lasky contract at the end of 1922 and moved back to New York. "There could be no leave of absence with the movies, and so the contract had to be broken."[92] Levien suffered none of the qualms that plagued Anzia Yezierska about entering or exiting contracts. When it became expedient, Sonya Levien simply broke her contract, retaining amicable relations with Paramount. She took an editorial position at *McClure's* magazine and continued doing freelance work.

Yezierska was back in New York preparing for the release of the *Hungry Hearts* film and the *Salome of the Tenements* novel when Sonya Levien published an article in the September 1922 issue of the *Metropolitan* called "My Pilgrimage to Hollywood." In this article Levien related some of her own experiences as a scriptwriter for Jesse Lasky at Famous Players–Lasky Paramount Pictures, and the anecdotes read like cautionary tales about Yezierska. "I was told," Levien wrote, "that most of the Eminent Authors brought de luxe to Hollywood were failures." Sonya Levien had learned how to collaborate as a magazine editor and writer without becoming precious and defensive about her writing. "The clever ones are those who make a point of never seeing their stories in the making or on the screen. When they think they can help the Director, they are about as welcome as a corn in a tight shoe."[93] This sounds like useful advice to Yezierska, but advice she would never accept.

Hire Power

Salome of the Tenements returned Sonya Levien to the movies. In 1924 her former bosses at Famous Players–Lasky asked Levien to write the film adaptation of Anzia Yezierska's novel. This job allowed Levien to remain in New York with her family. Levien was a logical choice, since she had edited and published so many of Yezierska's stories, she had known the author for fourteen years, and she was a close friend of Rose Pastor Stokes, on whose life the novel is partly based. Sonya Levien also is named in the novel as a role model admired by the heroine.

Yezierska might have recommended Levien to Paramount or requested that her friend and sometime publisher be hired as screenwriter, although there is no record of such a request. Levien was the most likely person to win Yezierska's approval for the screenwriting job. Helping Levien to get this job would have been an appropriate expression of gratitude for all the help Levien provided in launching Anzia's writing career. Yezierska would have welcomed such an opportunity to reciprocate Levien's kindness, and that of Rose Pastor Stokes, who had introduced the two young women to each other. Anzia did arrange for another friend, Irma Lerner, to be cast in the part of Gittel in the Salome film.[94] The job of adapting Yezierska's novel for film drew Levien back to the movie business, starting a career that would last more than three decades. Sonya Levien had helped Anzia Yezierska achieve success as a writer, and now Anzia Yezierska helped Sonya Levien achieve success as a screenwriter.

Circassian Dancer

In 1925, after finishing *Salome of the Tenements* for Famous Players–Lasky Paramount, Sonya Levien was hired by Samuel Goldwyn Pictures in story development and scenario editing (script doctoring). Like the *Salome of the Tenements* assignment, the Goldwyn job was in New York, but it only lasted a few months. Later that year Carl Hovey left the *Metropolitan*, which had by then been renamed *Hearst's International Magazine*. Carl Hovey and Sonya Levien and their kids moved to Hollywood. Carl went to work as a story editor for Cecil B. DeMille's new company, and Levien wrote screenplays for various film companies. Carl's contract granted him a salary of $150 a week for an initial period with renewal and raise options that DeMille never exercised. The money wasn't bad, about $110,000 a year in 2015 dollars,[95] but his wife was making three times as much. DeMille hired a full complement of writers, directors, and actors at that time for his start-up movie studio, among them the star Jetta Goudal who had played Sonya Mendel in *Salome of the Tenements*. DeMille and Goudal both had recently been pushed out of Famous Players–Lasky Paramount. Carl Hovey and Jetta Goudal became fellow employees at DeMille's fledgling studio.

Carl's career soon stalled. He lost his job with DeMille two years before DeMille fired Jetta Goudal. Although he continued writing, Hovey's efforts bore little fruit. He wrote two scripts for Fox Film Corporation in 1934, and pitched personality profiles to the *New Yorker* magazine that were never accepted. Sonya Levien published a profile of Samuel Goldwyn in the *New Yorker* in 1925 in which she described the movie mogul as "an inspired buccaneer" who coined "bon mots by the bushel," a fierce movie "genius" who, despite "insensitiveness to the feelings of others," was able "by sheer urge of some divine spark within him" to rise from humble beginnings as a poor Hungarian Jewish immigrant named Shmuel Gelbfisz to become "the head of the motion picture industry for a time."[96] His bon mots became widely known in Hollywood as "Goldwynisms."

Sonya Levien thrived in Hollywood. She wrote more than seventy screenplays between 1926 and 1955, the year she won an Academy Award for *Interrupted Melody*. She ended up supporting her family with the money she made as a screenwriter. At various times Cecil B. DeMille hired Levien to write for Metropolitan Pictures and Pathé; at other times she worked for MGM and Fox Films. In his 1957 autobiography, *I Blow*

14. Sonya Levien in hat with pearls and shawl. Sonya Levien Papers, Huntington Library, San Marino, California.

My Own Horn, Jesse Lasky recalled, "The pictures I made on the Fox lot included *Berkeley Square* with Leslie Howard, and *The White Parade* with Loretta Young, both with excellent screen plays by Sonya Levien, then a Fox contract writer, whom I had started as a scenarist in the early days of Paramount, and who developed into one of the best-known and most skilled craftsmen in her field."[97]

When Carl and Sonya moved to California in 1925, Clarence Day, the author, *New Yorker* contributor, and early supporter of women's suffrage, wrote her a letter of congratulations. Declaring, "what a modern career you are having!" he teased her about becoming a Hollywood screenwriter. "Sold yourself into slavery like a Circassian dancer, to amuse languid audiences."[98] Circassian women were reputed to be the most beautiful women in the world in legend and folklore dating to the early Ottoman Empire. These women were captured, enslaved, and forced into the harems of the most powerful sultans, for whom they danced and served as concubines, evoking comparisons to the stories of Queen Esther and Salome. The Circassians, from which the word Caucasian also derives, were a sect that was forcibly conquered by Slavic Russian armies. In this short sentence, Day alludes to Sonya Levien's childhood in Russia as an outsider from the dominant culture and compliments her physical beauty. By using the dance as a metaphor for Levien's performance as a screenwriter, he conflates her beauty with her creative intelligence.

Like the female icons Salome and Queen Esther, the beautiful Circassian harem slave struggles over agency with powerful, ruling men. These women deploy the power of feminine beauty and selective visibility. Clarence Day's quip ascribes agency to Sonya Levien by suggesting that she sold herself, she was not sold or coerced by others. The assertion was apt. Sonya Levien did indeed set her own agenda. She appeared only when and where she wanted to. In 1954 an article about Sonya Levien affirmed, "One of Hollywood's most interesting women is one whose face is never seen on the screen."[99] Levien preferred to lead from behind the scenes. "The most prolific Jewish woman writer was one whose name is little known" begins the entry on Sonya Levien in the encyclopedic *Jewish Women in America: An Historical Perspective*, edited by Paula Hyman and

Deborah Dash Moore.[100] She amplified her power by limiting her visibility. This allowed her to craft a successful public persona while protecting her private life.

Levien was skilled at corporate public relations when she arrived in Hollywood. She altered the birth year on her publicity bio to 1898 from the factual 1888 year of her birth, in deference to the reverence of youth that characterized an industry obsessed with physical appearance. In 1925 she was a thirty-seven-year-old wife and mother of two, claiming to be only twenty-seven. She had the good looks to maintain the illusion. She told a reporter that when she went to England in 1914 to report on the militant feminist movement, "I was only about twenty."[101] She actually had been twenty-six.

From Minsk to Malibu

Sonya Levien's success allowed her to complete a long journey from Minsk to Malibu, by way of Manhattan. She was able to integrate the roles of socialist and socialite, over time relinquishing the former and embracing the latter. Levien became famous among Hollywood insiders for hosting intellectual salons and celebrity parties at her Malibu beach house similar to the ones she had attended years earlier at Rose Pastor Stokes's Caritas Island and Mabel Dodge's apartment in New York City.

Dodge had moved to New Mexico and married Tony Luhan, who was a Pueblo Indian. In his memoir *Of Time and Change*, Frank Waters, author of Southwestern literature, recalled that his New Mexico friends Mabel Dodge and Tony Luhan visited California and stayed with "Carl Hovey and his wife, Sonya Levien, the top-notch screenwriter for Fox studios, on their large estate at Malibu Beach." Frank Waters had been a screenwriter, "with a shoestring motion-picture company turning out quickie cowboy-Indian thrillers."[102] He observed that many of the same writers, artists, and intellectuals who visited with Mabel Dodge and Tony Luhan in New Mexico ended up at Sonya Levien's get-togethers. Lady Dorothy Brett, an English painter, "stayed at the beach estate of Carl Hovey and his wife, Sonya Levien," who had by then become "MGM's top writer." Lady Brett and her close friends Frieda and D. H. Lawrence had enjoyed parties and repartee in New Mexico with the Luhans and in Malibu with Sonya

Levien.[103] At the Malibu beach house, "Every Sunday some fifty notables gathered for lunch, including Greta Garbo and Leopold Stokowski" and "Stokowski's bride, the young heiress Gloria Vanderbilt."[104] Vanderbilt was twenty-one years old when she married musical conductor Stokowski, who was her second husband.

The music at Levien's parties was legend. Composer Harold Arlen's biographer Edward Jablonski writes,

> So it was that the songwriters congregated in their own little world. A favorite center for their frolics was the home of the screenwriter Sonya Levien where some of their performances were recorded on acetate home recording discs. At one of these evening parties Arlen was asked to sing Gershwin, which he did, accompanied by the composer Milton Ager. To the delight of the company, he sang "Summertime" in the original key for soprano and followed with "There's a Boat Dat's Leavin' for New York" in its original key for baritone. His vocal range was phenomenal, his voice controlled, pliant, sensual. His vocal shadings came out of the synagogue and Harlem, with all stops between Broadway and Hollywood. A friend told him he had overheard a glamorous young woman exclaim after an Arlen vocal, "He sings as if his fly was open!"[105]

In his autobiography, Harpo Marx recalls "a party at the home of the late Sonya Levien" that he attended with the playwright and screenwriter S. N. ("Sam") Behrman and Oscar Levant, the pianist, composer, author, comedian, and actor. Harpo's anecdote recalls the post-party scene in *The Great Gatsby* in which a tipsy guest loses a tire while attempting to turn around in Gatsby's driveway:

> I went with Oscar, in his beat-up Ford. Sam, who had to leave early, followed in his rented Cadillac. When the party broke up, long after Sam had left, Oscar went for his car. . . . His car had been stolen! . . .
>
> While we waited for the cops to come, the car thief telephoned, asked for Oscar, and made a full confession. The thief was Sam Behrman.
>
> Driving home, Behrman had suddenly become aware that a car was following him. It didn't appear to be a police car, so Sam tried to shake it. He made several quick turns, then tried to outrace whoever it was. . . .

The car followed him all the way into the driveway and stopped right behind him. . . . But the car behind him was empty. It was Oscar Levant's Ford, locked bumper-to-bumper to the Cadillac. . . .

in parking, back at Sonya Levien's, he had whanged back into another car. But bashing other cars was a common occurrence with Sam, and he'd said nothing about it to anybody.[106]

In her novel *Among the Survivors*, Levien's daughter Tamara Hovey captures something of the cultural blend that characterized her mother's parties. The parties were imbued with "something handed down to [Sonya Levien] from her rabbinical forebears back in old Russia, who had spent their days in contemplation, the notion that there was nothing higher on earth nor more worthy of respect than the cultured 'learned' man."[107] This romanticized notion of the "cultured learned man" is actually a multicultural blending of the "rabbinical forebears" of Sonya Levien with the American, patrician intellectual forebears of Carl Hovey. It contrasts starkly with Anzia Yezierska's experience with her father, her rabbinic immediate forebear, as a religiously "learned man," not a "cultured" one, who lived off his family while providing them with no practical sustenance.

At Sonya Levien's gatherings in Malibu, even the catering was multicultural: "On the inlaid buffet at one end of the room lay a spread of hot buttered crumpets, cinnamon toast, and paper-thin English cookies from an expensive bakery on Beverly Drive. Side by side with this Anglo-Saxon offering were deep dishes of Baltic herring swimming in sour cream and onions, chopped liver, Russian black bread."[108]

Levien often spoke of her love of screenwriting and the Hollywood life it provided. She treasured "the opportunity of reading most current fiction while it is still in proof, or even in manuscript." Sonya Levien was thrilled to receive a draft of *The Great Gatsby* a year before it was published, one of the perks of her professional position and her friendship with F. Scott and Zelda Fitzgerald.[109] She also appreciated the "great moment" when "you see your words, your thoughts, your very feelings come to life on the sets, it is wonderful! There are gardens so beautiful that only dreams could have made them, rooms that were a joy to a woman to create, oriental streets glowing like opals, down which pad live camels laden with bright merchandise—fruits, and sloe-eyed, olive-skinned girls of the desert."[110]

Like her father, Levien retained a soft spot in her heart for political anarchists. She corresponded with Emma Goldman after Goldman was exiled from the United States. A letter from Goldman in London to Levien in November 1925, right around the time the film *Salome of the Tenements* was released, conveys the anarchist's gratitude that Sonya remained "a friend" even after Goldman and Rose Pastor Stokes had broken over political differences.[111] Goldman confesses to being surprised to hear from Levien, having "placed you among many others once my friends who have forgotten my existence." The mass starvation and brutality of the Russian civil war after World War I split socialists and anarchists who continued to support the Bolsheviks from those who renounced them. Rose Pastor Stokes remained a staunch supporter while Emma Goldman renounced the Bolsheviks. The violence and obliteration of civil liberties convinced the veteran anarchist that the Russian Revolution had failed. Goldman was unhappy "to find a number of people who were always friendly to me turn into bitter enemies because of my stand on Russia." Goldman's letter to Levien continued:

> I am very glad indeed that you are not among them. But Rose Pastor Stokes is. So much so that she presided at a meeting arranged by the Communists of New York and suggested that I be burned in effigy. To me such blind fanaticism is a sign of lack of individual thinking, not to speak of lack of humanity. Of course this ridiculous procedure only amused me. But it is one of the many proofs for the gangrene which the Bolshevik superstition has been spreading since it was foisted upon the world. Unless you can follow blindly everything done by Moscow you stand condemned in the eyes of such bigots as Rose Pastor Stokes and her comrades. All these years since she first entered the radical ranks have not taught her that there may be sincerity even among her enemies, and that no matter how much we are opposed to them, we still must learn to respect sincerity wherever we find it.[112]

Sonya Levien deftly navigated the movie studio system, and never trumpeted her personal political beliefs. She had learned as a little girl the painful price her father had paid for expressing his dissident political views, and she wished to protect herself and her family. Anarcho-syndicalist groups like the International Workers of the World, with their calls for direct action, including violent protest, held no appeal for Levien.[113]

Sonya Levien cultivated a quiet confidence that Anzia Yezierska could not muster. That confidence allowed Levien to be charmingly self-deprecating. "I can not cook," she told one interviewer, "nor sew. I am very stupid about things like that." In her own way she insisted, "I am domestic. I love my home; I love to make homes. And I have a passion for rebuilding old houses."[114] Anzia Yezierska earned a college degree in domestic science and was an excellent cook and seamstress, but she loathed doing these things.

Levien became an American patriot without losing her inmost self. She was a generous collaborator and an appreciative acolyte who attracted a series of caring mentors. Levien embodied a type that political scientist Bonnie Honig calls the "supercitizen immigrant."[115] This mythic creature manages to have it all, hard work that is rewarding and satisfying, close family, community ties, and eager participation in civic life. Honig states that "the supercitizen immigrant is the object of neither American hostility nor charity but of outright adoration."[116] Lisa Botshon notes that when the film *Hungry Hearts*, based on Anzia's short stories, was released, the author bridled at the publicity campaign that demonstrated the "Hollywood impulse to represent the Jew as the ideal immigrant," and specifically to present Yezierska "as an ideal immigrant" by manufacturing for the press the pretense of "her enthusiasm for the American system" and even to falsely suggest that the Jewish author had acquired vast "knowledge of Christianity."[117]

Sonya Levien fell in love with America. She thrived personally, socially, and professionally, and won the adoration of friends, family, and colleagues. The other women of the Salome Ensemble were to various degrees ambivalent about enacting American identities. Rose Pastor Stokes remained a staunch internationalist who dreamed of a united world, with nationalisms of diminished significance. Anzia Yezierska was conflicted by the desire to attain the full status of American personhood while retaining her margin of difference. Jetta Goudal still claimed to feel European even after living in America for more than seventy years.

Sonya Levien wrote the screenplay for the 1939 film *The Hunchback of Notre Dame*, starring Charles Laughton and Maureen O'Hara. Thirty-three years after they ended their youthful affair, Levien was called upon to co-write the screenplay for Sinclair Lewis's novel *Cass Timberlane*. The 1947 film starred Spencer Tracy and Lana Turner. It is the story of a civil court judge in his early forties who falls in love and marries a woman half his age. In the novel the judge is a divorcee, but in the film he is a widower. The young wife describes herself as a "wildcat," full of energy and seeking adventure. Having grown up poor, literally on the wrong side of the railroad tracks in their small town, she longs for a college education. When her husband calls her "my Ginny," she insists she is not his, but her own. She dreams that her future daughter will become the first woman president of the United States. She learns to pilot a plane. After various twists in which she temporarily becomes attracted to another man, she reconciles with her husband, providing the classic happy ending and preservation of the marriage plot. Levien and Lewis had traveled a long way from the days of *Hike and the Aeroplane*, but Sonya was still tweaking story elements, as she had done with *Salome of the Tenements*, to avoid controversy and make them acceptable to mass audiences. Divorce retained a stigma even in 1947, while widowhood evoked sympathy. Sonya Levien seems to have subscribed to the view that discretion is the better part of valor when confronted with potentially offensive elements in screenplays.

Levien was candid about some of the techniques required of a successful screenwriter. She advised aspiring screenwriters to suppress ego, learn to write with a team, and rewrite endlessly until a film is completed. She also suggested flattering the film's director, whom she archly referred to as the "Arrogant Animal." "[M]ilk him dry of all his own little bright ideas and put them into the yarn to save yourself the trouble, and if he hasn't any, as is often the case, then insinuate your own bright ideas into it and make him believe they are his."[118]

Next Generation

Sonya Levien's children pursued careers in creative arts. Her daughter, Tamara Hovey, became a writer and screenwriter like her mother. Tamara

Hovey's novel *Among the Survivors* included a thinly veiled fictionalized depiction of the Levien-Hovey family.[119] Mother and daughter co-wrote a story that MGM produced in 1949 as *That Midnight Kiss*. A musical comedy, it marked the screen debut of operatic tenor Mario Lanza. Tamara adapted the story for the screen with co-writer Bruce Manning. Tamara Hovey and Bruce Manning shared screenwriting credit while Sonya Levien received none; she allowed her name to vanish.[120] Two years later, in 1951, Mario Lanza achieved a popular hit with a recording that included "A Little Love, A Little Kiss," the song whose lyrics Anzia Yezierska had invoked almost thirty years before in a happy street scene in the novel *Salome of the Tenements*.[121] Also in 1951 Sonya Levien teamed up with William Ludwig to write the screenplay for *The Great Caruso*, in which Lanza starred as the famous tenor. The Caruso film was a pet project of Jesse Lasky, who recalled, "My friend Sonya Levien wrote the screen play in collaboration with William Ludwig."[122]

Like her father, Tamara Hovey wrote two biographies, one about her mother and father's old magazine colleague John Reed, and the other on the French novelist George Sand. Tamara Hovey also shared screen credit as the co-screenwriter of *Tamango* with her husband, Les Gold, and John Berry in 1959.

Sixty-three years after her grandfather Julius Opeskin was banished to Siberia as an anarchist, Tamara Hovey Gold and Les Gold were blacklisted as communist sympathizers in 1953, victims of McCarthyism. Tamara Hovey and Les Gold became part of a self-exiled community in Paris of blacklisted American communists. Sonya Levien made no public comments and left no private correspondence about the blacklist, and she continued working as a screenwriter.

Serge Hovey became a composer and musicologist whose artistic interests and achievements reflected the cultural mix of his parents' backgrounds.[123] He studied composition with Arnold Schoenberg and served as musical director of Berthold Brecht's *Galileo* in 1947 in Hollywood. In 1948 Serge Hovey composed music to accompany the Decca Records production of *Sholem Aleichem's Tales from the Old Country*, a recording voiced by Howard Da Silva reading English translations by Julius and Francis Butwin from the original Yiddish. This was followed by two theatrical scores, *Tevya and His Daughters* in 1953 and *The World of Sholem Aleichem* in 1957, composed by Serge Hovey to accompany plays by leftist internationalist Arnold Perl. These productions, also adapted from the stories of Sholem Aleichem, achieved critical acclaim and box office success. That success inspired Joseph Stein to write *Fiddler on the Roof*, based on some of the same Sholem Aleichem stories. Serge did not work on *Fiddler*, which debuted in New York in 1964. Serge Hovey also wrote *The Robert Burns Songbook* and recorded the seven-album *Songs of Robert Burns*. The subjects of Serge's works suggest a level of comfort with, even celebration of, his ethnic hybridity and a balance of influences from his parents. Serge Hovey married and had four sons.

From Russia with Love

Sonya Levien arrived in America a wary skeptic, but she turned into a patriot. She worked hard, married an Anglo-Saxon intellectual, had a family that she ended up supporting, achieved fame and fortune in Hollywood, and shed overt connections with the radicalism of her youth, but she never fully forsook those sympathies. While Anzia Yezierska remained all her life conflicted, undecided about her place in America, Sonya Levien overcame such conflicts. Levien embraced America and insinuated herself into the worlds of motion pictures, art, music, and letters. The role of screenwriter allowed Sonya Levien to thrive as an insider in an industry based on flamboyant spectacle while remaining behind the scenes, hidden for the most part from public view. Her name appeared in screen credits often as the second or third screenwriter. Sometimes she received no screen credit at all.

In 1955, at age sixty-seven, Sonya Levien won an Academy Award for the screenplay of *Interrupted Melody*, which she also co-wrote with William Ludwig. Even in the credits for that award-winning screenplay, Sonya's name appeared after that of her co-writer. Twenty-two years had passed since Rose Pastor Stokes died and Jetta Goudal left the movie business to become a labor activist and interior decorator. Anzia Yezierska published her last novel, *Red Ribbon on a White Horse*, five years earlier in 1950 at age seventy, although she continued writing book reviews and articles for the *New York Times*, *Commentary*, and other magazines.

While controlling and limiting her visibility, Sonya Levien made inroads as a woman, a Jew, and an immigrant, effacing social boundaries. She was a dynamo who generated energy without making noise. Instead, Sonya Levien created harmony. She arrived from Russia with love and brains and ambition, emerged from the darkness of the Russian Pale and the tenements of the Lower East Side, and made her way to the bright sunshine of Hollywood. Sonya Levien told one interviewer that among all of the movie stars she worked with, she retained a special fondness for Will Rogers, who was famous for claiming he had never met a man he didn't like.[124] Sonya Levien, who died at the age of seventy-two in 1960, appears never to have met a man or woman who didn't like her.

Mabel Dodge described Levien as "running things behind the scenes."[125] In a way this can be understood as a socialist sensibility, in that she appeared to subordinate her ego for the good of the collective. And yet she was known to have a strong will and a strong ego. She had a gift for boosting the confidence of her co-writers, owing to a quality Ross Posnock describes as the "power of sympathetic identification."[126] This was the ability to see and to know the emotional experiences of others, a capacity for empathy. Her ability to attract collaborators and bring out the best in others was one of the vital forces that pulled the women of the Salome Ensemble into each other's orbits. Her winning personality, positive outlook, strong drive, and enthusiasm for working with others allowed her to radiate magnetic charm, a kind of charisma. Sonya Levien was very smart and very pleasant, a powerful combination that allowed her to run things from behind the scenes.

| 5 |

Jetta Goudal Was the Forbidden Woman

Julie Henriette Goudeket was born in Amsterdam on July 12, 1891. There were approximately 82,000 Jews in The Netherlands at that time, less than 2 percent of the 4.5 million Dutch citizens.[1] The Goudekets were Orthodox Jews. Julie's father, Moses, was a diamond merchant born in 1860 and her mother, Geertruida Warradijn, was born in 1866. Julie was three years younger than her sister, Bertha. The Goudekets lived in Plantage Muidergracht in Amsterdam's former Jewish Quarter, or Jodenhoek, when their younger daughter was born. They moved a short distance to Sarphatistraat. These homes were located in the city center roughly one kilometer east of what is now the Rembrandt House Museum and three kilometers east of what became the Anne Frank House. Julie was raised in comfort in the Dutch capital, and no known trouble or trauma disturbed her childhood. But something happened along the way, because Julie Goudeket grew up to flee from home and heritance, permanently cut all ties to her family, and take on a new identity.

In New York Anzia Yezierska took the emotionally wrenching step of escaping the constricting environment of her Orthodox Jewish parents and moving to a room of her own. In Amsterdam, Julie Goudeket, who became Jetta Goudal, took the emotionally wrenching step of escaping from her Orthodox Jewish parents and moving to New York. Yezierska reappeared intermittently, never fully reconciling but never finally disappearing from the family and cultural community into which she was born. Throughout her life Yezierska kept in touch with her siblings, nieces, and nephews. Not Jetta Goudal. After Goudal vanished from her parents' sight around the age of twenty, she never reappeared, never saw them or her sister again, never spoke to them again, and never again allowed them

15. Jetta Goudal seated on a settee, in a messaline satin gown by Lanvin. Photograph by Edward Steichen in 1923. From *Vogue* magazine, November 1923.

to see her. That is, unless they chanced to see her on the screen years later, as a movie star.

Her mother, Geertruida, died in 1920 or 1921. Her father, Moses, remained in his Amsterdam home until his death in 1942. A younger cousin named Maurits Goudeket married the French novelist Colette, who was a music hall entertainer for a time and portrayed Salome on the stage.[2] Colette was a friend of Sarah Bernhardt.[3] During World War II Collette rescued Maurits Goudeket from the Nazis and helped him escape the Holocaust. Maurits wrote a book about their marriage, *Close to Collette: Intimate Portrait of a Woman of Genius.*[4]

Goudal emerged from the Dutch Jewish community that had excommunicated Baruch Spinoza 250 years earlier. It is not difficult to imagine her family rejecting her for behavior they considered apostasy, or her running away from their disapproval. For a woman from this community, transgressions such as dressing in modern clothing, socializing in public without parental permission, or mingling with Gentiles would have been sufficient grounds for ostracism. Like Spinoza, her banishment was permanent. Had she remained in Holland through World War II, she might have risked the same fate as Anne Frank and other Dutch Jews. But she left Europe right after World War I.

"I didn't come to the United States because I wanted to have a good time," she told film historian John Kobal. "I had gone through the war, and that had been more than I could take. . . . I knew that I was going to crack up . . . and I decided [to] start a whole new life."[5] She was a beautiful young woman, an ingénue and would-be leading lady possessed of natural acting talent and fluent in Dutch, French, English, and likely Yiddish and Ladino. Julie Goudeket arrived in America at a time of important new endings and new beginnings for the women of the Salome Ensemble. She moved into the Martha Washington Hotel a few months after Rose Pastor Stokes was convicted under the Espionage Act and John Dewey broke up with Anzia Yezierska. Sonya Levien was just starting to submit screenplays to movie studios.

As soon as she arrived in New York in 1918 at the age of twenty-seven, Julie began a slow, deliberate process of shedding her former identity and fashioning a new one. It took about three years to complete her transformation, her conversion experience. First she quietly disclaimed her Jewishness. She apparently feared anti-Semitism, and effacing her past as completely as possible might have seemed a prudent expedient to her. Then she took the name Jetta Goudal. As a child, her family called her Jetje, pronounced with a soft *j* so that the sound is similar to the pronunciation of Zsa-Zsa, as in Zsa-Zsa Gabor, the Hungarian actress who also has Jewish roots. To English speakers this might sound exotic, but for a Dutch family it was no more unusual than an American girl named Julie being nicknamed JJ. From Jetje she derived the name Jetta, and Goudal was a short substitute for Goudeket.

Finally she cast off her Dutch origins and grafted on fictitious French roots, only after the advent of her film career. She invented the story that she was a Christian born in Versailles, France. The Treaty of Versailles ending World War I represented a rebirth for Goudal. In that light the choice to proclaim Versailles as her birthplace makes sense. Her desire to conceal her Dutch background perhaps stemmed from fear that Americans would disdain an immigrant from a country that had remained neutral in the just-ended war.

Goudal presented herself to America anointed with a usable past in which controversial details were concealed, adorned with an exotic name, in the fine raiment of a movie star, radiant in the approving gaze of her public. For the rest of her life she clung to this fabricated biographical backstory concocted for American audience consumption. Occasionally this led to reprehensible or pathetic behavior. In one unfortunate example, as she grew older Goudal made vulgar anti-Semitic remarks in public, apparently to mask her own Jewishness. She also disavowed her Dutch Jewish family. Her sister Bertha died in the early 1940s, but Bertha had a daughter who immigrated to America after World War II. This niece attempted to contact her aunt Julie, but Jetta Goudal refused to speak with her, and falsely denied that she was the sister of the young woman's mother.

Julie supported herself with clerical office work during her first two years in New York. Then, beginning in 1921, she achieved some success on the theatrical stage. On July 23, 1921, the name Jetta Goudal appeared in a small item in the *New York Times* in a context that demonstrated her lingering association with her Dutch compatriots. The *Times* reported that the "Netherlands Aircraft Manufacturing Company of New York and Amsterdam" flew its Fokker F-3 monoplane, the *Half Moon*, in a demonstration flight over New York City for the first time to garner publicity for the plane, which was used in service between London and Amsterdam. Passengers on this publicity flight included the Netherlands consul in New York, the commercial representative of the Dutch Legation at Washington, DC, the secretary of the New York Chamber of Commerce for the Netherlands, and "Miss Jetta Goudal and a moving picture photographer."[6] It is a scene reminiscent of Sinclair Lewis's novel *Hike and the Aeroplane,* written a decade earlier.

By 1922 she displayed not only a flair for courting publicity, but a penchant for feminism, budding political activism, and a predilection for challenging corporate power. The *New York Times* reported on May 28, 1922, that "Miss Yetta Goudal, representing the theater," was among "the speakers and guests of honor" at the third annual convention of the New York State Federation of Business and Professional Women's Clubs held at the Hotel Pennsylvania.[7] Jetta Goudal listened as a letter from New York City Mayor John Francis Hylan was read to the assembly, in which corporate titans, "those engaged in monopolistic enterprises," were criticized for joining in "concerted action" to pass "legislation intended to benefit their own limited circles."[8] The mayor credited "the determination of the women of this state" for passage of "the human laws which now grace our statute books," and hoped that success would "band all women together in an insistence on an enactment of social legislation," addressing such issues as workplace safety and equal pay for women.[9]

Martha Washington

Jetta Goudal did not avail herself of the settlement houses in New York City, and she did not live in the tenements, but she did benefit from the largesse of philanthropic patrons. Upon arrival in the United States, Goudal moved into the Martha Washington Hotel for Women, a haven with a level of gentility not available to the immigrant denizens of the Lower East Side. At first glance life in the Martha Washington Hotel seems very different from the tenement lives of the other women of the Salome Ensemble. But in fact this hotel for women was part of the same philanthropic continuum as the settlement houses, designed to uplift, Americanize, and culturally assimilate immigrants, and integrate women into urban, industrial society. The benefactors of the Martha Washington were in the same wealthy set as philanthropists who funded the settlement houses attended by immigrant women like Rose Pastor Stokes, Anzia Yezierska, and Sonya Levien.

The Martha Washington Hotel is a twelve-story structure, extending from 29th Street to 30th Street in Manhattan, just east of Madison Avenue,[10] in a neighborhood historically known as Rose Hill.[11] It opened in 1903 as a hotel exclusively for women,[12] and operates today without gender restriction. It went co-ed in 1998.[13] The building was designed by the architect Robert W. Gibson, whose many achievements include the New York Botanical Garden Museum.[14] The Landmark Preservation Commission of the City of New York designated the Martha Washington Hotel a Historic Landmark in June 2012.[15]

The mission and the business of the hotel were developed by the Woman's Hotel Company, which was formed in March 1900 for that purpose.[16] The stockholders included John D. Rockefeller; William Schermerhorn; Mrs. Russell Sage; Miss Helen M. Gould, daughter of railroad magnate Jay Gould; Mrs. Elliott Shepard; and Mrs. C. Phelps-Stokes, a relative of Rose Pastor Stokes's husband.[17] The Board of Directors consisted of Lucian Warner, Charles F. Cox, Charles M. Jessup, and Charles D. Kellogg. This enterprise was conceived by its wealthy patrons to provide a "respectable" lodging for "the working girl of today," following principles articulated in 1844 by the Society for Improving the Condition of the Laboring Classes, "to provide the best accommodations at the least rent compatible with their desire to make a limited profit."[18] It did not work out so well for the investors, who found the room rates too low to cover business expenses. No profits meant no dividends, causing some to complain "that the enterprise was in fact a charity rather than a business."[19] This should hardly have been a surprise, given that many of the hotel company's stockholders, board members, and advisors also "served on the Board of the Charity Organization Society, a group started in 1882 by Mrs. Josephine Shaw Lowell."[20] The Charity Organization Society (C.O.S.) was committed to philanthropy guided by the principle of distinction between worthy and unworthy poor. Historian David Huyssen describes how the aggressive effort to ferret out and deny assistance to the unworthy poor undermined the Charity Organization Society's mission, earning it the disparaging sobriquet "Organization for the Prevention of Charity."[21] The C.O.S. also was entangled in a scandal when one of its presidents, Henry Weeks, embezzled funds from his law partners. Weeks fled to Costa Rica with money borrowed from a nephew who succeeded him as C.O.S. president, but he was extradited and sent to Sing Sing.[22] By 1918, when Jetta Goudal moved in, the Martha Washington

Hotel had been sold to Julius and William Manger, brothers who developed a chain of successful hotels.[23]

The Martha Washington at Mount Vernon theme of the hotel was a clear expression of its prescriptive purpose to help its residents become good American citizens. The investors expected the Martha Washington Hotel to be used by working women, and as a "headquarters for women business representatives from a distance."[24] The mission to empower women was accomplished sometimes in ways the well-intentioned investors might not have anticipated. Not just businesswomen, but suffragettes, flappers, and film stars also took shelter in the Martha Washington's modest facilities. On January 16, 1910, the hotel served as the setting for the founding of the Woman's Suffrage Party, a political party dedicated to winning the right to vote for women.[25]

The interior of the hotel was decorated by "Miss Kellogg, daughter of Charles D. Kellogg" and "Mrs. Davidge" in a manner designed to instruct and improve its residents. When it opened, the *New York Times* made a point of reporting that "nothing about any part of the building suggests the institutional or philanthropic elements so universally protested against in many existing hostelries for women exclusively."[26]

> On the second floor the dining room for guests on the American plan is situated. This is also in buff and white, with Colonial blue carpets and blue leather chairs. . . .
>
> The library in dark wood and deep red, is a particularly attractive room. The bookcases are mahogany, duplicates of those at Mount Vernon, and over the mantel is a fine relief of Martha Washington, flanked by symbolic figures of History and Literature.[27]

According to the *New York Times* report, except for bellhops, men were not allowed above the second floor of the building, which contained "public dining rooms and parlors." The roof "promenade" was designed to allow residents to "breathe air of a purity unknown to those who walk the streets." Silent film star Louise Brooks recounted her enjoyment of the air on the roof promenade during her brief experience in 1924 at the Martha Washington Hotel. Brooks, who was then seventeen years old, moved into the Martha Washington after the Algonquin evicted her. Some of the Algonquin's guests were scandalized by the sight of her in a provocative "short pink dress" on her way out clubbing at two o'clock in the morning. She wrote,

> The atmosphere of the Martha Washington Hotel was institutional. The women wore short hair, suits, and sensible shoes, and worked, I assumed, in offices. Two weeks after I had been assigned a cell under the roof, I went into the grim, nearly empty dining room for tea. To my amazement, sitting alone at a large table was the exotic star of the film *Java Head*, Jetta Goudal. While I ate a ham sandwich and drank iced tea, I watched her welcome to her table a group of girls, some of them bringing gifts. She was particularly pleased with a handmade shawl of white wool, which she threw over her shoulders. [Jetta had starred in the film *The Bright Shawl*.] . . .
>
> Before I could investigate Jetta Goudal's tea parties any further, I was asked to leave the Martha Washington, because people in a building overlooking the hotel had been shocked to see me on the roof, exercising in "flimsy pajamas."[28]

Anzia Yezierska understood the connection between settlement houses and hotels for women. In *Salome of the Tenements*, her protagonist Sonya Vrunsky moves out of a settlement house and into a woman's hotel after leaving her Brahmin millionaire husband. She stays at the hotel while pursuing a new career and self-reliance. The hotel in the novel is a way station on the main character's journey to financial self-sufficiency, just as the Martha Washington was for Jetta Goudal. Yezierska expresses disdain for the woman's hotel and the settlement houses as institutions whose philanthropic purposes are tainted by condescending attitudes and reductive functionalism. The protagonist Sonya Vrunsky decides the hotel is worse than the settlements:

> The room to which she was shown was narrow, cell-like, devoid of any touch of individuality. As she flung herself on the white-enameled bed and looked at the blank walls, she felt that the dark, dirty little rooms of Mrs. Peltz's Essex Street tenement were far more livable than this hard, institutional cleanliness deprived of one breath of human warmth.

But the complete sense of desolation did not take hold of Sonya until she got down to the dining room. The sea of segregated women buzzing at all the tables around made her feel lost in a desert of nonentities, as in a swarm of neuter bees. There were all kinds of professional and business women and working girls. But they had one thing in common: abnormal repression of femininity. . . . "This prison of females is more killing than a settlement!" Back in her cell of a room, the fear of her uncertain future thickened about her like a stifling fog. She was determined to get out of the dehumanizing atmosphere of the woman's hotel.[29]

The descriptions of Yezierska's fictional hotel and the Martha Washington are similar enough to raise the question of whether the author modeled the one in the novel on the very one that provided shelter for Jetta Goudal.

Shooting Starts

While Jetta Goudal was living at the Martha Washington Hotel in 1922, Anzia Yezierska was ensconced some twenty blocks away in Greenwich Village writing *Salome of the Tenements*.[30] They might have passed each other while shopping on lower Fifth Avenue. Goudal met Sidney Olcott, who was directing a film starring an actor who had been in a play with Jetta. At Olcott's invitation, Goudal took a screen test, and landed her first small cinematic role in *Timothy's Quest*, a film produced by Dirigo Films and distributed by American Releasing Corporation.[31] The film was released in September 1922. Goudal was thirty-one years old when she launched her film career.

In November, two months after the premiere of *Timothy's Quest*, Anzia Yezierska's novel *Salome of the Tenements* and the film adaptation of her short-story collection *Hungry Hearts* were released simultaneously for maximum tie-in publicity. Sonya Levien was spending most of her time in Hollywood by then, under a screenwriting contract with Famous Players–Lasky Paramount. From November 5 to December 5, 1922, Rose Pastor Stokes attended the Fourth Congress of the Communist International in Moscow, as a delegate to the Congress and a reporter for the Negro Commission.

Goudal became a rising star. In 1923 she appeared in *The Bright Shawl* with the screen idols Mary Astor, Edward G. Robinson, William Powell, and Dorothy Gish. Then came a second film directed by Sidney Olcott, *The Green Goddess*. Olcott, who remained the only director to work with Goudal on more than one film, directed her a third time in *Salome of the Tenements*. *The Green Goddess* was distributed by Samuel Goldwyn's company, Goldwyn-Cosmopolitan, and produced by Distinctive Pictures. Distinctive Pictures was impressed enough to sign Goudal to a multipicture contract. According to the contract, Jetta, referred to as the "Artiste," was to be a leading lady. The agreement was to run for an initial term of six months, with Goudal to be paid five hundred dollars per week. The studio was contractually obligated to place Goudal's name in advertisements and on screen "above any other female in the cast," and to "advertise and publicize her in a dignified and important manner."[32]

But obstacles arose as quickly as opportunities. Less than one month into the contract, on November 17, 1923, the company terminated the agreement. Goudal was fired, but she did not go away quietly. Just five years after she arrived in America and three years after American women won the right to vote, Jetta Goudal had the chutzpah to insist that her contractual rights had been violated by her employer. She did what many American women at that time would not have had the audacity to attempt. She sued.

Goudal viewed her contract as a pact between equals, not an indenture binding a servant to a master from which she could be summarily dismissed. Unlike Anzia Yezierska, Goudal had no phobia about signing an employment contract. Still, she refused to allow a corporation to disrespect her or diminish her social status. Unlike Sonya Levien, Goudal had no gift for inspiring the adoring comradery of coworkers. However, like Yezierska, Levien, and Rose Pastor Stokes, Goudal understood the power of American law over employers, landlords, and others who strong-arm or cheat women. Court papers indicate that Goudal was still living in the Martha Washington Hotel for Women in 1924 when she sued Distinctive Pictures for breach of contract.[33]

Goudal argued that she had been fired without cause. She demanded compensation of $100,000, including $11,000 of salary payments for the remainder of the six-month term of the contract and $89,000 for other damages. These other damages included impairment "to her professional reputation and her standing with the public," the loss of opportunities for "enhancing her skill and professional ability," and the loss of advertising and publicity, all of which caused her to be "hindered in obtaining other and similar work."[34] The claims for these other, special damages would generate the most heated arguments in the case.

Distinctive Pictures argued that Jetta was not obedient. She would not obey orders. Instead, she dared to challenge and argue with her colleagues on matters relating to "her role, her costumes and acting." She had "an ungovernable and furious temper," and made "persistent efforts" to "force the adoption of her personal opinions." She was "unremittingly insubordinate and combative." She uttered "disparaging and contemptuous remarks" to and about her co-workers.[35] Distinctive Pictures tried to convince the court that by committing these offenses Jetta, and not the studio, had "failed, neglected and refused to perform" her contractual obligations.[36]

However, nothing in her contract required Jetta to be fun to work with. The language of obedience and insubordination harkened back to outdated social status–based nineteenth-century legal doctrines, inappropriate for interpreting a twentieth-century contract. Disputes between employers and employees had a long history in English and American law of hinging on the assumption that differences in social class mandated unequal legal status between the parties. In addition to social class, women confronted entrenched attitudes and legal traditions of gender-based power asymmetries that reflexively favored men. Oliver Wendell Holmes Jr. wrote that viewing contracts this way leads to "the superfluous theory that a contract is a qualified subjection of one will to another, a kind of limited slavery."[37] Jetta Goudal was having none of that.

When Goudal brought her suit, contract law in American courts was undergoing a shift in which rights and obligations were increasingly recognized as arising from the agreement and not the social status of the contracting parties. The case was implicated in a debate over long-accepted legal theories characterized by legal scholar Grant Gilmore as "uneasily poised between past and future."[38] Karen Orren argues that nothing less than a "belated feudalism" in American law and politics retained influence on employment contracts.[39] Orren contends that "the law of master and servant was at the foundation of capitalist development and industrialism" in the United States at the turn of the twentieth century, and courts of law often deferred to "the hierarchical relation of master and servant."[40] Race, ethnicity, gender, and class all were implicated in this legal doctrine, which maintained that being a worker "was still a legal status"; that is, "an established position in society conferred upon an individual that does not arise from any specific action or from a contract but from the individual's personal characteristics."[41]

"In a democratic society who was master and who servant?"[42] asks Robert Wiebe in *The Search for Order, 1877–1920*. Amy Dru Stanley explains that American labor law of the late nineteenth century recognized a shift in which "wage work no longer belonged to the domestic realm,"[43] but maintained a contradictory "legal understanding of wage labor as both a free contract and a relation of authority and subordination." At the beginning of the twentieth century, labor law "used the new language of employer and employee interchangeably with the older one of master and servant."[44]

Even today the words *worker* and *servant* retain connotations of essential, personal characteristics, rather than voluntary affiliations. Werner Sollors describes this as the difference between "consent and descent," or status versus contract.[45] Amy Dru Stanley uses the starker language of the movement from "bondage to contract."[46] Ascribed, imposed, and coercively enforced distinctions are used to maintain the power imbalances of class and status hierarchies. That employees are obligated to be obsequious, obedient, and deferential to employers was assumed historically to be so clearly understood that it was considered not necessary to actually state this in the language of employment contracts.

Celebrated strikes and court battles between labor unions and employers expanded workers' rights in a series of landmark cases in the late-nineteenth and early-twentieth centuries. Less well known are cases such as those brought by Jetta Goudal, in which an individual sued her employer and successfully enforced her contractual rights while overturning archaic arguments based on social status of the parties. These legal cases also advanced the movement from social position to individual volition as the source of employee rights, the movement from status to contract.

Goudal's lawsuit against Distinctive Pictures also enabled her to participate in a legal vanguard on the question of reimbursable damages. Nothing more than unpaid salary would be awarded for breach of contract under classic legal theory. A separate lawsuit under tort, or personal injury law, would have been required for a plaintiff seeking further restitution under old doctrine. However by 1923, "Progressive legal thought had brought the distinction between contract and tort to the verge of collapse," explains legal historian Morton Horwitz.[47] "Duties deriving from contract and tort could not be distinguished in terms of the source of the obligation."[48] Moreover, the classical will theory of contracts required the legal resolution of disagreements to derive from the explicit language of the contract. As early as 1897 Oliver Wendell Holmes Jr. and others objected to the restrictions this placed on judges who were forced to parse the language of contracts that often failed to address the circumstances of the dispute. Increasingly, judicial discretion was deemed appropriate so that courts could infer or impose contractual conditions for the sake of fair and just outcomes. Arthur Corbin of Yale Law School asserted straightforwardly that "an obligation to pay damages for breach of contract is created by the law and not by the agreement."[49]

Goudal's claim for total damages of $100,000 was nearly ten times her lost wages. This demand inspired counsel for Distinctive Pictures to Shakespearean rhetorical flourish. Channeling Hamlet, defendant's attorney professed shock that Jetta was seeking "to make her contract ten times more valuable in the breach than in the observance."[50] But this statement precisely summarized Goudal's case. Distinctive Pictures' breach had in fact caused Jetta to suffer damages far beyond the loss of wages. That, Goudal's attorney argued, is why breaching the contract should cost the studio more than performing under it. The idea is encapsulated in Gus Kahn's lyrics to the 1928 song "Makin' Whoopie," which describes a judge's warning to a philandering husband in his courtroom: "You better keep her, I think it's cheaper."[51] More was at stake, for both Goudal and Distinctive Pictures, than her weekly paycheck.

During her single month under contract, Goudal had been cast as leading lady in two pending Distinctive Pictures films, *Blood and Gold* and *Martinique*. Press releases were issued and articles and photos placed in the press. Through these actions the studio expropriated the value of the actress's fame to promote its business. These initial notices also enhanced Goudal's reputation. Subsequently the company announced it was replacing Jetta with another actress in *Blood and Gold* and it had abandoned plans to produce *Martinique.*

This was a double blow to Goudal's growing celebrity. First, the public dismissal and cancellation destroyed any value she had derived from the initial notices, and second, they raised a cloud of doubt over her. She was not returned to the *status quo ante,* but rather damaged. It was not practical for the court to order the parties to resume specific performance of the terminated contract. Mutual antagonism eliminated any possibility of Distinctive Pictures and Jetta going back to working together.

Everyone is "free to break his contract if he chooses," Oliver Wendell Holmes Jr. asserted in his 1881 treatise *The Common Law,* if he is willing to face the consequences.[52] Holmes described entering a contract as "the taking of a risk" that a promise will be kept. If not, the party who broke the promise must pay. The law, Holmes asserted, will not interfere until after the promise has been broken. Mark Twain parodied Holmes in 1905 when he wrote of "the privilege of committing murder: we may exercise it if we are willing to take the consequences."[53]

The court decided that Distinctive Pictures had breached the contract, rejecting the company's argument that Jetta's behavior amounted to some form of constructive resignation. The company exercised its right to break the contract and it had to take the consequences. Still, it was not easy to quantify those consequences. The cash value of damage to a person's reputation is always difficult to ascertain. The language in the contract did not provide clarity. Goudal was promised lead roles, top billing, first-class travel, lodging, and all the fanfare and publicity appropriate for a leading lady. She was empowered to select her own wardrobe for each film role. She had promised not to work for, or allow her image to be used by any other employer while the contract was in force. Her salary was to be paid even during times when she was not working on a film. But Distinctive Pictures was not obligated to produce any minimum number of motion pictures for Goudal, and there was no explicit guarantee that she would be cast in even one film.

The company argued that it had not intended to assume the risk of special damages to the actress's reputation and that the court could not force it to do so. The actress argued that assumption of that risk was implicit and undeniable. The contract did state that its value was based upon Goudal's "personality and services being unique and extraordinary."[54] After entering the contract the studio damaged those unique and extraordinary qualities that had induced it to hire Goudal in the first place. Goudal argued that this was a foreseeable consequence of the company's breach. When a movie company enters a contract with a movie star based on her special talent, personality, and reputation, Goudal asserted, it assumes the responsibility not to damage that reputation, personality, and talent.

Since the parties disagreed on the meaning of the contract, the court had to decide. The company moved to strike any claims for damages not resulting from lost wages. The court denied that motion.[55] Distinctive Pictures appealed this denial, to no avail. Goudal was permitted to press her claims for compensation in excess of lost wages. The motion pleadings, hearings, order, appeal, and confirmation dragged on for more than a year until finally the main case was to move forward. A trial was to be held to determine if Goudal was due compensation for special damages, and if so, to determine the dollar amount. The trial was scheduled for September 28, 1925. A lack of further court records suggests that a settlement was reached. But despite the documentary fade-out, this was not the final scene in Jetta Goudal's serial courtroom drama. Her performances as a plaintiff were to be continued.

Commanding Performances

While prosecuting her lawsuit against Distinctive Pictures, Jetta Goudal signed a new three-picture contract with Famous Players–Lasky Paramount in May 1924. In December she moved to California to perform under that contract. Goudal's tenure with Paramount lasted longer than her one month with Distinctive Pictures, but not a lot longer. She completed three films with Paramount in ten months, *Open All Night*, *Salome of the Tenements*, and *The Spaniard*, and once again she was fired. However, unlike her unpleasant encounter with Distinctive Pictures, Goudal's brief time with Paramount propelled her to a higher professional, social, and economic status.

The Paramount Pictures company that signed Jetta Goudal had evolved through a series of mergers of smaller companies. The managers of the company had migrated from the live theater business into the film industry a decade before Goudal made the same transition. Adolph Zukor was a Hungarian immigrant who made money in Chicago as a furrier. In 1903, at the age of thirty, Zukor invested in penny arcades and nickelodeons in New York City, Newark, Boston, and Philadelphia. In 1912 he bought U.S. distribution rights to the French film *Queen Elizabeth*, starring Sarah Bernhardt, and exhibited the film in legitimate theaters instead of kinescope penny arcades and nickelodeon parlors, a bold initiative that paid off. The legitimate theaters lent an air of status and respectability to moviegoing. Previously films had been perceived as cheap, lowbrow curiosities, aimed primarily at the lower classes. The new venues opened up a whole new audience to cinema. On the strength of this success, Zukor founded a film production company that he named Famous Players. With Sarah Bernhardt as his first famous player whose celebrity generated box-office profits, Zukor set out to repeat that precedent by presenting more "famous players in famous plays."[56] He hired and nurtured the careers of stars such as Mary Pickford (née Gladys Smith).[57]

In 1913 vaudeville and legitimate theater impresario Jesse Lasky joined with playwright and stage actor Cecil B. DeMille, and Lasky's brother-in-law, a glove salesman named Samuel Goldfish (née Shmuel Gelbfisz),[58] who would later change his name to Goldwyn, to form a film production company called the Jesse L. Lasky Feature Play Company. Goldfish decided to leave the domestic glove business in part because the Underwood-Simmons Tariff Act of 1913 reduced tariffs on many items including imported gloves, thereby threatening his profit margins.[59] That act also reinstituted a federal income tax following the ratification of the Sixteenth Amendment on February 3, 1913.

Goldfish was a savvy, scrappy businessman who kept his eye on the main chance. Goldfish/Goldwyn was renowned for, among other flourishes, imparting the pearls of wisdom that Sonya Levien called "bon mots by the bushel."[60] Although he is sometimes quoted as saying, "A verbal agreement isn't worth the paper it's written on," it has been suggested that this was an inaccurate paraphrase of a comment Goldwyn actually made in praise of movie executive Joseph M. Schenk's trustworthiness. Referring to the producer whose nickname was "Honest Joe," Goldwyn is said to have asserted, "His verbal contract is worth more than the paper it's written on."[61] Whichever of the two versions is accurate, they convey Goldwyn's pragmatic business realism, which acknowledges that what a contract says is not always consistent with how the parties perform.

The Jesse L. Lasky Feature Play Company merged with Adolph Zukor's Famous Players in 1916. A film distribution company called Progressive was reorganized as Paramount in 1916 and acquired by Famous Players–Lasky in a hostile takeover in 1917.[62] This combination created a film production, distribution, and exhibition (movie theater) powerhouse that would remain intact until a consent decree in 1940 required the divestment

16. Jetta Goudal as Sonya Mendel in *Salome of the Tenements*, 1925. From Library of Congress Prints and Photographs Division, by permission of Paramount Pictures.

of the exhibition business. Following the mergers, the Paramount name survived. This was the company with which Sonya Levien signed a screen-writing contract in 1922, which she broke a year later. It also was the company that purchased the film rights to *Salome of the Tenements* from Anzia Yezierska and then rehired Sonya Levien to write the screenplay in 1924. And it was the company that signed a multipicture contract with Jetta Goudal in 1924 while she was in litigation against Distinctive Pictures. Jesse Lasky was the head of the combined studio during Jetta's time at Paramount, and Cecil B. DeMille was in charge of film production. However, Goudal and DeMille never got a chance to work together at Paramount.

Meant for the Part

In *Salome of the Tenements*, Jetta Goudal played Sonya Mendel. If ever an actress was meant for a role, Goudal was meant to portray Mendel. Both Goudal and Mendel were strong-willed Jewish immigrants in New York City who carefully crafted American identities. Both lived at hotels for single women while pursuing professional careers. Both sought the approval of older, powerful, Gentile men, with whom they suffered disillusion and painful breaks. Both rebounded from traumatic setbacks with hard work and training for a new artistic career. And both ended up with men with whom they shared empathetic, but not passionate, relationships. Sonya Mendel is compared to "a Bernhardt in her youth."[63] Jetta was "enchanted by Sarah Bernhardt."[64] Bernhardt, a French actress born in Paris in 1844 to a Dutch, Jewish mother named Julie from a prominent Amsterdam family, pioneered and cultivated the art of "female spectacle."[65] Jetta Goudal the actress and Sonya Mendel the character cunningly deployed the power of female spectacle, selective, elective visibility, following the examples of the salacious Salome and the beautiful Bernhardt. Critics and audiences praised Goudal's portrayal in *Salome of the Tenements* of a young girl who grows into a beautiful adult woman.[66] One reviewer thought that in the childhood scenes she looked like "a girl of ten"[67] while another saw her as "a girl of 16."[68] Goudal was thirty-three years old when she played the role.

In 1924 Sonya Levien told a reporter, "Now I am doing an adaptation of 'Salome of the Tenements,' by a Russian author, for Sidney Olcott, who is one of the three greatest directors in the world, you know."[69] She observed that "often a story has to be rewritten to suit a star. She finds that to act in a certain way would be entirely foreign to her nature, so a new part must be written on the spot, a new bit invented, or a piece of business improvised to suit the location where unexpected conditions often arise to change the story."[70] Jetta Goudal was the star Levien was working with when she made these remarks. In July 1925 Levien told the *Boston Post* that "[t]he motion picture people have lost so many thousands of dollars because those they employed had excess temperament."[71] Jetta Goudal was often described in the press as a "cocktail of temperament."[72]

Her performance in *Salome of the Tenements* drew Jetta Goudal into the Salome Ensemble with Rose Pastor Stokes, Anzia Yezierska, and Sonya Levien. However, Goudal was in some ways the odd woman out of this foursome. She was younger than the other three and the last to arrive in the United States. Goudal was Jewish like the others, but she was Dutch, not Russian, and she alone hid her religious and national origins. The Russian immigrant members of the Salome Ensemble fled with their families from humble beginnings. Goudal emerged from a Dutch society in which her family occupied a space of confusing status. The Goudekets were wealthy residents of cosmopolitan Amsterdam, who as members of the Jewish minority in a residential and commercial enclave were simultaneously connected and cut off, tolerated and disdained. The three from poor families in isolated shtetles in the Russian Pale knew physical discomfort but social clarity; they understood their status as pariahs. Jetta Goudal was proud and arrogant. In New York she strove to retain the trappings of status that the three Russians had not experienced as children. Rose, Anzia, and Sonya had to work in sweatshops, but Jetta did clerical work in more genteel office settings to support herself before launching her career as an actress on stage and screen. After moving to America, all four of them had to construct platforms to support professional, social, and personal ascent. Goudal, like the others, used American law and selective visibility as resources to achieve a successful career, social status, and political influence.

Clash of the Divas

The films Goudal made with Paramount were popular with critics and audiences, boosting her career and her paychecks. While the protracted

Distinctive Pictures lawsuit muddled through the New York courts, Goudal continued performing in front of the cameras and confronting new conflicts behind them. One rival prima donna proved capable of battling and beating Jetta. Goudal had been cast as the female lead opposite Rudolph Valentino in *The Sainted Devil*, but in a highly charged, tabloid-filling confrontation, Valentino's wife, Natacha Rambova (born Winifred Shaunessy in Salt Lake City), demanded that Jetta be dismissed from the film.[73] There are conflicting versions of the clash of the divas. Some allege that they fought over Goudal's proposed wardrobe for the film. Others suggest that Valentino and Goudal were attracted to each other and Rambova was jealous.

Rambova had been a movie art director, set designer, and scenario writer, and had worked on the 1923 silent film *Salome* starring the Russian ballerina Alla Nazimova, based on the Oscar Wilde play. Valentino biographer Robert Oberfirst writes that Rambova had "undisputed artistic talents, but she had never been permitted a voice in the actual production."[74] After marrying Valentino, she tried to control his films. "She intruded on every department with suggestions, criticisms, requests—and then demands—for changes."[75]

Alan Arnold, another biographer of Valentino, writes,

> Jetta Goudal was talented, exotic in her tastes, temperamental and very strong willed. By this time Natacha's power had grown. . . . From the beginning of the filming of The Sainted Devil it was clear that something was bound to happen between two such strong personalities as Jetta Goudal and Natacha. It was not long in coming about. . . . [Jetta] was to play a part which required elaborate costuming. Her exotic taste was nothing short of fantastic when exerted upon the process of conceiving her gowns for the film . . . Two eminent costume designers found them so difficult that they refused to accept the more spectacular designs. . . . Natacha swiftly settled the matter. Miss Goudal was *out* and another actress was *in*.[76]

There was simply not enough room on the sound stage for both of these imperious women according to Oberfirst. "Like Natacha, Jetta was beautiful, strong-willed and outspoken. She resented the 'advice' Natacha was giving on set and said so loudly and bitterly. The result was that she found herself out of the picture."[77] In her own memoir, Natacha Rambova insists she was falsely accused "of sacrificing Rudy for my own selfish ambitions—I wished 'to become a power in the industry.' Fortunately, my conscience is entirely free from this despicable accusation."[78]

Both Oberfirst and Arnold suggest that Goudal maliciously spread the false rumor that Valentino was attracted to her and that Rambova had her dismissed out of jealousy. According to Arnold, "The public believed there to be truth in her allegations. Was not Valentino the Screen's Greatest Lover, a man who had twice married, had once been arrested for bigamy, and did he not adore beautiful women? Such a man would hardly hesitate to make love to a woman of Jetta Goudal's beauty."[79] In his posthumously published memoir, Valentino refers only obliquely to this incident by acknowledging that "[i]t is quite true that I have listened to [Natasha's] advice . . . on the choice of actors for my support. . . . If all this is being henpecked, then I am indeed henpecked. What is more, I like it."[80]

Forty years after it occurred, the incident was rehashed in Rambova's 1966 *New York Times* obituary. "[Miss Goudal] insisted she had been dismissed because of Miss Rambova's jealousy. Miss Rambova said the quarrel began when she criticized Miss Goudal's wardrobe. 'A cinema star has no more use for durable clothes than a subway guard has for a course in etiquette,' she later declared."[81] The obit also alleges that after Goudal was dismissed from the starring role in *The Sainted Devil* she "was reported to have attempted suicide." It is not clear whether Jetta's emotional distress was a reaction to losing the man, losing the fight, or losing the film role. Rudolph Valentino and Natacha Rambova were divorced a year later. Rambova insisted that gossip had caused the divorce.

Mischief and Melodrama

While filming another Paramount picture, Goudal became enraged when she was soaked in a scene shot in artificial rain and no one brought her a towel. She stormed off the set and went home, costing the producers a day of filming. When posing for publicity shots, Goudal insisted that a full-length mirror be provided so she could see what she looked like before the photos were taken. For movie stars of today, these demands would hardly seem remarkable, but during the Roaring Twenties when Jetta rose to fame, studios generally wielded far more power than actors and actresses. The desire to redress this power imbalance and retain profits for themselves motivated Charlie Chaplin, Mary Pickford, D. W. Griffith, and Douglas Fairbanks to found the United Artists film studio in 1919. In March 1925, three months before Distinctive Pictures filed its answer in her lawsuit, Paramount fired Jetta Goudal.[82]

Film historian Anthony Slide writes, "Paramount did terminate her contract, claiming, in March 1925, that Goudal was too temperamental, entirely unmanageable, and that she delayed production for trivial reasons."[83] While her breach of contract suit with Distinctive Pictures was still being litigated, Goudal filed a new breach of contract suit against Paramount Pictures.[84] Jetta asked the court to order Paramount to pay her damages of $23,250, claiming that her contract had eighteen months to run and that she had been terminated without cause. Paramount argued that Goudal suffered no financial or career loss because she signed a multipicture leading lady deal with Cecil B. DeMille almost immediately at higher pay.[85] This lawsuit also appears to have been settled quietly.

When the trouble with Paramount occurred, Goudal quickly met with DeMille, who also had recently been fired by Paramount. DeMille was starting his own film production company, the Cecil B. DeMille Pictures Corporation. Although it did not provide her with job security, by the end of her Paramount period Jetta was successful enough to check out of the Martha Washington Hotel and move from New York to Los Angeles.[86] Goudal went to work at the new DeMille studio in Culver City, in which the "main administrative building was a striking replica of George Washington's home, Mount Vernon."[87] She left Martha Washington for George Washington, went west, and became a movie star. Jetta Goudal was living one version of the American Dream.

Commandments of the Director General

When he co-founded the Jesse L. Lasky Feature Play Company in 1913 with Lasky and Samuel Goldfish, Cecil B. DeMille was the only partner who brought no money to the new venture. The other partners perceived value in DeMille's reputation as an actor and playwright and a member of a famous Broadway theatrical family. His father and brother, both graduates of Columbia College in New York City, were celebrated playwrights, and his mother was a theatrical agent and promoter. Cecil had chosen to go to the Pennsylvania Military College and the American Academy of Dramatic Arts, where Anzia Yezierska had won a scholarship and studied in 1908 and 1909. Cecil had not achieved as much success and celebrity as his brother William. When the other partners raised $15,000 to start the Lasky Company, they granted DeMille ownership shares just for joining, and he was given the vaguely military-sounding title of director-general of the company. This established a pattern that DeMille would continue throughout his life of spending other people's money to make movies.

The film industry evolved from arcade kinescopes to nickelodeon parlors after 1905.[88] Historian Nan Enstad notes that early motion pictures were popular with a "predominantly working-class immigrant audience" prior to World War I, although some attempts were made to woo "a middle-class audience as early as 1908."[89] DeMille and his partners at the Lasky Company were determined to market movies to middle- and upper-class audiences. After 1913 they began to increase spending to improve production values and to produce long-form "feature films" based on adaptations of literary works or theatrical stage plays. These feature films eventually replaced short, ten-to-twenty-minute adventure serials and "labor-capital" films that depicted popular themes such as "working heroines who encountered adventures, gained inheritances, or married millionaires."[90] Film historian Sumiko Higashi writes that Cecil B. DeMille "inserted the photoplay into genteel culture by exploiting parallel discourses deemed highbrow in an era characterized by conspicuous racial, ethnic, and class distinctions."[91] This social class crossover appeal allowed DeMille to reach a wider audience and to pioneer the use of movies as vehicles of social engineering.

Cecile B. DeMille pursued an agenda with his films beyond the basic one of making money. He had a not uncommon nativist, paternalistic reaction to perceived threats to American society. Chief among his fears was the combination of mass immigration and concentration of the growing urban population. DeMille set out to use cinema to promote, if not impose, his vision of a healthy and virtuous social order as a bulwark against modern society's ills. To accomplish this goal, he made motion pictures designed to instruct an audience aspiring to upward mobility about his vision of proper civic behavior.

DeMille aimed at nothing less than defining American identity and encouraging immigrants to assimilate. Social historian Elizabeth Ewen affirms that "[t]he DeMille films openly attacked the customary assumptions, behavior, and style of their audience and pointed the way to the appropriation of a new definition of self. In this sense they became an agency of Americanization."[92] His early works reflected what Higashi calls an anxious "response to a pluralistic urban milieu populated by threatening strangers."[93] DeMille cast himself as a member of an elite leadership class charged with defending American civilization against an influx of barbarian hordes. Historian Paula Hyman explains that "[a]lthough the process of assimilation seemed inevitable to immigrants, the project of assimilation was complicated by the struggle of American elites with the potential impact of mass immigration on shifting definitions of American identity."[94] DeMille believed in the benevolence of his efforts to use film as an instrument of education, much as John Dewey believed in the benevolence of his own theories of education for living. Both men stumbled into the realms of coercive instrumentalism, their versions of social education descending into social engineering.

It is appropriate, then, that among DeMille's most enduring legacies are his two film versions of the biblical story of the foundational rules of law of a moral society, the Ten Commandments. In 1923 DeMille produced the silent epic *The Ten Commandments* for what was then a record high production budget of $1.5 million,[95] to the great consternation of his corporate colleagues. During the filming, when they questioned his mounting spending, he became enraged and asked if the moneymen wanted him to stop and release the incomplete film as *The Five Commandments*. DeMille prevailed and the film was released to great commercial success, with gross earnings almost triple its cost.[96] Nevertheless, two years later, Adolph Zukor and his long-time partner Jesse Lasky pushed DeMille out of the company after attempting without success to curb his production spending. In Lasky's autobiography, he describes DeMille's departure from the company in a chapter aptly titled "Thou Shalt Not Spend Wantonly."[97]

Nevertheless, DeMille had what might be described as the last laugh in this episode. In 1957 he produced a remake of *The Ten Commandments*, starring Charlton Heston, with a budget of more than $13 million, earning box office success and enduring value as a perennial television stalwart.

When Paramount fired him, DeMille created the Cecil B. DeMille Pictures Corporation, his own independent movie production company, and hired a staff of administrators, directors, writers, and actors, including Jetta Goudal. DeMille and Goudal commiserated about the shared experience of being fired by Paramount. Goudal believed that her role in the Paramount film *Salome of the Tenements* helped her land the new contract with DeMille. She later testified that during their initial meeting she showed DeMille critical reviews that praised her performance in *Salome of the Tenements*. She told the court that DeMille replied, "Yes, I saw the picture. That is the reason I wanted to talk to you."[98] After this talk, Goudal got the job. In 1925 she signed a multipicture contract with the brand-new DeMille studio.

DeMille also hired Sonya Levien's husband, Carl Hovey, that year. They did not work together, but Carl Hovey and Jetta Goudal were fellow employees of the same boss. Hovey lost the job with DeMille within a year, while Goudal stayed until September 1927. As Carl Hovey exited, his wife entered. In August 1926 DeMille hired Sonya Levien as a screenwriter, a position she held through June 1928. So, from August 1926 to September 1927, Levien and Goudal both worked for DeMille. At Paramount they had collaborated on *Salome of the Tenements*,[99] but in the vast enterprise that was the DeMille studio the two women did not work together. Perhaps they saw each other in the commissary.

In court testimony, DeMille recalled his first conversations with Jetta. "I called attention to the fact that she had just severed her relations with Famous Players Lasky Corporation under unpleasant circumstances," he testified. Lasky told DeMille that he fired Goudal because "she was impossible to get along with. That she was the Bolshevist note in the studio; that the situation in the wardrobe department was impossible; that she had torn a dress from her body."[100] But after hearing her side of the story, DeMille concluded, "You have convinced me that Mr. Lasky was unjust to you and that [Paramount] did not give you the right break; that you are right and they are wrong."[101] The judge found it remarkable that DeMille was inclined to trust Goudal's version of her departure from Paramount more than that of his long-time partner and friend Jesse Lasky.[102] However, this inclination is consistent with the strained relations that followed DeMille's own forced departure from Paramount. Goudal and DeMille gave very similar accounts of this conversation.

Cecil Blount DeMille was born in Ashfield, Massachusetts, to parents who had both had careers in live theater. He was a product of classic American polygenesis. His father, Henry deMille, was the scion of a Dutch Presbyterian family that traced its roots in the United States back to the seventeenth century, when an ancestor emigrated from the Netherlands to New York City, setting up house in Bowling Green.[103] DeMille's mother was a Sephardic Jewish immigrant from England who met her future husband when they performed in a play together. Under Jewish religious doctrine, which recognizes matrilineal descent in the children of intermarriages, Cecil B. DeMille would have been considered Jewish. However, like Jetta Goudal, DeMille hid his Jewish background, preferring to highlight the venerable Knickerbocker origins of his father's family. DeMille and Goudal both were "passing," concealing their Jewishness and presenting themselves as WASPs. For Jetta, this effort was about self-protection and personal gain. For DeMille, it fit with his crusade to embody and promote a concept of homogenized Americanism.

Goudal's lawsuits against Distinctive Pictures and Paramount remained unresolved when she entered the DeMille contract on May 19, 1925. This new contract had an initial term of one year, and it granted to the studio up to four annual renewal options for a potential total of five years. It was typical of film artist contracts of the era in granting the options to the studio in its sole discretion, with no compensation to the artist if the studio declined to exercise a renewal option. It did, however, provide for mandatory defined salary increases for Jetta at the end of each six-month period as long as the contract remained in effect, including the four renewal periods if the studio exercised its options.

During her first year with the DeMille Pictures Corporation, Goudal starred in two films, *The Coming of Amos* and *The Road to Yesterday*. Cecil

B. DeMille personally directed *The Road to Yesterday*, and he described his working relationship with Jetta as pleasant and productive. But she antagonized other directors and coworkers at the DeMille Company. Frank "Junior" Coghlan was a child actor who portrayed the younger brother of Jetta's character in the 1926 film *Her Man o'War*. In his autobiography, Coghlan remembered,

> Jetta Goudal was a good actress and very pleasant to me on the set; but from her I saw my first exhibitions of a temperamental actress. Our director was Frank Urson, one of the kindest men alive. He had worked his way up in the DeMille hierarchy, finally receiving codirector credit on some of C. B.'s films.
>
> This was Urson's first full directorial assignment and Jetta made life unbearable for him on the set. She would make demands and argue with him on the set in front of the entire company over her least little displeasure. Maybe she didn't like having a first time director on her starring vehicle.[104]

At the end of the first year of Jetta's contract, the DeMille company exercised its option to extend the agreement for a second year. In the second year, Jetta starred in *Three Faces East, Paris at Midnight*, and *Her Man o'War*. The company exercised its option to extend for a third year. In 1927 Jetta starred in *Fighting Love, White Gold*, and the prophetically titled *The Forbidden Woman*. She completed eight motion pictures for the DeMille company in almost two-and-a-half years. And then, on September 10, 1927, for the third time in her career Jetta endured the ignominious experience of being fired.

The Forbidden Woman was Jetta's final film with DeMille. As with all of Jetta's movies, tensions ran high during production. The actress argued with the director, David Stein, and with production executives and others working on the picture. Opinions differed as to whether this creative tension added quality or cost to the film. Cecil B. DeMille Pictures was a holding company that owned or worked with a group of subsidiaries and related corporations formed to manage budgets of individual films and other aspects of the business. William Sistrom was the studio manager for the William DeMille Picture Corporation, the corporate entity of Cecil B. DeMille's brother, and the entity that produced *The Forbidden Woman*. William DeMille supervised that film, and had also clashed with Jetta.

On August 30, 1927, Sistrom called Jetta for a meeting that set in motion the termination of her contract. Jetta testified she told Sistrom she was "discouraged" and "tired," because of "opposition" and "friction" she experienced working on the film.[105] She said, "I do not mind working, myself, sick, but I don't believe in fighting myself sick," and "You people have gotten me in a state of nervous collapse, and I had to go three months to a sanitarium, and I feel that I am going again. I am at the end of my rope." She told Sistrom that she would like to do her next picture "without making any suggestions at all, neither as to the story, [nor] as to my characterization." This would have been wrenchingly difficult for Jetta, who passionately believed that her creative vision was indispensable for the artistic success of any film in which she acted. Goudal felt it was her moral and contractual obligation to contribute proactively in every way she could. If she were merely to passively perform as directed by others she was genuinely concerned that this would detract from the picture's quality. However, apparently worn down by workplace combat, she told Sistrom, "let's try it."

"No, Jetta," Sistrom answered. "We don't want that. It would never be as good a Goudal picture. It will lack the very qualities that have made your pictures so far different."

Jetta was "amazed" and "flattered" by Sistrom's response. She momentarily let her guard down. She saw herself as a gifted actress who also was qualified to be a costume designer, a scriptwriter or at least a script doctor, and a director. Sistrom appeared to be validating this perception. Delighted that this producer might finally be acknowledging her inner auteur, Jetta's hopes began to rise. If Mr. Sistrom felt this way, perhaps he would agree that she should edit, shape, and punch up the script of her next picture in advance of filming. It was not so far-fetched a notion. This was, after all, the kind of respect that was paid to the great Sarah Bernhardt.

"I am not asking for any extra money," she quickly added. "I am not asking for $10,000.00, as you sometimes pay for script."

"We won't let you do it," Sistrom answered with devastating honesty. Jetta's hopes had been raised in vain only to be dashed. She had quite literally become the forbidden woman. This answer was a slap, stinging with clarity.

"I don't believe in staying where I am not wanted," Goudal replied haughtily after pausing to regain her composure. "Would you kindly ask Mr. DeMille to consider a proposition of release, Mr. Sistrom?" The precise meaning of this request fueled the legal dispute between the actress and the studio. The studio argued that Goudal had asked for permission to exit her agreement without penalty. Jetta insisted she meant she would negotiate to allow the company to compensate her for breaking their contract.

Experience had taught Jetta the futility of attempting to force the company to continue to perform under the contract. She knew that damage to her reputation and employability must be calculated and compensated. She also was aware of her duty to mitigate her damages by seeking other employment. Jetta was ready to discuss acceptable conditions for the dissolution of their contract without resort to judicial action. Nine months remained under the current annual term of her contract, and the studio retained two one-year renewal options.

Jetta met with Sistrom a week after she requested a proposal. At Cecil B. DeMille's instructions he prepared a short release for her to sign, surrendering all her rights under the contract. The studio offered her nothing in return but a release from her obligations to perform. If she would go away, they would permit her to go. It was a one-page document stating that the contract had been terminated by mutual agreement and the parties each held the other harmless. She would be paid for ten more days, during which the studio could require that she be available to shoot any "retakes" for the film she had just completed. After that, her paychecks would immediately cease, as would any contractual relationship between Goudal and DeMille.

Mr. Cecil B. DeMille remained invisible in this. He did not deign to appear at the meetings. Sistrom affected a disingenuous air of guileless innocence as he delivered the release form to Goudal, as if he were not aware of the insult he was adding to her injury. She disabused him of this pretended misperception, reminding Sistrom of the "great difference between talking terms and asking for a release."[106] Summoning her customary air of insouciant disdain and displaying a remarkable understanding of conflicting legal doctrines of status and contract, Goudal told Sistrom, "I think that is what one usually gives to a servant when you dismiss him, but not to an actress on a contract."[107] Having articulated her umbrage in the language of class discourse without regard to political correctness, she knew what she had to do next. Jetta disappeared temporarily, only to defiantly reappear in court where she could invoke the power and authority of American law to fight back. She sued. However, she did not do so lightly or without misgivings.

Mr. DeMille, I'm Ready for My Lawsuit

Goudal had learned from her prior lawsuits against film studios. She was acutely aware of the combative reputation she had acquired, and another lawsuit would serve to cement that negative image. Moreover, this dispute pitted Jetta against the revered and powerful Cecil B. DeMille, a man not likely to submit without a fight, a man who possessed the resources necessary to pursue that fight, and a man whose influence within the film industry could seriously jeopardize her future viability as a movie star. Adding to these impediments was the fact that Jetta liked and respected DeMille. On the one film on which they had worked together, *The Road to Yesterday*, they enjoyed mutual respect and a pleasant working relationship. She had become friends with DeMille's daughter. Goudal's disagreements had been with DeMille's underlings and employees, not with the man himself. But this was business, not personal.

On January 25, 1928, Jetta filed suit for breach of contract against Cecil B. DeMille Pictures Corporation in the Superior Court of Los Angeles County. Both parties waived the right to a jury trial, and the case was tried before Judge Leon Yankwich. Yankwich was himself a Rumanian immigrant who was later nominated by President Franklin Roosevelt to a seat on the U.S. District Court for the Southern District of California. Cecil B. DeMille's long-time attorney Neil McCarthy represented the defendant, and Jetta was represented by W. I. Gilbert.

William Isaac Gilbert was a prominent attorney involved in divorce, business, and even criminal cases of the Hollywood elite, including

Charlie Chaplin, Clara Bow, Aimee Semple McPherson, John Barrymore, J. Paul Getty, Alexander Pantages, and James Cagney. Gilbert represented Jetta Goudal's husband, Harold Grieve, in a lawsuit against Jean Harlow for an unpaid bill for Grieve's interior decorating services. Gilbert also represented Rudolph Valentino in his divorce from Goudal's former rival Natacha Rambova. This association must have raised Goudal's esteem for Gilbert given Goudal's earlier clash with Rambova.

The trial commenced on January 31, 1929, a year after DeMille had sold the Cecil B. DeMille Pictures Corporation to Pathé Exchange. DeMille told the court he no longer felt any connection with the company Goudal was suing, despite the fact that it had been his company and his decision to terminate her contract. When the judge asked DeMille on the witness stand about "your side" in the lawsuit, DeMille responded, "If I may interrupt, it is not my side. I haven't the remotest interest in it."[108]

The DeMille Pictures defense played like a remake of Goudal's court dramas with Distinctive Pictures and Paramount. The DeMille studio, which by this time was called Pathé, tested different strategies with the court. It told the judge that Goudal had not been fired at all, she had resigned. After this contention was quickly rejected, it moved on to offer three explanations to justify firing Goudal.

The company argued that Jetta deserved to be fired because she caused the studio to incur excessive film production costs. However, just as nothing in her Distinctive Pictures contract had required Goudal to be fun to work with, nothing in the DeMille contract required her to help limit film production costs, and she had no authority over spending. Moreover, Cecil B. DeMille had developed a well-established reputation for lavish spending on film production, which undermined the attempt to blame the actress.

Next, echoing the statements made five years earlier by Distinctive Pictures, her more recent employer expressed shock and offense at Jetta's disobedience and insubordination. Of course this should have been no surprise to anyone who knew her. Insubordination was Jetta Goudal's default mode. She would not subordinate herself socially or professionally. She was an actress, a leading lady, an artiste, and she insisted that her rights and her status be respected. Pathé argued that as a servant working for a master, Goudal owed the company obedience that she had failed to provide. It then argued that she breached specific provisions in the contract by refusing to take orders from film directors and others and by arriving late for work. This was essentially the previous argument couched in the language of modern contract law.

Goudal understood from her previous contract disputes that the studio's strategy was to debase and infantilize her. She testified that she called DeMille "Papa."[109] He referred to her as a "sweet child" and a "good girl" or a "bad girl."[110] When they disagreed, he asked her to promise to "be good."[111]

Once again Goudal found herself at the forefront of legal change. The Pathé Company's defense cited several hoary authorities who relied on status-based interpretations of the obligations of a servant to her master, including the Scottish Lord Patrick Fraser's 1846 *Treatise on Master and Servant According to the Laws of Scotland*:

> Where a servant deliberately violates his master's orders, or refuses to obey them when given, he is clearly guilty of the grossest breach of contract. His duty is to obey the master in all things for which he became bound expressly, or in which obedience is implied from the nature of the service undertaken. Of course the master cannot compel him to obey further than has been agreed between them, or than is consistent with law; but at the same time the servant is not entitled to enter upon a minute measurement of the exact limits of his service or to weigh in too nice a balance the precise kind and quantity of labour which he can in strict law be compelled to perform.[112]

Predictably the company carefully selected language from Fraser that appeared to support its position while omitting language that contradicted it. Fraser's *Treatise* distinguishes between the obligations of menial domestic servants, skilled and unskilled industrial servants, and servants of varying social status. The defendant did not cite the passage of the same chapter of the *Treatise* that states, "In the case of menial servants, external appearance is often the chief thing in the view of the master; but though a degree of respectful demeanor must be given by the servants of a tradesman, yet in this kind of service the object of real importance is the performance of the professional labour undertaken by the work-man."[113] In the case of "professional labour," Fraser points out that "the rank of the parties . . . stands much more on a level than" in the case of "menial labour." More to the point in Jetta's case, "A speech, therefore, which might justly be deemed insolent when coming from a menial ser-vant to his master, will admit of a different construction" when uttered by a professional worker of equal social rank with her employer.

Remarkably, the California court accepted the idea that social status sometimes has some weight in determining contractual rights. However it also accepted Jetta's insistence that she was deserving of higher social sta-tus than the studio was acknowledging. Invoking a racist characterization in support of Jetta's claim, trial court Judge Yankwich voiced his disap-proval that "an actress of Miss Goudal's standing and reputation, would be compelled to go around to the back door of the studio and knock, ask-ing for work, like a Mexican."[114] This eloquent expression of social class prejudice and race bigotry is preserved for all time in the official court transcript.

The court was equally reverent of the social status of Mr. DeMille, who had joined Metro-Goldwyn-Mayer by the time of the trial. The tran-script notes that the court convened at eight o'clock in the evening on Thursday, January 31, 1929, at the Metro-Goldwyn-Mayer Studio in Cul-ver City, to hear Mr. DeMille's testimony. Judge Yankwich was willing to accommodate Cecil B. DeMille, who would not be inconvenienced by being required to go to the court during normal business hours. DeMille's busy schedule and duties as a movie director were deemed worthy of suf-ficient deference to convince the court to move the judge, the attorneys, the plaintiff, and the court reporter to hold an evening session in Mr. De-Mille's office. Apparently movie-making was recognized by the court as a vital activity that must not be interrupted for so trivial a matter as a legal proceeding.

Jetta had rehearsed the role of plaintiff against Distinctive Pictures and Paramount. She was ready for a sequel. On the witness stand, facing a barrage of hostile questions from defendant's counsel, Goudal coquett-ishly solicited the judge's assistance, pleading, "I am not in the habit of testifying, you know." The transcript does not reveal whether or not she

batted her eyelashes. Her protestation of American jurisprudential innocence notwithstanding, this was Goudal's third breach-of-contract lawsuit against a movie production company, and it would not be her last.
Few actresses of the time could claim to be more in the habit of testifying.
Nevertheless, Jetta's ploys to win the court's sympathy apparently succeeded. The avuncular Judge Yankwich reassuringly explained to her,
"Our courts are a little different from those in Europe where they have
no rules of evidence, and where anyone is permitted to go on and tell his
story. We interrupt by asking questions."

"I see," replied an appreciative, doe-eyed Jetta. She had often relied
upon the kindness of strangers in judicial robes. Indeed, the foreign
immigrant Jetta Goudal seems to have understood the legal and practical
issues at least as well as the native-born American Cecil B. DeMille and
his attorneys.

Trouble

In high dudgeon, Pathé declared to the court that Jetta was "trouble."
There are dozens of references in the defendant's pleadings and witness
testimony to the vaguely defined "trouble" that Jetta Goudal caused. In
the nineteen-twenties the phrase "making trouble" was commonly used
as a euphemism to deride women who were considered subversive.[115]
"She was trouble" is a legally incoherent argument, but it sheds light
upon the social, cultural, and legal context. It was a gendered expression
of disrespect.

The court was impressed that somehow all of this trouble did not
prevent the parties from performing under the contract for two-and-a-
half years and releasing eight major motion pictures to general public and
critical acclaim and box office success. In fact, DeMille testified that "Miss
Goudal's pictures were always good in the market."[116] That is, they were
successful money-makers at the box office. All the trouble seemed only to
have become troubling quite recently.

Like her previous contract with Paramount, Goudal's contract with
Cecil B. DeMille Pictures Corporation promised that she would be the lead
actress in every motion picture in which she appeared, and would receive
top billing as the star. But the studio's pleadings were inconsistent with

her star status, casting her instead as a menial employee. They argued that Goudal's arriving late for work amounted to a breach of contract. The company cited a clause in her contract that required Jetta to perform "in accordance with and obedience to such rules and regulations as shall be issued from time to time by the Producer."[117]

Goudal questioned authority. She made trouble. Still, there was no disputing the fact that she did show up and did perform her duties as an actress, as was tangibly evidenced by the eight Cecil B. DeMille Pictures Corporation films in which she had starred. More damning for the company was the fact that it had twice exercised its options to extend her contract for additional one-year terms. If Goudal's behavior had truly been unacceptable, why did the company keep renewing her contract?

The gender, class, and ethno-racial attacks on Goudal were shown to be not just offensive but irrelevant. Goudal's attorney proffered an alternative motive for the studio's actions; the company was going broke. It needed to reduce costs by finding excuses to break expensive contracts such as Jetta's. Goudal's counsel attempted to introduce evidence demonstrating that Cecil B. DeMille Pictures Corporation was motivated by financial difficulties unrelated to Jetta Goudal. The company's counsel vehemently objected to inclusion of this financial evidence, but did not deny its veracity. Attorney Neil McCarthy declared, "it does not make any difference what the motivation was. The only question is whether grounds did exist for the discharge of this girl."[118] This "girl" was thirty-eight years old.

The court rejected all of the company's arguments about Goudal's allegedly bad behavior during the first two years under the contract, stating, "[I]f Mr. DeMille saw fit to buy a bucking horse he can't object if he gets thrown out of the saddle a time or two."[119] The company renewed Goudal's contract for a third time only four months before it fired her. That renewal was at the company's sole option, and Goudal was contractually obligated to go along. The renewal options, which were intended to favor the company in this case, backfired and helped the actress because they demonstrated that DeMille chose not to part with Jetta when he had the chance four months earlier. Whatever had happened before that latest renewal was irrelevant to the case, the judge declared. If DeMille believed there was a legally valid cause for firing Jetta Goudal, he would have to demonstrate that it arose during those last four months after he had renewed her contract.

Regarding the argument that she was combative and refused to passively follow orders, Goudal testified persuasively that her actions were motivated by zeal to achieve artistic excellence. The company argued that she had no right to question or do anything more than take instructions. She protested that she had to fulfill her moral and contractual obligation to do everything she could to make her films great. She explained that her creative input was required by her contract, and that therefore she would not have fulfilled her obligations if she had passively taken direction. Goudal's contract with Cecil B. DeMille Pictures Corporation stated, "the services to be performed by her hereunder are of a special, unique, unusual, extraordinary and intellectual character which gives them particular value."[120]

When Goudal's counsel asked DeMille if the actress "made many valuable suggestions which you accepted" on changes in scripts, wardrobes, and many other aspects of her films, DeMille answered, "She did." Pressed further about whether these valuable suggestions continued "throughout the term of her services," DeMille replied, "I think she did even in the last picture."[121] The questioning continued, "I presume you would allow even a star to have an opinion as to whether the story was good or not?" DeMille answered, "I am always delighted to get their opinions."[122]

Goudal had been determined to win DeMille's artistic approbation and confessed to being terribly stung when her contract was terminated. Jetta was wounded by Cecil B. DeMille's rejection as was Anzia Yezierska by John Dewey's rejection. When DeMille had snapped at Goudal, "You are not worth the trouble,"[123] it was not the word *trouble* but rather the word *worth* that held the key to his state of mind at the time. His company was in financial distress unrelated to Jetta Goudal, due in large part to the mogul's flawed judgment and inability to manage various business expenditures. DeMille was spending more than he was earning and he jettisoned Goudal as part of a last-ditch effort to cut costs. Goudal's attorneys kept stressing the studio's money problems.

While the company was going broke, Goudal was increasingly expensive. Her contract provided for salary increases every six months. From May through October 1925, she was paid $750 per week. From October 1925 through May 1926, her pay rose to $1,000 per week. The first one-year renewal option was exercised by the studio, and Jetta's pay rose to $1,250 per week from May through November 1926, and $1,750 per week from November 1926 through May 1927. Then the studio exercised its second one-year renewal option. From May through November 1927, her salary remained $1,750 per week. Under the terms of the contract, she was due a raise to $2,750 per week beginning November 29, 1927. Facing an obligation to increase her pay by $1,000 per week, the studio fired Goudal on September 10, 1927, two months before her next pay raise would have gone into effect.[124] The fact that she was considered difficult to work with provided a convenient excuse.

DeMille admitted in his testimony that "[t]he company operated at a loss."[125] Under cross-examination, DeMille described his response when he was told Jetta wanted a cash settlement before she would sign a release:

[PLAINTIFF'S COUNSEL]: What did you say?

[DEMILLE]: I said, "I think it is outrageous." . . . I said it would cost us more money than a lawsuit . . .

THE COURT: That keeping her would cost more than a lawsuit?

[DEMILLE]: Yes.

[PLAINTIFF'S COUNSEL]: You took a look at the question of a lawsuit, and with your previous experience with [your attorney], and then took a look at Miss Goudal and concluded [your attorney] was the cheapest?[126]

DeMille made the same mistake that Distinctive Pictures had made years earlier when terminating Goudal's contract. He failed to see that it would be cheaper to keep her.

In April 1927, four months before Jetta's contract was terminated, creditors took financial control of DeMille's company in what amounted to a foreclosure. The distribution subsidiary, Producers Distributing Corporation, had merged with another, better-financed distributor, the Pathé Exchange.[127] Cecil B. DeMille Pictures Corporation was renamed Pathé

Studios.[128] DeMille explained in his autobiography that "expansion of production, talent, and grounds and buildings, not to mention clipper ships, meant expansion of financing, too. Eventually the need of additional outside capital brought about a merger with—or I might better call it a submerging in—the Pathé Exchange, and brought again into the picture the bankers, in this case Blair & Company and the Chase National Bank."[129] This was all happening at the time DeMille fired Goudal. After DeMille released "a string of box-office flops" he faced increasing "pressure from his New York financiers."[130] Less than a year after terminating Goudal's contract, Cecil B. DeMille "had thrown in the towel in his marathon bout with the financiers."[131]

He had formed Cecil B. DeMille Pictures Corporation in 1925 after being forced out of Paramount for overspending. Jetta Goudal was dismissed in September 1927. Sonya Levien left her screenwriting position at the Cecil B. DeMille Pictures Company in June 1928. By August 1928 the Cecil B. DeMille Pictures Company had ceased to exist, because of the founder's overspending and under-earning.

DeMille sold his stock, resigned from Pathé, and signed a new three-picture contract as a director at Metro-Goldwyn-Mayer.[132] The three films DeMille produced for MGM were financial failures, and in 1932 DeMille returned to Famous Players–Lasky, which had become Paramount Publix Corporation. By then DeMille was "on the verge of bankruptcy and in the midst of litigation with the Internal Revenue Service."[133] Years later DeMille acknowledged the wisdom an old friend had imparted to him: DeMille belonged "behind a camera, not an executive's desk."[134] Although he possessed the skills of a great movie director, these did not qualify him to be a corporate business executive.

On May 8, 1929, the trial court rejected the studio's argument that Goudal had requested an unconditional release from her contract. It also rejected the studio's contention that Jetta had been terminated for a justifiable cause. The court held that the studio had breached the contract, stating, "That on the 10th day of September, 1927, the defendant [DeMille] breached the agreement of employment aforesaid thru discharging the plaintiff without cause."[135] The company appealed to the District Court of Appeal of the State of California, Second Appellate District, Division Two on September 20, 1929. The Great Stock Market Crash of 1929 commenced one month later.

The Appellate Court questioned the company's interpretation of an employee's duty of obedience, stating, "Even in the most menial forms of employment there will exist circumstances justifying the servant in questioning the order of the master."[136] Moreover, Jetta Goudal could not be classified as a menial laborer. Harking back to Lord Fraser, and taking Fraser's argument a step further, the court stated, "What may in the case of the extra girl be rank insubordination because of a refusal to do exactly what she is ordered to do by a director may be even praiseworthy cooperation in the interests of the employer when the refusal is that of an artist of the exceptional ability expressly stipulated in the contract here before us."[137] The Appellate Court continued, "one may well wonder who was temperamental and out of step when we note in connection therewith that in the picture in which Cecil DeMille directed Miss Goudal there was no trouble whatever."

In her trial testimony, Goudal recalled that in their first conversation, she had said, "Mr. DeMille, we are told in our contracts we must do, to the utmost of our ability, to the best of our ability. I have tried to do that."[138]

DeMille had answered, "I want my people, the people who work with me, to think. I don't want mannequins on the set; I want thinking people, and if you explain to me why you see something and why you want to do it that way, I will appreciate it."[139]

In forceful terms the Appellate Court asserted that it was wrong for the film company to try to compel Goudal to perform "unquestioningly" as directed.[140] The judges refused to permit the company to justify its breach of contract by reducing Goudal to "a mere puppet responding to the director's pull of the strings, regardless of whether or not he pulled the right or the wrong string."[141] The Appellate Court opinion reminded Mr. DeMille he told Goudal that "he did not want mannequins to work for him."

More than twenty years earlier, Rose Pastor Stokes had admonished working women, "I want you to be working *girls* not working *machines*. I want you all to be working, thinking women, not mere automatons!"[142] In Anzia Yezierska's short story "How I Found America," a character who is unhappy about her work in a sweatshop declares, "I didn't come to America to turn into a machine. I came to America to make from myself a person."[143]

"The case of *Goudal v. Cecil B. De Mille Pictures Corporation* constitutes a key moment in the history of labour-management relations in the motion picture industry," writes film historian Sean P. Holmes.[144] Jetta Goudal's legal victory over Cecil B. DeMille stands for the principle that, even when she is difficult to get along with, a lead actress who is a party to a major motion picture contract is not a puppet, not a mannequin, and not a machine, but rather a colleague, an artist, and a social and professional equal entitled to respect. Harvard Law School Professor Paul C. Weiler writes that "[t]he *Goudal* case highlights the tug-of-war between director and actor for control over the production of a movie."[145] The California courts recognized and enforced Goudal's legal rights. "As well as vindicating Goudal's position in her dispute with De Mille," Holmes states, "it also established the wider principle that leading screen performers were entitled to a say in how they were presented on screen."[146] This principle apparently was a novel concept to many of the prominent men in the movie business of the nineteen-twenties. When film historian Anthony Slide asked her almost fifty years later about the DeMille case, Jetta Goudal answered with understandable pride, "I established law in these United States."[147]

On November 19, 1931, the judgment of the lower court in Goudal's favor was affirmed by a three-judge panel in an opinion written by Judge J. Fricke. Jetta was awarded $34,531.23 in damages.[148] This would equal approximately $540,561.42 in 2015 dollars.[149] The money, while significant, mattered less to Jetta, to DeMille, to the motion picture industry, and to the press than the fact that a "mere" actress had defeated a film studio and the mighty Cecil B. DeMille. As Jetta expressed it succinctly, "I wanted my rights."[150] Never again would an American movie production company be able to dismiss an actor or actress under contract without considering the costs and the consequences of its actions. She had made a crack in a glass ceiling.

In his 1959 autobiography, DeMille recalled staying on good terms with Jetta, even after the lawsuit. "She was a good actress," he wrote, "but our professional temperaments did not exactly blend."[151] DeMille recounted his memory of the trial:

> The judge considerately consented to hear the case in my office. He first questioned Miss Goudal. Was Mr. deMille a bad director, had he ever been violent and abusive toward the plaintiff? Oh, not at all. He was an excellent director and a perfect gentleman. The judge then turned to me. Miss Goudal now, was she in my opinion a competent actress? Oh, yes, one of the best. Did I dislike her then? No, I did not dislike her at all. She was a fine person, and a particular friend of my daughter's. This was just a difference of opinion about some money due or not due. Jetta and I kept exchanging compliments and the judge kept getting more and more puzzled by such unusual litigants; but he finally decided in Jetta's favor. Perhaps the defendant had been too good a witness for the plaintiff. Incidentally, Jetta is still a good friend of Cecilia's. When Mrs. deMille and I celebrated our golden wedding anniversary in 1952, we had to limit the guests to a number our house could hold, but Jetta Goudal was one we particularly wanted to have with us.[152]

DeMille's personal recollections about Jetta were apparently softened by the intervening years. However, his attitudes concerning the rights of film actors were hardened by his experiences as a studio boss. DeMille actively fought against unionization of movie-company employees in the years after he lost Goudal's lawsuit, and he vigorously defended so-called "right to work" rules.

The phrase "right to work" is a linguistic inversion worthy of George Orwell. Companies used the phrase to demand that workers be protected from being forced to join unions and participate in collective bargaining. The pretense that the corporate managers were only protecting their workers was disingenuous. It was an attempt to obfuscate the fact that the workers wanted to unionize and that the protection they actually needed was from corporate management, not unions. Without the collective power of unions, workers had been forced to accept onerous terms of employment because as individuals they lacked bargaining leverage.

The right to work arguments echoed a doctrine of "freedom of contract" affirmed by the U.S. Supreme Court in the 1905 case of *Lochner v.*

New York. Right to work arguments were used as weapons against unions. Freedom of contract was used to attack labor laws passed to mandate safe working conditions and limit working hours. Under the Lochner doctrine employees and employers are assumed to be equal parties to employment contracts, despite vast disparities in bargaining power. Therefore any law passed to regulate minimum wages, maximum work hours, child labor, or safety conditions would be a violation of the constitutional rights of the employer and employee.[153] Historian Alice Kessler-Harris explains that "the pernicious idea of freedom of contract" was that it "ignored the vulnerable position of workers" and relied on "the fiction of a worker's liberty to negotiate fair terms for labor" to in reality protect "the rights of employers to offer even the most debilitating working conditions."[154] The court explicitly overturned this interpretation of freedom of contract in 1937, paving the way for legislation to protect workers from unfair or unsafe labor conditions. By fighting for her rights, Jetta Goudal refused to be victimized because of the unequal bargaining power she possessed as an individual worker compared to the consolidated power of a film corporation. In her contract disputes with film production companies, she fought for her rights individually, without the benefit of a labor union.

DeMille became an anti-union crusader, speaking frequently before audiences and even appearing before the U.S. Congress in 1948 on behalf of right to work legislation.[155] In 1944 DeMille was ejected from the American Federation of Radio Artists (AFRA, which after the advent of television became AFTRA), for refusing to pay a one-dollar union dues assessment to fund opposition to California legislation known as Proposition 12, which would have abolished the closed shop in which only union members could work in radio.

Jetta Goudal emerged from her experience with DeMille with a very different perspective on workers' rights. She had experienced the consequences that could result from challenging a powerful film studio, even if a court rules in one's favor. In a personal letter on April 16, 1928, Jetta asked a friend to help her find live theater work in New York because "Mr. de Mille manages to keep me out of picture work, at least for the time being."[156] Jetta's husband, Harold Grieve, was a founding member of the Actors Equity union. Goudal became active in the Actors Equity union's fight for unionization of film players, working with Grieve to promote movie actor rights to unionize and to insist on a closed shop in which only union members could work on films. "'Joan of Arc of Equity' she was dubbed by her fellow actors," according to film historian Anthony Slide.[157] Historian Mari Jo Buhle also refers to Rose Pastor Stokes as "a Joan of Arc,"[158] and film company chief William Fox asked Anzia Yezierska if she saw herself as "Joan of Arc."[159]

Jetta Goudal returned to the screen four more times, in *The Cardboard Lover*, produced by William Randolph Hearst as a star vehicle for his wife, Marion Davies; in *Lady of the Pavements*, directed by D. W. Griffith; in *Le Spectre Vert*, a silent film released with French intertitles by Metro-Goldwyn-Mayer; and then one final time in a film called *Business and Pleasure*, released in 1932. This last film was notable because it was the only "talking" picture in which Jetta performed. She appeared with a venerable cast, including the great Will Rogers, who was a friend of Anzia Yezierska and Sonya Levien. Audiences had mixed responses to Jetta's speaking voice, which revealed an accent not quite French, not quite Dutch, not quite identifiable, and not consistent with the voice that viewers of her silent films had imagined.

One Last Complaint

Jetta Goudal also returned one more time to the arena of legal dispute. After *Le Spectre Vert* was released, Jetta filed a complaint against MGM with the Actors Adjustment Committee of the Academy of Motion Picture Arts and Sciences. She demanded compensation, claiming that even though she had foregone any salary, MGM had failed to give her top billing in advertising and marketing the film.[160] This, she contended, was an unforgivable breach of her contract. Echoing Anzia Yezierska, Goudal told the Actors Adjustment Committee of the Academy of Motion Picture Arts and Sciences, "I am pretty strict about my contracts."[161] The dispute was settled after a series of hearings before the Actors Adjustment Committee and the Actors Branch Executive Committee in 1930.[162]

At the age of forty-one, she was no longer the gamine who had stepped off the New York stage and appeared briefly in *Timothy's Quest* ten years earlier. Her notoriety as the actress who sued and beat Cecil B. DeMille followed her within the movie industry, hindering her attempts to land worthy roles. Nervous exhaustion took a toll on her. The country plunged deeply into the Great Depression.

Jetta married Harold Grieve, a movie set-designer and interior decorator. Film historian Anthony Slide describes the Goudal-Grieve marriage as "a strange marriage but also presumably a happy one. If not outright gay, Harold Grieve was certainly bisexual. Jetta obviously tolerated her husband's lifestyle, provided he kept secret any sexual liaisons. She was happy to have a good-looking and successful man as a companion and, in all probability, expected no sexual contact in their marriage."[163] The marriage lasted fifty-five years, until Jetta's death in 1986 at the age of ninety-five. They had no children. It was not a marriage springing from a passionate love affair but rather a "marriage of convenience" or "marriage of reason" between friends who loved and respected each other. Jetta called her husband "Daddy."[164] Still, she never altered or surrendered her forceful, overbearing personality. She joined her husband as an interior decorator, working on the homes of wealthy, demanding denizens of Bel Air and the Hollywood community for whom her fading celebrity retained some luster. Working with Harold, Jetta volunteered her time as a spokesperson and fund-raiser for the Actors Equity Association (AEA) union. "Had Equity existed in the picture world," she told an audience of AEA members, "I would not have had to fight a battle all by my little self."[165] She transformed herself from actress to activist.

Jetta Goudal was neither the first nor the last narcissistic actress whose outsized ego got her in trouble. Nor was she the first or the last woman whose status as an equal work colleague or contracting partner was challenged by men who wished to exalt themselves by diminishing her. Conflicts between difficult actors and intransigent studio bosses became Hollywood legend and cliché, mirroring the experiences of professional women in every field.

"Goudal is credited today with establishing a star's rights within the film industry," writes one film history authority.[166] "All actors owe Jetta their gratitude for going to court to establish a star's rights," argues another.[167] Movie actors and actresses today walk in the legal footsteps of Goudal and many others who fought to advance their rights in courts, legislatures, union halls, executive suites, and boardrooms. In the years after Goudal's legal battles, Bette Davis and Olivia de Havilland sued movie studios to protect their contractual rights as actresses, following Jetta Goudal's lead.

Salome on Sunset Boulevard

Jetta Goudal struggled against the stereotype of the agitated, unstable diva who styles herself a femme fatale. The caricature of subversive female power is deployed alternatively as a cudgel against women and as a resource by women. Press and publicity materials, friends, foes, and fans perceived Jetta Goudal as exotic and temperamental. In *Salome of the Tenements*, when John Manning falls in love with Sonya Vrunsky, he sees her as "a vivid exotic."[168] The words *exotic* and *temperamental* are fraught with contradictory meanings, and they were used alternately to praise or deride Goudal. *Temperamental* conjures images of the actress as prone to losing her temper, of moodiness, emotional volatility and unpredictability. It also contains gender-related and ethnic and racial subtexts. The word *temperamental* applied to a male artist may suggest a level of respect that is more doubtful when applied to a female. A temperamental male artist is serious if erratic. Calling a female artist temperamental is more likely to imply derision and even ridicule. The dismissive and derogatory "hysterical" is used to describe women who are moody and volatile, as articulated by the scholar Sander L. Gilman in the phrase "mad like a hysterical woman."[169] The etymological root of the word *hysteria* is *hystéra*, Greek for uterus. Christine Stansell writes that prior to the growing awareness of Freudian psychoanalysis after 1920, "medical practice still relied on the diagnosis of hysteria to explain women's depression, [and] anger."[170] In testimony in Goudal's breach of contract lawsuit against his company in 1929, Cecil B. DeMille testified that the actress "got hysterical" when expressing creative disagreements with film directors.[171]

Exotic is also a loaded term. The first definition generally associated with *exotic* is "foreign." Positive and negative connotations are connected with exotic foreignness. These include outlandish, barbarous, strange, and uncouth, but also glamorous, striking, and beautiful. An exotic plant denotes a foreign species, transplanted but not acclimatized or naturalized, and therefore fragile. This meaning was not lost on Jetta herself. In a letter dated November 15, 1971, the screen actress Mary Pickford thanks Jetta for the gift of an "exotic anthurium," which is a tropical plant that Jetta apparently hoped would remind Pickford of her.[172] "Exotic clothing" is new, unusual, or colorful, which is consistent with Goudal's obsessive focus on fashion, costume, and dress. An "exotic dancer" is a "stripper" or "strip-teaser," like the biblical Salome performing the infamous Dance of the Seven Veils, or the Circassian dancers to whom Sonya Levien was compared.

Contemporary descriptions of Jetta Goudal as temperamental and exotic were thinly coded references to ethnic difference and foreignness. Sumio Higashi describes the silent film era as one "that stressed Americanization as a response to cultural diversity." Foreigners often were subjected to derisive depictions. One recurring theme in popular films was "a taste for sybaritic luxury and depraved sexuality" projected "onto new immigrants."[173]

The volatile prima donna, of whom Jetta Goudal became a symbol, occupies a position along the same continuum as Salome. Indeed, the two are linked. In the 1950 film *Sunset Boulevard*, the vulnerability beneath the dangerous exterior of the character type is explored by focusing on the aging diva in decline. The main character Norma Desmond, played by Gloria Swanson, is a has-been leading lady from the 1920s who spends years attempting to write a screenplay that will provide her with a starring role. William Holden plays the handsome young screenwriter Joe Gillis, whose no-nonsense skepticism confronts the self-deluding nature of Norma Desmond's confidence when she describes her dream project.

> NORMA: It's the story of Salome. I think I'll have DeMille direct it.
> GILLIS: Uh-huh.
> NORMA: We've made a lot of pictures together.
> GILLIS: And you'll play Salome?
> NORMA: Who else?[174]

"Salome—what a woman! What a part!" she rhapsodizes. "The Princess in love with a Holy man. She dances the Dance of the Seven Veils.

He rejects her, so she demands his head on a golden tray, kissing his cold, dead lips."[175]

Gillis reads the screenplay and questions the quality of the writing. Norma, wounded by the criticism, defends her writing with a line nearly identical to an expression of Anzia Yezierska. Norma tells Gillis, "I wrote that with my heart."[176] Yezierska once described her writing as "Little bits of human heart-pictures."[177] Frank Crane wrote that Yezierska had "dipped her pen in her heart" to write her short stories.[178]

The Norma Desmond character so closely resembles the public perception of Jetta Goudal that one is compelled to wonder whether the writer and the director were inspired by Goudal as a model. The silent film star Norma Talmadge has been identified as the role model on whom Norma Desmond was based,[179] but there is no evidence that Talmadge was the sole inspiration; the character appears to be an evocative conglomeration of elements drawn from real actresses and the writers' imaginations.

Norma Talmadge and Jetta Goudal were contemporaries, two beautiful movie stars of the nineteen-twenties whose careers ended with the introduction of talkies. At the beginning of her film career, Talmadge married the wealthy Joseph Schenk, known as "Honest Joe" in the film industry, about whom Samuel Goldwyn commented, "His verbal contract is worth more than the paper it's written on."[180]

If the screenwriters Billy Wilder, Charles Brackett, and D. M. Marshman Jr. had Norma Talmadge foremost in mind when they crafted the fictional Norma Desmond, they also knew the story of Jetta Goudal. In the film, Desmond has been withering in a deteriorating mansion for years. She is in a passionless marriage to a former film executive who functions as her caretaker, groundskeeper, butler, and preserver of her legacy.

Norma Desmond is afflicted not only by her own delusions, but also by cultural gender bias. She is disdained for her voracious hunger for public adoration, professional respect, and the sexual attention of a virile young man. She fights vainly but furiously against the diminishment of social power that attaches to women growing older, particularly in the youth-obsessed movie business, and for this she is subjected to ridicule and contempt. At Paramount Studios the Desmond character tells Cecil B.

DeMille, who plays himself onscreen, "Remember, I never start shooting before ten in the morning and never after four-thirty in the afternoon," as film crew members regard her with curiosity and mild amusement.[181] Everyone but Norma knows that her movie will never be made.

The film makes clear that the aging process diminishes women only; men appear to be exempt. When Norma Desmond arrives on the Paramount film lot, one executive says, "She must be a million years old." Cecil B. DeMille replies, "I hate to think where that puts me. I could be her father."[182] But DeMille was no object of ridicule. In this film, and in his life and career, he continued to earn public and professional approbation. DeMille kept making films until his death at age seventy-seven in January 1959.

Reflections of a Shooting Star

Sonya Levien wrote in 1922, "A movie queen once enthroned has quiet reigning," adding ominously, "for a few years anyway."[183] Goudal's reign was brief, but never quiet. She told a *Life* magazine interviewer, "I don't like being called a silent star. I was never silent."[184] Although few immigrants adapted to American life more effectively than Jetta Goudal, she insisted to the end of her life that she considered herself "European."[185] Henry James wrote of "the type of the intelligent foreigner whose conversation completes our culture."[186] This is how Jetta wished to be perceived, and when this image was not reflected in the gaze of her fans and contemporaries, she was crushed.

Jetta Goudal was a shooting star, but she was not gone in a flash. Something remains, even after such a shooting star disappears. She rose from the depths of obscurity and penury to the heights of the *status-sphere* and back again. Jetta never won an Oscar, but she did win a judgment and money damages in 1931 in her successful lawsuit against the powerful movie mogul Cecil B. DeMille. She insisted on deference to her status, always questioned authority, and refused to relinquish personal agency.[187]

Goudal subscribed to the audacious notion that orders were for others to obey; she preferred to give them. She played the sometimes contradictory roles of immigrant, celebrity, feminist, diva, temperamental artist, femme fatale, vixen, damsel-in-distress, leading lady, fallen star.

In what is the most collaborative of artistic endeavors, Goudal wanted to control many aspects of her films. She frequently clashed with costume designers and often worked overnight making and remaking her own film wardrobes. She challenged scriptwriters about story elements, and frequently offered her own rewrites of scenes. She even challenged film directors about the setups and action sequences in her scenes and about details large and small in the portrayals of her characters. But Jetta Goudal was no Charlie Chaplin or Woody Allen, or she was not permitted to be. Thrilled when directors, producers, costume designers, and screenwriters accepted her suggestions, Jetta became enraged, exasperated, and crestfallen when her ideas were rejected.

This might not appear to be the portrait of an artist likely to participate actively in and contribute significantly to the progression of the law of civil obligations from status to contract and the advancement of women's and workers' rights. But these achievements and a handful of leading lady performances precariously preserved in fading sepia tones on aging celluloid constitute Jetta Goudal's unlikely legacy. She became an agent of social change by opposing and defying those who cast her as a forbidden woman.

|6|

Novel Approaches

Salome has the next dance. The last four chapters presented overlapping biographical sketches, each from the perspective of one of the women of the Salome Ensemble, paying particular attention to their connections and collaborations. Their work comprises a collection of valuable artifacts of culture, class, ethnic, and gender relations. This chapter and the next focus on the meaning and value of *Salome of the Tenements* as literature, film, cultural transmission, and discourse on art and experience. This layered inquiry is proposed as an accurate, evocative, novel approach to the artists of the Salome Ensemble as individuals and agents of social change.

It begins with a tale as old as time. *Salome of the Tenements* tells the story of a female Russian Jewish immigrant who marries a wealthy Gentile American man and rises out of poverty. Yezierska's Salome does not wait demurely to be courted by her suitor. She aggressively pursues her American dream only to find that he fails to live up to her expectations. She wins her man, finds him wanting, and discards him to pursue her own destiny. Michael North describes Yezierska's novel as a "quintessentially American saga of self-realization."[1]

The poor girl rescued by marriage to a wealthy prince is a fantasy at least as old as *Cinderella*, variations of which exist in many languages dating back to antiquity. The virtuous factory girl who marries a millionaire was common in dime novels and serial films of the Progressive Era.[2] Rose Pastor Stokes became a living embodiment of this fairy tale when the Jewish former sweatshop worker married Gentile millionaire socialist James Graham Phelps Stokes in 1905. The press called the bride a "Cinderella of the Sweatshops."[3]

Anzia Yezierska attended her friend's wedding and took notes for a story based on the Stokes marriage. She set the project aside for years, only taking it up again in 1921. By that time, Yezierska had married and divorced twice and had a nine-year-old daughter. She had been through a romantic affair and traumatic breakup with the wealthy Gentile public intellectual John Dewey. When her collection of short stories, *Hungry Hearts*, was made into a Hollywood movie, Anzia Yezierska was called a Cinderella in 1921 newspapers, as Rose Pastor Stokes had been in 1905.[4] It had been twenty years since she worked in a sweatshop, and she was a self-supporting single woman attached to no Prince Charming.

Yezierska drew the contours of her novel's plot from the Stokes's marriage. However, she used her own personal experiences, her vast knowledge of literature, and her vivid imagination to flesh out the characters and dialogue. Mary Dearborn affirms that *Salome of the Tenements* is "emotionally informed by Yezierska's relationship with Dewey."[5] She also tried to bestow on the main character some of Sonya Levien's winning personality.

The Stokes's cross-class intermarriage was a tabloid sensation in 1905. More than economic and social upward mobility for the bride, this celebrity wedding celebrated a bride and groom who freely chose each other, not a marriage arranged by their parents. That made it more appealing or appalling, depending on one's point of view. Male scions of wealthy Protestant families with vast industrial holdings generally did not disregard their parents' wishes by choosing poor immigrant Jewish brides. Their social set would consider such behavior vulgar and déclassé. Female Russian Jewish immigrants in the early twentieth century did not take for granted the ability to choose whom to marry. The power to make that choice constituted a dramatic increase in status for these women. It was the attainment of a basic right of personhood and self-ownership that a patriarchal culture had previously denied them. Regarding intermarriage early in the twentieth century, Keren McGinity writes that "Jewish women who married non-Jews chose their mates rather than accept arranged marriages, evidence of the growing individualism in modern America."[6]

The fascination among Jewish immigrants with the shift from arranged to chosen marriage was the stuff of gossip, folklore, popular fiction, and Yiddish theater. Perhaps the most influential examples were Yiddish author Sholem Aleichem's stories about the character Tevye the Dairyman, particularly those that depicted the marriage, against her father's wishes, of Tevye's third daughter, Chava, to a Christian man, and her conversion to Christianity. The girl saw herself as a Cinderella who finds her prince, but to her parents it was a betrayal and to the Ukrainian Jewish community it was a scandal. The behavior of such a young woman was perceived as evil or insane, debased as that of a Salome. The distraught parents in Sholem Aleichem's story go so far as to "sit shiva," engaging in a ritual mourning for their daughter. Several editions of the Chava story were published between 1905 and 1909. In 1919 a production of *Tevye the Dairyman* was staged in New York with a focus "largely on the story of Chava and her non-Jewish love," writes historian Jeremy Dauber.[7] The great Yiddish writer immigrated to the United States in 1905, the year of the Stokes wedding.

As a practical matter, to choose a husband, especially from outside of her ethno-racial group, a Jewish immigrant needed opportunities to socialize and the ability to communicate across lines of class, ethnicity, and language. Language mattered deeply. George Bernard Shaw's *Pygmalion*, which premiered in London in 1912 and in New York in 1914, explicitly linked the Cinderella story with language as a barrier or bridge between social classes. In *Salome of the Tenements* the Jewish immigrant bride and the patrician Anglo-Saxon American groom struggle "to find a common language."[8]

Anzia Yezierska's great innovation, her novel approach to the story, was to merge the fairy tale Cinderella with the depraved Salome of the New Testament, the Oscar Wilde play, and the Richard Strauss opera. Yezierska pursues the seemingly impossible task of synthesizing two characters who appear to be polar opposites. Cinderella starts out at the ash-heap, while Salome is born a princess. Cinderella is virtuous while Salome is wicked. But Anzia Yezierska looked beyond the obvious to explore connections and similarities between these two characters. She contested them as stereotypes. She saw beneath Cinderella's innocence a seductress in a glamorous disguise. She saw beneath Salome's depravity an ingenuous virgin baring body and soul for love. Yezierska also understood that Cinderella and Salome share the inability to exist without a man. There could be no future for Cinderella without a Prince Charming to marry and live happily ever after. In Wilde's play and Strauss's opera Salome descends into madness and is killed after she takes Jokanaan's head. The opera premiered in New York in 1907. But reality confounds popular myth. The ancient historian Josephus writes that after the death of Jokanaan, the historical figure Salome lived on, married twice, and bore three sons.[9]

During the first two decades of the twentieth century a seemingly endless series of variations on the story of Salome was produced on vaudeville stages and movie screens. This phenomenon was labeled "Salomania," writes historian Susan Glenn.[10] The popular appeal arose from the appropriation of Salome, an icon of danger, depravity, and destructive force, and repurposing her as an icon of female power. Women celebrated the strength that could derive from the ability to inspire fear, and the freedom that could accompany divine decadence. Glenn argues that the Salome story became "what literary critics call an open text."[11] The character, "with all of her ambiguities and excesses was revised and subjected to varied uses as she wended her way from the high arts of painting, literature, drama and opera onto the vaudeville and revue stage, into the movies and then back again into literature and opera."[12]

In Yezierska's novel, the protagonist Sonya Vrunsky is repeatedly labeled a Salome, but her co-worker Gittel also calls her "my American Cinderella!" (8). This fusion allows the author to explore different interpretations of what "happily ever after" might really mean. Combining her own experiences with those of her friends and role models Rose Pastor Stokes and Sonya Levien, Anzia Yezierska created a new woman who would not depend on any man for her happiness. Many stories have been animated by a girl's dream to rise from poverty by marrying a millionaire. *Salome of the Tenements* reinterprets that dream.

From Nobody to Somebody

The novel follows Sonya Vrunsky on her quest for social acceptance, financial independence, personal fulfillment, and love. She eventually achieves these goals, but along the way her expectations are shattered.

Yezierska's narrative is a cautionary tale for aspiring social climbers hoping to marry up. Carol B. Schoen suggests that Yezierska set out to write "an antimyth," in which a woman who relies on "scheming duplicity" in her campaign "to trap a wealthy husband" might "not live happily ever after," but instead "end up in the divorce courts."[13]

Sonya Vrunsky begins as a reporter for the *Ghetto News*. She is assigned by the newspaper to interview millionaire philanthropist John Manning, who runs a Lower East Side settlement house and works to improve the lives of the poor. Their meeting results in love at first sight, another fairy tale conceit interrogated by Yezierska. Sonya is mesmerized by Manning, "the product of generations of Puritans" (33), and he is intoxicated by her. He asks her out for lunch, and then proposes to call at her home for tea, a genteel gesture that makes Sonya swoon. Sonya Vrunsky's ardor for Manning devolves into obsession. She tells her co-workers, "I'll rob, steal or murder if I got to" in order to capture John Manning's head (8). In a rare moment of self-awareness she thinks, "What a selfish, unfeeling person I am," but she neither wavers nor desists (9). To Sonya Vrunsky, Manning offers the possibility of full acceptance into American society, which she sees as conferring personhood, a magical transition in which a "nobody" becomes a "somebody" (48).

She aspires to be "somebody of my own making" (48). As the reader attempts to identify Sonya Vrunsky, the character desperately seeks to identify herself. She is surprised that the millionaire John Manning admires "me—a nobody?" (1). She wonders why dressmaker Jacques Hollins would trouble himself "for a penniless nobody like me?" (28). She believes she occupies the lowest rung of the status hierarchy, and she yearns to establish self-worth. Although financial security matters to her, that is not her only priority. Sonya Vrunsky desires to behold beauty and to have basic dignity. If she can fulfill these desires, she says, "it wouldn't bother me if we have Bolshevism or Capitalism" (27). Her dream is "the democracy of beauty" (26). The author and the character are concerned with a concept of personal value that transcends cash value. It is a quest for status, recognition, and respect as a human being. To Yezierska, to be a person means to not be a slave or a "machine" (129). It means possessing "human rights" (54).

17. Jetta Goudal as Sonya Mendel in *Salome of the Tenements*. The poster she is admiring is a reproduction of the 1870 painting *Salomé* by the French artist Henri Regnault. This painting was donated to the Metropolitan Museum of Art in New York in 1916. From Library of Congress Prints and Photographs Division, by permission of Paramount Pictures.

In Sonya Vrunsky's imagination, John Manning holds the key to social acceptance, financial security, and moral rectitude, which is ironic given her avowed willingness to transgress moral boundaries in order to reach him. She believes, as Natalie Friedman writes, that "[s]exual access to Manning will mean complete access to America."[14] Ann Shapiro calls this the illusory ideal of "The Ultimate Shaygets."[15] "Shaygets" is Yiddish derogatory slang for Gentile male, the feminine form of which is "shiksa."

Sonya Vrunsky's identity is neither fixed nor definite. Her backstory, her emotional affect, and the focus of her ambitions change as rapidly and dramatically as her clothing. Described variously as "the eternal mystery" (150), "an unknown personality" (150), a "flame" (37), and a "longing" (37), she cannot be pinned down. The author's portrait of this character is deliberately unstable, recalling Marcel Duchamp's cubist surrealist *Nude Descending a Staircase*, which scandalized New Yorkers when it was displayed at the 1913 Armory Show. Duchamp's painting contains a series of abstract representations of a nude figure at various positions on a staircase. The shapes combine in the active viewer's mind into a composite impression of a body in motion. Sonya Vrunsky, who similarly does not remain static long enough to become a fixed image, emerges as a composite character in motion, assembled in the mind of the active reader from the different, conflicting fragments crafted by the author. But Sonya Vrunsky does not descend. She is a woman ascending the ladder of social status, financial independence, and self-realization. Sonya Vrunsky fantasizes that "[e]ven the crooked stairs that led to her hall-room changed into a Jacob's ladder that led skyward where dreams opened upon dreams" (4).

Her origins are indeterminate. At first Sonya Vrunsky self-identifies as an immigrant, comparing herself with Rose Pastor Stokes, Mary Antin, and Sonya Levien (83). She remembers when she was "a little girl, holding on to my aunt's skirts, on the ship to America," forced to cross the ocean "herded, like cattle, in the steerage, choked with bundles and rags and seasick humanity" (34). She is stung when a salesgirl insults her immigrant status, taunting, "Did you ever wear anything but a shawl over your head in the old country? . . . The minute they come to America nothing is good enough for them" (14). John Manning cannot stop thinking about "this immigrant girl" (37). Later in the novel, however, Sonya Vrunsky is no longer described as an immigrant. She remembers a different past, in which she was "[b]orn in the blackest poverty of a Delancey Street basement." In this alternative past she was a child crying defiantly, "I ain't no immigrant" (83). In one episode she proclaims, "I am a Russian Jewess" (37), and in another she insists, "I'm an American—not a crazy Russian!" (94).

Her family background also remains uncertain. "I have no one," she cries. "No father, no mother, no money, no friends" (47). She believes it is her greedy landlord's obligation to help her because "it's the duty of every good Jew to help an orphan" (43). Later she remembers "her overworked, care-crushed mother" and her "father, a dreamy-eyed religious fanatic" (83). She feels guilty for the worry she caused her parents during her Lower East Side childhood. These apparent contradictions demonstrate

Yezierska's deliberate retention of a margin of ambiguity, a state of fluctu-
ation, an element of discontinuity in the central character's identity. John
Dewey said, "Apparent contradictions always demand attention."[16] These
irreconcilable descriptions of Sonya Vrunsky allow her to think of herself as "nobody from nowhere" (46) while they compel the active reader
to fill in blanks, resolve contradictions, and imaginatively complete the
character.

Sonya finds working at the newspaper preferable to her previous
sweatshop job, but she earns barely enough to make ends meet. She abhors
the squalor of the Lower East Side, and the meager pay from her job por-
tends a bleak future from which she recoils. Her co-workers include Lipkin, a Jewish editor who writes poetry in his solitary hours away from
the office. He is in love with Sonya Vrunsky but she disdains what she
perceives as his ineffectuality. Gittel Stein, a fellow female journalist a
few years older than Sonya, alternately envies and resents the younger
woman, but cannot help admiring her.

Sonya Vrunsky's only possessions of value, her only assets, are personal resources, aspects of her self. These include intelligence, unwavering
self-regard, strong will, the capacity for hard work, and an appreciation
of beauty that amounts to aesthetic empathy. She feels the strength of her
youth and takes pride in being physically attractive, but beyond pride she
knows that her looks give her power. She does not have money, and she
is certain that it will take more than lip rouge to make all of her qualities visible to John Manning. The dance she must perform to seduce her
prince must convey not only beauty, but worthiness. Such a performance
requires costumes, props, sets, choreography, and acting talent. Sonya tai-
lors her appearance to win John Manning, recalling the tale of the scriptural Queen Esther's preparations to compete for the favor of the Persian
king. A persistent tension for Sonya Vrunsky and Queen Esther during
these preparations arises from the precarious position they occupy, teeter-
ing between innocent Cinderella at the ball and seductive, strip-teasing
Salome. Sonya Vrunsky sees her performance as an act of combined sup-
plication and deception, which she describes as "subterfuge" (46).

Sonya decides that her cheap clothes and her dingy room are inad-
equate for receiving a gentleman of Manning's status. She must appear

to have fine but modest clothing and a suitable parlor to demonstrate her worthiness. Yezierska's focus on "beautiful, expensive clothing" contains "shades of Edith Wharton's *The House of Mirth*," Meredith Goldsmith argues, which are "telling," and "not accidental." Yezierska's characters exhibit a passion, "like Lily Bart, who considers clothing the frame with which beautiful young women must advertise their suitability for marriage.[17] Because she cannot afford to buy fine things, Sonya Vrunsky uses her youthful beauty, street smarts, and strong will to acquire them. Because she has no money, she relies on moxie.

Cunning, Guile, and Chutzpah

To win the American Gentile man of her dreams, Sonya enlists the help of three Jewish immigrant men. She beguiles them like a fairy tale princess with magic powers of cunning, guile, and chutzpah. One of these men responds to Sonya Vrunsky with empathy, but she must appeal to the baser instincts of lust and greed to recruit the other two.

First, Sonya enchants Jacques Hollins, a haute couture clothing designer who plies his trade in an atelier on Fifth Avenue. Hollins is, like Sonya, a Russian Jewish immigrant. He is a former denizen of the Lower East Side whose name used to be Jaky Solomon. He transformed himself with innate talent, hard work, and a stint as an expat in France. After a few years toiling in garment industry sweatshops, Hollins saved money to leave New York and study fashion in Paris. There he acquired Western European sophistication and shed Eastern European immigrant behaviors he believed would hinder his progress. Returning to New York, Hollins presents himself as a French-American. He discards the ethnically laden name Jaky Solomon and takes the deracinated moniker Jacques Hollins. His successful strategy is to adopt a new identity that, while still vaguely foreign, is of a type that helps him gain social acceptance in American culture and achieve upward mobility. Jetta Goudal used a similar strategy in denying her Dutch Jewish roots and reinventing herself as a French Gentile. Sonya Vrunsky recognizes that Hollins has successfully reinvented himself while retaining his artistic, poetic temperament and a margin of ethnic difference that Americans find acceptable. But she also sees the fellow immigrant striver beneath the polished façade.

18. Jetta Goudal in *Salome of the Tenements*, 1925, rejecting the cheap, ready-made hat offered by a Lower East Side milliner. From Library of Congress Prints and Photographs Division, by permission of Paramount Pictures.

Jacques Hollins and Sonya Vrunsky both resist the increasing pressure to conform that accompanied industrial capitalism in general and the clothing industry in particular. Ready-made clothing represented a democratization of fashion beginning in the second half of the nineteenth century. The standardization and low costs of mass-produced clothing empowered working people to dress for success by imitating the wealthy and professional classes. But Sonya Vrunsky and Jacques Hollins are offended by "the ready-made shoddiness" (57) of mass-produced clothing. They believe that identical clothing erases individual identity. Uniform garb degenerates into imprisoning uniforms, inhibiting self-expression. Sonya Vrunsky longs for the luxury of expensive bespoke couture. She is painfully envious of a rich young woman in Hollins's store because "[t]he world is made to order for her" (47). Sonya raises her arms "with the abandon of a tragedy queen" when she cannot find a suitable new hat among the "cheapness of the ready-mades" (14, 15).

In 1903 Rose Pastor wrote about the great equalizing effect of factory-made clothing on working-class Jewish immigrant women she observed at a party. "Who is the girl in that elegant gown of violet crepe de chine, trimmed in velvet and fine laces? . . . She works in the same factory as my cousin Jennie; she's a necktie maker. . . . If I didn't know that all the girls here are working girls, I would think her papa was a railroad magnate or someone who owned a few millions at the least."[18] Demonstrating proto-modernist attitudes, Hollins and Sonya Vrunsky disdain the egalitarian-ism of factory clothing. They aspire to express their individualism, taste, and refinement through custom-made clothes.

"I feel I know you," Sonya Vrunsky tells Jacques Hollins the first time they meet (22).

"You know me—don't you feel like you know me?" she implores him (22).

They form a bond of empathy. She describes a feeling of knowing, a form of emotional recognition. In this first meeting, Sonya reveals herself to Hollins in stark contrast to the way she conceals herself from Manning. She tells the clothing designer about her "consuming passion for beauty," and her revulsion at the offerings of the gaudy bargain shops on Orchard Street, "hideous ready-made stuff." She tells him that "only an artist like you" can understand her. Sonya is an "inspiration," a "stimulus" to Hollins. Her emotions become his own. She "brought back to him the thrill of his own emotion" (22, 23).

Sonya Vrunsky and Jacques Hollins are kindred souls who share aesthetic empathy. Hollins is attracted to Sonya's looks, and even more to her fiery temperament and intelligence. He admires her audacity in asking him to custom-make a beautiful dress, hat, and shoes for her for free. The material success Hollins has achieved allows him to indulge poetic, creative longings that transcend the profit motive. Sonya's "maddening hunger for beautiful clothes" makes him feel "starved for something more than appreciation of his art in terms of money" (23).

Hollins fulfills her request because he wants to see beautiful Sonya wearing beautiful clothing that he creates for her. He tells her, "you have given me the first chance of my life to work for love" (28). When she dons the apparel he designs for her, Hollins says, "Now, I see before me a new Esther, dazzling the King of the Persians" (26). He tells Vrunsky, "you can be your own, free, individual self" (27), articulating one of her most cherished desires, and she is thrilled. Manning also sweeps her off her feet when he tells Sonya Vrunsky, "you are distinctly yourself" (2).

After captivating Hollins, Sonya Vrunsky confronts her greedy landlord, Benjamin Rosenblat. The single room that Sonya sublets and the hallways and entry of the tenement building in which she dwells need paint and maintenance that Rosenblat withholds. She is loath to allow John Manning to see these squalid conditions. But she encounters no empathic receptivity in Rosenblat. Wearing humble work clothes, Sonya visits the landlord and asks him to spruce up the building. He refuses and summarily dismisses her from his office with the invective "You Bolshevik!" (43).

Sonya will not be deterred. Keenly grasping the landlord's way of seeing, she alters her appearance to take advantage. She dresses in the clothing made for her by Jacques Hollins and finds the unwitting Rosenblat in a restaurant. He fails to recognize this beautifully attired Sonya Vrunsky as the same importuning tenant he previously dismissed, because in these clothes Sonya is "transformed" (27). She derives power by controlling her visibility. Adding to his confusion, she "vamps" for him, pretending to flirt (57). The married, hypocritical landlord takes the bait, responding with seamy, leering attraction. Sonya Vrunsky pretends to be receptive. When he offers to keep her in a fine apartment as his mistress, Sonya reveals her true identity, scoffs at him, and threatens to publicly expose his sordid offer. She tells him that she had hoped to appeal to his respect for "human rights" (54). When that proved futile, she resorted to entrapment and blackmail. Now she will use her position as a newspaper reporter to publicize his immorality unless he repaints her room and the building lobby. She reminds him that such exposure would alert his wife. But her final threat, the clincher, is, "I'll tell John Manning, who has put more than one landlord in prison for bad housing" (54).

Here Yezierska introduces the language of civil law and rights that a Russian Jewish immigrant of the nineteen-twenties would have perceived as quintessentially American. The power of the wealthy landlord can be trumped by the power of American law. Any moral authority she claims is diminished by her perpetration of blackmail. However, the author, the narrator, and the main character justify this because the landlord is a scoundrel, and the reader is inclined to go along. Landlord Rosenblat surrenders to Sonya Vrunsky, and pays to have her room and the building's common areas freshly painted. He even expresses grudging admiration for his tormentor.

The neighborhood loan shark is the third Jewish man whose help Sonya enlists. She wants money to buy a sofa, a samovar, flowers, and accessories to complete the image of worthiness for Manning. She has neither collateral to support a loan nor income to repay one. But Sonya Vrunsky believes fervently that armed with the necessary resources, she will entice John Manning to marry her. She purveys her confidence to the cynical loan shark "Honest Abe" Levy (64), persuading him to lend her a hundred dollars against her future marriage and wealth as security. He agrees, but insists that for a hundred-dollar loan, Sonya must pay five hundred dollars one month after she marries Manning. The amount owed will increase if repayment is delayed. If she doesn't marry Manning, that loan will become a terrible burden. But this is a risk she willfully, recklessly undertakes. The pawnbroker understands that he is granting not freedom but servitude, for he expects to extract his pound of flesh in the form of usurious cash returns. But Sonya Vrunsky sees the loan document as her personal Emancipation Proclamation signed by "Honest Abe."

Writing this loan is a creative act by which Sonya authors her own desirable future. It is a time-honored method for pursuing self-transformation from immigrant to American. Jennifer Baker writes that debt and borrowing have been represented as "essential to immigration, settlement and national independence," and "both individual opportunity and communal cohesion," beginning with the earliest American literature.[19] Moreover, "the archetypal American" as a literary figure harbors faith that "indebtedness might convert dreams into reality."[20] It appears that borrowing is as American as apple pie.

As a teenager, Sonya Levien borrowed thirty-six dollars to pay for a stenography course that helped her escape the sweatshops and launch her

19. Displaying the fabricated simplicity she has carefully arranged, Jetta Goudal as Sonya Mendel in *Salome of the Tenements*, 1925, pouring tea from an elegant samovar for her rich beau, John Manning, played by Godfrey Tearle. From Library of Congress Prints and Photographs Division, by permission of Paramount Pictures.

career. It took her four years to repay that loan. Sonya Vrunsky's experience with borrowing is far less successful than Levien's. Like Lily Bart's debt to Gus Trenor in *The House of Mirth*, Sonya Vrunsky's debt to Honest Abe pushes her to a crisis.

Revealing and Concealing

After finagling the three *lanzmen* (fellow Jewish immigrants), Sonya Vrunsky turns her sights back on John Manning. She calculates how much to reveal to the unwitting Manning and how much to conceal to maximize the power of female display. With new custom-made clothing cajoled from the dress designer, a fresh coat of paint extorted from the landlord, and money borrowed from the loan shark, she creates a beautiful "tableaux vivant" for Manning.[21]

Sonya trains her keen aesthetic intelligence on pursuit of the beauty of simplicity. This is not beauty as truth, but a fabrication, the illusion of simplicity as an instrument of deception. The goal is to achieve the appearance that Tolstoy describes as *"very simple,* that is to say, very elegant,"[22] while avoiding the "excessive affected assumption of simplicity."[23] Using the magician's technique of misdirection, Sonya Vrunsky draws John Manning's gaze to the carefully staged appearance of simplicity while diverting his attention from the reality of her extravagant contrivance.

Sonya Vrunsky performs for John Manning like Salome dancing with her seven veils or Cinderella in her glass slippers at the ball. Sonya's appearance, her bearing, her clothing, and the artfully understated décor of her room hit Manning right in the receptors. But this is not empathy. It is rather the dazzling allure of the exotic other. Sonya Vrunsky's performance deliberately reinforces Manning's preconceptions about the worthy poor. He is oblivious of the effort required to construct the simplicity he sees. He asks Sonya to become his secretary at the settlement house he endows and manages. It does not take long after this for Sonya Vrunsky to marry the boss and move in with him at the settlement house.

Unsettling

Anzia Yezierska had mixed feelings about settlement houses. She worried that these institutions were not as benevolent as they pretended to be. While she knew that settlement houses provided real help to poor immigrants, Yezierska was dismayed by what she perceived as their tendency to drift across a fine line from social services into social engineering, from altruism to coercive instrumentalism. Sonya Vrunsky's utterances on the subject reflect the author's conflicted attitude. Yezierska herself made good use of the resources provided by settlements. Settlement houses sponsored activities in which she made friends, including Rose Pastor Stokes and Sonya Levien. Settlement houses and similar institutions provided her with room and board when she needed them, and even a scholarship to fund her college tuition. But for Yezierska these things came with great psychic cost, leaving her feeling demeaned.

Initially Sonya Vrunsky disdains what she perceives as the condescending tone of settlement house workers. But her cherished John

Manning is a wealthy philanthropist who supports and manages a prominent settlement house. She cannot allow herself to think ill of him or his work. To reconcile this dilemma, Sonya searches for reasons to applaud the settlement house movement. The character acknowledges her ambivalence, but she refers to the author's real-life friends as examples of the successful women who derived great benefits from settlement houses: "'Where else can a poor girl like me meet her millionaire if not in the settlement?' Sonya rationalized her inconsistency. 'How did Rose Pastor catch on to Graham Stokes? . . . How did Sonya Levien, a plain stenographer, rise to be one of the biggest editors?'" (82–83). The character's disapprobation for the settlement houses returns when her initial excitement over John Manning abates. Once again she finds herself "depressed" by the drab décor, the cold institutional character, and the "faked, futile home economy" offered by these institutions to the "worthy poor" women who are told to make do with "[m]ilkless, butterless, eggless cake" (134–35). To Yezierska and Sonya Vrunsky, the settlement houses offered an emotionally detached pity, a patronizing sympathy tainted with disdain that failed to recognize the humanity and the emotional pain of the recipients. This kind of charity denied dignity to those in need. The author and the character wanted assistance informed by empathy.

At the end of the novel, Sonya Vrunsky plans to open a clothing store on the Lower East Side to sell beautiful clothing at affordable prices, freeing tenement dwellers from the tyranny of "the ready-mades." This, she declares, will be "my settlement" (178). Having escaped the Russian Pale of Settlement and the settlement houses in New York, Yezierska aspired to create some idealized sanctuary that would be a home and a place for personal expression. Through Sonya Vrunsky she gave voice to this aspiration.

Something to Offend Everyone

Sonya Vrunsky and John Manning are presented as opposites that attract. These two are posited as antithetical, not to attempt to synthesize them but to explore whether it is possible for them to establish empathetic bonds. Manning and Vrunsky are defined against each other as man and woman, rich and poor, Jew and Gentile, American and immigrant. These external attributes are paired with inward traits that supposedly define the essences of the characters. Thus, if Sonya Vrunsky is excessively emotional, John Manning is reserved; if Vrunsky is passionate, Manning is repressed; if she is impulsive, he is deliberate. She is chaos to his control, crazy to his sane, depravity to his rectitude, entropy to his order. The central weakness of this technique is that it reduces characters to stereotypes.

Many of Yezierska's characters are guilty of reductive, oppositional identity thinking. The author exaggerates ethnic and what she calls racial behavioral markers, and cultural distances between social classes. Yet she oscillates in drawing conclusions about essential, inherent human differences. She insists that people are irreconcilably different, and that we are all the same. These inconsistencies arise from Yezierska's personal quest to define her identity and affiliation as a Russian Jewish female immigrant American. She relies on personal recollections of her relationship with John Dewey as a literary device through which to articulate ambivalences. That is why it is important to recognize that much of the dialogue between Sonya Vrunsky and John Manning is modeled not on Rose and Graham Stokes, but on Yezierska's conversations and philosophical debates, remembered or reimagined, with John Dewey.

At the beginning of their affair, John Manning tells Sonya Vrunsky, "It's because we come from opposite ends of civilization that we fuse so perfectly" (107). He calls their love "the mingling of the races" (108). Sonya starts out strongly attracted to Manning's reserved, proper, refined personality, but after spending more time with him, she is surprised to find herself repelled by that same aristocratic demeanor. Later, when their marriage is breaking up, Sonya Vrunsky decides "that just as fire and water cannot fuse, neither could her Russian Jewish soul fuse with the stolid, the unimaginative, the invulnerable thickness of the New England puritan (*sic*)" (147). During a moment of passion, Manning cries out, "Oh, my beautiful maddening Jewess!" (181). When she finally reveals that Honest Abe is demanding payment on the note secured by Sonya's great expectations of marriage, John Manning erupts in rage at the mention of the loan shark, whom he reviles as "that Jew!" (151). He decides to pay off the note, declaring with contempt, "Your Jew won't refuse cash" (151).

Their focus on the external social markers of their backgrounds hinders their ability to see each other as individuals. Vrunsky and Manning are passionately drawn together, Yezierska suggests, by forces of sexual attraction and irrational love. However, they cannot fulfill each other's fantasies. As individuals, when they inevitably deviate from the confining stereotypical identity thinking that ignites their attraction, their attempts to form bonds of empathy are thwarted. They do not fully recognize, that is, they do not assimilate or vicariously experience, each other's emotional interiority. Instead, they keep trying to clothe each other in prefabricated illusions that do not fit.

At their wedding reception, Sonya makes a dramatic entrance in a simple, elegant gown designed by Hollins. For a moment she envisions herself as mistress of a "shining palace of pleasure" (120). Unfortunately that "palace of pleasure" is as illusory as the unattainable "house of mirth" from which Lily Bart is cast out.[24] Sonya Vrunsky quickly perceives the invisible barriers and mutual distrust that separate Manning's wealthy friends and relatives from her own poor, Lower East Side, immigrant guests. This party scene is a stark contrast to the parties that Jewish screenwriter Sonya Levien and her WASP intellectual husband Carl Hovey hosted at their Malibu beach house a few years after the *Salome of the Tenements* film. The Levien and Hovey brunches reflected a comfortable mixing, with high tea, finger sandwiches, and scones sharing tables with chopped liver, and schmaltz herring with sour cream and onions.

The different groups of Manning and Vrunsky's wedding guests resist mixing as stubbornly as oil and water. Manning's friends are put off by Sonya's "Jewish fervor" (121). She is stung by cutting remarks she overhears from some of the haughty upper-class guests.

"Russian Jewesses are always fascinating to men" because they are "creatures of sex," one snobbish socialite comments (128, 127). Another society lady stoops so low as to mock Sonya as a "pet monkey." "Giving a dinner for a pet monkey is one thing and marrying one is quite another" (128, 127).

Yezierska's Jews and Gentiles are equally willing to dehumanize others by comparing them to animals. When Sonya Vrunsky works as a waitress, she calls the rude customers "low-down beasts," who do not hesitate to reach out with a "thick paw" to grope her (164–65). She complains to her boss who "put a hairy, gorilla-like hand upon her shoulder," but he shows no sympathy (164–65). Sonya's greedy Jewish landlord is described as a "brute" whose "thick hairy paw" reaches out to take Sonya's hand (50, 51). "Yezierska retained many stereotypes that accentuated the less attractive aspects of Jewish immigrants," Carol Schoen writes, "so there was, in effect something in the book to offend everyone."[25]

Honeymoon to Heartache

After hearing the unkind remarks of the wealthy wedding guests, Sonya vanishes upstairs to hide away from the party, refusing to display herself before Manning and his cohort. When Manning finds her in their bedroom, he responds with anger instead of the empathy she hopes for. Unable to feel what she feels, he tells her to stifle her emotions. He commands her to return to the party and make herself visible to the guests. She is devastated, but she complies. She feels temporarily powerless, an intolerable sensation, and a "terrible sense of defeat," while Manning is delighted because "[s]he had obeyed him" (130). This opens a rift between the newlyweds that will widen. "They looked at each other with strange eyes" (131). As their relationship deteriorates, Sonya tells Manning, "I won't take orders" (151). Manning finds himself increasingly attracted to Sonya's passion and physicality, but he worries about her inability to fit in with his family and wealthy contemporaries. He becomes concerned about how her behavior might impact his social position. Sonya begins to question her decision to marry John Manning.

Yezierska conveys sexual feeling as a vital component of self, in language that is absorbing without being salacious. Throughout the text when Sonya Vrunsky is excited, passionate, happy, or sad, she imagines herself naked. Disgusted by the "ugliness" of cheap clothing, Sonya would prefer to "walk the streets naked" (23). Jacques Hollins is inspired by Sonya's "naked, passionate youth" (23). Her "nakedness staggered" John Manning (33). Responding to Manning's critical male gaze, "she felt herself stark naked" (114). When Hollins meets Sonya, he surveys her with "aesthetic delight," noting that her "neck was like the stalk of a flower, and through the coarse serge of her shabby suit the bud-like breasts" (24). In a dressing-room, changing into a dress Hollins has designed for her, Sonya is delighted to find "undergarments and every little detail of the toilette laid out on the dresser—obviously for her—even shoes and silk stockings" (27). Without discussing it, Hollins understands that Sonya will discard her "coarse, cotton undergarments" (27). She arouses empathy and desire in Hollins. Sonya is "radiant" in the elegant clothing Hollins provides (29). She "felt in each movement of her supple body her skin vibrate with the luxuriant feel of her silken undergarments" (29).

Manning's physical attraction to Sonya burgeons into "an overwhelming madness to thrust civilization aside, tear the garments that hid her beauty from him, put out his hands over her naked breasts and crush her to him till she surrendered" (106) But irrational love and sexual attraction, Yezierska suggests, are not the same thing as empathy, and the difference becomes increasingly pronounced and important.

"I hate love," Sonya Vrunsky intones melodramatically. "What's love but bondage?" (91).

After they are married, Manning and Sonya slowly remove performative veils to reveal their naked bodies and personalities to each other. On their honeymoon, "without shame they surrendered themselves" to each other. "She was all love that wrapped itself around him," their "flesh merging" (107). The newlywed Sonya loves to make love with her husband; "the more she gave, the more bottomless became her urge" (109)

At first Manning is equally enchanted. But soon he withdraws, becoming reserved and less physically expressive. Yezierska signals that this is Manning's way of regressing to his accustomed mien. Sonya Vrunsky's anxiety rose as "the first veil of illusion fell between them" (109)

Honest Abe reappears to demand his payment, threatening to reveal her deception to her husband if Vrunsky defaults. The amount she owes rises each week, soon surpassing one thousand dollars for what was a one-hundred-dollar loan. Although now married to a wealthy man, a thousand dollars is more than she can obtain in cash without alerting Manning. This fact confirms her subordinate, dependent status. She offers to pay the loan shark "three hundred dollars, her pin money allowance for the month" (140). Abe takes the three hundred, and forces Sonya to sign a new note for fifteen hundred dollars.

She becomes withdrawn, fretting over her marriage, the settlement house's shortcomings, and fear of exposure by Honest Abe. Manning comes home one night to find Sonya in bed, feigning sleep. In recent days he has missed her "over-demonstrativeness" (143). He is possessed by "carnal indelicacy," desiring "her naked body," imagining her "breasts . . . her hips . . . her slender flanks . . . the whiteness of her flesh" (144). He reaches out to his wife and "his hand closed over her breast" (144). Sonya has longed for him to show his desire for her, but she is "in no mood for his caresses now" (145). She wants to tell him about Honest Abe. Driven by "hot desire," Manning's hand "slipped into the valley of her breast" (145).

"Don't, don't! I'm so tired!" she pleads (145).

A few moments later, Manning tries again, but now, "Sonya's mood had imperceptibly changed," as "propinquity had softened her resistance" (145). Moreover, an opportunity occurs to her. She will share with her husband a "moment of love" and "yielding closeness" (146). Then, in the afterglow she will reveal her debt to Honest Abe and the deceptions she committed to win Manning's love. He still cannot truly see her, and she still cannot stop trying to manipulate him.

The disconnect between desire and empathy becomes insurmountable. Sonya looks to Manning for comfort and understanding. She needs his tender reassurance at the moment when he needs her passionate physicality. Timing is everything, and their timing is off.

When Manning realizes that Sonya has surrendered to his advances, "he abandoned all subtlety" (146). This is not the tender lovemaking that Sonya anticipates. Manning exacts an "instant of thrilling triumph," that leaves him "tinged swiftly with shame" (146). Sonya is filled with "shame and disillusion" (146). This has been a "disaster to her thwarted love," and "Her flesh was raw and hurt by the insult" to her "wounded, quivering body" (146). But Sonya Vrunsky will not sink into helpless victimhood. Instead she reacts with anger to "her roused and unsatisfied desire" (147).

Manning experiences their sexual act as an emotional breakthrough in their relationship, strengthening their connection as husband and wife, while for Sonya it creates a breach that cannot be repaired. The next morning they have a heated argument. Determined to wound him, Sonya reveals the truth about her debt to Honest Abe. Manning reacts with uncharacteristic rage to what he perceives as a double betrayal. Not only has Sonya deceived him, but Honest Abe is one of the corrupt predators that Manning has been attempting to banish.

Vrunsky asks Manning if he wants a divorce. "There has never been a divorce in the Manning family," he answers "with frigid contempt" (152). He vows that he will not grant her a divorce.

"I am married to you. We stay under one roof. But we are through" (152).

This is another echo of Tolstoy. When Anna Karenina pleads in vain for a divorce, her husband refuses because he fears it will subject him to public disgrace. Like John Manning, Count Karenin insists on maintaining an "external status quo." He resolves to "have nothing to do with" his wife. "She does not exist for me."[26]

"The Karenins, husband and wife, continued living in the same house, met every day, but were complete strangers to one another."[27] For a while Anna Karenina submits to this arrangement.

But Sonya Vrunsky will not even consider John Manning's suggestion. Convinced that they cannot reconcile their differences, wracked with guilt and anger, she packs up and leaves. Manning is astonished when his wife runs away. She simply withdraws, vanishes, disappears. The forces that attract them to each other cannot make up for their inability to communicate emotionally, their failure to create bonds of understanding empathy.

There is a particular resonance with Jewish culture in these disputes in which the wife wants a divorce that the husband refuses to grant. Jewish tradition provides a husband the power to give or withhold permission for divorce. This permission is called a "get." Throughout recorded Jewish history, and continuing to the present day, numbers of observant Jewish women have been placed in a marital state of limbo, no longer with their husbands but barred under Jewish law from remarrying because their husbands have refused to grant them a get. This sexist power imbalance is decried, particularly by the women who suffer its effects, as outrageously unjust. Even under civil law women could face daunting obstacles to exiting a marriage in the 1920s. Rose Pastor Stokes was forced to submit to the humiliation of admitting adultery to obtain a divorce when her

Gentile husband James Graham Phelps Stokes would not agree to submit any other grounds acceptable under 1925 New York State divorce laws. Yezierska did not have to fight with either of her two Jewish ex-husbands for a get, but she did confront the reality of the gender power imbalance inherent in the rules. She recognized the parallels in Anna Karenina, and recalled them in *Salome of the Tenements*.

Sonya Vrunsky does not hesitate to leave her husband while waiting for a divorce. Moreover, Vrunsky does not addle her mind with morphine and throw herself under a train like Anna Karenina, or overdose on chloral hydrate like Lily Bart. Sonya Vrunsky will not be sedated. She does not seek sleep, insisting instead on pursuing her waking dreams.

Reinvention and Redemption

Sonya Vrunsky checks into a drab women's hotel, remarkably similar to the Martha Washington Hotel where Jetta Goudal lived before her acting career took off. Vrunsky goes to work, first as a waitress, then as an apprentice to a dress designer. She abjures her husband's financial support, and submits to drudgery and obscurity. Wharton's Lily Bart also "longed to drop out of the race and make an independent life for herself," but unlike Sonya Vrunsky, Lily could not imagine a way "to live contentedly in obscurity."[28] Slowly Sonya learns how to design clothing. She earns redemption with hard work. Yezierska's protagonist withdraws from the marriage and reinvents herself as an independent, self-sufficient woman, much as Anzia had done herself. Sonya Vrunsky finds a way to support herself and an outlet for artistic expression.

Eventually Jacques Hollins sees Sonya's dresses in a shop window and he seeks her out. Now able to meet Hollins as an equal, not a dependent or supplicant, she determines that he is her true soul mate. They retain the bond of empathy formed when they first met. She feels a thrill of enthusiasm for clothing design that she could not muster for work in a settlement house. Her relationship with the former Jaky Solomon grows from one of respect and empathy into romantic love, but there are no erotic scenes between them and their interactions display a curious lack of physical passion that contrasts with her volatile affair with Manning.

The bond between Hollins and Vrunsky is not based on the kind of irrational desire she experienced with Manning. This new connection appears not to contain the same intense sexual passion. It is a bond of empathetic receptivity and recognition, emotional and aesthetic communication, and mutual affection. Their relationship is curiously evocative of chivalric love, or what Yezierska described as "mental companionship" when she described her expectations about marriage to her first husband.[29]

Sonya Vrunsky and Jacques Hollins become partners in business and personal life. She assumes that Manning has commenced divorce proceedings against her, but this is never confirmed. The dangling thread of uncertainty about Sonya's marital status is consistent with a literary modernist resistance to finality. It is one of many instances in which Yezierska's deliberate ambiguity serves as both irritant and stimulant. Sonya tells Hollins, "you know Manning's trip West means that he's divorcing me, and I want to wait until I'm free and clear from all that" (177). But the reader never is told if or when she becomes free and clear. "The lack of resolution," Natalie Friedman writes, "is, perhaps, the most interesting part of the entire novel."[30]

Sonya and Jacques get engaged, but "[a]s the day for her marriage to Hollins drew near, a vague, unutterable sadness possessed Sonya" (179). Manning arrives unexpectedly at her door one evening as Vrunsky and Hollins prepare for supper. The formerly reserved gentleman is unhinged, struggling to maintain his composure as he says, "I must see you alone." For a moment Sonya is a young professional woman forced to choose between two handsome suitors, recapitulating a model upon which countless romance novels have been constructed. Sonya tells Hollins to leave so that she can speak with Manning. "The eyes of the two men clashed like swords," as Hollins withdraws, flashing "hatred for hatred" (181).

The scene that follows between Sonya and Manning is shocking. Natalie Friedman describes it as "a surprising scene of attempted rape."[31] And while this is an accurate reading, it also is clear that Yezierska intended it to demonstrate Sonya Vrunsky's strength, not her weakness or defeat. Once Manning and Sonya are alone, they fall to shouting at each other. Manning is undone by desire.

"You belong to me," he cries out to her, implying that their marriage has not been legally dissolved.

"I want you. I can't live without you. . . . I'm hungry for you." He grabs Sonya and "every vestige of civilization had left him. He was a primitive man starved into madness for the woman." He pulls at her hair, her neck, her breasts, and "her whole body." He becomes "lost in his passion" as he kisses her helplessly (181).

But she "struggles against him" (181). She will not surrender to his advances as she had done in the past. "'No—no,' she cried, 'let me—let me go'" (181). Then, "With a violent twist of both arms she pushed him from her" (181). There Sonya stands, staring down John Manning. Her hair is disheveled, her shirt torn open to reveal her "heaving bosom" (181).

Yet she has been empowered, not diminished. Sonya is "superb, ravishing in her fury" (181). She mocks John Manning, derisively reminding him how cold he was to her when she desperately desired him. She laughs, recalling "how she had lain beside him night after night, sleepless, nerves unstrung, hungering in vain for a kiss, for a breath of response, for a sign of his need of her" (182).

"Now I don't want you," she says with withering contempt, exulting in this demonstration of his weakness and her power (182).

"This," we are told, "was her moment." Manning's descent from genteel man to would-be rapist is his ultimate defeat and Sonya's "triumph of her sex" (182). The storm of their argument passes and calm returns.

"I'm sorry," Manning says. And then, more significantly, "I didn't know, I didn't understand" (182).

"I'm sorry too," Sonya answers (182).

The chapter is titled "Revelation" (179). Manning and Vrunsky have finally revealed themselves to each other. Sonya now is able to forgive John Manning and appreciate the significance to each of them of the love they shared. He can sadly let her go. They seem at last to have reached an empathetic understanding at the very end of their relationship. They part amicably, as Sonya rejects her handsome, wealthy Gentile American for her handsome, wealthy Jewish immigrant.

Even after this emotional storm Sonya remains burdened with "doubt and uncertainty." She wonders, "Whom do I really love? Manning or

Hollins? Or do I love both? Or do I love neither?" (182). In Deweyan prag-matist fashion, she decides that "Manning was an experience which had burned forever into the texture of her life," and by marrying Hollins she will be "[g]oing into a new experience" (183). But the book ends before the wedding day arrives.

In her 1923 review of *Salome of the Tenements*, although she lavished praise on Yezierska's novel, Gertrude Atherton declared that "the end of the story is too abrupt."[32] Sonya Vrunsky's ambivalence, she asserted, illustrates "the mysticism and eternal dissatisfaction of the Russian." Moreover, "it is doubtful if for that aspiring and wholly unreasonable soul there is any earthly fulfillment of desire."[33]

Atherton imagines that in the future Sonya Vrunsky "will have far more interesting men in love with her than" either Manning or Hollins.[34] The relationship with Hollins, the critic suggests, "promises to be an even briefer incident in her life." Natalie Friedman agrees that "[t]he ending leaves the reader guessing: Will Sonya marry Hollins? Will her old love for Manning prevent her from joining forces with her new love interest? Will she reject both Manning and Hollins for a life on her own?"[35]

Naming and Necessity

The act of naming is an exercise of power. The women of the Salome Ensemble learned this when they arrived in the United States as immigrants and chose American names for themselves. Anzia Yezierska became Hattie Mayer for many years before reclaiming her original name. Sara Opeskin became Sonya Levien. Julie Goudeket became Jetta Goudal. Yezierska, Pastor Stokes, Levien, and Goudal each confronted the question of whether to take their husbands' surnames. They had many opportunities to ponder the meanings of names of works of art and fictional characters.

Critic Thomas J. Ferraro admonishes that "using Yezierska's fiction to reconstruct her life is not the same as using her life to reorient our approach to her fiction."[36] They are not the same, but they are both useful. The author deliberately tempts readers to look in both directions. In *Salome of the Tenements*, Yezierska uses names to convey connections, occasionally subtle but more frequently conspicuous, to her own lived experiences, to the lived experiences of others, and to works of art from which she drew inspiration.

One example is Gittel Stein, Sonya Vrunsky's newspaper co-worker. The name Gittel is the Yiddish diminutive for Gertrude, so this frumpy, frustrated journalist friend of the protagonist is named Gertrude Stein (69). It appears the author's intention here was merely to amuse those who would recognize the reference. However, soon after she finished writing *Salome of the Tenements*, Yezierska traveled to Europe where she sought out Gertrude Stein and asked about her writing process.

"Why worry?" Gertrude Stein told Anzia Yezierska. "Nobody knows how writing is written, the writers least of all!"[37]

At other times Yezierska employs character names as repositories of meaning hidden in plain sight. They evince premeditation and purpose, beginning with the name of the book: *Salome of the Tenements*. Since the biblical Salome was a royal princess who did not dwell in tenements, the book's title signals "a number of dichotomies" that, Michael North writes, suggest "a whole series of other dichotomies."[38] The title introduces the animating tension of the main character as a combination of dissonant components, a Cinderella and a Salome. The jarring juxtaposition focuses attention on the protagonist's agency, morality, and even sanity.

The main character's name, Sonya Vrunsky, is packed with meaning. The name Sonya was indelibly linked in Yezierska's mind with her friend and editor Sonya Levien. Levien had published many of Anzia's short stories in the *Metropolitan* magazine. While Anzia was writing *Salome of the Tenements*, Sonya Levien was working as a screenwriter in Hollywood for Famous Players–Lasky Paramount Pictures, the studio that ended up producing the film. The film of Anzia's previous book, *Hungry Hearts*, was in post-production at Samuel Goldwyn Studios, to be released in November 1922 at the same time as the publication of the novel *Salome of the Tenements*. Three months before the simultaneous releases, Anzia told an interviewer that "Sonya Levien of the *Metropolitan* was the first editor to accept a manuscript from me" when "I began to emerge from obscurity."[39]

Yezierska was displeased with the screenplay for *Hungry Hearts*, written by Julian Josephson and Montague Glass. She hoped to have a better experience with a screenwriter for *Salome of the Tenements*. Naming her protagonist Sonya hints that Anzia had Levien in mind right from the start. Disinclined to be subtle, Yezierska goes so far as to have the protagonist Sonya Vrunsky applaud Sonya Levien as a role model (83). The sequence of events is suggestive. First Yezierska names her main character Sonya and has her extol Sonya Levien in the text. Then Yezierska proclaims admiration and gratitude for Sonya Levien in a publicity interview shortly before the book's publication, at the same time that Levien is working at Paramount. It could hardly have been a surprise when Paramount Pictures chose Sonya Levien to write the screenplay.

20. The Strunsky sisters at Caritas Island. Yale University Library, Manuscripts and Archives, Rose Pastor Stokes Papers, MS 573, microfilm.

The name Vrunsky is no less determined and purposeful. One referent is a connection with Tolstoy. Tolstoy figures prominently among Yezierska's literary influences, and many scenes in the story of *Anna Karenina* bear striking resemblances to Anzia's personal experiences. Like Tolstoy's tragic heroine, Anzia wished for a handsome Count Vronsky type to rescue her from her unsatisfying life as a wife and mother. John Dewey filled that symbolic role for her for one exciting year. A legacy of Anna Karenina is discernible in the character Yezierska named Vrunsky, separated by only one letter from Vronsky.

Yezierska unequivocally acknowledges her inspiration by Tolstoy. Early in *Salome of the Tenements*, Sonya Vrunsky tells Jacques Hollins that John Manning is "a born saint—a follower of Tolstoy" (31). Hollins disdains Tolstoy as a "faker." To this "sacrilege," Vrunsky retorts that "Manning is a follower of Tolstoy but he's no faker" (31). She goes on to write an article for the *Ghetto News* about John Manning, declaring that he has "[t]he face of a Lincoln, the soul of a St. Francis, an American Tolstoy" (32).

"I must love and live," Anna Karenina cries after leaving her husband; "he has not once even thought that I'm a live woman who must have love."[40]

"I cannot live without love," Sonya Vrunsky wails at John Manning. "I'm dying under your eyes. And you don't see it. You don't know it" (149).

Anna Karenina runs off with Count Vronsky. Sonya flees from her role as Mrs. Manning and goes back to being Miss Vrunsky.

Yezierska's change in spelling from Vronsky to Vrunsky evokes the rhyming surname of the Strunsky family, with whom the author was well acquainted. Rose and Anna Strunsky were Russian Jewish immigrants who arrived in the United States in 1886 and moved between San Francisco and New York. The Strunsky sisters became active socialists, intellectuals, journalists, and writers. They were prominent participants in the intellectual scene in San Francisco that attracted Anzia Yezierska during repeated visits there. They had a brother, Albert Strunsky, whose daughter Lenore married composer Ira Gershwin.[41]

Anna Strunsky married William English Walling and the couple lived for several years with Rose Pastor and Graham Stokes on the Stokes's privately owned Caritas Island off the Connecticut shore of Long

Island Sound. Yezierska likely met Anna Strunsky at the Stokes wedding or at Caritas. Caritas is the model for the fictional Greenwold in *Salome of the Tenements*, the estate to which John Manning takes Sonya Vrunsky on their honeymoon. For several years William Walling and Rose Pastor Stokes were fellow contributors to the *Masses*. Both the Walling and Stokes marriages eventually ended, in part because of political differences between the spouses over America's participation in World War I.

Anna's sister Rose Strunsky was at one time Sonya Levien's rival for the affections of Sinclair Lewis. Levien and Yezierska might have known that Lewis wrote love poems to Rose Strunsky. In 1917 Rose Strunsky translated and published *The Journal of Leo Tolstoi*, a work with which Anzia would have been familiar.[42] Wittingly or unwittingly, Yezierska appears to have melded Vronsky and Strunsky to derive Vrunsky.

Yezierska's attention to names is evident throughout *Salome of the Tenements*. Jacques Hollins, the clothing designer who becomes Sonya's lover, is Jaky Solomon when he arrives as a poor immigrant in New York. "Solomon" and "Salome" are masculine and feminine forms of the same Hebrew name, both of which derive from *shalom*, which means "peace." Jaky's "real" surname, Solomon, labels him as a male counterpart to Sonya Vrunsky as Salome. Natalie Friedman calls Jaky Solomon "a kind of exotic mirror, a masculine version of Sonya."[43] This Salome and Solomon, possessors of the male and female Hebrew names for peace, together achieve peace of mind.

When Sonya marries John Manning, Hollins calls her "Mrs. Manning" (117). To the dress designer, Sonya has taken on a new identity as Sonya Manning, reenacting his own identity transformation from Jaky Solomon to Jacques Hollins. At the end of the novel, these two become engaged, but Sonya never becomes Mrs. Hollins.

Sonya's greedy landlord Benjamin Rosenblat is a meaner version of Sim Rosedale, the Jewish landlord in *The House of Mirth*.[44] Wharton's Rosedale is a noveau riche social climber motivated to use his wealth to achieve heightened social status. Yezierska's Rosenblat is a base individual for whom wealth is an end in itself, not a means to any loftier goal. Wharton's Jewish landlord is intelligent and reasonable. Yezierska's is coarse and volatile. It is remarkable that the Gentile, genteel Edith Wharton, who espoused overt if dispassionate anti-Semitism, depicts a complex, nuanced Jewish landlord in Rosedale, while the Jewish, sentimental Anzia Yezierska creates a crude, vulgar stereotype in Rosenblat, the cheap Jew.

Even though he is coldly calculating and selfish, Rosedale displays real empathy for Lily Bart. Wharton uses this character to convey the fact that financial wealth and social acceptance are separate things; it is quite possible to have one without the other. Yezierska's Rosenblat is a repellant caricature, devoid of empathy or fellow feeling for the poor Jewish tenants whom he overcharges while allowing his tenements to crumble and decay.

Rosedale seeks acceptance by American socialites. He has amassed wealth, but has not yet gained entrée at the beginning of *The House of Mirth*. At that point Lily Bart does not have money, but she possesses beauty and membership in the elite with which he can transform his wealth into the status he covets. This membership represents to Rosedale great value that cannot be measured in cash. Rosedale desires Lily sexually, but that is only one component of his complex motivation. He is refined and intelligent enough to behave with some grace and respect for Lily as a person. Rosenblat cannot see Sonya Vrunsky at all until she dons beautiful apparel to dress to impress, and then he can conjure nothing more than sexual desire. Sonya must threaten him in order to win Rosenblat's cooperation.

John Manning's name is one of his most cherished possessions. He is outraged to learn that his name appears in Sonya's written marker to the loan shark. The Manning name has increased in value with each passing generation from colonial times. It has a value measurable in cash, but it also has a noneconomic value that transcends any cash nexus. John Manning is a scion to whom the family name is sacred. This name has been left to him as a steward. It is to be honored and protected. Here Manning is again like Tolstoy's Count Karenin, who demands that his "name is not disgraced," that "his name would remain unsullied."[45] Manning's view is that Sonya has debased his good name by using it as collateral for her loan. "My name," he shouts in disbelief, barely able to contain himself (151). Although Manning is furious, he pays Honest Abe to ensure that this blight on his name is expunged immediately. After she leaves Manning,

Sonya Vrunsky tells a friend, *"His name*, that's all he cares about!"(157, emphasis in original).

Influence and Inspiration

Salome of the Tenements eludes easy categorization. On one level it is an assimilation story similar to those produced by early twentieth-century Jewish immigrant authors such as Abraham Cahan, Mary Antin, Israel Zangwill, Henry Roth, and Mike Gold. Antin's and Zangwill's work unabashedly celebrated immigrant assimilation in America, the very topic about which Yezierska's writings reflected her never-ending irresolution. Writers like Cahan, Roth, Gold, and Yezierska shaded their depictions of immigrant experience with varying levels of ambivalence. *Salome of the Tenements* also shares characteristics of regional and immigrant assimilation stories from non-Jewish writers of various ethnic and national backgrounds, including Jacob Riis, Ole Edvart Rølvaag, Zora Neale Hurston, and Jean Toomer. Andrew Delbanco connects Yezierska to Gish Jen, Chang-Rae Lee, and other contemporary immigrant writers."[46]

As a narrative of female empowerment and gender relations, *Salome of the Tenements* exhibits affinities with Kate Chopin's *The Awakening* and *The Yellow Wallpaper* by Charlotte Perkins Gilman. Carol Schoen argues that Sonya Vrunsky's "all-consuming egoism is reminiscent of Sister Carrie, and the seduction of Manning is as inevitable as that of Hurstwood."[47] I have demonstrated that Yezierska took inspiration from *The House of Mirth* and *Anna Karenina*, and crafted *Salome of the Tenements* as a tale in which a Lily Bart or an Anna Karenina survive, surmounting all obstacles. *The House of Mirth* was published in 1905, the year of the Stokes wedding.

Yezierska's novel also fits in a long line of cross-ethnic and cross-class literary romances and marriages, particularly those between Jewish and Gentile lovers. The latter include Charles Brockden Brown's *Arthur Mervyn*, Sir Walter Scott's *Ivanhoe*, Pearl S. Buck's *Peony*, Jacques Halévy's opera *La Juive*, and many others reaching back to Queen Esther and King Achashverosh. Even the catastrophic confrontation of Salome and John the Baptist functions as a cautionary tale against romance between Christian and Jew. Anthony Trollope's *Nina Balatka* is a nineteenth-century story set in Prague in which a poor Gentile woman marries a wealthy Jewish man. In George Eliot's *Daniel Deronda*, a man raised in a wealthy Anglican household discovers that he was born Jewish. He falls in love and marries a poor Jewish woman while retaining a chaste friendship with a beautiful Gentile woman who loves him. In *Daniel Deronda*, the proto–Lily Bart is Gwendolyn Harleth, who seeks financial security by marrying a wealthy man, only to discover that his emotional cruelty forces her to pay a terrible price. The kind, empathetic Deronda remains unattainable to her. Wharton's *The House of Mirth* profits from the influence of *Daniel Deronda* and Henry James's *The Portrait of a Lady*.

Anzia Yezierska's knowledge of the canons of Western literature, Yiddish literature, and high and popular culture is illustrated by voluminous references in her writing. Yezierska's compulsion to refer overtly and covertly to her many literary influences demonstrates both the loftiness of her aspirations as a writer and the intensity of her longing for respect. The author of *Salome of the Tenements* was determined to let readers know that she intended to enter the ring with a pantheon of literary greats. Meredith Goldsmith describes Yezierska as "[a] highbrow reader who admired Galsworthy, James, Wharton, and the modernists."[48] In *Salome of the Tenements*, the narrator or the main character refer explicitly to Shakespeare's *Merchant of Venice*; Cervantes's *Don Quixote*; Israel Zangwill, who wrote the play *The Melting Pot*; the prodigy violinist Jascha Heifetz, whose American debut was at Carnegie Hall in 1917; the playwright David Pinski; Sarah Bernhardt; the opera singer Jeritza; Queen Esther; Heinrich Heine; Keats; Shelly; Gorky; Tolstoy; St. Francis; Abraham Lincoln; Chaucer; Tchaikovsky; Rembrandt; Kant's *Critique of Pure Reason*; the *Atlantic Monthly*; and Browning's *Pippa Passes*, among many others. Yezierska pours forth a torrent of popular and literary references. The author contrasts her main character's intense emotional expressiveness with the seeming restraint of the *Mona Lisa*. As if to ensure that the reference is not missed, the painting also is identified as "La Giaconda" and "the smiling fifteenth century siren" (84, 90).

A minor character, a rich, snobbish Jewish banker's wife, brags that she is going to take her daughter, Sadie, "to the swellest hotel in Long Branch where come the richest of the rich American Jews," to give Sadie "a chance to marry herself good" (8, 17, 19, 28, 45). Here Yezierska's garish banker's wife unabashedly celebrates the same Long Branch that worried Henry James. In *The American Scene*, James laments that "German Jewry" replaced "the old superseded shabbiness of Long Branch," with the "big brown wooden barracks of the hotels" and "the chain of big villas" that strike him as "more or less monstrous pearls."[49]

Yezierska draws strength from her refusal to adhere to strictures of genre. In fact, the author's deliberate straddling of literary genres allows her to connect with readers and transcend her limitations as a stylist. Her fiction works as overemotional romantic sentimentalism, melodrama, and social and psychological realism.[50] It also fits under the broad umbrella of modernism.

The agitated energy, sentimentalism, and melodrama of Anzia's style constituted an effective method of engaging the empathy of active readers and soliciting their solidarity. Yezierska's overwrought tone is comparable to the sensationalist mode of some journalism of the era. She combined sentimentalism with realism, and unabashedly mixed biographical sociology with diverse literary influences.

Richard Hofstader calls realism the "dominant note in the best thought of the Progressive era," articulated in the "literature and journalism" of the time, by the "most fertile thinkers of the age" in "philosophy, law, and economics."[51] In particular, Hofstader describes the muckraking journalism of the late nineteenth and early twentieth centuries, characterized by a provocative writing style designed to elicit strong emotional reactions from readers. This style of journalism, practiced by Jacob Riis, H. L. Mencken, Ida Tarbell, Lincoln Steffens, Hutchins Hapgood, and many others, combined different writing styles and thrived concurrently with various forms of literary sentimentalism and realism. "Indeed, the marriage of biographical sociology to literature marked the most original journalism of the turn of the century," wrote Moses Rischin in 1902.[52] Aviva Taubenfeld describes Jacob Riis as "[d]eliberately straddling the old and new genres of sentimentalism and journalistic realism."[53]

Hofstadter refers to "the vulgarity and sentimentality of sob-sister journalism."[54] Film director Paul Bern, who later worked with Sonya Levien and Jetta Goudal, once told Yezierska, "You're what I call a natural-born sob sister."[55] Will Rogers affectionately called Anzia Yezierska a "[s]ad, sad, sad little sister" and told her, "You got success on a tear-jerker."[56] While the "manifest function" of this kind of writing was to "exploit sentiment for the sake of sales," Hofstadter writes, it also contained a "latent function," which was "to help create an urban ethos of solidarity and to put some limits on the barbarization of urban life."[57] The strategy is to convey emotion, to trigger vicarious experience and solidarity, to evoke empathy.

When the author calls Sonya Vrunsky a "Lily Out of an Ash-Can," (56), she links the character not only to the social realism of Wharton's *The House of Mirth*, but also to the Ash Can school of art. The Ash Can artists produced paintings and photographs depicting stark urban realism, including harsh aspects of modern life. One example is a painting by George Bellows called *Cliff Dwellers*, which also was displayed at the 1913 Armory Show that featured Duchamp's *Nude Descending a Staircase*. The *Cliff Dwellers* painting depicts a crowded street scene of New York City tenement residents much like scenes in *Salome of the Tenements*.

In Carol Schoen's view, the most prominent literary mode discernible in *Salome of the Tenements* is literary naturalism.[58] This mode is consistent with Yezierska's repeated emphasis on essential, immutable characteristics of race, ethnicity, and national origin. Sonya Vrunsky struggles endlessly to exert her free will, "her indomitable will" (97), but she confronts the obstacles imposed by her irrational overemotionalism, which she attributes to her Russian Jewish heritage. When Sonya Vrunsky meets Jacques Hollins, they are both thrilled by "the racial oneness of the two of them" (25). Edith Wharton's Lily Bart is similarly described as "the product of her heredity, environment, and the historical moment," unable to break free of the constraints imposed by her origins.[59]

The commitment Yezierska demonstrates in *Salome of the Tenements* to indeterminacy, unresolved dualisms, irreconcilable ambiguity, and experimentation is characteristic of literary modernism.[60] To Natalie Friedman, "Yezierska was a modernist, a contemporary of Fitzgerald, Hemingway, and Joyce."[61] But Michael North insists that "Yezierska is not in any traditional sense a modernist."[62] She has been variously labeled an exemplar of "ethnic modernism,"[63] "middlebrow modernism,"[64] and "vernacular modernism."[65] Lori Harrison-Kahan compares Yezierska with African

American female writers of the Jazz Age and Harlem Renaissance such as Nella Larsen and Jessie Fauset, who "formulate new conceptions of identity" in which apparent contradictions "are no longer antithetical but rather operate in" what she calls a "distinctly modernist . . . dialectic of identity."[66] Michael North suggests rather that in Sonya Vrunsky, Yezierska created "a very early example of a personality commonly associated with postmodernism, one who derives a certain measure of autonomy and even agency from her consumption of mass-market images."[67]

A Tale of Two Lilies

Apparent opposites can be kindred spirits, even those as outwardly dissimilar as Salome and Cinderella. Anzia Yezierska, the daughter of penniless Russian Jewish immigrants, and Edith Wharton, the child of an Old New York family of great wealth and high social status, had more in common than their vastly different backgrounds would indicate. The work of both of these artists was influenced by and bears stylistic attributes consistent with literary social realism and psychological realism. Their writing styles differ greatly in tone and perspective, but they frequently arrive at similar meanings and messages. Wharton's consummate virtuosity in composing sublime sentences contrasts sharply with Yezierska's strategic use of dialect and broken English. The artistic mastery and evocative emotional austerity of Wharton's language differs markedly from Yezierska's hyper-emotionalism and pursuit of the inexpressible. Nevertheless, these authors pursue a shared desire to provoke their readers' empathetic connection to their characters.

Yezierska was wounded by her father's disapproval, and Wharton was injured by her mother's "coldness and rejection."[68] Each of these women had difficulty reconciling sexual desire with a repressive upbringing. Each of them married and divorced. Each of them grappled with anxiety and depression. They found the act of writing to be therapeutic. Cynthia Griffin Wolff contends that "Edith Wharton wrote herself to health."[69] Yezierska also turned to writing as an outlet for her overwhelming emotions, and a method of pursuing a fragile and fleeting equanimity. John Dewey might have been thinking of Yezierska when he argued that aesthetic creation can function as problem-solving behavior.[70] Kristian Berg notes that "[w]hile Wharton and Yezierska moved in very different social worlds and had very different concerns, they both were interested in the plight of women who struggled against the constraints of class and convention."[71]

Some scenes in *Salome of the Tenements* and *The House of Mirth* line up neatly for comparison. However, for Yezierska, inspiration did not result in imitation. Sonya Vrunsky is no Lily Bart, and never was intended to be. In fact Vrunsky is a kind of anti–Lily Bart. Unlike Wharton's beautiful, fading hothouse flower cast out upon the gritty soil of a material world where she cannot sink stable roots, Sonya Vrunsky fights with streetwise tenacity to achieve her place in the sun. Tolstoy described Anna Karenina as "a faded flower."[72] In striking contrast, Yezierska calls Sonya Vrunsky a "Lily Out of an Ash-Can" (56) whose intelligence and strong will give her an advantage over "hothouse debutantes" (47). Sonya Vrunsky displays a capacity for self-preservation that Lily Bart and Anna Karenina fatally lack. Lily Bart wilts and dies in the unprotected urban landscape while Sonya Vrunsky tenaciously blossoms through the pavement.

Both characters long for beauty in a world that confronts them with vulgar realities. Lily Bart teeters on the precipice of the privileged social class into which she was born, always in danger of falling, "actually struggling for a foothold on the broad space which had once seemed her own for the asking."[73] Lily "revolted from the complacent ugliness" of the house in which she lived with her aunt, Mrs. Peniston.[74] Sonya Vrunsky considers herself "trapped by poverty in a prison of ugliness" (150), and hates the "depressing squalor" (41) of her "mean and dingy" tenement (4). Lily Bart also "hated dinginess."[75] Orphaned without sufficient means to maintain her position, Lily depends upon the largesse of rich friends and relatives. Sonya also is described as an orphan, but she was born into poverty, not privilege, and she works to support herself. Sonya longs to climb. Her friend Gittel calls her "a creature consumed by the madness to rise" (7).

Gittel Stein in *Salome of the Tenements* recalls Gerty Farish in *The House of Mirth*. Gittel and Gerty admire and would like to emulate Sonya Vrunsky and Lily Bart. But Gerty and Gittel are resigned to being sidekicks, viewing their pretty friends as if through a department store window, noses pressed against the glass. These plain but good-hearted women serve as foils for the protagonists, embodying alternative visions of how differently the two heroines might react to their circumstances if they had more modest expectations and self-images. Just as Gerty Farish pines in vain for Lawrence Selden, who in turn loves Lily, so Gittel loves Lipkin the editor poet who is in love with Sonya. "For all his fine poetry," scoffs Sonya Vrunsky, Lipkin is "a pitiful *nebich* [ineffectual fool]" (7). Gittel is neither materialistic nor ambitious like her co-worker Sonya; Gittel is enthralled by Lipkin, sighing, "How I could love that poet!" (11). But Gittel, like Gerty Farish, does not feel entitled.

Gittel Stein and Gerty Farish harbor envy and anger toward the leading ladies who capture the hearts of the men they love. Yet both Gittel and Gerty also feel affection for Sonya Vrunsky and Lily Bart. Gerty Farish takes Lily into her home, comforts her with tea and sympathy and a safe place to sleep after Gus Trenor menaces and traumatizes her. Yezierska inverts the scene, with Sonya taking care of the ailing Gittel, who is touched when she sees Sonya Vrunsky "on her knees before the rusty grate coaxing the kettle to boil, while Gittel lay helpless with an aching chest" (7). Gerty Farish overcomes her jealousy and forms a mutual bond of empathy with Lily Bart. Gittel remains ambivalent toward Sonya Vrunsky. "Gittel Stein," the narrator informs us, "had never been Sonya's real friend" (123).

In both novels the main characters have strong reactions to differences between indoor and outdoor spaces, indicating the extent to which Yezierska and Wharton are concerned with implications of control of women's visibility. Irene Billeter Sauter notes stark contrasts in aesthetic depiction and emotional tone in Wharton's and Yezierska's presentations of interior and exterior New York City scenes and settings.[76] These contrasts are connected to contemporary cultural transformations that undermined notions of separate spheres of domesticity for women and public life for men. Rejection of the myth of separate spheres coincides with and affirms assertions of female agency. Both authors locate their protagonists in a variety of indoor spaces, some deplorably dingy and others grand. Sonya Vrunsky often seems oppressed and unhappy indoors, even in her husband's grand townhouse. Lily Bart appreciates the beautiful homes of her wealthy friends and covets Lawrence Selden's apartment. The approach to outdoor scenes is markedly different. When Lily Bart walks in the streets, she is vulnerable, frightened, and searching for an indoor safe haven. Sonya Vrunsky is at home on the sunny streets of New York. Yezierska's protagonist sings and dances with children on sidewalks and gutters.

Sonya Vrunsky worries that her hyperexpressive emotionality marks her as flawed and different from native-born Americans (66, 121, 143). She does not doubt her own intelligence, "all my brains" (66), but she fears that her strong emotions hinder her ability to think and communicate clearly. "You got a head," Sonya Vrunsky tells John Manning. "I got only feelings" (38). Lily Bart retains her outward composure even at moments when she is under intense pressure. With no safety valve for her stress, Lily turns to drugs. When her emotional pain becomes overwhelming, she uses chloral hydrate to sedate herself, even unto death. Sonya Vrunsky's overemotionality turns out to be a resource, a release of emotional pressure that restores her combative refusal to accept defeat.

On the day appointed for John Manning to call on Sonya Vrunsky for afternoon tea, she calls in sick to stay home from work and get ready. The editor and poet Lipkin rushes over to see if she is all right. He shows her a love poem he composed for her, but she coldheartedly brushes him off. She is preoccupied with Manning's impending visit. At this moment Sonya is in a state of emotional intensity and calculation, a predator, frightened but focused. Without apparent self-awareness she asks Lipkin, "Ain't there some way I can learn to get myself cold in the heart and clear in the head like sensible people?" (68). To the lovesick Lipkin, Sonya has never seemed so cold, clear, and ruthless.

Lipkin recites, "Bitter and sweet it is to love the moon" (68), a line from a poem, "Villanelle of Poor Pierrot," published in 1919 by Walter Adolphe Roberts.[77] Roberts was a Jamaican-born Afro-Caribbean poet, historian, novelist, journalist, and editor of *Ainslee's Magazine*. Roberts also worked at the *Metropolitan* and *Hearst's International* while Carl Hovey and Sonya Levien were still active at those magazines. He is credited as the first African American to write a detective novel. In that novel, *The Haunting Hand*, published in 1926, the crime-solving detective is a white woman employed by a movie studio in Astoria, in Queens, New York, the studio where *Salome of the Tenements* was filmed.[78] Roberts's interview with

Yezierska appeared in *American Hebrew* magazine while she was finishing writing *Salome of the Tenements*.[79] Flattering Roberts by quoting his poem was a shrewd tactic in Yezierska's campaign for self-promotion. Currying his favor might encourage him to review her novel favorably or publish work she might later submit to him. Sure enough, Roberts reviewed *Salome of the Tenements* in the *New York Tribune* in December 1922, asserting that the novel was "shot through with genius."[80]

Roberts also wrote a poem called "Tiger Lily," published in 1920 in *Ainslee's Magazine*.[81] *Ainslee's* was the magazine that published Sonya Levien's short story in 1912 after it was rejected by Carl Hovey at the *Metropolitan*. Roberts's "Tiger Lily" is an ode to the strength of the Tiger Lily flower, praised because it blossoms "Bravely apart" and remains "vivid, free." The Tiger Lily "has no heed for paler" flowers; she "knows Pity nor pride." Even when "Tattered by autumn storms, she will not fling Herself to sullen foes."[82] Sonya Vrunsky is a strong, tenacious Tiger Lily, not a fragile Lily Bart in need of shelter from the storms.

Cinderella Salome

Anzia Yezierska broke new ground with *Salome of the Tenements* by challenging the totalizing identity thinking that oppressed her as a woman and an immigrant. She contested false dichotomies by interrogating personality types posited as polar opposites and exposing their connections. She used Sonya Vrunsky to reveal ambiguities and inconsistencies within common stereotypes. This was the author's way to oppose the kind of reductionism that demeans and dehumanizes. While acknowledging natural affinities and willed affiliations, she denounced the prejudice of relegating individuals to artificial ethnic or gender categories. Ironically and unfortunately Yezierska fell into the trap of writing characters who behaved as thin stereotypes in order to drive her plot.

Yezierska's innovative, novel approach consisted in combining the iconic Salome and Cinderella to model her main character. She explored the tensions in her own life and the lives of her contemporaries caused by social pressures on women to inhabit the role of Salome or Cinderella, exotic foreigner or genteel American, sexual dynamo or demure innocent. Mary Dearborn identifies how such dichotomies have been deployed by and against female immigrants in America beginning with the story of Pocahontas.[83] In addition to her identity as an immigrant, Yezierska was particularly sensitive to the implications of her Jewishness. Sander Gilman argues that the femme fatale and the *belle juive* are "two related images of difference . . . which usually function in two different cultural contexts, the one misogynist, the other anti-semitic."[84] Both cultural contexts were oppressive to Yezierska. The anti-Semitic element distinguishes the duality of Salome and Cinderella from that other misogynist binary of Madonna and whore.

Sonya Vrunsky is "one of Yezierska's more complex heroines," in Mary Dearborn's estimation.[85] Vrunsky is too complicated to be identified simply as either a Cinderella or a Salome. This is a great strength of Yezierska's novel. Many of the immigrants and native-born American characters in *Salome of the Tenements* can be separated by their display of ascribed, defining characteristics of overemotionality or calm rationality, hypersexualized savagery or civilized rationalism, propensity to act either on impulse or intelligence. Still, the most revelatory moments involve characters transgressing the boundaries of their presumed social group behavior. Sonya Vrunsky displays warm intelligence and cool emotions. John Manning comports himself as a genteel aristocrat and a crude savage. Sonya Vrunsky succeeds when she embraces her differences while recognizing that some things do connect all human beings.

The book reviews were mixed. Scott Nearing titled his 1923 review of *Salome of the Tenements* in the *Nation* "A Depraved Spirit," calling it "an unwholesome book" and the protagonist "a devouring monster."[86] Michael North adds that "many readers objected that she was altogether too reprehensible to gain their sympathy."[87] James Harvey Robinson endorsed the novel's authenticity, and admonished "every sociologist and social psychologist and miscellaneous moralizer" to read *Salome of the Tenements* so they might be disabused of facile assumptions about poor immigrants.[88] Robinson's flattering review appeared in the *Literary Digest International Book Review* at the time Yezierska was having an affair with that journal's editor, Clifford Smyth.[89]

Walter Adolphe Roberts was not the only reviewer of *Salome of the Tenements* to use the word *genius*. The writer and feminist Gertrude Atherton started her 1923 *New York Herald* review of the novel by asserting, "One hesitates a long while before applying the word genius to a new author."[90] But once she overcame her initial reluctance, Atherton did not hesitate to use the word repeatedly in the glowing review, declaring "the genius of Anzia Yezierska" to be "the most remarkable case of sheer genius fighting its way through an impenetrable thicket and imposing itself upon an unsympathetic world that I have any knowledge of."[91] Atherton was well known for scathing criticism of those with whom she did not agree, but she and Yezierska were fellow former members of Samuel Goldwyn's group of Eminent Authors. They met during Anzia's brief time in Hollywood. Atherton's accolades for *Salome of the Tenements* were perhaps partly motivated by her own ties with the novel's publisher. Boni and Liveright had published some of Atherton's books in the past, and the firm was about to release her novel *Black Oxen*. The desire to maintain good relations with Boni and Liveright would logically have provided some incentive to do what she could to boost the sales of a fellow author in the publisher's catalog. Atherton hoped that Yezierska would someday write a sequel to *Salome of the Tenements*, to show a mature, successful, and happy Sonya Vrunsky. No sequel ever was written, but an altered version of the story was brought to the silver screen.

|7|

Moving Pictures

Although *Salome of the Tenements* was her first novel, Anzia Yezierska was no novice when she wrote it. She had published short stories in prominent popular magazines for seven years. Her first book, a collection of short stories called *Hungry Hearts*, had been turned into a film by Samuel Goldwyn Studios. She had firsthand knowledge of the worlds of publishing and movies, and the publicity machines that served them. While the *Hungry Hearts* film was in post-production, Yezierska started writing *Salome of the Tenements*, confident the novel would be made into a movie. Anzia rushed through the project, completing the book in a matter of months. This rush allowed the novel *Salome of the Tenements* to be released simultaneously with the opening of the movie version of *Hungry Hearts* during Thanksgiving 1922, a publicity coup.[1]

By writing a book intended to be turned into a film, Yezierska implicitly acknowledged that her story would be handed off to others to participate in a retelling. She knew this, but she did not like the idea. Anzia hated the way her stories had been reinterpreted for the *Hungry Hearts* movie. The separate stories in the *Hungry Hearts* collection were blended together by the studio for the film, which made rewriting unavoidable. Yezierska labored to create in *Salome of the Tenements* a plot both linear and tightly focused on the main character to limit the need for rewrites. Generational conflicts between immigrant parents and their increasingly Americanized children are central to the stories in *Hungry Hearts*. These conflicts are absent from *Salome of the Tenements*, which reduces the potential to veer off on plot tangents. In the novel the protagonist's narrative arc is uncomplicated by parents or siblings.

21. Movie theater promotional lobby card for the film *Salome of the Tenements*, 1925, produced by Paramount Pictures and starring Jetta Goudal and Godfrey Tearle. From Library of Congress Prints and Photographs Division, by permission of Paramount Pictures.

Key passages of *Salome of the Tenements* betray the author's intentions for the film adaptation. Unfortunately, scenes that appear to be taken from or intended for the movies do not always make good reading. When the novel was released, the *New York Times* book reviewer, Louise Maunsell Field, said the John Manning character was a poorly drawn stick-figure stereotype, and that Yezierska "seems to have taken her ideas of the type and its surroundings from the cheaper 'movies.'"[2] Michael North disparages a scene in which the protagonist fantasizes about throwing handfuls of money to poor children in the street (13) as "so obviously a scene from the movies, complete with pantomimic expressions of gratitude and joy, that it is impossible to take at face value."[3] In a subsequent, equally saccharin passage, Sonya Vrunsky tosses not money but red roses to a group of children who hunger for beauty (72). Yezierska's self-conscious attempts to write cinema-worthy prose provide an early example of a common pitfall. "Hardly a major novelist in the last hundred years," Phillip Lopate writes, "has not been profoundly influenced by the movies."[4]

Yezierska displayed courage by presenting a powerful female protagonist sure to offend many readers. Levien, subscribing to the belief that offensiveness would depress box office receipts, tried to fashion a more sympathetic main character.[5] The screenwriter has the female Jewish immigrant achieve not personal empowerment through hard work but redemption through love and intermarriage. Lead actress Jetta Goudal, hoping to please her adoring fans, tried to infuse a fetching personality into her screen performance, and strove to arouse empathy for the young woman she portrayed. The actress and the screenwriter discussed the script and collaborated in the attempt to depict the heroine more as a Cinderella than a Salome. A film review in the *Los Angeles Examiner* noted that "readers of the Yezierska novel may find that the story itself has undergone some changes."[6]

Levien changed the main character's name from Sonya Vrunsky to Sonya Mendel, eliminating Yezierska's references to *Anna Karenina*. The name Sonya stayed, and the screenwriter rewrote liberally to create a character to whom she could relate. Sonya Levien bestowed upon the protagonist the surname Mendel, a name with many connotations for the screenwriter. The name evokes the character Mendel Quixano in Israel Zangwill's play, *The Melting Pot,* and Gregor Mendel, the father of modern genetic science. Levien picked up on Zangwill's deliberate choice of the name Mendel Quixano as a link to Gregor Mendel, and the useful implications of this connection for *Salome of the Tenements.*

Levien's great friend Theodore Roosevelt was a fan and promoter of Zangwill's play. Levien met Zangwill in 1914 when she traveled to England to report on the women's suffrage movement there. Yezierska also met Zangwill, but only after writing *Salome of the Tenements.* In the play, Mendel Quixano is the main character's uncle. Zangwill's theme is that America is strengthened by the genetic mixing of different groups. Werner Sollors remarks that the Uncle "Mendel" character "reflects, as his name suggests, the mixture of Jewishness and American surrounding."[7]

In his 1914 afterword to the play, Zangwill made explicit his play's invocation of the "Mendelian language" of genetics.[8]

By changing Vrunsky to Mendel, Sonya Levien signaled the important shift she wanted to accomplish in the story's emphasis. In Levien's version, genetic mixing eliminates lines separating races and social classes, and consecrates ethnic intermarriage. In the book, the main character's marriage ends. In the movie, husband and wife reconcile. Yezierska demonstrates that breaking up is hard to do but not impossible for a strong, self-possessed woman. Sonya Levien eliminates the plot elements of adultery, love triangles, and divorce, and replaces them with situations closer to her own experiences. Yezierska shows a strong woman who works hard, mends herself, and moves on, independent of the man who broke her heart. Levien's heroine is rescued by her husband.

These changes lead to very different visions of immigrant assimilation, American identity, and gender relations. Yezierska's vision insists on retention of ethnic difference while acknowledging a common humanity. Levien's approach attempts to efface lines of difference. Her screenplay displays a heightened sensitivity to American audience attitudes about ethnic mixing. Yezierska's novel follows the heroine's quest for personal fulfillment and refusal to be destroyed by unhappy romance. The failure of the marriage of Jew and Gentile in the book followed by the engagement between the two Jews, Sonya Vrunsky and Jacques Hollins, would have been viewed with approval by those who disdained ethnic mixing. But Levien apparently worried that the protagonist's disrespect for the marriage bond and cruelty to her husband would not play well in Peoria.

Under Sonya Levien's guidance, the film became about a female immigrant's assimilation and upward mobility through intermarriage to a wealthy American man. For Sonya Levien, love was the answer. Levien inverted Yezierska's narrative arc of resistance to immigrant assimilation and female subordination. Anzia's book depicts a journey to female self-reliance. The film substitutes a typical celebration of immigrant renunciation of foreign affiliation and female submission to male dominance, with marriage and security the rewards for a spirited, creative young woman who surrenders autonomy. The novel is in harmony with themes of female empowerment and independence. Yezierska's Salome learns that she can and must refuse to capitulate to male authority. She never stops desiring a loving relationship with a man, but she insists that any such relationship be on her terms of equality. Levien's protagonist surrenders herself to her husband. In return, the benevolent husband forgives, protects, and supports her, and they live happily ever after.

In America, the women of the Salome Ensemble freed themselves from the type of paternal authority to which Rose Pastor Stokes's mother, Hindl Lewin, had fallen victim more than forty years earlier in Russia. They would never submit, as Hindl had been forced to do, to an unwanted marriage arranged by their parents. Nor would they accept a status subordinate to their husbands. They had seized sufficient autonomy to choose for themselves. For these women, as for the heroine they created, marriage was a result of consent, not descent, a matter of contract, not bondage.

22. Jetta Goudal as Sonya Mendel in *Salome of the Tenements*, 1925, borrowing from the loan shark, Banker Ben, to decorate her shabby room to impress her rich beau. From Library of Congress Prints and Photographs Division, by permission of Paramount Pictures.

Like their creators, Sonya Vrunsky and Sonya Mendel are drawn to wealthy, patrician, white Anglo-Saxon Protestant men. Sonya Levien said that Jewish men reminded her of her brothers and cousins, and she found herself more attracted to Gentile men. Levien achieved self-reliance and an American identity, and if intermarriage had not been a prerequisite, it had not been a hindrance to her. Her marriage to New England blue-blood Carl Hovey embodied the successful mixing of ethnicities, races, cultures, and gene pools, consistent with precepts of Mendelian science. In Levien's film script the lead character ends up back with Gentile John Manning, their intermarriage presumably destined to issue what Zangwill had referred to as "the hybrid posterity" that would constitute a new American race.[9] The marriage of John Manning and Sonya Mendel is an allegory of assimilation through genetic mixing. Lori Harrison-Kahan says Anzia Yezierska strives "to bring the two worlds together" in a Hegelian synthesis and create "a new identity as a hybrid self."[10] In the novel, John Manning declares that he and Sonya Vrunsky are "[t]he oriental mystery and the Anglo-Saxon clarity that will pioneer a new race" (108). But in Yezierska's book that hybridization experiment fails when the marriage ends. In the film, Sonya Levien resurrects the intermarriage, and the project of breeding hybrid Americans can go on.

Removing Pictures

The depiction of divorce was still considered risqué in Hollywood movies of 1925 although many films dared to include social controversy. The influence of nineteenth-century genteel tradition was not completely effaced from mass culture. "It was all but impossible to imagine a happy ending that outstripped the marriage plot," writes Christine Stansell, even for some writers who had moved beyond romanticism and genteel tradition and embraced social realism and modernism.[11] Sonya Levien deferred to Hollywood convention by providing a happily-ever-after with the marriage intact, restoring a fairy tale ending for a Cinderella. But the film eliminates the main character's empowerment and earned redemption through hard work. Anzia Yezierska dispensed with marriage and saccharin happy endings in her writing and her personal life, but Sonya

Levien embraced them. Levien turned the book into a moving picture by removing pictures that Yezierska had drawn.

The main character's self-reinvention and achievement of self-reliance through ennobling effort and fortitude, central to the novel, are absent from the film. Instead, the tension that drives the film plot to its climax comes from the easily identifiable villain, the banker. Levien changed the loan shark's name from Honest Abe to Banker Ben. The sarcasm implicit in the appellation "Honest Abe" might be obvious in a novel, but confusing for a silent film audience, and the ironic reference to Lincoln might be lost. Apparently it was as easy then as it is today to direct anger at an evil banker. The film Manning has been working to expose the loan shark and others in the neighborhood for systematic exploitation, extortion, and corruption.

Jacques Hollins's role in the movie is reduced to that of just a friend, not a lover. The character's name is changed to the less macho Julian.[12] With the romantic tension about Sonya's choosing between two lovers removed, the film focuses instead on her pursuit of upward economic and class mobility and Americanization through intermarriage. Unfortunately this focus risks putting the main character in an unflattering light as little more than a social climber. True love is meant to vanquish such cynicism and doubt.

The screenwriter endeavored to make the main character more appealing than she appears in the book. In the book, the adult Sonya Vrunsky encounters poor children playing in the streets of the Lower East Side. She talks and dances with them and even gives them a bunch of roses. But she retains some emotional distance from the children. In the movie, Sonya Mendel is shown as a twelve-year-old child playing on the streets and sidewalks of the Lower East Side with a group of girls and boys. She evokes empathy as one of these poor children, not merely as an adult observing them. In another Levien embellishment, the adult Sonya Mendel climbs on a table to admire herself in a small wall-mirror in her fine clothing from the dress designer. When Jetta Goudal obligingly made that climb for the cameras, she fell off the wobbly table and broke several ribs. The next day she had to shoot additional scenes with her ribs taped up underneath her costume.[13]

When Sonya Mendel does not pay her debt, Banker Ben tricks her into stealing the loan agreement. He leaves her alone in a room where the note sits unattended. Then he bursts in, catches her in the act of taking the document, and threatens to have her arrested. He confronts Manning with Sonya's signed IOU. He demands that Manning quit his campaign against the neighborhood extortionists, or face the scandal of public exposure of the loan and his wife's arrest for theft. In a twist taken from an earlier Levien screenplay called *Who Will Marry Me*, Sonya Mendel protests that she is willing to go to jail. However, Manning saves the day and "shrewdly shows the banker that the whip hand is his own."[14]

Unlike landlord Rosenblat, Manning refuses to capitulate. In the novel, the loan shark's blackmail magnifies the married couple's growing alienation from each other, leading to a final breach. In Levien's filmscript, the attempted blackmail draws the couple closer together as they join to fight a common enemy. In contrast to the novel, the film places great importance on the civic and social institutions of society. Marriage as an institution is treated as a contingent expedient in the book, lightly discarded. But the sanctity of marriage is preserved in the film. Also, greater emphasis is placed on the authority of American law and community action in the movie than in the novel. In the book the landlord arranges to have Sonya Vrunsky's room and building lobby painted. In the film the young woman's neighbors join to help paint and redecorate in a tenement version of a barn-raising or quilting-bee.[15]

True to her background as a lawyer, Levien brought the film to a climax with John Manning threatening Banker Ben with criminal indictment. The movie Manning pays his wife's debt, and presses on with his crusade against corruption. There is a dramatic scene in a courtroom or community hall that does not occur in the novel, replete with what appears to be a grim presiding judge, a jury of righteous American citizens, a prominent American flag, and a solemn portrait of George Washington. The corrupt capitalist cronies are vanquished. The outraged majesty of the law is avenged.

Sonya Mendel runs off, but the benevolent John Manning follows her to the Lower East Side, embraces her, and showers her with love and forgiveness. The reconciled couple lives happily ever after. It was cleverly

23. In a scene from *Salome of the Tenements*, 1925, the American flag and a portrait of George Washington preside over a courtroom or community meeting in which the majesty of the law is restored and corrupt landlords and bankers are punished. From Library of Congress Prints and Photographs Division, by permission of Paramount Pictures.

subversive of Sonya Levien to use the happy marriage ending to win the approval of 1925 American audiences of an ethnically and religiously mixed marriage, an implicit affirmation of the screenwriter's own mixed marriage. The married couple in the film resembles Sonya Levien and Carl Hovey more closely than either Graham and Rose Pastor Stokes or Anzia Yezierska and John Dewey. By the time the book was published, Rose Pastor Stokes and Graham Stokes were estranged, and by the time the film was released, they had divorced. But Hovey and Levien remained happily married until Carl's death in 1956. Sonya Mendel's path of upward economic and class mobility requires her acceptance by and marriage to the wealthy, white, Protestant American. Conjugal love is her salvation. A film review in the *Atlanta Constitution* took a sympathetic view of Sonya Mendel, describing her as concerned with "simplicity, hard work, the creation of beauty, the love of her own kind."[16] But the film character receives salvation as a gift from her uxorious husband in contrast to the hard work, talent, and luck that benefit the protagonist of the novel. As Natalie Friedman writes, in the novel *Salome of the Tenements*, Yezierska "condemns marriage and romance as the means by which to achieve success."[17] But this is precisely what the movie celebrates.

Sonya Levien had of course seen the *Hungry Hearts* film before she worked on *Salome of the Tenements*. She had not only read the *Hungry Hearts* short-story collection, she had bought, edited, and published some of those stories in the *Metropolitan* magazine. When the Goldwyn studio ordered a new, happy ending to be added to the scenario for *Hungry Hearts*, Anzia Yezierska was outraged. She complained to an interviewer that the studio bosses had meddled "with the inviolate lines that had been wrought with pain and agony. Little bits of human heart-pictures that took me weeks and months to portray truthfully—*were cut out*. A happy ending was appended. A happy ending! To my story."[18] Just weeks before *Salome of the Tenements* was published, Yezierska told Walter Adolphe Roberts, "Art is inevitably preoccupied with tragedy, yet it is difficult to find a publisher here for a story with an unhappy ending."[19] Anzia had written a deliberately unresolved ending to the novel *Salome of the Tenements* that left open the possibility of happiness. But in Sonya Levien's opinion, it was not happy enough for the movies. Despite her deep familiarity with Yezierska's earlier work and artistic intentions, Levien made the changes she believed necessary to adapt the *Salome of the Tenements* story for the screen. Levien cut out many of Yezierska's "heart-pictures" and reworked the ending into one that would appear happier and less controversial.

Parting Shots and Fadeout

The film was shot in New York. This location allowed Sonya Levien to work on it while remaining at home with her family, which by that time included her son Serge and her newborn daughter, Tamara. It also allowed Anzia Yezierska to monitor the film's progress from the sidelines. Yezierska was less involved than she had attempted to be with the filming of *Hungry Hearts*. But apparently she retained some influence. Yezierska modeled the character Gittel Stein after her friend Irma Lerner, who had been her fellow student at the Academy of Dramatic Arts almost twenty years earlier. Lerner was a reporter for *Variety,* and she was chosen to play Gittel in the film. According to Yezierska's daughter Louise, "Anzia actually obtained the role of Gittel for her in the movie later made of *Salome.*"[20] The review in *Moving Picture World* said Irma Lerner "might have been brought up from the fringe of Seward Park so true to type does she play her part."[21]

Sonya Levien's biographer Larry Ceplair writes that "Levien's diary entry of December 26, 1924, notes Yezierska's name and telephone number."[22] Their collaboration on *Salome of the Tenements* was a culmination of Yezierska and Levien's twelve-year-long personal and professional relationship. The project allowed these two to pay homage to their mutual friend Rose Pastor Stokes with an artistic representation built on the framework of the Stokes marriage. Yezierska had ample reason to trust Levien, who had edited and published many of her short stories. What today would be called Anzia's "shout-outs" to Levien in the novel and in press interviews illustrate that Yezierska held Levien in high regard. Levien's supportive personality qualified her to contend with Yezierska's emotional intensity and authorial preciousness. These women were connected by bonds of mutual empathy. Nevertheless, the way the screenplay altered the story must have strained their relationship.

New York Times reviewer Mourdant Hall had generally positive comments on the screenplay. "Occasionally the subtitles are a little strained," he opined, "but many of them are quite good."[23] He was particularly moved by a scene in which Sonya Mendel takes dictation as John Manning's stenographer. "This is followed by a real O. Henry touch. Sonya is taking down letters, when Manning comes over to her and picks up her notebook, and observes penciled clearly on different lines, 'I love you, John Manning.' It is not to be wondered that he succumbs to this artful attack."[24] This was Sonya Levien's embellishment. In the book, the character takes dictation but does not reveal her feelings this way.

The *Atlanta Constitution* called the film "the clamor of the Ghetto blending with the glamour of Fifth avenue, pathos intermingling with rich comedy" in a "vigorous commentary on the strange blend of civilization which is Americanism."[25] In Atlanta the movie was approved by the "Better Films committee" and the "Parent-Teacher Better Films committee."[26]

The filming in New York of *Salome of the Tenements* became an exciting event. One of the largest film sets ever built was constructed in Astoria, Queens, at the Famous Players–Lasky Paramount Studio. The *New York Times* reported that "[i]t showed a section of Hester, Orchard and Ludlow Streets, peopled by 500 'extras,' some of whom declared that the reproduction was so good that they could recognize their own dwellings."[27] A Yiddish interpreter shouted directions through a megaphone. A horse pulled "an old-time horse car" alongside "stone paving, the street car tracks, the fire escapes and the densely-thronged streets."[28]

Among the many extras recruited from the Lower East Side to appear in the film were some elderly residents of the Home of Old Israel on Henry Street. Mrs. Jenny Freeman, who was 108 years old at the time, and Mrs. Esther Baron, a youthful 70, attended the opening of the movie at the Rialto Theatre at Broadway and 42nd Street in Times Square, to celebrate their screen debut. One of their fellow residents of the Home, Mrs. Fanny Weintraub, age 85, also appeared in the film, but she died of a heart attack on the morning of the New York premiere, apparently overcome by excitement at her impending celebrity.[29]

The prints and negatives of the *Salome of the Tenements* film have been lost. The film has vanished, disappeared. A decade-long search of film archives, the corporate records of Paramount Pictures, the Library of Congress, the Academy of Motion Picture Arts and Sciences, and other institutions supports the conclusion that the movie, filmed on nitrate film stock, must have spontaneously combusted, disintegrated, or been carelessly discarded, sharing the fate of countless thousands of silent movies. Paramount Pictures renewed the copyright registration for the seven-reel film in 1952, but this does not prove that the film physically existed even by that time, since the renewal application was part of the form reregistration of a long list of titles within the studio's library. The film's ultimate fate remains ambiguous. No movie company official, film historian, collector, or archivist has confirmed how many prints were made, where they were stored, or when or how they were lost or destroyed. This leaves open a remote, but tantalizing possibility that the film, or a portion of it, might still someday be found; that having vanished, it might yet reappear. The Library of Congress possesses hundreds of still photographs from the film. These pictures are in pristine condition on sturdy cloth backing. Other still photographs consisting of screen captures, publicity shots, posters, and on-set candid photos are located in collections in the George Eastman House, the Huntington Library, and the Margaret Herrick Library at the American Academy of Motion Picture Arts and Sciences.

It is possible that Rose Pastor Stokes, Anzia Yezierska, Sonya Levien, and Jetta Goudal sat one evening in December 1924 in a darkened private screening room in New York City with other Paramount Pictures insiders, friends, and family, watching the newly completed film *Salome of the Tenements* just weeks before its theatrical release to the public. Sonya Levien and Jetta Goudal would have reacted positively while reserving some space for self-criticism, or in Goudal's case, self-celebration. Anzia Yezierska and Rose Pastor Stokes would have dismissed the film as superficial mush for mass audiences.

Rose Pastor Stokes would have recognized the outlines of her own marriage to Graham Stokes. But Rose knew how different the important details of her life were from the simple confection that appeared on the screen. Perhaps these differences encouraged her to write her own memoir. Rose would have preferred Anzia Yezierska's book to Levien's filmscript, but she would have recognized how much the characters in that book were modeled on John Dewey and Yezierska, and how little they reflected her experiences with Stokes. Rose also would have detected reflections in the novel of the many conversations she and Anzia had shared.

Eight years later Rose penned her version of the story of the young ghetto-dwelling journalist who married a millionaire. Rose Pastor Stokes, in the months before her untimely death in 1933, wrote her unfinished autobiography, which was published posthumously six decades later in 1992. Pastor Stokes's book tells a quixotic political love story that led an idealistic young woman inexorably to disillusionment. In 1942 the writer Gershon Einbinder, who used the pseudonym Chaver Paver, wrote a novel in Yiddish based on the life of Rose Pastor Stokes, called *Rose of the East Side*. It was serialized in the New York Yiddish newspaper *Morgn Freiheit*, a testament to the enduring fascination inspired by Pastor Stokes.[30] This story written in Yiddish nearly a decade after the death of Rose Pastor Stokes suggests a lingering connection between this secularized socialist and the Jewish community she left behind.

Jetta Goudal recalled *Salome of the Tenements* as the best performance of her career. She told film historian John Kobal in 1982, "I call that my tour de force."[31] Goudal exited the movie industry in 1933 and followed a path remarkably similar to that of the fictional Sonya Vrunsky. Jetta became an interior decorator to the wealthy and famous denizens of Hollywood, providing herself an independent means of support and artistic expression. She became a union activist. She married Harold Grieve, a movie art director with whom she reportedly shared mutual bonds of empathy but not passion. The marriage lasted until she died in 1985 at age ninety-four.

After working with the temperamental Jetta Goudal and Anzia Yezierska, Sonya Levien likely welcomed the opportunity to move on to different projects. Levien went on to a long career as a screenwriter after *Salome of the Tenements*, leaving behind the world of magazine editing and winning an Academy Award in 1955 for the screenplay of *Interrupted Melody*. Sonya Levien died in 1960 at age seventy-two.

Anzia Yezierska no doubt would have been as dismayed by the film of her novel as she had been with the earlier film of her book of short stories. Her novel approach had been mostly abandoned in the movie. Yezierska published her last novel, *Red Ribbon on a White Horse*, in 1950, but continued writing for the *New York Times*, *Commentary* magazine, and other publications until shortly before she died in 1970 at age ninety. *Salome of the Tenements* was the last work by Anzia Yezierska to be transformed into cinema.

| 8 |

Taming the Bewilder-ness: To Affinity and Beyond

America at the beginning of the twentieth century contained millions of metaphorical fish out of water. These were the masses of workers who flowed from farms to factories, the myriad rural dwellers who flooded into big cities, and the multitudes of immigrants who poured across American shores. Their pilgrimage was no less terrifying than that of the Puritans or the first Dutch sailors and traders of the West India Company. The untamed savage forces these later pilgrims encountered were as unfamiliar and threatening as those confronted by their seventeenth-century predecessors. The predecessors had found unimproved wilderness, wide open spaces, a misunderstood native population whose presence and intentions seemed ominous, and the awesome powers of nature and divinity.

The challenges faced by the new arrivals and internal migrants between 1880 and 1920 were very different but equally as daunting. These more modern times presented a *bewilder-ness* that they had to decipher, assimilate, integrate, and cultivate, a forbidding metropolitan brutalism, an unfathomable urban labyrinth of modern machine power and population density, and a cacophony of linguistic and cultural diversity. To this was added the clash of socioeconomic classes exacerbated by the concentration of capital for industry, and the economic distress of a labor force thwarted by the retention of ancient legal rules of master and servant.

Anzia Yezierska emphasized the Pilgrim connection. "Weren't the Pilgrim fathers immigrants two hundred years ago?" a character asks in a story called "How I Found America" from her 1920 collection *Hungry Hearts*.[1] In another story, "America and I," from her 1923 collection *Children of Loneliness*, a character asserts, "I saw that it was the glory of America that it was not yet finished. And I, the last comer, had her share to give, small or great, to the making of America, like those Pilgrims who came in the Mayflower."[2] Producing *Salome of the Tenements* helped the women of the Salome Ensemble find their way through the early twentieth-century American bewilder-ness.

Some fifty years earlier Darwin and Spencer had challenged divinity, and in the subsequent decades technology and industry seemed to subjugate nature. Experience was trumping preconceived notions and undermining religious faith. Frederick Lewis Allen reported that people who worriedly rejected any scientific teaching that conflicted with the Christian Bible "began in 1921 to call themselves Fundamentalists."[3] From the leisure class to the laboring class, Americans confronted previously unknown forces, accelerating change, unfamiliar forms of modernity, and new kinds of fear. Self-styled urbane sophisticates and genteel cosmopolitans suffered from neurasthenia. Historian Jackson Lears cites *American Nervousness*, published in 1880, in which "the neurologist George Miller Beard identified 'neurasthenia,' or 'lack of nerve force,' as the disease of the age."[4] The idea of lack of nerve force was interpreted as an abhorrent weakness of will. "The worst kind of melancholy is that which takes the form of panic fear," wrote William James after he and his father experienced emotional breakdowns that their family called "vastations."[5] As a result of "overcivilization," middle- and upper-class Americans suffered from "a sense that they had somehow lost contact with the palpitating actuality of 'real life.'"[6] Lears describes this as "desperate anxiety" and "yearning for rebirth."[7] Henry Adams, appearing to have eerily presaged World War I, perceived a world of ever-increasing force and complexity that would inevitably spin beyond human control.[8]

The immigrants experienced desperate anxieties and yearnings no less traumatic than the native-born. Theodore Roosevelt advocated the embrace of a strenuous life as curative, and as quintessentially American. The ability to conquer one's emotions was deemed a virtue, and in some literature, film, and journalism, derision was cast on those who could not. Women often were denigrated as hysterical, and immigrants as neurotic. The depravity of Salome represented the lowest depth of this affliction. In *Ugly Feelings*, her 2005 book of "studies in the aesthetics of negative emotions,"[9] Sianne Ngai explains that "exaggerated emotional expressiveness" functions in American literature and film as a disdainful marker "of racial or ethnic otherness in general."[10] This surfeit of emotional expressiveness is presented as base, vulgar, threatening, and possibly contagious. Ngai cites as an example of this trope the writing of Anzia Yezierska, whose female immigrant protagonists struggle with what they perceive to be "problematic overemotionality" that influences their "trajectory toward cultural assimilation."[11] Gilded Age and Progressive Era Americans who perceived an epidemic of neurasthenia sought to distance themselves from those they viewed as uncivilized ethnics and immigrants who appeared to suffer from the symptoms of this dire emotional ailment. Shelley Reuter, a scholar of sociology and anthropology, writes that in the first decades of the twentieth century, "The fact that Jewish immigrants continued to display their nervous tendencies in America where they were free from persecution was seen as proof of their biological inferiority and raised concerns about the degree to which they were being permitted free entry into the US."[12]

Growing apprehension over problematic overemotionality and the multiplicity of technological and cultural changes sparked artistic tension and inspired literary exploration of the friction of contradictions. For Anzia Yezierska, contradictions are like the electromagnetic dynamos that fascinated Henry Adams.[13] They generate power and must be acknowledged and pondered, not resolved. In her introduction to the 1996 edition of Anzia's 1927 novel *Arrogant Beggar*, Katherine Stubbs relates that "Yezierska had once complained, 'My greatest tragedy in life is that I always see the two opposites at the same time.' In retrospect, this ability to see two sides of an issue appears not as a tragedy but as a primary source of her writing's complexity and strength."[14]

Yezierska was hardly alone in perceiving ethnic others as contradictions or opposites in need of reconciliation. Wealthy white Protestant American men stood atop the social hierarchy in the America the Salome

Ensemble entered. American men were the alluring, elusive others whom these young women sought to know and to emulate. They were the opposites that these women hoped to attract. Although money and social class were important, the perception that these men possessed the key to entrée into the exclusive club of "American-ness" carried significance beyond the pecuniary.

Writers of literary realism and literary modernism opposed and attacked modernity, challenging the affectations of the rising bourgeoisie, aspiring to offer what Ross Posnock calls "art as imaginative salvation from modernity's philistine vulgarity."[15] Writers such as Theodore Dreiser, F. Scott Fitzgerald, Ernest Hemingway, Sinclair Lewis, Henry James, and William Dean Howells stood as inheritors of an imagined white, male, Calvinist, Puritan, patrician legacy and peered with sympathy or derision from America's shores at ethnic minorities, immigrants, women, and the other nations of the world as they grappled with modernity and identity. Anzia Yezierska and her cohort of women, Jewish, immigrant, and nonwhite writers confronted many of the same issues of alienation, emotional malaise, secular modernism, industrial capitalism, and spiritual homelessness as those white male American literary modernists. But they were outsiders looking in, carrying their own intellectual and cultural baggage.

The urban fish out of water gazed apprehensively at one another, illuminated by recently electrified city lights. Indeed, some scenes in the 1925 *Salome of the Tenements* movie take place in the *finsternish* darkness of gaslit rooms with visible jet flames flaring from chandeliers and wall sconces. Individuals searched for comprehensible signs, reassuring glances, familiar words and facial expressions. They were afraid but drawn to each other. Stephen Marche writes, "For the great French-Jewish philosopher Emmanuel Levinas, the encounter with another's face was the origin of identity—the reality of the other preceding the formation of the self. . . . And from the infinity of the face comes the sense of inevitable obligation, the possibility of discourse, the origin of the ethical impulse."[16] The reliance on lingering closeups of actors' faces accounts for much of the emotional power of silent films.

It is human nature to seek and cultivate affinities and form connections. These are among the conditions precedent to the formation of the kind of "imagined communities" described by historian Benedict Anderson.[17] As Anderson and E. J. Hobsbawm explain,[18] such formations require, if not a spoken and written shared language, then at least some medium of communication accessible to those who would imagine themselves members of such communities, a vernacular lingua franca through which people can connect. In previous eras, Anderson demonstrates, written language, printing, and books provided the media of communication, and these took centuries to permeate European societies.[19] Hobsbawm discusses the development of "national" languages through written literary or administrative idioms, and oral forms useful to "preachers or the reciters of songs and poems common to a wider cultural area."[20] Eighteenth-century American legal, political, and literary writers consciously participated in what Robert Ferguson calls "The struggle for a collective identity,"[21] which was the process of imagining the new republic, and an affiliation beyond the shared use of the English language. Ludwig Wittgenstein published the seminal *Tractatus Logico-Philisophicus* in 1921, aspiring to define the relationship between language and reality, and initiating a linguistic turn in modern philosophy. Ralph Ellison states that "American literature is both an art of discovery and an artistic agency for creating a consciousness of cultural identity."[22]

Theatrical performances, photography, and movies established a new visual vernacular that facilitated widening imagined affiliation. Jonathan Freedman sees "the late nineteenth and early twentieth centuries as a crucial moment in the formulation of this understanding of the visual, its powers, and its limitations."[23] The visual display of women provided a semiotics available in any language. Movies expanded the audience far beyond the largest individual theater or town square. Women deployed the power of female spectacle in music halls, on burlesque and vaudeville stages, at lecture podiums, and on movie screens. Clothing provided a pliable resource for harnessing the power of female visibility in public and private spaces, allowing measured disclosure and concealment, and the use of color, style, and material as chosen signifiers of social class, ethnic, and other characteristics.

Constructive Collision and Translational Motion

Historian Robert Wiebe argues that what Americans longed for was a way out of what seemed to be chaos. "The search for order" drove social, cultural, and political change.[24] Wiebe describes how urbanization, industrialization, and soaring immigration impacted "the perspective of the threatened community"[25] among native-born Americans in the decades after Frederick Jackson Turner declared the closing of the frontier. By the turn of the century, anti-immigration sentiment among nativists was challenged in part by a "process of ethnic maturation,"[26] through which creolized children of immigrants grew politically confident and assertive. As for the urban proletariat, Wiebe writes, "No pot melted these bits and pieces into a class. Fearful of each other's ways, they lived in mutual suspicion, as separated into groups of their own kind as they could manage."[27]

Nevertheless, they could not avoid proximity in the increasingly dense population. Proximity is at the root of the concept of translational motion, which gained currency among physicists in the early twentieth century. Translational motion describes how influence, force, and energy pass between moving bodies whose proximity results in close encounters, collisions, connections, and entanglements. If the early twentieth-first century is an "Age of Fracture" as Daniel Rodgers argues,[28] then the early twentieth century in which the women of the Salome Ensemble interacted was more an Age of Collision and Translational Motion, as various forms of power centralized, cities filled up with diverse populations, large corporations amassed capital, labor unions organized, and government institutions grew. Human differences did not melt away in this milieu but they did collide, connect, impact, influence, and entangle. People were forced by circumstances to encounter and mingle with others from different groups and backgrounds with vastly different experiences.

These social encounters and collisions allowed individuals to move beyond inherent or inherited affinities and form chosen, willed affiliations. As exemplified by the women of the Salome Ensemble, they moved beyond ethnicity to make connections of the type highlighted by Werner Sollors, based on consent, not descent.[29] Invoking a 1903 statement by W. E. B. DuBois, David Hollinger identifies race in the sense of totalizing identity thinking as the overarching social challenge of the twentieth century. In the twenty-first century, Hollinger suggests, the greatest issue is the deliberate construction of solidarity.[30] He describes solidarity as "an experience of willed affiliation" that satisfies the deep "human need for belonging." Further, "one can have multiple affiliations," and "[t]hat we all have multiple identities . . . and are capable of several solidarities is widely understood."[31] He emphasizes the distinction between "particularist" and "universalist" solidarities, with the former being smaller, more intimate groupings and the latter defined as broader alliances that foster mutual protection and defense in addition to providing useful tools for achieving social and cultural experience.[32] The Salome Ensemble was a particularist solidarity. The participants engaged in larger universalist solidarities, and what Robert Wuthnow calls communities of discourse.[33]

The novel *Salome of the Tenements* was released at the end of 1922, although the copyright date is 1923.[34] In 1922 James Joyce published *Ulysses* and T. S. Eliot published *The Waste Land*. Willa Cather published the novel *One of Ours* in 1922, for which she was awarded the Pulitzer Prize in 1923. More than twenty million immigrants arrived in the United States between 1880 and 1924, the year *Salome of the Tenements* was filmed. In 1924 while Sonya Levien wrote the *Salome of the Tenements* screenplay, surging nativism and anti-immigrant sentiment in the United States was manifested in the passage of the National Origins Act.[35] This law set strict quotas limiting the number of legal immigrants permitted to enter the United States each year from individual European nations, and excluded most Asians. The contestation over immigration policy in America was as full of contradictions in the first decades of the twentieth century as it is in the first decades of the twenty-first.

When the movie *Salome of the Tenements* opened in 1925, Calvin Coolidge was the new president of the United States. Coolidge's inauguration was the first to be broadcast on radio. The first public radio broadcast had taken place in 1907, but the first commercial radio broadcast occurred in 1920. Charlie Chaplin released the film *The Gold Rush* in 1925; his *Modern Times* would arrive eleven years later. Former President William Howard Taft was chief justice of the Supreme Court. The *New Yorker* magazine began publication in February 1925. The Chrysler Corporation was founded that year, and F. Scott Fitzgerald published *The Great Gatsby*. It was the year of the Scopes trial, and the first public demonstration of television, at that time called "radiovision," by an American scientist named Charles Francis Jenkins. It also was the year of the publication of *Mein Kampf*.

Among the important lessons imparted by the women of the Salome Ensemble are the facts and the impact of their distinct particularities. At the start of this inquiry into their lives their similarities were most noticeable. It was not their uniqueness but rather their exemplariness that focused attention. They began as poor, Jewish women, immigrants, talented, and avid for knowledge and self-expression. They pursued a vigorous quest for status and aggressively questioned authority. They were motivated by the longing to belong and the desire for autonomy. They developed strategies to attain power by controlling their public visibility in an oscillating movement between Salome and Cinderella.

And while the similarities between these women are crucial to understanding them as exemplars of a particular historical context, the superficiality of those similarities is revealed upon close examination. Each member of an ensemble plays a distinct, specific part. The women of the Salome Ensemble retained their separate, individual selves. It is a practical and moral necessity to recognize this truth about all human aggregations. Nations, families, affinity ensembles, willed affiliations, and other collectivities of people "are composed of individuals, who never do fuse," says Martha Nussbaum, and respect for "the separate reality of individual lives" is a logical and ethical imperative, regardless of the kinds of groups to which they belong.[36] Nevertheless, to ignore the fact of willful affiliation is to miss nuanced comprehension of the individuals who do coalesce into an ensemble. In 1918, the year of his affair with Anzia Yezierska, John Dewey said that "democracy is concerned . . . with associated individuals in which each by intercourse with others somehow makes the life of each more distinctive."[37] Rose, Anzia, Sonya, and Jetta associated, collaborated, and influenced each other in ways that made the life of each more distinctive. They were as interdependent and independent as any frontier rugged individualists at a barn-raising or a quilting bee.

This work set out to study the connections between Rose Pastor Stokes, Anzia Yezierska, Sonya Levien, and Jetta Goudal and to concentrate attention on their collaboration on *Salome of the Tenements*. The thesis has been to illuminate how the lives of these individuals expose the broader contours of the social and cultural landscape in which they lived. The focus on them, particularly as immigrants and as women, is consistent with historian Ronald Hoffman's admonition to probe individual life experiences for deeper meaning,[38] and Jill Lepore's exhortation to concentrate on "solving small mysteries about a person's life as a means to exploring the culture."[39]

By turning ideas into action, the women of the Salome Ensemble sought deeper meaning and helped to fashion the culture. Men and women today are better off because Rose Pastor Stokes and others fought for suffrage and birth control and freedom of speech. Workers still benefit because Rose Pastor Stokes and Jetta Goudal fought, each in her own way, for labor unions, and workers' rights, and equal legal status for employees and employers. Movies with screenplays written by Sonya Levien still edify and entertain, as do the works of writers whose careers she enabled by editing and publishing their stories in magazines. Among those writers is Anzia Yezierska, who reaches a growing audience larger than the one she attracted during her lifetime.

For all the social change that has occurred since the women of the Salome Ensemble first told their stories, much of today's American society would appear familiar to them. Much of the world is not yet safe for democracy. The Espionage Act has never gone out of style. Class, ethnicity, and race remain as preeminent challenges. Immigration and naturalization are still confronted with strident nativism. Debate still rages over definitions of the worthy and unworthy poor, and how to diminish human suffering. The desire for autonomy still confronts the longing to belong to a community. America is still a nation of individuals striving for status and questioning authority. That every Salome is a Cinderella and every Cinderella a Salome is continuously revealed and repeated on social media and reality television.

The story of *Salome of the Tenements* was inspired in part by the life of Rose Pastor Stokes. Anzia Yezierska told that story in her novel. Sonya Levien retold it in her screenplay. Jetta Goudal enacted it on the silver screen. But that was not all. Rose Pastor Stokes wrote her own version of the story in a memoir she called *I Belong to the Working Class*, which was published fifty-nine years after her death. There was at least one other version. Gershon Einbinder, who used the pseudonym Chaver Paver, published a novel called *Reizel of the East Side* based on the life of Rose Pastor Stokes. The novel was written in Yiddish nine years after she died and was serialized from January through March 1942 in the daily newspaper the *Morgn-Frayhayt* (Morning Freedom).[40]

Rose Pastor Stokes, Anzia Yezierska, Sonya Levien, and Jetta Goudal each had stories to tell and different ways of telling and retelling. Storytelling, cultural transmission via oral, written, cinematic, or other media, has functioned as a cohesive and clarifying force throughout this investigation and apprehension of the Salome Ensemble. Storytelling also serves an adaptive function for tellers and listeners. It is a coping mechanism with which to navigate the fluidity of cultural and social identities. The character of a culture is shaped by the stories it tells itself. The social identity of an individual is shaped by the stories she tells herself, her listeners, and her wider culture.

The history of the Salome Ensemble merits, compels, obliges telling more than ninety years after *Salome of the Tenements* the movie was released, and ninety-three years after the novel was first published.[41] Their collective, connective tale remains relevant and recognizable even from this distance. Rose Pastor Stokes, Anzia Yezierska, Sonya Levien, and Jetta Goudal still fascinate, illuminate, clarify, edify, and entertain. The story of these finders and founders of America who pursued art and experience, empathy and affiliation, self-sufficiency and social visibility, is worthy to be told and retold. They tamed a bewilder-ness and journeyed to affinity and beyond.

Chronology | Notes | Bibliography | Index

Chronology

1859 John Dewey born.

1872 James Graham Phelps Stokes born.

1875 Carl Hovey born.

1878 Hindl Lewin's forced marriage to Jacob Wieslander.

1879 Rose Harriet Wieslander (Raisel Chana Wieslander) born in Augustowo, Russia.

1880 Anzia Yezierska born (no birth certificate).

1881 Assassination of Czar Alexander II followed by pogroms and May Laws.

1882 Jacob Wieslander abandons his family.

1883 Rose and Hindl move to London.

1886 Women permitted to practice law in New York State.

1888 Sarah Opeskin born.

1890 Yezierska family moves to New York. Anzia becomes Hattie Mayer.
Rose Pastor arrives in New York and moves to Cleveland.
Julius Opeskin banished to Siberia.

1891 Julie Goudeket born in Amsterdam.
Julius Opeskin escapes Siberia and immigrates to America via Shanghai.

1892 Oscar Wilde's play *Salome* is banned in London.

1896 Sarah Opeskin arrives in New York and becomes Sonya Levien.

1899 Anzia Yezierska moves to Clara de Hirsch Home for Girls.

1900 Women's Hotel Company formed to build and manage Martha Washington Hotel for Women.

1901 Rose Pastor moves to New York to work at the *Jewish Daily News*.
Harold Grieve born.

1903 Rose Pastor meets and interviews James Graham Phelps Stokes.
Rose Pastor Stokes serves as counselor for a group of girls, including Sonya Levien, at the Jewish Educational Alliance and the University Settlement.
Kishineff Pogrom in Russia.

1904   Anzia Yezierska graduates from Teachers College at Columbia University.

1905   Rose Harriet Pastor marries James Graham Phelps Stokes.

1907   Strauss opera *Salome* premieres in New York.
       Sholem Aleichem play *Stempenyu* premieres in New York.

1908   Sonya Levien meets Sinclair Lewis.

1909   Sonya Levien graduates from NYU Law School.
       Israel Zangwill play *The Melting Pot* premieres in New York and
       Washington, DC.

1910   Anzia Yezierska marries Jacob Gordon.

1911   Anzia Yezierska annuls Jacob Gordon marriage, marries Arnold
       Levitas, religious-only ceremony.

1912   Anzia Yezierska gives birth to daughter Louise.

1917   President Wilson brings America into World War I combat to make the
       world "safe for democracy."
       Sonya Levien marries Carl Hovey.
       Rose Pastor Stokes and Anzia Yezierska commiserate during
       Thanksgiving.
       Rose Pastor Stokes declines invitation to dine with President Wilson.
       Anzia Yezierska bursts into John Dewey's office and introduces herself.

1918   Rose Pastor Stokes indicted, tried, and convicted under Espionage Act.
       World War I Armistice.
       Julie Goudeket arrives in New York, begins transformation to Jetta
       Goudal.

1919   Sonya Levien receives first on-screen credit for original story for the
       film *Who Will Marry Me*, produced by Bluebird Photoplays.
       Treaty of Versailles.
       Prohibition begins with Eighteenth Amendment and Volstead Act.

1920   Sonya Levien gives birth to son Serge Hovey, born March 10.
       Anarchist terrorists detonate a bomb at the corner of Wall Street and
       Broad Street in NYC on Black Thursday, killing forty, injuring three
       hundred.
       Hungry Hearts published by Houghton Mifflin.

1921   Espionage case against Rose Pastor Stokes withdrawn by Harding
       administration.
       Famous Players–Lasky Paramount signs Sonya Levien to a
       screenwriting contract after purchasing her stories "The Heart of
       Youth" and "Baby Doll."

Rose Pastor Stokes forms Proletarian Theater and performs in *King Arthur's Socks*, written by Floyd Dell, at theater at 66 East 4th Street.

Samuel Goldwyn buys film rights to *Hungry Hearts* for $10,000.

1922 Novel *Salome of the Tenements* published. The copyright date is 1923, but the book is released at the end of 1922.

Jetta Goudal appears in her first film, *Timothy's Quest*.

Film version of *Hungry Hearts* released.

1923 Jetta Goudal enters contract with Distinctive Pictures Company that is terminated one month later.

Sonya Levien terminates her contract with Famous Players Lasky Paramount in order to return to New York and her family.

Sonya Levien gives birth to daughter Tamara Hovey.

1924 Jetta Goudal signs three-picture contract with Paramount Pictures.

Famous Players–Lasky Paramount asks Sony Levien to adapt *Salome of the Tenements* for the screen.

National Origins Act, also known as the Johnson-Reed Act or Immigration Act of 1924, sets immigration quotas by country of origin.

1925 Silent film *Salome of the Tenements* released.

Jetta Goudal enters film contract with Cecil B. DeMille Productions.

Rose Pastor Stokes and James Graham Phelps Stokes divorce. Rose's black-and-white drawings and pastels exhibited by the Society of Independent Artists on the Waldorf Astoria roof.

James Graham Phelps Stokes remarries.

Carl Hovey enters a contract with Cecil B. DeMille Productions.

1927 Cecil B. DeMille Productions terminates Jetta Goudal contract, September 10.

Rose Pastor Stokes at age forty-seven marries V. J. Jerome.

1929 Great stock market crash.

1930 Jetta Goudal marries Harold Grieve.

1932 Jetta Goudal appears in her last film, *Business and Pleasure*, costarring Will Rogers.

1933 Rose Pastor Stokes Jerome dies in Germany at age fifty-four.

Prohibition repealed by Twenty-First Amendment.

1950 Yezierska publishes *Red Ribbon on a White Horse*.

1952 John Dewey dies.

1955 Sonya Levien wins an Oscar for the screenplay of *Interrupted Melody*.

1956 Carl Hovey dies.

1960   Sonya Levien dies at age seventy-two.

James Graham Phelps Stokes dies.

Jetta Goudal is honored with a star on the Hollywood Walk of Fame. Discovering the star placed on Vine Street, she demands that it be moved to Hollywood Boulevard. The Hollywood Chamber of Commerce complies.

1970   Anzia Yezierska dies at age ninety.

1985   Jetta Goudal dies at age ninety-four.

1993   Harold Grieve dies.

Notes

Introduction

1. Anzia Yezierska, *Salome of the Tenements* (New York: Grosset and Dunlap, 1923; Urbana: Univ. of Illinois Press, 1996).

2. Richard Rorty, *Contingency, Irony, and Solidarity* (New York: Cambridge Univ. Press, 1989); Harriet Marla Sigerman, "Daughters of the Book: A Study of Gender and Ethnicity in the Lives of Three American Jewish Women" (PhD diss., Univ. of Massachusetts, 1992), 16, 17.

3. Inge Clendinnen, "Fellow Sufferers: History and Imagination," *Australian Humanities Review* 3 (Sept.–Nov. 1996).

4. Ibid.

5. Ronald Hoffman and Mechal Sobel, *Through a Glass Darkly: Reflections on Personal Identity in Early America*, ed. Fredrika J. Teute (Chapel Hill: Univ. of North Carolina Press, 1997), viii.

6. Jessica Lang, "Jewish and American, Historical and Literary: The (Un)Ifying Experience of Reading Text," *Studies in American Jewish Literature* 31, no. 1 (2012): 76, 77, 82.

7. Ibid.

8. Simon Schama, "Clio Has a Problem," *New York Times Magazine*, Sept. 8, 1991. Sigerman, "Daughters of the Book," 17.

9. Lytton Strachey, *Eminent Victorians* (London: Chatto and Windus, 1918), preface.

10. Albert Einstein, "Einstein's Reply to Criticisms," in *Albert Einstein: Philosopher-Scientist*, ed. Paul Arthur Schilpp (Cambridge, UK: Cambridge Univ. Press, 1949, 663.); Albert Einstein, *Physics and Reality*, trans. Jean Piccard, *Journal of the Franklin Institute* 221, no. 3 (1936): 376, accessed Nov. 2, 2015, http://www.kostic.niu.edu/physics_and_reality-albert _einstein.pdf.

11. Louis Menand, *The Metaphysical Club* (New York: Farrar, Straus and Giroux, 2001).

12. Benedict Anderson, *Imagined Communities* (London: Verso, 1983, 1991).

13. Casey Blake, *Beloved Community* (Chapel Hill: Univ. of North Carolina Press, 1990).

14. Edmund Burke, *Reflections on the Revolution in France and on the Proceeding in Certain Societies in London Relative to That Event in a Letter Intended to Have Been Sent to a Gentleman in*

Paris. The Works of the Right Honourable Edmund Burke, vol. 3 of 12 (New York: P. F. Collier and Son, [1790] 1909–14), available online as Project Gutenberg ebook #15679, 2005.

15. Horace M. Kallen, "Democracy Versus the Melting Pot: A Study of American Nationality," *Nation*, Feb. 25, 1915.

16. David A. Hollinger, "From Identity to Solidarity," *Daedalus* 135, no. 4 (Fall 2006). David A. Hollinger, *Cosmopolitanism and Solidarity: Studies in Ethnoracial, Religious, and Professional Affiliation in the United States* (Madison: Univ. of Wisconsin Press, 2006).

17. Werner Sollors, *Beyond Ethnicity: Consent and Descent in American Culture* (New York: Oxford Univ. Press, 1986).

18. Robert Wuthnow, *Communities of Discourse: Ideology and Social Structure in the Reformation, the Enlightenment, and European Socialism* (Cambridge, MA: Harvard Univ. Press, 1989).

19. Michael North, *Reading 1922: A Return to the Scene of the Modern* (Oxford, UK: Oxford Univ. Press, 1999). As North notes, "Though the copyright date of *Salome* is 1923, reviews make it clear that it was issued late in 1922" (236n164).

20. Hoffman and Sobel, *Through a Glass Darkly*, viii.

21. Jill Lepore, "Historians Who Love Too Much: Reflections on Microhistory and Biography," *Journal of American History* 88, no. 1 (June 2001): 133, 141.

22. Ibid.

1. Character Building

1. Leon Wieseltier, "Intellectuals and Their America, Symposium: Part I," *Dissent* (Winter 2010): 40.

2. Nan Enstad, *Ladies of Labor, Girls of Adventure* (New York: Columbia Univ. Press, 1999).

3. Kathy Peiss, *Cheap Amusements, Working Women and Leisure in Turn-of-the-Century New York* (Philadelphia, PA: Temple Univ. Press, 1986), 62; Janet Floyd, Alison Easton, R. J. Ellis, and Lindsey Traub, *Becoming Visible: Women's Presence in Late Nineteenth-Century America* (Amsterdam: Rodopi, 2010); R. J. Ellis, "People Will Think You Have Struck an Attitude: Fashionable Space in Emma Dunham Kelley-Hawkins' Novels," in Floyd et al., *Becoming Visible*, 186.

4. *Oxford English Dictionary*.

5. Ross Posnock, "Henry James, Veblen and Adorno: The Crisis of the Modern Self," *Journal of American Studies* 21, no. 1 (1987): 46; Ross Posnock, *The Trial of Curiosity: Henry James, William James, and the Challenge of Modernity* (New York: Oxford Univ. Press, 1991), 135.

6. James T. Kloppenberg, *Uncertain Victory: Social Democracy and Progressivism in European and American Thought, 1870–1920* (New York: Oxford Univ. Press, 1986); Louis Menand, *The Metaphysical Club* (New York: Farrar, Straus and Giroux, 2001).

7. Casey Blake, *Beloved Community* (Chapel Hill: Univ. of North Carolina Press, 1990).

8. Dara Horn, "Jewish Surnames [Supposedly] Explained," *Mosaic Magazine*, Jan. 21, 2014.

9. Matthew Frye Jacobson, *Special Sorrows: The Diasporic Imagination of Irish, Polish, and Jewish Immigrants in the United States* (Berkeley: Univ. of California Press, 2002).

10. Matthew Frye Jacobson, "A Ghetto to Look Back To: World of Our Fathers, Ethnic Revival, and the Arc of Multiculturalism," *American Jewish History* 88, no. 4 (Dec. 2000): 463–74; Marcus Klein, "Heritage of the Ghetto," *Nation*, Mar. 27, 1976, 373.

11. Kloppenberg, *Uncertain Victory*, 330. Kloppenberg refers to the 1896 work *Solidarité*, by French philosopher and statesman Léon Bourgeois, stating, "According to Bourgeois, every group of men is either voluntarily or involuntarily an *'ensemble solidaire.'*"

12. Edward Bradford Titchener propounded the term *empathy* in 1909. Sigmund Freud wrote about the concept as early as 1905. Prior to 1900, psychologists generally used the German term *Einfühlung*, or "feeling-into," and in 1759 Adam Smith expounded extensively on "sympathy," "fellow-feeling," "compassion," and related ideas with regard to economic and moral behavior, which he makes clear are equivalent to our modern concept of empathy. Adam Smith, *The Theory of Moral Sentiments* (London: "printed for A. Millar, in the Strand; and A. Kincaid and J. Bell, in Edinburgh," 1759); Louis Agosta, "Empathy and Intersubjectivity," in *Empathy I*, ed. Joseph Lichtenberg, Melvin Bornstein, and Donald Silver (Hillsdale, NJ: Analytic Press, Lawrence Erlbaum Associates, 1984); Edward Bradford Titchener, *Lectures on the Experimental Psychology of the Thought-Processes* (New York: MacMillan, 1909), "Lecture on Introspection and Empathy" reprinted in Edward Bradford Titchener, "Introspection and Empathy: History of Mental Concepts, Crossing Dialogues Association," *Dialogues in Philosophy, Mental and Neuro Sciences* 7, no. 1 (2014), accessed Nov. 2, 1015, http://www.crossingdialogues.com/Ms-E14-01.pdf.

13. Olivia Lang, "Never Hurts to Ask: Review of the Empathy Exams by Leslie Jamison," *New York Times*, Apr. 6, 2014, 26.

14. Lionel Trilling, *The Liberal Imagination* (New York: New York Review of Books, 1950), 46.

15. Ann Mikkelsen, "From Sympathy to Empathy: Anzia Yezierska and the Transformation of the American Subject," *American Literature* 82, no. 2 (2010), 363, 362.

16. Agosta, "Empathy and Intersubjectivity," 44.

17. Robert B. Westbrook, *John Dewey and American Democracy* (Ithaca, NY: Cornell Univ. Press, 1991), 44.

18. Agosta, "Empathy and Intersubjectivity," 60.

19. Arthur Zipser and Pearl Zipser, *Fire and Grace: The Life of Rose Pastor Stokes* (Athens: Univ. of Georgia Press, 1989), 7.

20. Mary V. Dearborn, *Love in the Promised Land* (New York: Free Press, 1988), 39.

21. Benedict Anderson, *Imagined Communities* (London: Verso, 1991).

22. Richard Hofstadter, *The Age of Reform, from Bryan to F.D.R.* (New York: Vintage Books, 1955), 202.

23. Ibid., 238.

24. Ibid.

25. Robert A. Ferguson, *Law and Letters in American Culture* (Cambridge, MA: Harvard Univ. Press, 1984), 11.

26. Ibid.

27. E. J. Hobsbawm, *Nations and Nationalism since 1780* (Cambridge, UK: Cambridge Univ. Press, 1990), 58.

28. Robert H. Wiebe, *The Search for Order, 1877–1920* (New York: Hill and Wang, 1967).

29. Robert Cover, "Obligations: A Jewish Jurisprudence of the Social Order," in *Narrative, Violence, and the Law: The Essays of Robert Cover,* ed. Michael Ryan, Martha Minow, and Austin Sarat (Ann Arbor: Univ. of Michigan Press, 1995), 243.

30. Ibid., 245.

31. Ibid., 241.

32. Louise Levitas Henriksen, *Anzia Yezierska: A Writer's Life* (New Brunswick, NJ: Rutgers Univ. Press, 1988), 154.

33. Floyd, et al. *Becoming Visible*, 1–2.

34. Susan A. Glenn, *Female Spectacle: The Theatrical Roots of Modern Feminism* (Cambridge, MA: Harvard Univ. Press, 2000), 6, 7.

35. Ibid., 5, 6.

36. Ibid.

37. Sander L. Gilman, *Love + Marriage = Death and Other Essays on Representing Difference* (Stanford, CA: Stanford Univ. Press, 1998), 79.

38. Glenn, *Female Spectacle*, 98.

39. Gilman, *Love + Marriage = Death*, 79.

40. Karen Beckman, *Vanishing Women—Magic, Film, and Feminism* (Durham, NC: Duke Univ. Press, 2003).

41. Ibid., 23.

42. Ibid., 19.

43. Nathaniel Hawthorne, *The Scarlet Letter and Other Writings*, Norton Critical Edition (New York: W. W. Norton and Co., 2005).

44. Werner Sollors, *Beyond Ethnicity, Consent and Descent in American Culture* (New York: Oxford Univ. Press, 1986), 166.

45. Flavius Josephus, *Josephus, the Complete Works*, trans William Whiston (Nashville, TN: Thomas Nelson Publishers, 1988), 582.

46. Glenn, *Female Spectacle*, 96, 99.

47. Larry Ceplair, *A Great Lady: A Life of the Screenwriter Sonya Levien* (Lanham, MD: Scarecrow Press, 1996), 63, quoting letter of Clarence Day to Sonya Levien, Aug. 27, 1925.

48. Charles C. Benham, "Jetta Goudal: The Exotic," *Classic Images* 291 (Sept. 1999), accessed Jan. 10, 2007, http://www.classicimages.com/1999/september99/goudal.htm).

49. Mari Jo Buhle, *Women and American Socialism, 1970–1920 (Working Class in American History)* (Urbana: Univ. of Illinois Press, 1983), 320.

50. Anzia Yezierska, *Red Ribbon on a White Horse* (New York: Persea, 1987 [1950]), 87; Nathan Rothman, "An Artist Unfrozen," Margaret Herrick Library, Academy of Motion Picture Arts and Sciences, *Saturday Review of Literature*, Nov. 4, 1950; Stephen Birmingham, *"The Rest of Us": The Rise of America's Eastern European Jews* (1984; Syracuse, NY: Syracuse Univ. Press, 1999), 112.

2. Rose Pastor Stokes Was beyond the Pale

1. Rose Pastor Stokes, *I Belong to the Working Class: The Unfinished Autobiography of Rose Pastor Stokes*, ed. Herbert Shapiro and David L. Sterling (Athens: Univ. of Georgia Press, 1992), 3–4.

2. Hanna Shpayer-Makov, "The Reception of Peter Kropotkin in Britain, 1886–1917," *Albion: A Quarterly Journal Concerned with British Studies* 19, no. 3 (Autumn 1987): 378.

3. Anzia Yezierska, *Bread Givers*, forward and introduction © 1999 by Alice Kessler-Harris (1925; New York: Persea Books, 2003).

4. Arthur Zipser and Pearl Zipser, *Fire and Grace: The Life of Rose Pastor Stokes* (Athens: Univ. of Georgia Press, 1989), 17.

5. Stokes, *I Belong to the Working Class*, 44, 15; Stanley Ray Tamarkin, "Rose Pastor Stokes: The Portrait of a Radical Woman, 1905–1919" (PhD diss., Yale Univ., 1983).

6. Zipser and Zipser, *Fire and Grace*, 21.

7. Ibid., 23.

8. Ibid., 23–25.

9. Tony Michels, *A Fire in Their Hearts: Yiddish Socialists in New York* (Cambridge, MA: Harvard Univ. Press, 2005), 94.

10. Ibid., 106.

11. Ibid., 94.

12. Rose Harriet Pastor, "Views of Settlement Workers: A Talk with Miss Lillian D. Wald," *Jewish Daily News*, 1903, Manuscripts and Archives, Rose Pastor Stokes Papers, Ms 573, Yale Univ. Library.

13. Zipser and Zipser, *Fire and Grace*, 9.

14. Rose Pastor Stokes, *The Woman Who Wouldn't* (New York: G. P. Putnam's Sons, 1916).

15. Patrick Renshaw, "Rose of the World: The Pastor-Stokes Marriage and the American Left, 1905–1925," *New York History: Quarterly Journal of the New York Historical Association* 62, no. 4 (Oct. 1981): 420.

16. Rose Harriet Pastor, "The Views of a Settlement Worker: Talk with J. G. Phelps Stokes," *Jewish Daily News*, 1903, Manuscripts and Archives, Rose Pastor Stokes Papers, Ms 573, Yale Univ. Library.

17. Stokes, *I Belong to the Working Class*, 104; Zipser and Zipser, *Fire and Grace*, 43–44); Bettina Berch, *From Hester Street to Hollywood: The Life and Work of Anzia Yezierska* (New York: Sefer International, 2009), 40; Mary V. Dearborn, *Love in the Promised Land* (New York: Free Press, 1988), 69.

18. Stokes, *I Belong to the Working Class*, xxv–xxvi.

19. Alexander Berkman to Rose Pastor Stokes, Jan. 20, 1913, Yale Univ. Library, Manuscripts and Archives, Rose Pastor Stokes Papers, MS 573, microfilm.

20. "Miss Goldman Upheld as Trial Begins, Her Views Approved at 'Birth Control' Dinner," Manuscripts and Archives, Rose Pastor Stokes Papers, Ms 573, microfilm, Yale Univ. Library; *New York Evening Sun*, Apr. 20, 1916.

21. Rose Pastor Stokes, "The Second Carnegie Hall Meeting," *Mother Earth*, 1916, Manuscripts and Archives, Rose Pastor Stokes Papers, MS 573, microfilm, Yale Univ. Library.

22. Stokes, *I Belong to the Working Class*, xxvii–xxviii, n26.

23. Rose Pastor Stokes, "Rose Pastor Stokes Flays Capitalist Press," "Socialist newspaper in Boston," Feb. 24, 1914, Yale Univ. Library, Manuscripts and Archives, Rose Pastor Stokes Papers, MS 573, microfilm reel 5; Rose Pastor Stokes, letter to the editor, *New York Times*, Nov. 1, 1917, 14.

24. Margaret C. Jones, *Heretics and Hellraisers: Women Contributors to the Masses, 1911–1917* (Austin: Univ. of Texas Press, 1993), 59.

25. Zipser and Zipser, *Fire and Grace*, 136.

26. Stokes, *I Belong to the Working Class*, xiii, from an article by Rose Pastor in the Oct. 9, 1901, issue of the *Jewish Daily News*.

27. Stokes, "The Second Carnegie Hall Meeting."

28. Renshaw, "Rose of the World," 422.

29. Zipser and Zipser, *Fire and Grace*, 77.

30. Ibid.

31. Ibid.

32. Anne C. Rose, *Beloved Strangers: Interfaith Families in Nineteenth-Century America* (Cambridge, MA: Harvard Univ. Press, 2001), 159, quoting James Graham Phelps Stokes, 1925.

33. Zipser and Zipser, *Fire and Grace*, 65n20.

34. David M. Kennedy, *Over Here: The First World War and American Society* (New York: Oxford Univ. Press, 1980), 11.

35. Eric Rauchway, *Blessed among Nations, How the World Made America* (New York: Hill and Wang, 2006), 70.

36. Kennedy, *Over Here*, 24.

37. Benedict Anderson, *Imagined Communities* (1983; London: Verso, 1991).

38. Gary Gerstle, *American Crucible: Race and Nation in the Twentieth Century* (Princeton, NJ: Princeton Univ. Press, 2001), 19.

39. Israel Zangwill, *The Melting Pot* (1909; New York: Macmillan Co., 1914).

40. Gerstle, *American Crucible*, 50–51.

41. Horace M. Kallen, "Democracy Versus the Melting Pot: A Study of American Nationality," *Nation*, Feb. 25, 1915.

42. Randolph S. Bourne, *War and the Intellectuals: Collected Essays 1915–1919*, ed. Carl Resek (Indianapolis, IN: Hackett Publishing Co., 1964), 107.

43. Stokes, *I Belong to the Working Class*, xv, quoting Rose Pastor Stokes, "Kishineffing It," *Jewish Daily News*, June 9, 1903.

44. Flora Merrill, "Women Must Choose 'Babies or Business' Says Noted Author— Wife of Boston Editor," *Boston Sunday Post*, July 5, 1925, Sonya Levien Papers, Huntington Library, San Marino, CA, quoting Pastor Stokes's letter of resignation to the Women's Peace Party, Mar. 17, 1917.

45. Ibid.

46. John Fabian Witt, *Patriots and Cosmopolitans: Hidden Histories of American Law* (Cambridge, MA: Harvard Univ. Press, 2007), 9–10.

47. Bonnie Honig, *Democracy and the Foreigner* (Princeton, NJ: Princeton Univ. Press, 2001), 13.

48. Rose Pastor Stokes, letter to the editor, *New York Times*, Nov. 1, 1917.

49. Rose Pastor Stokes, "A Confession," *Century*, Nov. 1917, excerpted in Zipser and Zipser, *Fire and Grace*, 172–73.

50. Stokes, *I Belong to the Working Class*, xxxi.

51. Milton Friedman, *Capitalism and Freedom* (1962), excerpted in David A. Hollinger and Charles Capper, eds., *The American Intellectual Tradition*, vol. 2, *1865 to the Present* (New York: Oxford Univ. Press, 2006).

52. Harry W. Laidler, Intercollegiate Socialist Society to Rose Pastor Stokes, Sept. 17, 1917, Tamiment Library and Robert F. Wagner Labor Archives, Rose Pastor Stokes Papers.

53. Woodrow Wilson, "President Woodrow Wilson's War Message to Congress," Woodrow Wilson, War Messages, 65th Cong., 1st Sess. Senate Doc. No. 5, Serial No. 7264, 1917, 3–8, passim. (1917).

54. John Reed, *Ten Days That Shook the World* (New York: Boni and Liveright, 1919).

55. Emma Goldman, *My Disillusionment in Russia* (Garden City, NY: Doubleday, Page and Co., 1923); Emma Goldman, *My Further Disillusionment in Russia* (Garden City, NY: Doubleday, Page and Co., 1924).

56. Capper, *The American Intellectual Tradition*, 144.

57. Wilson, "President Woodrow Wilson's War Message to Congress."

58. Ibid.

59. Jane Addams, "Patriotism and Pacifists in War Time," *City Club [of Chicago] Bulletin* 10 (June 16, 1917): 184–90, in Jane Adams Memorial Collection, reel 47-1543-1549, Library, Univ. of Illinois at Chicago.

60. Espionage Act of June 15, 1917, Pub.L 65-24, 40 Stat, 217.

61. Louis Menand, *The Metaphysical Club* (New York: Farrar, Straus and Giroux, 2001), 418.

62. Stokes, *I Belong to the Working Class*, 147.

63. Ibid., 148.

64. Ibid., 146.

65. Zipser and Zipser, *Fire and Grace*, 189; Rose Pastor Stokes, undated note on the unfairness of New York State divorce laws of the 1920s, Manuscripts and Archives, Rose Pastor Stokes Papers, Ms 573, Yale Univ. Library.

66. Rose, *Beloved Strangers*, 157, quoting Rose Pastor Stokes, Mar. 6, 1925.

67. Rose, *Beloved Strangers*, 160, quoting Stokes; Zipser and Zipser, *Fire and Grace*, 256.

68. Keren R. McGinity, *Still Jewish: A History of Women and Intermarriage in America* (New York: New York Univ. Press, 2009), 4.

69. Zipser and Zipser, *Fire and Grace*, 266–67.

70. Louis W. Mack to Rose Pastor Stokes, Oct. 31, 1917, Manuscripts and Archives, Rose Pastor Stokes Papers, Ms 573, Yale Univ. Library.

71. Alice Guy-Blaché and Rose Pastor Stokes, "Shall the Parents Decide?" Rose Pastor Stokes Papers, microfilm, 1917, Tamiment Library and Robert F. Wagner Labor Archives, New York.

72. Stokes, *I Belong to the Working Class*, 147.

73. Ibid., 147.

74. Martin F. Norden, "Alice Guy Blaché, Rose Pastor Stokes, and the Birth Control Film That Never Was," in *Researching Women in Silent Cinema: New Findings and Perspectives*, ed. Victoria Duckett, Monica Dall'Asta, and Lucia Tralli (Bologna, Italy: Department of Arts, Univ. of Bologna, in association with the Victorian College of the Arts, Univ. of Melbourne and Women and Film History International, 2013), 39.

75. Zipser and Zipser, *Fire and Grace*, 180.

76. Ibid., 181.

77. Bourne, *War and the Intellectuals*; Zipser and Zipser, *Fire and Grace*, 181; Randolph S. Bourne, "The War and the Intellectuals," *Seven Arts*, June 1917, 14.

78. Kennedy, *Over Here*, 26.

79. Zipser and Zipser, *Fire and Grace*, 177.

80. Michael P. Donnelly, "Capital Crime and Federal Justice in Western Missouri: Four Cases" (Thesis, Univ. of Missouri, 2001).

81. Ibid.

82. Randolph S. Bourne, "The Collapse of American Strategy," *Seven Arts*, Aug. 1917, in Bourne, *War and the Intellectuals*, 33.

83. Rose Pastor Stokes, letter to the editor, *Kansas City Star*, Mar. 19, 1918.

84. Espionage Act of June 15, 1917.

85. Zipser and Zipser, *Fire and Grace*, 184.

86. Donnelly, "Capital Crime and Federal Justice in Western Missouri," *Stokes v. United States*, *Federal Reporter* 18, 264 (1920); *United States of America v. Rose Pastor Stokes*, Bull. Dept. of Justice 106 (W. D. Mo., 1917), National Archives and Records Administration, Central Plains Region, Kansas City, MO.

87. Stokes, *I Belong to the Working Class*, xxxiv.

88. Honig, *Democracy and the Foreigner*, 97.

89. Zipser and Zipser, *Fire and Grace*, 188. *Stokes v. United States, Federal Reporter* 18, 264 (1920); *United States of America v. Rose Pastor Stokes, Bull. Dept. of Justice* 106 (W. D. Mo., 1917), National Archives and Records Administration, Central Plains Region, Kansas City, MO.

90. Christine Stansell, *American Moderns, Bohemian New York and the Creation of a New Century* (New York: Metropolitan Books, Henry Holt and Co., 2000), 316.

91. Honig, *Democracy and the Foreigner*, 46, 75.

92. Ibid., 84.

93. Stokes, *I Belong to the Working Class*, xxxiii.

94. Donnelly, "Capital Crime and Federal Justice in Western Missouri"; *Stokes v. United States, Federal Reporter* 18, 264 (1920). *United States of America v. Rose Pastor Stokes, Bull. Dept. of Justice* 106 (W. D. Mo., 1917), National Archives and Records Administration, Central Plains Region, Kansas City, MO.

95. Zechariah Chafee, "Freedom of Speech in War Time," *Harvard Law Review* 32, no. 8 (June 1919): 932.

96. Woodrow Wilson, *The New Freedom: A Call for the Emancipation of the Generous Energies of a People* (New York: Doubleday, Page and Co., 1913), excerpted in Stokes, *I Belong to the Working Class*, xxxiv.

97. Louis D. Brandeis, *Other People's Money and How the Bankers Use It* (1913; New York: McClure Publications; Frederick A. Stokes Co.; Martino Publishing, 2009), 46, 47, 48, 51, 92.

98. Stokes, *I Belong to the Working Class*, xxxiv–xxxv.

99. Ibid., xxxv.

100. Clarence Darrow, *The Story of My Life* (New York: Charles Scribner's Sons, 1932; unabridged paperback ed., Da Capo Press, 1996), 69; Zipser and Zipser, *Fire and Grace*, 189–90.

101. Stokes, *I Belong to the Working Class*, xxxvii.

102. Ibid., xxxvii.

103. Eugene V. Debs, "The Canton, Ohio Speech, Anti-War Speech; June 16, 1918," E. V. Debs Internet Archive, 2001, accessed Nov. 3, 2015, http://www.marxists.org/archive/debs/works/1918/canton.htm.

104. Zipser and Zipser, *Fire and Grace*, 193.

105. "When the Pacifist Comes to the Test," *New York Times*, May 25, 1918.

106. *Stokes v. United States*, Federal Reporter 18, 264 (1920); *United States of America v. Rose Pastor Stokes, Bull. Dept. of Justice* 106 (W. D. Mo., 1917), National Archives and Records Administration, Central Plains Region, Kansas City, MO.

107. Schenck v. United States, 249 U.S. 47 (1919).

108. Ibid.

109. Abrams v. United States, 250 U.S. 616 (1919).

110. Ibid.

111. Chafee, "Freedom of Speech in War Time," 958, 960.

112. *Stokes v. United States, Federal Reporter* 18, 264 (1920); *United States of America v. Rose Pastor Stokes, Bull. Dept. of Justice* 106 (W. D. Mo., 1917), National Archives and Records Administration, Central Plains Region, Kansas City, MO.

113. Zipser and Zipser, *Fire and Grace*, 235, 236, 288.

114. Ibid., 237; Cedric J. Robinson, *Black Marxism: The Making of a Black Radical Tradition* (London: Zed Press, 1983; repr., Chapel Hill: Univ. of North Carolina Press, 2000).

115. Mari Jo Buhle, *Women and American Socialism, 1970–1920* (Urbana: Univ. of Illinois Press, 1983), 320–21.

116. Emma Goldman to Sonya Levien, Nov. 6, 1925.

117. Ibid.

118. Zipser and Zipser, *Fire and Grace*, 250, 257, 264, 268.

119. Ibid., 257.

120. Stokes, undated note on the unfairness of New York State divorce laws.

121. Zipser and Zipser, *Fire and Grace*, 280.

122. Ibid., 298.

123. Witt, *Patriots and Cosmopolitans*, 187.

3. Anzia Yezierska Was between the Lines

1. She also changed her reported age whenever it suited her. When she had newly arrived in Hollywood for the filming of her book *"Hungry Hearts,"* a studio publicist was assigned to assist Anzia with press relations. He told her that for publicity purposes she should say that she was about thirty-five. "I'll say I'm about thirty," she instantly replied. She was in fact around forty-two. Anzia Yezierska, *Red Ribbon on a White Horse* (New York: Charles Scribner's Sons, 1950; New York: Persea, 1987), 80. Citations refer to the Persea edition.

2. Shana Alexander, *Happy Days: My Mother, My Father, My Sister and Me* (New York: Doubleday, 1995), 124; Henriksen, *Anzia Yezierska: A Writer's Life*.

3. Bettina Berch, *From Hester Street to Hollywood, The Life and Work of Anzia Yezierska* (New York: Sefer International, 2009), 20.

4. Mary Antin, *The Promised Land* (Boston: Houghton Mifflin Co., 1912).

5. Jacobson, "A Ghetto to Look Back To," 463–74; Marcus Klein, "Heritage of the Ghetto," *Nation*, Mar. 27, 1976, 373.

6. Sholem Aleichem, *Stempenyu: A Jewish Romance*, trans. Hannah Berman (Sweden: Folksbibliotek, 1888; first publication in English by Methuen and Co., London, 1913; Brooklyn, NY: Melville House, 2008).

7. Jan Lisa Huttner, "Everybody's Fiddler: A Researcher Finds a Link—Long Denied—between Chagall and Sholom Aleichem," *Forward*, Sept. 5, 2003.

8. *Bye Bye Birdie* (New York: Columbia Pictures, 1963). Based on the 1960 play by Michael Stewart with music by Charles Strouse and lyrics by Lee Adams.

9. Henriksen, *Anzia Yezierska: A Writer's Life*, 20.

10. Anzia Yezierska, *Bread Givers*, forward and introduction by Alice Kessler-Harris (1925; New York: Persea Books, 2003), 85–88.

11. Carol B. Schoen, *Anzia Yezierska* (Boston: Twayne Publishers, 1982), 7.

12. Henriksen, *Anzia Yezierska: A Writer's Life*, 13–14; Gay Wilentz, introduction to *Salome of the Tenements* by Anzia Yezierska (New York: Boni and Liveright, 1923; Urbana: Univ. of Illinois Press, 1996), x–xi.

13. Andrew S. Dolkart, *Biography of a Tenement House in New York City: An Architectural History of 97 Orchard Street* (Santa Fe, NM: Center for American Places, 2006).

14. Irving Howe, *World of Our Fathers: The Journey of the East European Jews to America and the Life They Found and Made* (New York: Galahad Books, 1976), 110.

15. Anzia Yezierska, *Salome of the Tenements* (Urbana: Univ. of Illinois Press, 1996), 150.

16. Kathy Peiss, *Cheap Amusements: Working Women and Leisure in Turn-of-the-Century New York* (Philadelphia, PA: Temple Univ. Press, 1986), 73.

17. Virginia Woolf, *A Room of One's Own* (London: Hogarth Press, 1929).

18. Thomas Pynchon, *Vineland* (Boston: Little, Brown and Co., 1990).

19. Stokes, *I Belong to the Working Class*, 1992), 104; Zipser and Zipser, *Fire and Grace*, 1989), 43–44; Berch, *From Hester Street to Hollywood*, 40; Dearborn, *Love in the Promised Land*, 69.

20. John Dewey, "My Pedagogic Creed," *School Journal* 54 (Jan. 1897).

21. Jackson Lears, *Rebirth of a Nation: The Making of Modern America, 1877–1920* (New York: HarperCollins, 2009), 237.

22. Dearborn, *Love in the Promised Land*, 32.

23. Anzia Yezierska, *Arrogant Beggar* (New York: Doubleday, Page and Co., 1927; Durham, NC: Duke Univ. Press, 1996).

24. Ibid., 5.

25. Katherine Stubbs, introduction to *Arrogant Beggar* by Anzia Yezierska (Durham, NC: Duke Univ. Press, 1996), xxix.

26. Ibid.

27. Sonya Levien, "The Franks Case Makes Me Wonder," *Hearst's International*, Dec. 1924, Sonya Levien Papers, Huntington Library, San Marino, CA.

28. Yezierska, *Salome of the Tenements*, 43.

29. Robert Cover, "Obligations: A Jewish Jurisprudence of the Social Order," in *Narrative, Violence, and the Law: The Essays of Robert Cover*, ed. Michael Ryan, Martha Minow, and Austin Sarat (Ann Arbor: Univ. of Michigan Press, 1995); Yezierska, *Arrogant Beggar*. Yezierska's unflattering depiction of philanthropists in *Arrogant Beggar* and throughout her fiction proceeds from a tradition exemplified by Melville's satirical presentation of "The Man With Gold Sleeve-Buttons" in *The Confidence Man*. The man with the gold sleeve buttons was said to be a parody of Abbott Lawrence, who with his brother cofounded the textile town of Lawrence, Massachusetts, and donated large sums to Harvard to create the Lawrence Scientific School later attended by William James. Herman Melville, *The Confidence Man, His*

Masquerade (London: Longman, Brown, Green, Longmans, and Roberts, 1857; New York: Penguin Classics, 1990). A classic skewering of an "arrogant beggar" is Charles Dickens's character Harold Skimpole in *Bleak House*.

30. Lears, *Rebirth of a Nation*, 237.

31. Ibid.

32. Blake, *Beloved Community*, 92, referencing Robert Westbrook on John Dewey.

33. Catherine Rottenberg, "Salome of the Tenements: The American Dream and Class Performativity," *American Studies* 45, no. 1 (2004).

34. Sianne Ngai, *Ugly Feelings* (Cambridge, MA: Harvard Univ. Press, 2005), 89.

35. Dearborn, *Love in the Promised Land*, 75.

36. Henriksen, *Anzia Yezierska: A Writer's Life*, 27.

37. Ibid., 35.

38. Ibid., 35–36.

39. Ibid., 40.

40. Dearborn, *Love in the Promised Land*, 76.

41. Henriksen, *Anzia Yezierska: A Writer's Life*, 37.

42. Ibid., 37; Dearborn, *Love in the Promised Land*, 76.

43. Ellen Key, *Love and Marriage*, trans. Arthur G. Chater (New York: G. P. Putnam's Sons, 1911; New York: Source Book Press, 1970).

44. Henriksen, *Anzia Yezierska: A Writer's Life*, 45.

45. Dearborn, *Love in the Promised Land*, 77.

46. Anzia Yezierska to Rose Pastor Stokes, July 25, 1917, Anzia Yezierska Collection, Box 4, Special Collections of the Howard Gotlieb Archival Research Center, Boston Univ. Library.

47. Yezierska, *Salome of the Tenements*, 34.

48. Henriksen, *Anzia Yezierska: A Writer's Life*, 71.

49. Ibid., 69.

50. Ibid.

51. Christine Stansell, *American Moderns: Bohemian New York and the Creation of a New Century* (New York: Henry Holt and Co., 2000), 131.

52. Ibid., 185.

53. Henriksen, *Anzia Yezierska: A Writer's Life*, 139.

54. Ibid., 75.

55. Anzia Yezierska to Rose Pastor Stokes, July 25, 1917, Anzia Yezierska Collection, Box 4, Special Collections of the Howard Gotlieb Archival Research Center, Boston Univ. Library.

56. Henriksen, *Anzia Yezierska: A Writer's Life*, 170.

57. Rose Pastor Stokes, letter to the editor, *New York Times*, Nov. 1, 1917.

58. Rose Pastor Stokes, "A Confession," *Century*, Nov. 1917, excerpted in Zipser and Zipser, *Fire and Grace*, 172–73.

59. Henriksen, *Anzia Yezierska: A Writer's Life*, 123.

60. Ibid.

61. Ibid., 30.

62. Jo Ann Boydston, *The Poems of John Dewey* (Carbondale: Southern Illinois Univ. Press, 1977), 18.

63. Randolph Bourne, "The War and the Intellectuals," *Seven Arts*, June 1917.

64. Bourne, *War and the Intellectuals*.

65. Blake, *Beloved Community*, 159.

66. Bourne, "The War and the Intellectuals."

67. Dearborn, *Love in the Promised Land*, 20.

68. Robert B. Westbrook, "On the Private Life of a Public Philosopher: John Dewey in Love," *Teachers College Record* 96, no. 2 (1994): 184.

69. Ibid.

70. Ibid., 185. Westbrook quotes from John Dewey, letter to William James, Mar. 27, 1903, in *The Thought and Character of William James*, ed. Ralph Barton Perry (Boston: Little, Brown, 1935), 522.

71. Blake, *Beloved Community*, 119.

72. Dearborn, *Love in the Promised Land*, 138.

73. Westbrook, "On the Private Life of a Public Philosopher," 184.

74. Boydston, *The Poems of John Dewey*, 15.

75. Yezierska, *Salome of the Tenements*, 66.

76. Henry James, *The Ambassadors* (Boston: North American Review, 1903; Oxford, UK: Oxford World's Classics, 1998).

77. Ibid., 35.

78. Yezierska, *Red Ribbon on a White Horse*, 109.

79. Ibid., 108.

80. James, *The Ambassadors*, 153.

81. In the 1961 novel *V.*, Thomas Pynchon utilizes the power of a woman's offstage presence to drive the multigenerational plot, which examines philosophy and world politics from pre–World War I through the late 1950s. V, the title character, might or might not have existed, or might have been a conflation of several different individuals, and might or might not ever directly appear within the scene of the novel's action. Yet all of the other characters revolve around her. It appears that Pynchon was mindful of Melville's *The Confidence Man* in exploring this theme. Thomas Pynchon, *V.* (Philadelphia: J. B. Lippincott Co., 1961).

82. Westbrook, "On the Private Life of a Public Philosopher," 193.

83. Yezierska, *Red Ribbon on a White Horse*, 113.

84. Yezierska, *Salome of the Tenements*, 13.

85. Adrian Ross (English lyrics), Lao Silesu (music), and Nilson Fysher (French lyrics), "A Little Love, A Little Kiss" (London: Chapell and Co., 1912).

86. Boydston, *The Poems of John Dewey*, xlv, n55.

87. Dearborn, *Love in the Promised Land*, 121, 119.

88. Boydston, *The Poems of John Dewey*, xlv, n55.

89. Henriksen, *Anzia Yezierska: A Writer's Life*, 121.

90. Westbrook, "On the Private Life of a Public Philosopher," 193.

91. Schoen, *Anzia Yezierska*, 13.

92. Yezierska, *Red Ribbon on a White Horse*, 116.

93. Schoen, *Anzia Yezierska*, 13.

94. Rose, *Beloved Strangers*, 141.

95. Henry James, *The American Scene* (New York: Harper and Brothers, 1907; New York: Penguin Books, 1994), 66, 67.

96. Henriksen, *Anzia Yezierska: A Writer's Life*, 116.

97. Stokes, *I Belong to the Working Class.*

98. Lears, *Rebirth of a Nation*, 1.

99. Lori Harrison-Kahan, "'Drunk with the Fiery Rhythms of Jazz': Anzia Yezierska, Hybridity, and the Harlem Renaissance," *Modern Fiction Studies* 51, no. 2 (2005).

100. Schoen, *Anzia Yezierska*, 13–14.

101. Groucho Marx, *The Groucho Letters: Letters from and to Groucho Marx*, with an introduction by Arthur Sheekman. (New York: Simon and Schuster, 1967), 8.

102. Henriksen, *Anzia Yezierska: A Writer's Life*, 6; Blake, *Beloved Community.*

103. Alice Kessler-Harris, introduction to *Bread Givers* by Anzia Yeziersak (New York: Persea Books, 2003), xi.

104. Andrew Delbanco, *The Real American Dream: A Meditation on Hope* (Cambridge, MA: Harvard Univ. Press, 1999), 5.

105. Thomas Pynchon, *Against the Day* (New York: Viking Penguin, 2006).

106. Vivian Gornick, introduction to *How I Found America* by Anzia Yezierska (New York: Persea Books, 1991), vii.

107. Wilentz, introduction to *Salome of the Tenements*, xii.

108. Boydston, *The Poems of John Dewey*, xxxix; Henriksen, *Anzia Yezierskaa: A Writer's Life*, 123.

109. Boydston, *The Poems of John Dewey*, xxxvi.

110. Norma Rosen, *John and Anzia: An American Romance* (New York: E. P. Dutton, 1989; Syracuse, NY: Syracuse Univ. Press, 1997).

111. Zipser and Zipser, *Fire and Grace*, 220.

112. Anzia Yezierska, "This Is What $10,000 Did to Me," *Cosmopolitan*, Oct. 1925.

113. Henriksen, *Anzia Yezierskaa: A Writer's Life.*

114. Ibid., 149.

115. Ibid.

116. Waldo David Frank, *Our America* (New York: Boni and Liveright, 1919).

117. Anzia Yezierska, *Hungry Hearts* (1920; New York: Penguin Books, 1997), 179; Frank, *Our America.*

118. Blake, *Beloved Community*, 5, 3.

119. Ibid., 8.

120. Julie Altman, "Margaret Naumburg," in *Jewish Women: A Comprehensive Historical Encyclopedia 1 March 2009*, Jewish Women's Archive, Dec. 5, 2009, http://qa.jwa.org /encyclopedia/article/naumburg-margaret.

121. Boydston, *The Poems of John Dewey*; Waldo David Frank, "The Man Who Made Us What We Are," *New Yorker* 2:1926; Waldo David Frank and Alan Trachtenberg, *Memoirs of Waldo Frank* (Boston: Univ. of Massachusetts Press, 1973).

122. Boydston, *The Poems of John Dewey*; Frank, "The Man Who Made Us What We Are"; Frank and Trachtenberg, *Memoirs of Waldo Frank*.

123. Yezierska, *Red Ribbon on a White Horse*, 56.

124. Larry Ceplair, *A Great Lady: A Life of the Screenwriter Sonya Levien* (Lanham, MD: Scarecrow Press, 1996), 58.

125. Yezierska, *Red Ribbon on a White Horse*, 56.

126. Ibid., 59.

127. Yezierska, "This Is What $10,000 Did to Me."

128. Yezierska, *Red Ribbon on a White Horse*, 86.

129. Henriksen, *Anzia Yezierskaa: A Writer's Life*, 140.

130. Alice Guy-Blaché and Rose Pastor Stokes, "Shall the Parents Decide?," New York: Tamiment Library and Robert F. Wagner Labor Archives, Rose Pastor Stokes Papers, microfilm, 1917.

131. Henriksen, *Anzia Yezierskaa: A Writer's Life*, 184–85.

132. Ibid., 174.

133. Ibid.

134. Werner Sollors, *Ethnic Modernism* (Cambridge, UK: Cambridge Univ. Press, 2002; Cambridge, MA: Harvard Univ. Press, 2008), 10; Michael North, *Reading 1922: A Return to the Scene of the Modern* (Oxford, UK: Oxford Univ. Press, 1999). As North notes, "Though the copyright date of *Salome* is 1923, reviews make it clear that it was issued late in 1922" (236n164).

135. Henriksen, *Anzia Yezierskaa: A Writer's Life*, 179.

136. Ibid., 182.

137. Yezierska, *Red Ribbon on a White Horse*, 68.

138. Ibid.

139. Henriksen, *Anzia Yezierskaa: A Writer's Life*, 196.

140. Ibid., 235.

141. Anzia Yezierska to Rose Pastor Stokes, Sept. 15, 1932, Anzia Yezierska Collection, Box 4, Special Collections of the Howard Gotlieb Archival Research Center, Boston Univ. Library.

142. Fyodor Dostoevsky, *Notes from Underground* (1864; Baltimore, MD: BN Publishing, 2009), 17.

143. Ross Posnock, "The Politics of Nonidentity: A Genealogy," *Boundary* 2 19, no. 1 (1992): 36. Later published in *National Identities and Post-Americanist Narratives*, ed. Donald E. Pease (Durham, NC: Duke Univ. Press, 1994).

144. Ross Posnock, "Going Astray, Going Forward: Du Boisian Pragmatism and Its Lineage," in *The Revivial of Pragmatism: New Essays on Social Thought, Law, and Culture*, ed. Morris Dickstein (Durham, NC: Duke Univ. Press, 1999), 178, quoting W. E. B. Du Bois, "My Evolving Program for Negro Freedom," in *What the Negro Wants* (Chapel Hill: Univ. of North Carolina Press, 1944), 57–58.

145. Henriksen, *Anzia Yezierska: A Writer's Life*, 257.

146. Kessler-Harris, introduction to *Bread Givers*, xvii.

147. Ann R. Shapiro, "The Ultimate Shaygets and the Fiction of Anzia Yezierska," *MELUS* 21, no. 2 (Summer 1996).

148. John Dewey, "Nationalizing Education," *Journal of Proceedings and Addresses of the National Education Association* (Washington, DC: National Education Association, 1916), 183; J. Christopher Eisele, "John Dewey and the Immigrants," *History of Education Quarterly* 15, no. 1 (Spring 1975): 72–73.

149. Wilentz, introduction to *Salome of the Tenements*, xi.

150. Blanche H. Gelfant, introduction to *Hungry Hearts*, by Anzia Yezierska (1920; New York: Penguin Books, 1997), xxix.

151. Ibid., xxx.

152. Rosen, *John and Anzia*, 16.

153. Schoen, *Anzia Yezierska*, preface.

154. Henriksen, *Anzia Yezierska: A Writer's Life*, 1.

4. Sonya Levien Was behind the Scene

1. Tony Michels, *A Fire in Their Hearts: Yiddish Socialists in New York* (Cambridge, MA: Harvard Univ. Press, 2005), 11. Historian Tony Michels writes, "Legal restrictions, which tightened or loosened depending on the reigning czar, hindered integration of Jews into Russian society."

2. Yezierska, *Salome of the Tenements*, 37.

3. Ceplair, *A Great Lady*.

4. Daniel T. Rodgers, *Atlantic Crossings: Social Politics in a Progressive Age* (Cambridge, MA: Belknap Press of Harvard Univ. Press, 1998), 20, 1.

5. Kloppenberg, *Uncertain Victory, Social Democracy and Progressivism in European and American Thought*, 207. Kloppenberg convincingly elucidates "the movement of ideas back and forth across the Atlantic."

6. Ibid., 3.

7. Michels, *A Fire in Their Hearts*, 3–5.

8. Ibid. "Contrary to an old misperception, eastern European Jews did not import a pre-existing socialist tradition to the United States," Tony Michels writes. In Russia, "A distinct

movement of Yiddish-speaking Jewish Workers did not come into existence until the mid-1890s, and did not gain a mass following until early in the twentieth century, almost two decades after the Jewish labor movement arose in New York." Beginning in the 1880s, Russian Jewish immigrants on New York's Lower East Side "discovered a thriving socialist labor movement among German (mostly non-Jewish) immigrants, who constituted the majority of the area's population into the 1880s. . . . With their help, Russian Jews created their labor movement in a German image. They experienced an unusual kind of Americanization, one guided not by native-born elites but by a larger, already established immigrant group. Through socialism, Russian Jews did not become so much Americanized as German-Americanized" (3–5).

9. Jackson Lears, "Teddy Roosevelt, Not-So-Great Reformer: What Washington-Focused Liberals Miss About Progressivism," *New Republic*, Mar. 14, 2014.

10. "Stokes Charges Socialist Wing Is Pro-German," *New York Tribune*, May 4, 1917. James Graham Phelps Stokes accused Morris Hillquit of being "Pro-German," noting that the socialist movement in America was of German origin. This was remarkable given that Stokes was himself a vociferous member of the Socialist Party of America at that time. Still, the party officially opposed President Wilson's war effort. The socialists in America also were accused of promoting a separate peace between Russia and Germany that would eliminate Russia's military support of America's allies. Primarily because he supported President Wilson's war effort and the party opposed it, Stokes soon resigned from the Socialist Party of America. His wife, Rose Pastor Stokes, opposed the war effort. This difference caused an irreparable rift in their marriage, which ended in 1925.

11. Hollinger, *Cosmopolitanism and Solidarity*, 162.

12. Merrill, "Women Must Choose 'Babies or Business' Says Noted Author."

13. Yezierska, *Salome of the Tenements*, 83.

14. Ibid., 34.

15. Stokes, *I Belong to the Working Class*, 91.

16. Ibid., 90–91.

17. Merrill, "Women Must Choose 'Babies or Business' Says Noted Author."

18. Stokes, *I Belong to the Working Class*, 104; Zipser and Zipser, *Fire and Grace*, 43–44; Berch, *From Hester Street to Hollywood*, 40; Dearborn, *Love in the Promised Land*, 69.

19. New York State Supreme Court—Appellate Division for the First Judicial Department, *In the Matter of the Application of Sara A. Levien for Admission to the Bar*, Sept. 1909, Sonya Levien Papers, Huntington Library, HM56591.

20. Witt, *Patriots and Cosmopolitans*, 165. Witt writes that "[n]o woman was admitted to practice law in [the] state of New York until 1886. By 1910, there were only 133 women among the 17,000 lawyers across the state, and only 558 women among the more than 114,000 lawyers nationwide. Even as late as 1920, women would make up 5 percent of all physicians and 4.7 percent of all scientists, but only 1.4 percent of all lawyers in the country."

21. Diane Heckert, "Prize-Winning Movie Scripter Tells of Law-to-Writing Switch," *Dayton Daily News*, Nov. 30, 1954, Sonya Levien Papers, Huntington Library, San Marino, CA, 26.

22. Sonya Levien to Phillip Allan Friedman, Dec. 4, 1953, Sonya Levien Papers, Huntington Library, HM56302; Sonya Levien to Phillip Allan Friedman, Dec. 10, 1953, Sonya Levien Papers, Huntington Library, HM56303; Philip Allan Friedman to Sonya Levien, Nov. 19, 1953, Sonya Levien Papers, Huntington Library, HM55988; Philip Allan Friedman to Sonya Levien, Dec. 8, 1953, Sonya Levien Papers, Huntington Library, HM55989; Philip Allan Friedman to Sonya Levien, July 9, 1957, Sonya Levien Papers, Huntington Library, HM55990; Ceplair, *A Great Lady*, 14.

23. Nan Enstad, *Ladies of Labor, Girls of Adventure* (New York: Columbia Univ. Press, 1999), 177; Mary Kingsbury Simkhovich, *The City Worker's World in America* (New York: Macmillan, 1917), 132.

24. Sonya Levien, "The Franks Case Makes Me Wonder," *Hearst's International*, Dec. 1924, Sonya Levien Papers, Huntington Library, San Marino, CA.

25. Dearborn, *Love in the Promised Land*, 94.

26. "672nd Dinner, Twilight Club, Friday, February 27, 1914 at the Aldine Club, the Wages of Shame Vs. The Shame of Wages," New York City, Tamiment Library and Robert F. Wagner Labor Archives, Rose Pastor Stokes Papers, microfilm, Feb. 27, 1914.

27. Sinclair Lewis, *Hike and the Aeroplane* (New York: Frederick A. Stokes Co., 1912).

28. Stansell, *American Moderns*, 130.

29. Ceplair, *A Great Lady*, 12–16.

30. "Mr. Hovey's Life of Morgan," *New York Times*, Feb. 1, 1912. After publishing his biography of J. P. Morgan in 1911, Hovey wrote a letter to the *New York Times* in which he forcefully asserted his ethical standards. "[T]he book was not authorized by Mr. Morgan. . . . May I go on to say that I would never put myself in a position of describing a man's life from his dictation. . . . In writing the book I felt that there was a definite advantage in gathering my material independently, and that is the way in which it was done."

31. Ceplair, *A Great Lady*, 16

32. Sonya Levien, "New York City's Motion Picture Law," *American City*, Oct. 1913, 319–21.

33. Stokes, *I Belong to the Working Class*, 99.

34. Tamarkin, "Rose Pastor Stokes," 11.

35. Nancy J. Rosenbloom, "In Defense of the Moving Pictures: The People's Institute, the National Board of Censorship and the Problem of Leisure in Urban America," *American Studies* 33, no. 2 (Fall 1992): 41.

36. Ibid., 42.

37. Ibid., 52.

38. Ibid., 52, 53.

39. Norden, "Alice Guy Blaché, Rose Pastor Stokes, and the Birth Control Film That Never Was," 32.

40. Ceplair, *A Great Lady*, 20.

41. Ibid.

42. Couzens was offended by Ford's overt anti-Semitism. The two men had a series of disagreements and Couzens eventually left the Ford Motor Company, after having accumulated a vast fortune.

43. "The Ford Bonus to Employees," *New York Times*, Jan. 7, 1914.

44. Reed, *Ten Days That Shook the World*.

45. F. Scott Fitzgerald and Zelda Fitzgerald to "Sonya Hovey" and to "Carl and Sonya Hovey," Sonya Levien Papers, Huntington Library, HM 55974-55978; HM 55979.

46. Ibid.

47. Merrill, "Women Must Choose 'Babies or Business' Says Noted Author." May Sinclair was the pseudonym of British novelist and suffragist Mary Amelia St. Clair.

48. Robert E. Hewes, "Noted Writer in Hollywood, Miss Sonia Levien Here to Join Lasky Studio as Special Playwright, Has Achieved Fame," *Hollywood Daily Citizen*, Dec. 17, 1921, 8, Sonya Levien Papers, Box 32, Huntington Library, San Marino, CA.

49. Alexandra Kropotkin, "To the Ladies," *Liberty*, 1927–43.

50. Mabel Dodge Luhan, *Intimate Memories* (Albuquerque: Univ. of New Mexico Press, 1999; Santa Fe, NM: Sunstone Press, 2008, 125. Luhan writes, "[O]ne Evening, when many artists were present, there had been a great deal of talk about the corrupting influence of money, of trying to please the public taste for money, of the sacred freedom of the artist, and all that, and among them all Carl Hovey was there, listening with a smile on his intelligent lean face. Following that talk I wrote him a letter. He was co-editor of the *Metropolitan Magazine*. This magazine was the most popular, and the most expensively printed and illustrated, ten-cent periodical of the day. . . . So I asked Hovey to come for an Evening and to bring his art editor, Will Bradley, to meet the editors and artists of *The Masses*, a small radical affair that was the very antithesis of the plutocratic *Metropolitan*."

51. Sonya Levien, "Col. Roosevelt in Our Office," *Metropolitan Bulletin*, May 1915, 5, Sonya Levien Papers, Box 35, Huntington Library, San Marino, CA.

52. Sonya Levien, "Milk," 1918, Sonya Levien Papers, Huntington Library, San Marino, CA.

53. Ibid.

54. Ibid.

55. Hewes, "Noted Writer in Hollywood," 8.

56. Ibid.

57. Levien, "Milk."

58. Aviva F. Taubenfeld, *Rough Writing: Ethnic Authorship in Theodore Roosevelt's America* (New York: New York Univ. Press, 2008), 88, quoting a personal letter from Jacob Riis dated 1903.

59. Levien, "Milk."

60. Ibid.

61. Charles Dickens, *Bleak House* (1853; Oxford, UK: Oxford Univ. Press, 1989). In Dickens's *Bleak House* Mrs. Pardiggle is a self-appointed social worker who visits the poor and admonishes them to behave properly and keep clean and sober, strongly implying that they are solely responsible for their own poverty. She ignores or cannot see the squalor of their surroundings, their dire circumstances, and the anguish that they suffer. Esther Summerson responds to the same poor people with empathy and compassion, withholding judgment and offering whatever help she can. Comparing and contrasting these two women, another character, Mr. Jarndyce, remarks that "there were two classes of charitable people; one, the people who did a little and made a great deal of noise; the other, the people who did a great deal and made no noise at all." Here is an ironic inverted echo of Theodore Roosevelt's motto, "Speak softly and carry a big stick." Mrs. Pardiggle is a caricature of a type of heartless social worker depicted in the fiction of Anzia Yezierska.

62. "Calls Roosevelt Ignorant, Mrs. Rose Pastor Stokes Say He Should Learn What Socialism Is," *New York Times,* July 15, 1908; Zipser and Zipser, *Fire and Grace,* 65–66; Edward Allan Brawley, "A Jewish Cinderella," *New York History Review,* Aug. 21, 2010.

63. "Calls Roosevelt Ignorant"; Zipser and Zipser, *Fire and Grace,* 65–66; Brawley, "A Jewish Cinderella."

64. Sonya Levien, "The Great Friend," *Woman's Home Companion,* Oct. 1919, Sonya Levien Papers, Huntington Library, San Marino, CA.

65. Libbian Benedict, "The Story of Sonya Levien, Writer in the Motion Picture Field Whose Experiences Have Been Arduous and Varied," *American Hebrew,* June 19, 1924, Sonya Levien Papers, Huntington Library, San Marino, CA.

66. Taubenfeld, *Rough Writing, Ethnic Authorship,* 47.

67. Ibid., 4.

68. Benedict, "The Story of Sonya Levien."

69. Levien, "The Great Friend."

70. Merrill, "Women Must Choose 'Babies or Business' Says Noted Author."

71. Ibid.

72. Dearborn, *Love in the Promised Land,* 138.

73. Ibid. Dearborn is quoting Yezierska's "Mostly About Myself," from *Children of Loneliness.*

74. Rottenberg, "Salome of the Tenements."

75. This was the case for Jay Gatsby, for whom Daisy represented entrée and acceptance into a higher level on the status hierarchy to which he aspired. Gatsby amasses his fortune and then attempts to hide his shady, criminal associations with the Jewish Meyer Wolfsheim, so that he may move into the social circles to which the Gentile Daisy can provide access. For Daisy, an element of Gatsby's allure arose from the inference that his status as an outsider would have precluded her parents' approval of the match.

76. Merrill, "Women Must Choose 'Babies or Business' Says Noted Author."

77. Ceplair, *A Great Lady*, 29.

78. Ibid.

79. Rose Pastor Stokes to Sonya Levien, Nov. 11, 1917, Sonya Levien Papers, Huntington Library, HM56594.

80. Janiss Garza, "Plot Synopsis—Who Will Marry Me," *Allmovie Guide*, accessed Nov. 3, 2015, www.allmovie.com.

81. Ceplair, *A Great Lady*, 53.

82. Sonya Levien to Rose Pastor Stokes, Dec. 29, 1919, Sonya Levien Papers, Huntington Library, HM56336.

83. Rose Pastor Stokes to Sonya Levien, Oct. 29, 1910, Sonya Levien Papers, Huntington Library, HM56592.

84. Sonya Levien to Rose Pastor Stokes, Oct. 5, 1921.

85. Alida S. Malkus, "She Came to America from Russia: The Story of Sonya Levien," *Success*, Jan. 1925, 57, Sonya Levien Papers, Huntington Library, San Marino, CA.

86. U.S. Department of Labor, Bureau of Labor Statistics, "CPI Inflation Calculator," accessed Nov. 3, 2015, http://www.bls.gov/Data/Inflation_Calculator.htm.

87. Malkus, "She Came to America from Russia," 57.

88. Hewes, "Noted Writer in Hollywood," 8.

89. Henriksen, *Anzia Yezierska: A Writer's Life*, 164.

90. Oliver Wendell Holmes Jr., *The Common Law* (Boston: Little, Brown, and Co., 1881; Cambridge, MA: Harvard Univ. Law School Library, 2003, accessed Nov. 3, 2015, http://library.law.harvard.edu/suites/owh/index.php. Holmes states that every person is "free to break his contract if he chooses," as long as he or she is prepared to pay for the consequences (Lecture 8—Contract. 2—Elements, at 301).

91. Walter Adolphe Roberts, "My Ambitions at 21 and What Became of Them—Anzia Yezierska," *American Hebrew*, Aug. 25, 1922.

92. Malkus, "She Came to America from Russia," 121.

93. Sonya Levien, "My Pilgrimage to Hollywood," *Metropolitan*, Sept. 17, 1922, 36, 114, Sonya Levien Papers, Box 32, Huntington Library, San Marino, CA.

94. Henriksen, *Anzia Yezierska: A Writer's Life*, 171.

95. U.S. Department of Labor, "CPI Inflation Calculator."

96. Sonya Levien, "The Celluloid Prince," *New Yorker*, Apr. 25, 1925, Sonya Levien Papers, Huntington Library, San Marino, CA.

97. Jesse L. Lasky, *I Blow My Own Horn* (New York: Doubleday, 1957), 245.

98. Ceplair, *A Great Lady*, 63, quoting a letter of Clarence Day to Sonya Levien, Aug. 27, 1925.

99. Heckert, "Prize-Winning Movie Scripter."

100. Deborah Dash Moore and Paula Hyman, eds. *Jewish Women in America: An Historical Encyclopedia* (New York: Routledge, 1997), 439.

101. Merrill, "Women Must Choose 'Babies or Business' Says Noted Author."

102. Frank Waters, *Of Time and Change* (Denver, CO: MacMurray and Beck, 1998), 60.

103. Michael Squires, *Living at the Edge: A Biography of D. H. Lawrence and Frieda Von Richtofen* (Madison: Univ. of Wisconsin Press, 2002), 412.

104. Waters, *Of Time and Change*, 143.

105. Edward Jablonski, *Harold Arlen: Rhythm, Rainbows, and Blues* (Boston: Northeastern Univ. Press, 1996), 125.

106. Harpo Marx with Rowland Barber, *Harpo Speaks!* (New York: Bernard Geis Assoc., 1962; New York: Proscenium Publishers, 2000), 353, 354.

107. Tamara Hovey, *Among the Survivors* (New York: Grossman, 1971), 39.

108. Ibid., 38.

109. Benedict, "The Story of Sonya Levien."

110. Malkus, "She Came to America from Russia," 57.

111. Emma Goldman to Sonya Levien, Nov. 6, 1925. Sonya Levien Papers, Huntington Library, HM56011.

112. Ibid.

113. Ceplair, *A Great Lady*, 7.

114. Malkus, "She Came to America from Russia," 121.

115. Honig, *Democracy and the Foreigner*, 77–78. Honig also notes that "exceptionalist accounts of American democracy are inextricably intertwined with the myth of an immigrant America" (74). Familiar immigrant stereotypes are recruited to reinforce idealized values of commitment to hard work, family, community, and democracy, and to elicit nativist feelings of hostility or charity.

116. Ibid., 77.

117. Lisa Botshon, "Anzia Yezierska and the Marketing of the Jewish Immigrant in 1920s Hollywood," in *Middlebrow Moderns: Popular Women Writers of the 1920s*, ed. Meredith Goldsmith and Lisa Botshon (Boston: Northeastern Univ. Press, 2003), 220.

118. Levien, "My Pilgrimage to Hollywood," 114.

119. Ceplair, *A Great Lady*; Hovey, *Among the Survivors*.

120. "M-G-M," *New York Times*, Oct. 11, 1947; "Bruce Manning," *New York Times*, June 26, 1948; "Metro's 'That Midnight Kiss' Introduces Mario Lanza to Film Fans at Capitol," *New York Times*, Sept. 23, 1949.

121. Ross, Silesu, and Fysher, "A Little Love, A Little Kiss."

122. Lasky, *I Blow My Own Horn*, 267.

123. Esther Hovey, "The Genesis of Serge Hovey's the Robert Burns Songbook," *Studies in Scottish Literature* 30, no. 1 (1998).

124. Heckert, "Prize-Winning Movie Scripter."

125. Luhan, *Intimate Memories*, 125.

126. Ross Posnock, *The Trial of Curiosity: Henry James, William James, and the Challenge of Modernity* (New York: Oxford Univ. Press, 1991), 228.

5. Jetta Goudal Was the Forbidden Woman

1. Aart C. Liefbroer, Hanna van Solinge, and Frans van Poppel, "Joden in Nederland," *Demos* 17 (Oct./Nov. 2001): 77–80.

2. Susan A. Glenn, *Female Spectacle: the Theatrical Roots of Modern Feminism* (Cambridge, MA: Harvard Univ. Press, 2000), 219.

3. Robert Gottlieb, *Sarah: The Life of Sarah Bernhardt* (New Haven: Yale Univ. Press, 2010).

4. Maurice Goudeket, *Close to Colette: An Intimate Portrait of a Woman of Genius* (New York: Farrar, Straus and Cudahy, 1957).

5. John Kobal, "John Kobal Interview with Jetta Goudal," Jan. 2, 1982, from the private collection of Kevin Brownlow. John Kobal was an eminent film historian who died in 1991. Kobal bequeathed his extensive collection of photographic negatives and fine art photographs of Hollywood subjects to the John Kobal Foundation. Kobal interviewed Jetta Goudal in 1982, but this interview is not in the possession of the John Kobal Foundation. A transcript of this interview is held in the private collection of Kevin Brownlow. Brownlow also is an eminent film historian, author, and filmmaker, and founder and principal of Photoplay Productions, a British company that preserves an extensive archive of silent films and produces documentaries.

6. "Fokker Flies over City," *New York Times*, July 23, 1921.

7. "Business Women of State Convene: Mrs. Marlan Booth Kelley Elected President at Third Annual Meeting of Federation, Mayor Sends His Greeting, Predicts Benefits from Active Feminine Participation in Public Affairs," *New York Times*, May 28, 1922.

8. Ibid.

9. Ibid.

10. Jeff Hirsh, *Images of America: Manhattan Hotels, 1880–1920* (Charleston, SC: Arcadia Publishing, 1997), 90.

11. Norval White and Elliot Willensky, *A.I.A. Guide to New York City*, 4th ed. (New York: Three Rivers Press, 2000), 212.

12. "Martha Washington Hotel," Library Collections: Hotel Files, George B. Corsa Hotel Collection, New-York Historical Society Museum and Library, New York; "Martha Washington Hotel Designation Report," Landmarks Preservation Commission, City of New York, June 12, 2012, Designation List 456, Amended Landmark Site, June 19, 2012, Designation List 456a, LP-2428.

13. "Martha Washington Hotel Designation Report."

14. Building permit Nb# 1224, Manhattan New Building Database, Office for Metropolitan History, New York, accessed Nov. 4, 2015, www.metrohistory.com.

15. "Martha Washington Hotel Designation Report."

16. "Property Profile Overview, Manhattan 10016," Bin #1080777, 29 East 29 Street, 27–31 East 29 Street, 30 East 30 Street, Record #Nb 1224-01, Tax Block: 859, Tax Lot: 26, New York City Department of Buildings.

17. "Midtown Hotel Sold at Auction," *New York Times*, Aug. 9, 1933; "Martha Washington Hotel Designation Report."

18. "Martha Washington Hotel Designation Report."

19. Ibid.

20. Ibid.

21. David Huyssen, *Progressive Inequality: Rich and Poor in New York, 1890–1920* (Cambridge, MA: Harvard Univ. Press, 2014), 64–65, 86–87.

22. Ibid.

23. "Martha Washington Hotel Designation Report."

24. "Women's Hotel Opens," *New York Times*, Feb. 4, 1903.

25. "Form a Suffrage Party: New Organization Perfected at Martha Washington," *New York Times*, Jan. 16, 1910.

26. "Women's Hotel Opens."

27. Ibid.

28. Louise Brooks, *Lulu in Hollywood* (1974; Minneapolis: Univ. of Minnesota Press, 2000), 16.

29. Yezierska, *Salome of the Tenements*, 162–63.

30. Henriksen, *Anzia Yezierska: A Writer's Life*, 175; Dearborn, *Love in the Promised Land*, 151.

31. Charles C. Benham, "Jetta Goudal: The Exotic," *Classic Images* 291 (Sept. 1999).

32. "Complaint," Jetta Goudal v. Distinctive Pictures Corporation, Appelate Divison of the Supreme Court of New York, 215 App. Div. 674, 212 N.Y.S. 818 (Oct. 1925), 2, Archives of the New York County Clerk.

33. Ibid.

34. Ibid., 3.

35. "Answer," *Jetta Goudal v. Distinctive Pictures Corporation*, 4.

36. Ibid., 2.

37. Holmes, *The Common Law*, lecture 8.

38. Grant Gilmore, *The Death of Contract* (1974; Columbus, OH: Ohio State Univ. Press, 1995), 72. Legal scholar Grant Gilmore called the first *Restatement of Contracts*, published in 1932, "uneasily poised between past and future," because its drafters were caught in debates between classical legal theory and emerging legal realism.

39. Karen Orren, *Belated Feudalism: Labor, the Law, and Liberal Development in the United States* (Cambridge, UK: Cambridge Univ. Press, 1991).

40. Ibid., 70, 74.

41. Ibid.

42. Wiebe, *The Search for Order*, 43.

43. Amy Dru Stanley, *From Bondage to Contract: Wage Labor, Marriage, and the Market in the Age of Slave Emancipation* (New York: Cambridge Univ. Press, 1998), 82.

44. Ibid., 83.

45. Sollors, *Beyond Ethnicity*.

46. Stanley, *From Bondage to Contract*.

47. Morton J. Horwitz, *The Transformation of American Law, 1870–1960* (New York: Oxford Univ. Press, 1992), 51.

48. Ibid., 49.

49. Ibid.

50. "Memorandum On Behalf of the Defendant in support of a Motion to Strike out Certain Matter in the Complaint," *Jetta Goudal v. Distinctive Pictures Corporation*, 21.

51. "Makin' Whoopee," lyrics by Gus Kahn, music by Walter Donaldson (N.p.: Donaldson Publishing Co., 1928).

52. Holmes, *The Common Law*.

53. Mark Twain, "The Privilege of the Grave (1905)," *New Yorker*, Dec. 22 and 29, 2008.

54. "Agreement between Distinctive Pictures Corporation and Jetta Goudal" (Oct. 22, 1923). This agreement is included as "Exhibit A, Attached to Complaint," in Jetta Goudal v. Distinctive Pictures Corporation, Appelate Divison of the Supreme Court of New York, 215 App. Div. 674, 212 N.Y.S. 818 (Oct. 1925).

55. *Jetta Goudal v. Distinctive Pictures Corporation*, Order issued by Hon. Francis B. Delehanty, Justice, New York Supreme Court, County of New York, Special Term—Part I (May 1, 1924).

56. Simon Louvish, *Cecil B. DeMille: A Life in Art* (New York: St. Martin's Press, 2007), 56; A. Scott Berg, *Goldwyn: A Biography* (New York: Alfred A. Knopf, 1989), 44.

57. Cecil B. DeMille, *The Autobiography of Cecil B. DeMille*, ed. Donald Hayne (Englewood Cliffs, NJ: Prentice-Hall, 1959), 58.

58. Louvish, *Cecil B. DeMille: A Life in Art*, 43.

59. DeMille, *The Autobiography of Cecil B. DeMille*, 68.

60. Levien, "The Celluloid Prince."

61. Peter F. Boller and John George, *They Never Said It: A Book of Fake Quotes, Misquotes and Misleading Attributions* (Oxford, UK: Oxford Univ. Press 1989), 42; Berg, *Goldwyn: A Biography*, 113.

62. Robert S. Birchard, *Cecil B. DeMille's Hollywood* (Lexington: Univ. of Kentucky Press, 2004), 89.

63. Yezierska, *Salome of the Tenements*, 24.

64. Benham, "Jetta Goudal: The Exotic."

65. Glenn, *Female Spectacle*.

66. Florence Lawrence, "'Last Laugh' Is Unique Example of Cinema Art; Jetta Goudal Meets Test," *Los Angeles Examiner*, Mar. 9, 1925.

67. "Salome of Tenements Big Rialto Feature," *Atlanta Constitution*, Mar. 1, 1925.

68. "Hundreds Throng Gigantic Setting," *New York Times*, Dec. 7, 1924.

69. Malkus, "She Came to America from Russia," 57.

70. Ibid.

71. Merrill, "Women Must Choose 'Babies or Business' Says Noted Author."

72. "Jetta Goudal, 'Cocktail of Temperament,'" *New York Morning Telegraph*, May 22, 1927.

73. "Miss Rambova, 69, Film Figure, Dead—2d Wife of Valentino—Was Ballerina and Columnist," *New York Times*, June 8, 1966.

74. Robert Oberfirst, *Rudolph Valentino: The Man Behind the Myth* (New York: Citadel Press, 1962), 329.

75. Ibid.

76. Alan Arnold, *Valentino* (New York: Library Publishers, 1954), 110–11.

77. Oberfirst, *Rudolph Valentino*, 240.

78. Natacha Rambova, *Rudy: An Intimate Portrait of Rudolph Valentino by His Wife Natacha Rambova* (London: Hutchinson and Co., 1926), 133.

79. Arnold, *Valentino*, 111.

80. Rudolph Valentino, *The Intimate Journal of Rudolph Valentino* (New York: William Faro, 1931), 181.

81. "Miss Rambova, 69, Film Figure, Dead."

82. Reporter's Transcript, *Jetta Goudal v. Cecil B. DeMille Pictures Corporation*, 455, District Court of Appeal, Second Appellate District, State of California, Division 2; 118, Cal. App. 407 (Cal. Ct. App. 1931); Appellate Court Case #2Civ6752, On appeal from Jetta Goudal vs. Cecil B. De Mille Pictures Corporation, Case No. 243415, Superior Court of the State of California, in and for the County of Los Angeles, Department 31. The Reporter's Transcript is that section of the documentation that contains the court stenographer's record of testimony of witnesses. The Clerk's Transcript contains pleading papers, including Complaints, Answers, Motions, and Judgments. Full transcripts and documentation of these cases provided by the California State Archives of the Office of the Secretary of State.

83. Anthony Slide, *Silent Players: A Biographical and Autobiographical Study of 100 Silent Film Actors and Actresses* (Lexington: Univ. Press of Kentucky, 2002), 149.

84. Jetta Goudal v. Famous Players–Lasky Corporation, Case No. 166251 (Mar. 27, 1925), Superior Court of the State of California in and for the County of Los Angeles.

85. Benham, "Jetta Goudal: The Exotic."

86. Ibid.

87. Frank "Junior" Coghlan, *They Still Call Me Junior* (Jefferson, NC: McFarland and Co., 1993), 27.

88. Nan Enstad, *Ladies of Labor, Girls of Adventure* (New York: Columbia Univ. Press, 1999), 163.

89. Ibid., 165.

90. Ibid., 162.

91. Sumiko Higashi, *Cecil B. DeMille and American Culture: The Silent Era* (Berkeley: Univ. of California Press, 1994), 1.

92. Elizabeth Ewen, *Immigrant Women in the Land of Dollars* (New York: Monthly Review Press, 1985), 223.

93. Higashi, *Cecil B. DeMille and American Culture*, 2.

94. Paula E. Hyman, *Gender and Assimilation in Modern Jewish History: The Roles and Representation of Women* (Seattle: Univ. of Washington Press, 1995), 94.

95. Higashi, *Cecil B. DeMille and American Culture*, 199.

96. Ibid., 200.

97. Jesse L. Lasky, *I Blow My Own Horn* (New York: Doubleday, 1957).

98. Reporter's Transcript, *Jetta Goudal v. Cecil B. DeMille Pictures Corporation*, 457.

99. Ceplair, *A Great Lady*, 67.

100. Reporter's Transcript, *Jetta Goudal v. Cecil B. DeMille Pictures Corporation*, 437.

101. Ibid., 106–7.

102. Ibid., 136.

103. Louvish, *Cecil B. DeMille: A Life in Art*, 6.

104. Coghlan, *They Still Call Me Junior*, 29.

105. Reporter's Transcript, *Jetta Goudal v. Cecil B. DeMille Pictures Corporation*, 73. The quotations from the August 23 meeting are all from the Reporter's Transcript.

106. Ibid., 500.

107. Ibid., 80.

108. Ibid., 66.

109. Reporter's Transcript on Appeal, *Jetta Goudal v. Cecil B. DeMille Pictures Corporation*, 463, 491, 499.

110. Western Union Telegram to Miss Jetta Goudal at the Ambassador Hotel, Los Angeles, CA, from Cecil B. De Mille, Apr. 4, 1926; Reporter's Transcript on Appeal, *Jetta Goudal v. Cecil B. DeMille Pictures Corporation*, 595.

111. Reporter's Transcript on Appeal, *Jetta Goudal v. Cecil B. DeMille Pictures Corporation*, 166.

112. Patrick Fraser, *Treatise on Master and Servant, Employer and Workman, and Master and Apprentice According to the Laws of Scotland*, 3rd ed. updated by William Campbell (1846; 1872; Edinburgh: T. and T. Clark, 1882), 71, 72, quoted in Appellant's Opening Brief, *Jetta Goudal v. Cecil B. DeMille Pictures Corporation*, 31.

113. Ibid., 71.

114. Reporter's Transcript, *Jetta Goudal v. Cecil B. DeMille Pictures Corporation*, 98, para. 292. The following information about this court appearance is from the Reporter's Transcript, 101, 254, 106, 153.

115. Glenn, *Female Spectacle*, 109.

116. Reporter's Transcript, *Jetta Goudal v. Cecil B. DeMille Pictures Corporation*, 131.

117. Appellate Brief, *Jetta Goudal v. Cecil B. DeMille Pictures Corporation*, 4.

118. Reporter's Transcript, *Jetta Goudal v. Cecil B. DeMille Pictures Corporation*, 206.

119. Ibid., 46, 106, 107.

120. Exhibit "A," *Jetta Goudal v. Cecil B. DeMille Pictures Corporation*, 3.

121. Reporter's Transcript, *Jetta Goudal v. Cecil B. DeMille Pictures Corporation*, 142.

122. Ibid., 144.

123. Ibid., 75.

124. Exhibit "A," *Jetta Goudal v. Cecil B. DeMille Pictures Corporation*.

125. Reporter's Transcript, *Jetta Goudal v. Cecil B. DeMille Pictures Corporation*, 206.

126. Ibid., 185.

127. Birchard, *Cecil B. DeMille's Hollywood*, 273.

128. Reporter's Transcript, *Jetta Goudal v. Cecil B. DeMille Pictures Corporation*, 435.

129. DeMille, *The Autobiography of Cecil B. DeMille*, 273–74.

130. Birchard, *Cecil B. DeMille's Hollywood*; DeMille, *The Autobiography of Cecil B. De-Mille*, 234.

131. Louvish, *Cecil B. DeMille: A Life in Art*, 282.

132. Ibid.

133. Higashi, *Cecil B. DeMille and American Culture*, 201.

134. DeMille, *The Autobiography of Cecil B. DeMille*, 290.

135. Trial Court Findings of Fact and Conclusions of Law, Paragraph XVI, Appellant's Opening Brief, *Jetta Goudal v. Cecil B. DeMille Pictures Corporation*, 59.

136. Appellate Opinion, *Jetta Goudal v. Cecil B. DeMille Pictures Corporation*, Nov. 19, 1931, 8.

137. Ibid., 9, 5.

138. Reporter's Transcript, *Jetta Goudal v. Cecil B. DeMille Pictures Corporation*.

139. Ibid., 458–59.

140. Appellate Opinion, *Jetta Goudal v. Cecil B. DeMille Pictures Corporation*, 3.

141. Ibid., 3, 4.

142. Stokes, *I Belong to the Working Class*, xiii, from an article by Rose Pastor in the Oct. 9, 1901, issue of the *Jewish Daily News*.

143. Yezierska, *How I Found America* (New York: Persea Books, 1991), 115.

144. Sean P. Holmes, "No Room for Manoeuvre: Star Images and the Regulation of Actors' Labour in Silent Era Hollywood," in *Working in the Global Film and Television Industries*, ed. Andrew Dawson and Sean P. Holmes (New York: Bloomsbury Academic, 2012), 85.

145. Paul C. Weiler, *Entertainment Media and the Law: Text Cases Problems*, 3rd ed. American Casebook Series (St. Paul, MN: Thomson/West, 2006), 720.

146. Holmes, "No Room for Manoeuvre," 85.

147. Anthony Slide interview with Jetta Goudal, 1979, transcript in the Oral History of the New York Motion Picture Industry collection of the Museum of the Moving Image, New York.

148. *Jetta Goudal v. Cecil B. DeMille Pictures Corporation*.

149. U.S. Department of Labor, Bureau of Labor Statistics, "CPI Inflation Calculator," accessed Nov. 4, 2015, http://www.bls.gov/Data/Inflation_Calculator.htm.

150. Kobal, "John Kobal Interview with Jetta Goudal," Jan. 2, 1982.

151. DeMille, *The Autobiography of Cecil B. DeMille*, 269.

152. Ibid.

153. *Lochner v. New York*, 198 U.S. 45 (1905).

154. Alice Kessler-Harris, *A Woman's Wage: Historical Meanings and Social Consequences* (Lexington: Univ. Press of Kentucky, 1990), 38–40.

155. Birchard, *Cecil B. DeMille's Hollywood*, 375; Louvish, *Cecil B. DeMille: A Life in Art*, 435.

156. Jetta Goudal to "My Dear Messmore," Apr. 16, 1928, sent on stationary of the Ambassador Hotel, Los Angeles, Margaret Herrick Library of the Academy of Motion Picture Arts and Sciences, Jetta Goudal Papers.

157. Benham, "Jetta Goudal: The Exotic."

158. Buhle, *Women and American Socialism*, 320.

159. Yezierska, *Red Ribbon on a White Horse*, 87; Nathan Rothman, "An Artist Unfrozen," *Saturday Review of Literature*, Nov. 4, 1950; Birmingham, *"The Rest of Us,"* 112.

160. Sean P. Holmes, "The Hollywood Star System and the Regulation of Actors' Labor, 1916–1934," *Film History* 12, no. 1 (2000): 107–8, 114.

161. Goudal, Jetta v. MGM Case #58, June 26, 1930, Statement of Jetta Goudal before the Actors Adjustment Committee, Academy of Motion Picture Arts and Sciences Collection, Conciliation Committee Files, Margaret Herrick Library, Los Angeles, CA.

162. *Goudal, Jetta vs. MGM Case #58*, Aug. 8, 1930; Holmes, "No Room for Manoeuvre."

163. Slide, *Silent Players*, 150.

164. Ibid.

165. Jetta Goudal speech at a general meeting of the Actors Equity Association, transcript titled "MEETING HELD AT WOMEN'S CLUB OF HOLLYWOOD, THURSDAY, JUNE 27, 1929, 8:30P.M." contained in the Actors' Equity Association Records, WAG.011 Series II: Foundations of Actors' Equity, 1913–1933, Box 3, folder 20, Tamiment Library and Robert F. Wagner Labor Archives, New York Univ. Library.

166. "Jetta Goudal," *An Encyclopedic Dictionary of Women in Early American Films, 1895–1930* (Binghamton, NY: Haworth Press, 2005).

167. Benham, "Jetta Goudal: The Exotic."

168. Yezierska, *Salome of the Tenements*, 106.

169. Gilman, *Love + Marriage = Death and Other Essays on Representing Difference* (Stanford, CA: Stanford Univ. Press, 1998), 48.

170. Stansell, *American Moderns*, 302.

171. Reporter's Transcript, *Jetta Goudal v. Cecil B. DeMille Pictures Corporation*.

172. Mary Pickford to Jetta Goudal, Nov. 15, 1971, Jetta Goudal Papers, Margaret Herrick Library of the Academy of Motion Picture Arts and Sciences.

173. Higashi, *Cecil B. DeMille and American Culture*, 3.

174. Ibid.

175. Ibid.

176. Ibid.

177. Henriksen, *Anzia Yezierska: A Writer's Life*, 167.

178. Ibid., 149.

179. Dave Kehr, "An Independent Woman, Nobly Suffering in Silents," *New York Times*, Mar. 11, 2010.

180. Boller and George, *They Never Said It*, 42; Berg, *Goldwyn: A Biography*, 113.

181. Wilder, *Sunset Boulevard*.

182. Louvish, *Cecil B. DeMille: A Life in Art*, 392.

183. Levien, "My Pilgrimage to Hollywood," 36.

184. Benham, "Jetta Goudal: The Exotic."

185. Ibid.

186. Henry James, *The Princess Casamassima* (1886; London: Everyman's Library, 1991), 66.

187. Stanley, *From Bondage to Contract*, 20.

6. Novel Approaches

1. North, *Reading 1922*, 105.

2. Enstad, *Ladies of Labor, Girls of Adventure*, 162.

3. Buhle, *Women and American Socialism*, 320.

4. "Cinderella Story of a Servant Girl," *Cedar Rapids Evening Gazette*, Mar. 5, 1921.

5. Dearborn, *Pocahontas's Daughters: Gender and Ethnicity in American Culture* (New York: Oxford Univ. Press, 1986), 122.

6. McGinity, *Still Jewish*, 23.

7. Jeremy Dauber, *The Worlds of Sholem Aleichem* (New York: Random House, 2013), 334.

8. Yezierska, *Salome of the Tenements*, 132.

9. Josephus, *Josephus, the Complete Works*, 582.

10. Glenn, *Female Spectacle*, 96, 99.

11. Ibid.

12. Ibid., 97–98.

13. Schoen, *Anzia Yezierska*, 39.

14. Natalie Friedman, "Marriage and the Immigrant Narrative: Anzia Yezierska's Salome of the Tenements," *Legacy* 22, no. 2 (2005): 184.

15. Ann R. Shapiro, "The Ultimate Shaygets and the Fiction of Anzia Yezierska," *MELUS* 21, no. 2 (Summer 1996).

16. John Dewey, "The Ethics of Democracy," in *Pragmatism: A Reader*, ed. Louis Menand (1888; New York: Vintage Books, 1997), 182.

17. Meredith Goldsmith, "The Coming of Age of a Jewish Female Intellectual, Anzia Yezierska's Red Ribbon on a White Horse," in *The New York Public Intellectuals and Beyond: Exploring Liberal Humanism, Jewish Identity, and the American Protest Tradition*, ed. Ethan Goffman and Daniel Morris (West Lafayette, IN: Purdue Univ. Press, 2009), 180.

18. Enstad, *Ladies of Labor*, 29; Rose Pastor, "Just between Us Girls," *Yiddishes Tageblatt*, Dec. 27, 1903.

19. Jennifer J. Baker, *Securing the Commonwealth* (Baltimore, MD: Johns Hopkins Univ. Press, 2005), 4.

20. Ibid., 23.

21. Wharton, *The House of Mirth*.

22. Leo Tolstoy, *Anna Karenina*, trans. Amy Mandelker (1877; New York: Barnes and Noble, 2003), 199.

23. Ibid., 632.

24. Edith Wharton took the title for her novel from the passage in Ecclesiastes 7:3–4, which states that "the heart of fools is in the house of mirth."

25. Schoen, *Anzia Yezierska*, 39.

26. Tolstoy, *Anna Karenina*, 261, 264.

27. Ibid., 331.

28. Wharton, *The House of Mirth*, 39.

29. Henriksen, *Anzia Yezierska: A Writer's Life*, 37; Dearborn, *Love in the Promised Land*, 76.

30. Friedman, "Marriage and the Immigrant Narrative," 184.

31. Ibid., 176.

32. Gertrude Atherton, "Fighting Up from the Ghetto," *New York Herald*, Jan. 7, 1923.

33. Ibid.

34. Ibid.

35. Friedman, "Marriage and the Immigrant Narrative," 184.

36. Thomas J. Ferraro, *Ethnic Passages: Literary Immigrants in Twentieth-Century America* (Chicago: Univ. of Chicago Press, 1993), 56.

37. Henriksen, *Anzia Yezierska: A Writer's Life*, 188, 195; Alexander, *Happy Days*, 139.

38. North, *Reading 1922*, 100.

39. Roberts, "My Ambitions at 21 and What Became of Them."

40. Tolstoy, *Anna Karenina*, 273.

41. Alexander, *Happy Days*.

42. Leo Tolstoi, *The Journal of Leo Tolstoi*, trans. Rose Strunsky (New York: A. A. Knopf, 1917).

43. Friedman, "Marriage and the Immigrant Narrative," 183.

44. Cynthia Griffin Wolff draws a connection between Sim Rosedale and the Rothschilds. Wharton might have had the Rothschilds in mind in naming her fictional Jewish landlord. Wolff, introduction to *The House of Mirth*, xxv. In 1891 Simon Rosendale, born in Albany, became the New York State attorney general, the first Jew elected to statewide public office in New York. His career continued for decades after that. Howe, *World of Our Fathers*, 367. The similarity of the name and the correspondence in time with the writing careers of Wharton and Yezierska of the real Simon Rosendale permit a question of whether

Wharton or Yezierska or both drew upon Rosendale's name when naming the characters Sim Rosedale or Benjamin Rosenblat.

45. Tolstoy, *Anna Karenina*, 297, 331.

46. Andrew Delbanco, "American Literature: A Vanishing Subject?" *Daedalus*, Mar. 22, 2006, 8, 13, 14, 15.

47. Schoen, *Anzia Yezierska*, 48.

48. Goldsmith, "The Coming of Age of a Jewish Female Intellectual," 189.

49. Henry James, *The American Scene* (New York: Penguin Books, 1994), 9, 10. First published in 1907, New York: Harper and Brothers.

50. Aviva F. Taubenfeld, *Rough Writing, Ethnic Authorship in Theodore Roosevelt's America* (New York: New York Univ. Press, 2008). Taubenfeld writes of Jacob Riis, "Deliberately straddling the old and new genres of sentimentalism and journalistic realism" (54). I believe the statement also is applicable to Anzia Yezierska.

51. Hofstadter, *The Age of Reform*, 198.

52. Moses Rischin, introduction to *The Spirit of the Ghetto (1902)*, by Hutchins Hapgood, ed. Moses Rischin (Cambridge, MA: Belknap Press of Harvard Univ. Press, 1967), xxx.

53. Taubenfeld, *Rough Writing*, 54.

54. Hofstadter, *The Age of Reform*, 190n2.

55. Yezierska, *Red Ribbon on a White Horse*, 45.

56. Ibid., 68.

57. Hofstadter, *The Age of Reform*, 190n2.

58. Schoen, *Anzia Yezierska*, 48.

59. Donald Pizer, "The Naturalism of Edith Wharton's *The House of Mirth*," *Twentieth Century Literature* 41, no. 2 (Summer 1995). Pizer is quoting Blake Nevius.

60. Katherine Stubbs, introduction to *Arrogant Beggar*, by Anzia Yezierska (Durham, NC: Duke Univ. Press, 1996), xvii. First published in 1927 by Doubleday, Page and Co.

61. Friedman, "Marriage and the Immigrant Narrative," 184.

62. North, *Reading 1922*, 106.

63. Sollors, *Ethnic Modernism*; Delia Caparoso Konzett, *Ethnic Modernisms, Anzia Yezierska, Zora Neale Hurston, Jean Rhys, and the Aesthetics of Dislocation* (New York: Palgrave Macmillan, 2002).

64. Botshon, "Anzia Yezierska and the Marketing of the Jewish Immigrant in 1920s Hollywood," 203–26.

65. Brooks E. Hefner, "'Slipping Back into the Vernacular': Anzia Yezierska's Vernacular Modernism," *MELUS* 36, no. 3 (Fall 2011).

66. Lori Harrison-Kahan, "'Drunk with the Fiery Rhythms of Jazz': Anzia Yezierska, Hybridity, and the Harlem Renaissance," *Modern Fiction Studies* 51, no. 2 (2005): 417.

67. North, *Reading 1922*, 103.

68. Griffin, introduction to *The House of Mirth*, xii.

69. Ibid., xvi.

70. Ibid., xvii. Wolff writes, "In *Psychoanalytic Explorations in Art*, the distinguished psychiatrist Ernst Kris writes: 'Aesthetic creation, as Dewey has convincingly set forth in *Art as Experience*, may be looked on as a type of problem-solving behavior.'"

71. Kristian Berg, *American Passages: A Literary Survey 09: Social Realism*, videorecording (Burlington, VT: Annenberg Media, 2003), Learner.org, Oregon Public Broadcasting with Annenberg Foundation–Corporation for Public Broadcasting.

72. Tolstoy, *Anna Karenina*, 336.

73. Wharton, *The House of Mirth*, 38.

74. Ibid., 99.

75. Ibid., 39.

76. Irene Billeter Sauter, *New York City, 'Gilt Cage' or 'Promised Land'?: Representations of Urban Space in Edith Wharton and Anzia Yezierska* (Bern, Switzerland: Peter Lang AG, 2011).

77. Walter Adolphe Roberts, *Pierre Wounded and Other Poems* (New York: Britton Publishing Co., 1919), 41.

78. Walter Adolphe Roberts, *The Haunting Hand* (New York: Macaulay Co., 1926).

79. Roberts, "'My Ambitions at 21.'"

80. Walter Adolphe Roberts, "Hungry Souls," *New York Tribune*, Dec. 17, 1922, 26.

81. Walter Adolphe Roberts, "Tiger Lily," *Anthology of Magazine Verse for 1920*, ed. William Stanley Braithwaite (Boston: Small, Maynard, and Co., 1920). Originally published in *Ainslee's Magazine*.

82. Ibid.

83. Dearborn, *Pocahontas's Daughters*.

84. Gilman, *Love + Marriage = Death and Other Essays*, 71.

85. Dearborn, *Pocahontas's Daughters*, 123.

86. Scott Nearing, "A Depraved Spirit," *Nation*, June 6, 1923, 675–76.

87. North, *Reading 1922*, 100.

88. James Harvey Robinson, "Review of Salome of the Tenements by Anzia Yezierska," *Literary Digest International Book Review*, Feb. 1923; Henriksen, *Anzia Yezierska: A Writer's Life*, 181.

89. Henriksen, *Anzia Yezierska: A Writer's Life*, 188–89.

90. Atherton, "Fighting Up from the Ghetto."

91. Ibid.

7. Moving Pictures

1. Henriksen, *Anzia Yezierska: A Writer's Life*, 171.

2. Louise Maunsell Field, "Review of *Salome of the Tenements* by Anzia Yezierska," *New York Times*, Dec. 24, 1922, 22.

3. North, *Reading 1922*, 101.

4. Phillip Lopate, "Adapt This into Film," *Book Forum*, June/July/Aug. 2007, accessed Nov. 5, 2015, www.bookforum.com.

5. Kevin Brownlow, *Behind the Mask of Innocence* (New York: Knopf, 1990), 404; Mordaunt Hall, "The Screen," *New York Times*, Feb. 24, 1925; "Hundreds Throng Gigantic Setting," *New York Times*, Dec. 7, 1924; "'Salome of the Tenements' Appeals to All Emotions," *Atlanta Constitution*, Feb. 23, 1925; "Salome of Tenements Big Rialto Feature," *Atlanta Constitution*, Mar. 1, 1925; Epes W. Sargent, "'Salome of the Tenements' Sidney Olcott Makes a Fine Production of an Exotic Story for Paramount," *Moving Picture World*, Mar. 7, 1925; Bettina Berch, *From Hester Street to Hollywood: The Life and Work of Anzia Yezierska* (New York: Sefer International, 2009), 114–16; Ceplair, *A Great Lady*, 61.

6. Florence Lawrence, "'Last Laugh' Is Unique Example of Cinema Art; Jetta Goudal Meets Test," *Los Angeles Examiner*, Mar. 9, 1925.

7. Sollors, *Beyond Ethnicity*, 71.

8. Zangwill, afterword to *The Melting-Pot*.

9. Ibid.

10. Harrison-Kahan, "'Drunk with the Fiery Rhythms of Jazz,'" 417.

11. Stansell, *American Moderns*, 31.

12. Rob Reel, "Picture of the Ghetto Has Tender Fascination," *Chicago Evanston American*, Feb. 24, 1925; Sonya Levien, "1925 Synopsis of Story 'Salome of the Tenements,'" Sonya Levien Papers, Margaret Herrick Library of the Academy of Motion Picture Arts and Sciences, Los Angeles, 1925.

13. Slide, *Interview with Jetta Goudal*, Oral History of the New York Motion Picture Industry collection, Museum of the Moving Image, New York, 1979.

14. Sargent, "'Salome of the Tenements.'"

15. Slide, *Interview with Jetta Goudal*.

16. "Salome of Tenements Big Rialto Feature."

17. Friedman, "Marriage and the Immigrant Narrative," 177.

18. Henriksen, *Anzia Yezierska: A Writer's Life*, 167.

19. Walter Adolphe Roberts, "'My Ambitions at 21 and What Became of Them—Anzia Yezierska,'" *American Hebrew*, Aug. 25, 1922.

20. Henriksen, *Anzia Yezierska: A Writer's Life*, 171.

21. "Hundreds Throng Gigantic Setting."

22. Ceplair, *A Great Lady*, 61.

23. Hall, "The Screen."

24. Ibid.

25. "'Salome of the Tenements' Appeals to All Emotions."

26. Ibid.

27. "Hundreds Throng Gigantic Setting."

28. Ibid.

29. "Little Old Lady Who Acted a Bit in a Film Dies of Excitement as It Opens on Broadway," *New York Times*, Feb. 24, 1925.

30. Chaver Paver (pseudonym of Gershon Einbinder), "Rose of the East Side" ("Reizel Fun Der East Side"), *Morgn Freiheit* (Morning Freedom), New York, Sunday, Jan. 4, 1942, to Monday, Mar. 23, 1942.

31. Kobal, "John Kobal Interview with Jetta Goudal."

8. Taming the Bewilder-ness

1. Yezierska, *How I Found America*, 127.

2. Ibid.; Joyce Antler, *The Journey Home: How Jewish Women Shaped Modern America* (New York: Free Press, 1997), 33.

3. Frederick Lewis Allen, *Only Yesterday: An Informal History of the 1920s* (1931; New York: HarperCollins, 2000), 173.

4. Jackson Lears, *Rebirth of a Nation: The Making of Modern America, 1877–1920* (New York: HarperCollins, 2009), 7.

5. William James, "The Varieties of Religious Experience: A Study in Human Nature," in *William James, Writings 1902–1910* (1902; New York: Library of America, 1987), 149.

6. Lears, *Rebirth of a Nation*, 8.

7. Ibid.

8. Henry Adams, *The Education of Henry Adams*, Oxford World's Classics ed. (1918; New York: Oxford Univ. Press, 1999).

9. Sianne Ngai, *Ugly Feelings* (Cambridge, MA: Harvard Univ. Press, 2005), 1.

10. Ibid., 94.

11. Ibid.

12. Shelley Reuter, "The Genuine Jewish Type: Racial Ideology and Anti-Immigrationism in Early Medical Writing about Tay-Sachs Disease," *Canadian Journal of Sociology* 31, no. 3 (Summer 2006): 311.

13. Adams, *The Education of Henry Adams*.

14. Stubbs, introduction to *Arrogant Beggar*, xxi–xxii.

15. *The Trial of Curiosity*, 224.

16. Stephen Marche, "The Epidemic of Facelessness," *New York Times*, Feb. 14, 2015.

17. Anderson, *Imagined Communities*.

18. E. J. Hobsbawm, *Nations and Nationalism since 1780* (Cambridge, UK: Cambridge Univ. Press, 1990).

19. Anderson, *Imagined Communities*.

20. Hobsbawm, *Nations and Nationalism since 1780*, 52.

21. Robert A. Ferguson, *Law and Letters in American Culture* (Cambridge, MA: Harvard Univ. Press, 1984), 5.

22. Ralph Ellison, *Going to the Territory* (New York: Random House, 1986), 9.

23. Jonathan Freedman, "The Ambassadors and the Culture of Optical Illusion," *Raritan*, Winter 2015, 134.

24. Wiebe, *The Search for Order.*

25. Ibid., 65.

26. Ibid., 50–51.

27. Ibid., 14.

28. Daniel T. Rodgers, *Age of Fracture* (Cambridge, MA: Belknap Press of Harvard Univ. Press, 2011).

29. Sollors, *Beyond Ethnicity.*

30. David A. Hollinger, *Cosmopolitanism and Solidarity: Studies in Ethnoracial, Religious, and Professional Affiliation in the United States* (Madison: Univ. of Wisconsin Press, 2006), xv.

31. David A. Hollinger, "From Identity to Solidarity," *Daedalus* 135, no. 4 (Fall 2006): 23–32.

32. Ibid., 23–32.

33. Robert Wuthnow, *Communities of Discourse: Ideology and Social Structure in the Reformation, the Enlightenment, and European Socialism* (Cambridge, MA: Harvard Univ. Press, 1989).

34. North, *Reading 1922.* As North notes, "Though the copyright date of *Salome* is 1923, reviews make it clear that it was issued late in 1922" (236n164); Sollors, *Ethnic Modernism*, 10.

35. Also called the Johnson-Reed Act or the Immigration Act of 1924.

36. Martha C. Nussbaum, *Sex and Social Justice* (New York: Oxford Univ. Press, 1999), 62.

37. John Dewey, "Philosophy and Democracy," in *The American Intellectual Tradition*, ed. David A. Hollinger and Charles Capper (1918; New York: Oxford Univ. Press, 2006), 209.

38. Ronald Hoffman, Mechal Sobel, and Fredrika J. Teute, eds. *Through a Glass Darkly: Reflections on Personal Identity in Early America* (Chapel Hill: Univ. of North Carolina Press, 1997), viii.

39. Jill Lepore, "Historians Who Love Too Much: Reflections on Microhistory and Biography," *Journal of American History* 88, no. 1 (June 2001): 133, 141.

40. Chaver Paver (pseudonym of Gershon Einbinder), "Rose of the East Side" ("Reizel Fun DerEast Side") *Morgn-Frayhayt* (Morning Freedom), New York, Sunday, Jan. 4, 1942, to Monday, Mar. 23, 1942.

41. After going out of print, Anzia Yezierska's fiction was rediscovered by Alice Kessler-Harris in the late 1960s. *Salome of the Tenements* was republished in 1995. Anzia Yezierska, *Bread Givers* (1925; New York: Persea Books, 2003), foreword and introduction by Alice Kessler-Harris, 1999, ix.

Bibliography

Libraries and Archives

Anthology Film Archives, New York, NY

American Film Institute, Louis B. Mayer Library, Los Angeles, CA

Boston University Library, Howard Gotlieb Archival Research Center and Anzia Yezierska Papers, Boston, MA

California State Archives, Office of the Secretary of State, Sacramento, CA

Columbia University Butler Library, Rare Books Collection, New York, NY

George Eastman House, Rochester, NY

The Huntington Library, Art Collections and Botanical Gardens, Sonya Levien Papers, San Marino, CA

Library of Congress, Moving Image Section; Motion Picture, Broadcasting and Recorded Sound Section; Manuscripts Section, Washington, DC

Margaret Herrick Library, Sonya Levien Papers; Jetta Goudal Papers, Academy of Motion Picture Arts and Sciences, Los Angeles, CA

Museum of the Moving Image, The Oral History of the New York Motion Picture Industry, New York, NY

National Archives and Records Administration, Central Plains Region, Kansas City, MO

National Center for Jewish Film, Brandeis University, Waltham, MA

National Film Information Service, Beverly Hills, CA

New York City Department of Buildings, New York, NY

New York County Archives, New York County Clerk, Business Section, New York, NY

New York Historical Society, Corsa Collection, New York, NY

New York Public Library, Dorot Jewish Division; Dewitt Wallace Periodical Room; New York Public Library for the Performing Arts, New York, NY

New York State Archives Partnership Trust, Albany, NY

Office for Metropolitan History, New York, NY

Tamiment Library and Robert F. Wagner Labor Archives, New York University, Rose Pastor Stokes Papers, New York, NY

U.S. National Archives and Records Administration, College Park, MD

Women's Film Preservation Fund, New York, NY

Yale University Library, Manuscripts and Archives, Rose Pastor Stokes Papers, New Haven, CT

YIVO Library, Center for Jewish History, New York, NY

Books, Periodicals, and Websites

"672nd Dinner, Twilight Club, Friday, February 27, 1914 at the Aldine Club, the Wages of Shame vs. The Shame of Wages." Rose Pastor Stokes Papers, microfilm, Feb, 27, 1914, Tamiment Library and Robert F. Wagner Labor Archives, New York.

"1925 Synopsis of Story 'Salome of the Tenements' by Sonya Levien." Sonya Levien Papers, Margaret Herrick Library of the Academy of Motion Picture Arts and Sciences, Los Angeles.

Adams, Henry. *The Education of Henry Adams.* Oxford World's Classics ed. New York: Oxford Univ. Press, 1999. First published in 1918.

Addams, Jane. "Patriotism and Pacifists in War Time." *City Club [of Chicago] Bulletin* 10 (June 16, 1917): 184–90. In Jane Addams Memorial Collection, reel 47-1543-1549, Library, Univ. of Illinois at Chicago.

Agosta, Louis. "Empathy and Intersubjectivity." In *Empathy I,* edited by Joseph Lichtenberg, Melvin Bornstein, and Donald Silver. Hillsdale, NJ: Analytic Press, 1984.

"Agreement between Distinctive Pictures Corporation and Jetta Goudal." "Exhibit A, Attached to Complaint, Oct. 22, 1923," in *Jetta Goudal v. Distinctive Pictures Corporation,* Appellate Divison of the Supreme Court of New York, 215 App. Div. 674, 212 N.Y.S. 818 (Oct. 1925).

Aleichem, Sholem. *Stempenyu: A Jewish Romance.* Translated by Hannah Berman. Brooklyn, NY: Melville House, 2008. First published in 1888 by Folksbibliotek; first published in English in 1913 by Methuen and Co., London.

Alexander, Shana. *Happy Days: My Mother, My Father, My Sister and Me.* New York: Doubleday, 1995.

Allen, Frederick Lewis. *Only Yesterday: An Informal History of the 1920s.* New York: HarperCollins, 2000. First published by Harper and Row, 1931.

Altman, Julie. "Margaret Naumburg." In *Jewish Women: A Comprehensive Historical Encyclopedia.* Mar. 1, 2009. Jewish Women's Archive. http://qa.jwa.org /encyclopedia/article/naumburg-margaret. Accessed Dec. 5, 2009.

Anderson, Benedict. *Imagined Communities.* London: Verso, 1991.

Antin, Mary. *The Promised Land.* Boston: Houghton Mifflin, 1912.

Antler, Joyce. *The Journey Home: How Jewish Women Shaped Modern America.* New York: Schocken Books, 1997.

Arnold, Alan. *Valentino.* New York: Library Publishers, 1954.

Atherton, Gertrude. "Fighting Up from the Ghetto." *New York Herald,* Jan. 7, 1923.

Baker, Jennifer J. *Securing the Commonwealth.* Baltimore, MD: Johns Hopkins Univ. Press, 2005.

Beckman, Karen. *Vanishing Women: Magic, Film, and Feminism.* Durham, NC: Duke Univ. Press, 2003.

Benedict, Libbian. "The Story of Sonya Levien, Writer in the Motion Picture Field Whose Experiences Have Been Arduous and Varied." *American Hebrew,* June 19, 1924, 207. Sonya Levien Papers, Huntington Library, San Marino, CA.

Benham, Charles C. "Jetta Goudal: The Exotic." *Classic Images,* Sept. 1999. Vol. 291. Accessed Jan. 10, 2007. http://www.classicimages.com/1999/september99 /goudal.htm.

Berch, Bettina. *From Hester Street to Hollywood: The Life and Work of Anzia Yezierska.* New York: Sefer International, 2009.

Berg, A. Scott. *Goldwyn: A Biography.* New York: Alfred A. Knopf, 1989.

Berg, Kristian. *American Passages: A Literary Survey 09: Social Realism.* Videorecording. Burlington, VT: Annenberg Media, 2003. Learner.org, Oregon Public Broadcasting with Annenberg Foundation–Corporation for Public Broadcasting.

Birchard, Robert S. *Cecil B. Demille's Hollywood.* Lexington: Univ. of Kentucky Press, 2004.

Birmingham, Stephen. *"The Rest of Us": The Rise of America's Eastern European Jews.* Syracuse, NY: Syracuse Univ. Press, 1999. First published by Little, Brown and Co., 1984.

Blake, Casey. *Beloved Community.* Chapel Hill: Univ. of North Carolina Press, 1990.

Botshon, Lisa. "Anzia Yezierska and the Marketing of the Jewish Immigrant in 1920s Hollywood." In *Middlebrow Moderns, Popular Women Writers of the 1920s,* edited by Meredith Goldsmith and Lisa Botshon. Boston: Northeastern Univ. Press, 2003.

Bourne, Randolph. "The Collapse of American Strategy." *Seven Arts*, Aug. 1917.

———. "The War and the Intellectuals." *Seven Arts*, June 1917.

———. *War and the Intellectuals: Collected Essays, 1915–1919*. Edited by Carl Resek. Indianapolis, IN: Hackett Publishing Co., 1964.

Boydston, Jo Ann. *The Poems of John Dewey*. Carbondale: Southern Illinois Univ. Press, 1977.

Brandeis, Louis D. *Other People's Money and How the Bankers Use It*. Martino Publishing, 2009. First published by Frederick A. Stokes Co., 1914.

Brawley, Edward Allan. "A Jewish Cinderella." *New York History Review*, Aug. 21, 2010.

Brooks, Louise. *Lulu in Hollywood*. 1974; Minneapolis: Univ. of Minnesota Press, 2000.

Brownlow, Kevin. *Behind the Mask of Innocence*. New York: Knopf, 1990.

"Bruce Manning." *New York Times*, June 26, 1948.

Buhle, Mari Jo. *Women and American Socialism, 1970–1920*. Urbana: Univ. of Illinois Press, 1983.

Burke, Edmund. *Reflections on the Revolution in France and on the Proceeding in Certain Societies in London Relative to That Event in a Letter Intended to Have Been Sent to a Gentleman in Paris*. Vol. 3 of 12. *The Works of the Right Honourable Edmund Burke*. 1790; New York: P. F. Collier and Son, 1909–14. Project Gutenberg ebook, 2005. https://www.gutenberg.org/ebooks/15679.

"Business Women of State Convene: Mrs. Marlan Booth Kelley Elected President at Third Annual Meeting of Federation, Mayor Sends His Greeting, Predicts Benefits from Active Feminine Participation in Public Affairs." *New York Times*, May 28, 1922.

Bye Bye Birdie. George Sidney, director; Fred Kolmar, producer; Irving Brecher, screenplay based on the 1960 play by Michael Stewart with music by Charles Strouse and lyrics by Lee Adams. Culver City, CA: Columbia Pictures, 1963.

"Calls Roosevelt Ignorant, Mrs. Rose Pastor Stokes Says He Should Learn What Socialism Is." *New York Times*, July 15, 1908.

Capper, David A., and Charles Hollinger, eds. *The American Intellectual Tradition*. Vol. 2: *1865 to the Present*. New York: Oxford Univ. Press, 2006.

Ceplair, Larry. *A Great Lady: A Life of the Screenwriter Sonya Levien*. Lanham, MD: Scarecrow Press, 1996.

Chafee, Zechariah. "Freedom of Speech in War Time." *Harvard Law Review* 32, no. 8 (June 1919): 932–73.

"Cinderella Story of a Servant Girl." *Cedar Rapids Evening Gazette*, Mar. 5, 1921.

Clendinnen, Inge. "Fellow Sufferers: History and Imagination." *Australian Humanities Review*, Sept.–Nov. 1996.

Coghlan, Frank "Junior". *They Still Call Me Junior*. Jefferson, NC: McFarland and Co., 1993.

Cover, Robert. "Obligations: A Jewish Jurisprudence of the Social Order." In *Narrative, Violence, and the Law: The Essays of Robert Cover*, edited by Michael Ryan, Martha Minow, and Austin Sarat. Ann Arbor: Univ. of Michigan Press, 1995.

Darrow, Clarence. *The Story of My Life*. Boston: Da Capo Press, 1996. First published by Charles Scribner's Sons, 1932.

Dauber, Jeremy. *The Worlds of Sholem Aleichem*. New York: Nextbook Schocken Books, Random House, 2013.

Dearborn, Mary V. *Love in the Promised Land*. New York: Free Press, 1988.

———. *Pocahontas's Daughters: Gender and Ethnicity in American Culture*. New York: Oxford Univ. Press, 1986.

Debs, Eugene V. "The Canton, Ohio Speech, Anti-War Speech, June 16, 1918." *The Call*, E. V. Debs Internet Archive, 2001. http://www.marxists.org/archive /debs/works/1918/canton.htm.

Delbanco, Andrew. "American Literature: A Vanishing Subject?" *Daedalus*, Mar. 22, 2006.

———. *The Real American Dream: A Meditation on Hope*. Cambridge, MA: Harvard Univ. Press, 1999.

DeMille, Cecil B. *The Autobiography of Cecil B. Demille*. Edited by Donald Hayne. Englewood Cliffs, NJ: Prentice-Hall, 1959.

Dewey, John. "The Ethics of Democracy." In *Pragmatism, a Reader*, edited by Louis Menand. New York: Vintage Books, 1997. First published in 1888.

———. "My Pedagogic Creed." *School Journal* 54 (Jan. 1897): 77–80.

———. "Nationalizing Education." *Journal of Proceedings and Addresses of the National Education Association* 54 (1916).

———. "Philosophy and Democracy." In *The American Intellectual Tradition*, edited by David A. Hollinger and Charles Capper. New York: Oxford Univ. Press, 2006. First published in 1918.

Dewey, John, to William James, Mar. 27, 1903. In *The Thought and Character of William James*, edited by Ralph Barton Perry. Boston: Little, Brown and Co., 1935.

Dickens, Charles. *Bleak House*. Oxford, UK: Oxford Univ. Press, 1989. First published in 1853.

Dolkart, Andrew S. *Biography of a Tenement House in New York City: An Architectural History of 97 Orchard Street*. Santa Fe, NM: Center for American Places, 2006.

Donnelly, Michael P. "Capital Crime and Federal Justice in Western Missouri: Four Cases." Thesis, Univ. of Missouri, 2001.

Dostoevsky, Fyodor. *Notes from Underground*. Baltimore, MD: BN Publishing, 2009. First published in 1864.

Einstein, Albert. "Einstein's Reply to Criticisms." In *Albert Einstein: Philosopher-Scientist*, edited by Paul Arthur Schilpp. Cambridge, UK: Cambridge Univ. Press, 1949.

———. *Physics and Reality*. Translated by Jean Piccard. *Journal of the Franklin Institute* 221, no. 3 (1936): 376. http://www.kostic.niu.edu/physics_and_reality-albert_einstein.pdf.

Eisele, J. Christopher. "John Dewey and the Immigrants." *History of Education Quarterly* 15, no. 1 (Spring 1975).

Ellison, Ralph. *Going to the Territory*. New York: Random House, 1986.

Enstad, Nan. *Ladies of Labor, Girls of Adventure*. New York: Columbia Univ. Press, 1999.

Espionage Act of June 15, 1917. Pub.L. 65-24, 40 Stat. 217, June 15, 1917.

Ewen, Elizabeth. *Immigrant Women in the Land of Dollars*. New York: Monthly Review Press, 1985.

Ferguson, Robert A. *Law and Letters in American Culture*. Cambridge, MA: Harvard Univ. Press, 1984.

Ferraro, Thomas J. *Ethnic Passages: Literary Immigrants in Twentieth-Century America*. Chicago: Univ. of Chicago Press, 1993.

Field, Louise Maunsell. "Review of *Salome of the Tenements* by Anzia Yezierska." *New York Times*, Dec. 24, 1922.

Floyd, Janet, Alison Easton, R. J. Ellis, and Lindsey Traub, eds. *Becoming Visible: Women's Presence in Late Nineteenth-Century America*. Amsterdam: Rodopi, 2010.

"Fokker Flies Over City." *New York Times*, July 23, 1921.

"The Ford Bonus to Employees." *New York Times*, Jan. 7, 1914.

"Form a Suffrage Party: New Organization Perfected at Martha Washington." *New York Times*, Jan. 16, 1910.

Frank, Waldo David. "The Man Who Made Us What We Are." *New Yorker* 2 (1926): 15–16.

———. *Our America*. New York: Boni and Liveright, 1919.

Fraser, Patrick. *Treatise on Master and Servant, Employer and Workman, and Master and Apprentice According to the Laws of Scotland*. Edinburgh: T. and T. Clark, 1846; 2nd ed. 1872; 3rd ed. 1882, updated by William Campbell.

Freedman, Jonathan. "The Ambassadors and the Culture of Optical Illusion." *Raritan*, Winter 2015.

Friedman, Natalie. "Marriage and the Immigrant Narrative: Anzia Yezierska's *Salome of the Tenements*." *Legacy* 22, no. 2 (2005): 176–86.

Garza, Janiss. "Plot Synopsis—Who Will Marry Me." *Allmovie Guide*. http://www.allmovie.com/movie/who-will-marry-me-v116871.

George, John, and Peter F. Boller. *They Never Said It: A Book of Fake Quotes, Misquotes and Misleading Attributions*. Oxford, UK: Oxford Univ. Press, 1989.

Gerstle, Gary. *American Crucible: Race and Nation in the Twentieth Century*. Princeton, NJ: Princeton Univ. Press, 2001.

Gilman, Sander L. *Love + Marriage = Death and Other Essays on Representing Difference*. Stanford, CA: Stanford Univ. Press, 1998.

Gilmore, Grant. *The Death of Contract*. Columbus: Ohio State Univ. Press, 1995. First published in 1974.

Glenn, Susan A. *Female Spectacle: The Theatrical Roots of Modern Feminism*. Cambridge, MA: Harvard Univ. Press, 2000.

Goldman, Emma. *My Disillusionment in Russia*. Garden City, NY: Doubleday, Page and Co., 1923.

———. *My Further Disillusionment in Russia*. Garden City, NY: Doubleday, Page and Co., 1924.

Goldsmith, Meredith. "The Coming of Age of a Jewish Female Intellectual: Anzia Yezierska's Red Ribbon on a White Horse." In *The New York Public Intellectuals and Beyond: Exploring Liberal Humanism, Jewish Identity, and the American Protest Tradition*, edited by Ethan Goffman and Daniel Morris, 176–93. West Lafayette, IN: Purdue Univ. Press, 2009.

Gottlieb, Robert. *Sarah: The Life of Sarah Bernhardt*. New Haven: Yale Univ. Press, 2010.

Goudal, Jetta, to "My Dear Messmore," Apr. 16, 1928. Sent on stationary of the Ambassador Hotel, Los Angeles, California. Margaret Herrick Library of the Academy of Motion Picture Arts and Sciences, Jetta Goudal Papers.

Goudal, Jetta. "Speech at Meeting of Actors Equity Association." 1929. Transcript titled "MEETING HELD AT WOMEN'S CLUB OF HOLLYWOOD, THURSDAY, JUNE 27, 1929, 8:30P.M." Actors' Equity Association Records WAG.011 Series II: Foundations of Actors' Equity, 1913–1933, Box 3, folder 20, Tamiment Library and Robert F. Wagner Labor Archives, New York Univ. Library.

———. Conciliation Committee Files, Aug. 8, 1930. Academy of Motion Picture Arts and Sciences Collection, Margaret Herrick Library, Los Angeles, CA.

Goudeket, Maurice. *Close to Colette: An Intimate Portrait of a Woman of Genius*. New York: Farrar, Straus and Cudahy, 1957.

Hall, Mordaunt. "The Screen." *New York Times*, Feb. 24, 1925.

Harrison-Kahan, Lori. "'Drunk with the Fiery Rhythms of Jazz': Anzia Yezierska, Hybridity, and the Harlem Renaissance." *Modern Fiction Studies* 51, no. 2 (2005): 416–38.

Hawthorne, Nathaniel. *The Scarlet Letter and Other Writings*. Norton Critical Edition. New York: W. W. Norton and Co., 2005.

Heckert, Diane. "Prize-Winning Movie Scripter Tells of Law-to-Writing Switch." *Dayton Daily News*, Nov. 30, 1954. Sonya Levien Papers, Huntington Library, San Marino, CA.

Hefner, Brooks E. "'Slipping Back into the Vernacular': Anzia Yezierska's Vernacular Modernism." *MELUS* 36, no. 3 (Fall 2011): 187–211.

Henriksen, Louise Levitas. *Anzia Yezierska: A Writer's Life*. New Brunswick, NJ: Rutgers Univ. Press, 1988.

Hewes, Robert E. "Noted Writer in Hollywood, Miss Sonia Levien Here to Join Lasky Studio as Special Playwright, Has Achieved Fame." *Hollywood Daily Citizen*, Dec. 17, 1921. Box 32, 8, Sonya Levien Papers, Huntington Library, San Marino, CA.

Higashi, Sumiko. *Cecil B. DeMille and American Culture: The Silent Era*. Berkeley: Univ. of California Press, 1994.

Hirsh, Jeff. *Images of America: Manhattan Hotels, 1880–1920*. Charleston SC: Arcadia Publishing, 1997.

Hobsbawm, E. J. *Nations and Nationalism since 1780*. Cambridge, UK: Cambridge Univ. Press, 1990.

Hoffman, Ronald, Mechal Sobel, and Fredrika J. Teute, eds. *Through a Glass Darkly: Reflections on Personal Identity in Early America*. Chapel Hill: Univ. of North Carolina Press, 1997.

Hofstadter, Richard. *The Age of Reform, from Bryan to F.D.R.* New York: Vintage Books, 1955.

Hollinger, David A. *Cosmopolitanism and Solidarity: Studies in Ethnoracial, Religious, and Professional Affiliation in the United States*. Madison: Univ. of Wisconsin Press, 2006.

———. "From Identity to Solidarity." *Daedalus* 135, no. 4 (Fall 2006).

Holmes, Oliver Wendell, Jr. *The Common Law*. Cambridge, MA: The President and Fellows of Harvard College, 2003. http://www.law.harvard.edu/library/collections/special/online-collections/common_law/index.php. First published by Little, Brown and Co., Boston, 1881.

Holmes, Sean P. "The Hollywood Star System and the Regulation of Actors' Labor, 1916–1934." *Film History* 12, no. 1 (2000): 97–114.

———. "No Room for Manoeuvre: Star Images and the Regulation of Actors' Labour in Silent Era Hollywood." In *Working in the Global Film and Television Industries*, edited by Andrew Dawson and Sean P. Holmes. New York: Bloomsbury Academic, 2012.

Honig, Bonnie. *Democracy and the Foreigner*. Princeton, NJ: Princeton Univ. Press, 2001.

Horn, Dara. "Jewish Surnames [Supposedly] Explained." *Mosaic Magazine*, Jan. 21, 2014.

Horwitz, Morton J. *The Transformation of American Law, 1870–1960*. New York: Oxford Univ. Press, 1992.

Hovey, Esther. "The Genesis of Serge Hovey's 'The Robert Burns Songbook.'" *Studies in Scottish Literature* 30, no. 1 (1998).

Hovey, Tamara. *Among the Survivors*. New York: Grossman Publishers, 1971.

Howe, Irving. *World of Our Fathers: The Journey of the East European Jews to America and the Life They Found and Made*. New York: Galahad Books, 1976.

"Hundreds Throng Gigantic Setting." *New York Times*, Dec. 7, 1924.

Huttner, Jan Lisa. "Everybody's Fiddler: A Researcher Finds a Link—Long Denied—between Chagall and Sholom Aleichem." *Forward*, Sept. 5, 2003.

Huyssen, David. *Progressive Inequality: Rich and Poor in New York, 1890–1920*. Cambridge, MA: Harvard Univ. Press, 2014.

Hyman, Paula E. *Gender and Assimilation in Modern Jewish History: The Roles and Representation of Women*. Seattle: Univ. of Washington Press, 1995.

Hyman, Paula E., and Deborah Dash Moore, eds. *Jewish Women in America: An Historical Encyclopedia*. New York: Routledge, 1997.

Jablonski, Edward. *Harold Arlen: Rhythm, Rainbows, and Blues*. Boston: Northeastern Univ. Press, 1996.

Jacobson, Matthew Frye. "A Ghetto to Look Back To: World of Our Fathers, Ethnic Revival, and the Arc of Multiculturalism." *American Jewish History* 88, no. 4 (Dec. 2000): 463–74.

———. *Special Sorrows: The Diasporic Imagination of Irish, Polish, and Jewish Immigrants in the United States*. Berkeley: Univ. of California Press, 2002.

James, Henry. *The Ambassadors*. Oxford, UK: Oxford Univ. Press, 1998. First published as a serial in *North American Review*, 1903.

———. *The American Scene*. New York: Penguin Books, 1994. First published by Harper and Brothers, 1907.

———. *The Princess Casamassima*. London: Everyman's Library, 1991. First published in 1886.

James, William. "The Varieties of Religious Experience: A Study in Human Nature." In *William James, Writings 1902–1910*. New York: Library of America, 1987. First published in 1902.

"Jetta Goudal." *An Encyclopedic Dictionary of Women in Early American Films, 1895–1930*. Binghamton, NY: Haworth Press, 2005.

"Jetta Goudal, 'Cocktail of Temperament.'" *New York Morning Telegraph*, May 22, 1927.

Jones, Margaret C. *Heretics and Hellraisers: Women Contributors to the Masses, 1911–1917*. Austin: Univ. of Texas Press, 1993.

Josephus, Flavius. *Josephus, the Complete Works*. Translated by William Whiston. Nashville, TN: Thomas Nelson Publishers, 1988.

Kallen, Horace M. "Democracy Versus the Melting Pot: A Study of American Nationality." *Nation*, Feb. 25, 1915.

Kehr, Dave. "An Independent Woman, Nobly Suffering in Silents." *New York Times*, Mar. 11, 2010.

Kennedy, David M. *Over Here: The First World War and American Society*. New York: Oxford Univ. Press, 1980.

Kessler-Harris, Alice. *A Woman's Wage: Historical Meanings and Social Consequences*. Lexington: Univ. Press of Kentucky, 1990.

Key, Ellen. *Love and Marriage*. Translated by Arthur G. Chater. New York: Source Book Press, 1970. First published by G. P. Putnam's Sons, 1911.

Klein, Marcus. "Heritage of the Ghetto." *Nation*, Mar. 27, 1976.

Kloppenberg, James T. *Uncertain Victory: Social Democracy and Progressivism in European and American Thought, 1870–1920*. New York: Oxford Univ. Press, 1986.

Kobal, John. "John Kobal Interview with Jetta Goudal." Jan. 2, 1982. Private collection of Kevin Brownlow, Photoplay Productions, London.

Konzett, Delia Caparoso. *Ethnic Modernisms: Anzia Yezierska, Zora Neale Hurston, Jean Rhys, and the Aesthetics of Dislocation*. New York: Palgrave Macmillan, 2002.

Kropotkin, Alexandra. "To the Ladies." *Liberty*, 1927–43.

Lang, Jessica. "Jewish and American, Historical and Literary: The (Un)Ifying Experience of Reading Text." *Studies in American Jewish Literature* 31, no. 1 (2012): 76–83.

Lang, Olivia. "Never Hurts to Ask: Review of the Empathy Exams by Leslie Jamison." *New York Times*, Apr. 6, 2014.

Lao Silesu (music), Adrian Ross (English lyrics), and Nilson Fysher (French lyrics). "A Little Love, A Little Kiss." London: Chapell and Co., 1912.

Lasky, Jesse L. *I Blow My Own Horn*. New York: Doubleday, 1957.

Lawrence, Florence. "'Last Laugh' Is Unique Example of Cinema Art; Jetta Goudal Meets Test." *Los Angeles Examiner*, Mar. 9, 1925.

Lears, Jackson. *Rebirth of a Nation: The Making of Modern America, 1877–1920*. New York: HarperCollins, 2009.

———. "Teddy Roosevelt, Not-So-Great Reformer, What Washington-Focused Liberals Miss about Progressivism." *New Republic*, Mar. 14, 2014.

Lepore, Jill. "Historians Who Love Too Much: Reflections on Microhistory and Biography." *Journal of American History* 88, no. 1 (June 2001): 129–44.

Levien, Sonya. "The Celluloid Prince." *New Yorker*, Apr. 25, 1925. Sonya Levien Papers, Huntington Library, San Marino, CA.

———. "Col. Roosevelt in Our Office." *Metropolitan Bulletin*, May 1915. Sonya Levien Papers, Box 35, Huntington Library, San Marino, CA.

———. "The Franks Case Makes Me Wonder." *Hearst's International*, Dec. 1924, 18–19, 107–8. Sonya Levien Papers, Huntington Library, San Marino, CA.

———. "The Great Friend." *Woman's Home Companion*, Oct. 1919. Sonya Levien Papers, Huntington Library, San Marino, CA.

———. "Milk." Sonya Levien Papers, Huntington Library, San Marino, CA, 1918.

———. "My Pilgrimage to Hollywood." *Metropolitan*, Sept. 17, 1922. Sonya Levien Papers, Box 32, Huntington Library, San Marino, CA.

———. "New York City's Motion Picture Law." *American City*, Oct. 1913, 319–21.

Lewis, Sinclair. *Hike and the Aeroplane*. New York: Frederick A. Stokes Co., 1912.

"Little Old Lady Who Acted a Bit in a Film Dies of Excitement as It Opens on Broadway." *New York Times*, Feb. 24, 1925.

Lopate, Phillip. "Adapt This into Film." *Book Forum*, June/July/Aug., 2007. www.bookforum.com.

Louvish, Simon. *Cecil B. Demille: A Life in Art*. New York: St. Martin's Press, 2007.

Luhan, Mabel Dodge. *Intimate Memories*. Santa Fe, NM: Sunstone Press, 2008. First published by Univ. of New Mexico Press, 1999.

"M-G-M." *New York Times*, Oct. 11, 1947.

"Makin' Whoopee." Lyrics by Gus Kahn, music by Walter Donaldson. N.p.: Donaldson Publishing Co., 1928.

Malkus, Alida S. "She Came to America from Russia: The Story of Sonya Levien." *Success*, Jan. 1925, 55–57, 121. Sonya Levien Papers, Huntington Library, San Marino, CA.

Marche, Stephen. "The Epidemic of Facelessness." *New York Times*, Feb. 14, 2015.

"Martha Washington Hotel Designation Report." Designation List 456, June 12, 2012; Amended Landmark Site, Designation List 456a, LP-2428, June 19, 2012. Landmarks Preservation Commission, City of New York.

Marx, Groucho. *The Groucho Letters: Letters from and to Groucho Marx*. With an introduction by Arthur Sheekman. New York: Simon and Schuster, 1967.

Marx, Harpo, with Rowland Barber. *Harpo Speaks!* New York: Proscenium Publishers, 2000. First published by Bernard Geis Associates, 1962.

McGinity, Keren R. *Still Jewish: A History of Women and Intermarriage in America*. New York: New York Univ. Press, 2009.

Melville, Herman. *The Confidence Man, His Masquerade*. New York: Penguin Classics, 1990. First published in 1857 in London by Longman, Brown, Green, Longmans, and Roberts.

Menand, Louis. *The Metaphysical Club*. New York: Farrar, Straus and Giroux, 2001.

Merrill, Flora. "Women Must Choose 'Babies or Business' Says Noted Author— Wife of Boston Editor." *Boston Sunday Post*, July 5, 1925. Sonya Levien Papers, Huntington Library, San Marino, CA.

"Metro's 'That Midnight Kiss' Introduces Mario Lanza to Film Fans at Capitol." *New York Times*, Sept. 23, 1949.

Michels, Tony. *A Fire in Their Hearts: Yiddish Socialists in New York*. Cambridge, MA: Harvard Univ. Press, 2005.

"Midtown Hotel Sold at Auction." *New York Times*, Aug. 9, 1933.

Mikkelsen, Ann. "From Sympathy to Empathy: Anzia Yezierska and the Transformation of the American Subject." *American Literature* 82, no. 2 (2010): 361–88.

"Miss Goldman Upheld as Trial Begins, Her Views Approved at 'Birth Control' Dinner." *New York Evening Sun*, Apr. 20, 1916. Yale Univ. Library, Manuscripts and Archives, Rose Pastor Stokes Papers, Ms 573, microfilm.

"Miss Rambova, 69, Film Figure, Dead—2d Wife of Valentino—Was Ballerina and Columnist." *New York Times*, June 8, 1966.

"Mr. Hovey's Life of Morgan." *New York Times*, Feb. 1, 1912.

Nearing, Scott. "A Depraved Spirit." *Nation*, June 6, 1923.

Ngai, Sianne. *Ugly Feelings*. Cambridge, MA: Harvard Univ. Press, 2005.

Norden, Martin F. "Alice Guy Blaché, Rose Pastor Stokes, and the Birth Control Film That Never Was." In *Researching Women in Silent Cinema: New Findings and Perspectives*, edited by Victoria Duckett, Monica Dall'Asta, and Lucia Tralli. Bologna: Dept. of Arts, Univ. of Bologna, in association with the

Victorian College of the Arts, Univ. of Melbourne, and Women and Film History International, 2013.

North, Michael. *Reading 1922: A Return to the Scene of the Modern*. Oxford, UK: Oxford Univ. Press, 1999.

Nussbaum, Martha C. *Sex and Social Justice*. New York: Oxford Univ. Press, 1999.

Oberfirst, Robert. *Rudolph Valentino: The Man Behind the Myth*. New York: Citadel Press, 1962.

Orren, Karen. *Belated Feudalism—Labor, the Law, and Liberal Development in the United States*. Cambridge, UK: Cambridge Univ. Press, 1991.

Pastor, Rose. "Just between Us Girls." *Yiddishes Tageblatt*, Dec. 27, 1903.

———. "The Views of a Settlement Worker: Talk with J. G. Phelps Stokes." *Jewish Daily News*, 1903.

———. "Views of Settlement Workers: A Talk with Miss Lillian D. Wald." *Jewish Daily News*, 1903.

Paver, Chaver. "Reizel of the East Side." *Morgn-Frayhayt*, Jan.–Mar. 1942.

Pease, Donald E., ed. *National Identities and Post-Americanist Narratives*. Durham, NC: Duke Univ. Press, 1994.

Peiss, Kathy. *Cheap Amusements: Working Women and Leisure in Turn-of-the-Century New York*. Philadelphia, PA: Temple Univ. Press, 1986.

Pizer, Donald. "The Naturalism of Edith Wharton's *The House of Mirth*." *Twentieth Century Literature* 41, no. 2 (Summer 1995): 241–48.

Posnock, Ross. "Going Astray, Going Forward: Du Boisian Pragmatism and Its Lineage." In *The Revivial of Pragmatism: New Essays on Social Thought, Law, and Culture*, edited by Morris Dickstein. Durham, NC: Duke Univ. Press, 1999.

———. "Henry James, Veblen and Adorno: The Crisis of the Modern Self." *Journal of American Studies* 21, no. 1 (1987): 31–54.

———. "The Politics of Nonidentity: A Genealogy." *Boundary 2* 19, no. 1 (1992).

———. *The Trial of Curiosity: Henry James, William James, and the Challenge of Modernity*. New York: Oxford Univ. Press, 1991.

"Property Profile Overview," Manhattan 10016, Bin #1080777, 29 East 29 Street, 27–31 East 29 Street, 30 East 30 Street, Record #Nb1224-01, Tax Block: 859, Tax Lot: 26. Dept. of Buildings, City of New York.

Pynchon, Thomas. *Against the Day*. New York: Viking Penguin, 2006.

———. *V*. Philadelphia: J. B. Lippincott Co., 1961.

————. *Vineland*. Boston: Little, Brown and Co., 1990.

Rambova, Natacha. *Rudy: An Intimate Portrait of Rudolph Valentino by His Wife Natacha Rambova*. London: Hutchinson and Co., 1926.

Rauchway, Eric. *Blessed among Nations: How the World Made America*. New York: Hill and Wang, 2006.

Reed, John. *Ten Days That Shook the World*. New York: Boni and Liveright, 1919.

Reel, Rob. "Picture of the Ghetto Has Tender Fascination." *Chicago Evanston American*, Feb. 24, 1925.

Renshaw, Patrick. "Rose of the World: The Pastor-Stokes Marriage and the American Left, 1905–1925." *New York History: Quarterly Journal of the New York Historical Association* 62, no. 4 (Oct. 1981): 415–38.

Reuter, Shelley. "The Genuine Jewish Type: Racial Ideology and Anti-Immigrationism in Early Medical Writing about Tay-Sachs Disease." *Canadian Journal of Sociology* 31, no. 3 (Summer 2006): 291–323.

Rischin, Moses. Introduction to *The Spirit of the Ghetto*, by Hutchins Hapgood, edited by Moses Rischin. Cambridge, MA: Belknap Press of Harvard Univ. Press, 1967. First published in 1902.

Roberts, Walter Adolphe. *The Haunting Hand*. New York: Macaulay Co., 1926.

————. "Hungry Souls." *New York Tribune*, Dec. 17, 1922.

————. "My Ambitions at 21 and What Became of Them: Anzia Yezierska." *American Hebrew*, Aug. 25, 1922.

————. *Pierre Wounded and Other Poems*. New York: Britton Publishing Co., 1919.

————. "Tiger Lily." *Anthology of Magazine Verse for 1920*. Edited by William Stanley Braithwaite. Boston: Small, Mayard and Co., 1920.

Robinson, Cedric J. *Black Marxism: The Making of a Black Radical Tradition*. London: Zed Press, 1983; Repr., Chapel Hill: Univ. of North Carolina Press, 2000.

Robinson, James Harvey. "Review of Salome of the Tenements by Anzia Yezierska." *Literary Digest International Book Review*, Feb. 1923.

Rodgers, Daniel T. *Age of Fracture*. Cambridge, MA: Belknap Press of Harvard Univ. Press, 2011.

Rodgers, Daniel T. *Atlantic Crossings: Social Politics in a Progressive Age*. Cambridge, MA: Belknap Press of Harvard Univ. Press, 1998.

Rorty, Richard. *Contingency, Irony, and Solidarity*. New York: Cambridge Univ. Press, 1989.

Rose, Anne C. *Beloved Strangers: Interfaith Families in Nineteenth- Century America*. Cambridge, MA: Harvard Univ. Press, 2001.

"Rose Pastor Stokes Flays Capitalist Press." "Socialist Newspaper in Boston," Feb. 24, 1914. Yale Univ. Library, Manuscripts and Archives, Rose Pastor Stokes Papers, MS 573, microfilm reel 5.

Rosen, Norma. *John and Anzia: An American Romance*. Syracuse, NY: Syracuse Univ. Press, 1997. First published in 1989 by E. P. Dutton.

Rosenbloom, Nancy J. "In Defense of the Moving Pictures: The People's Institute, the National Board of Censorship and the Problem of Leisure in Urban America." *American Studies* 33, no. 2 (Fall 1992): 41–60.

Rothman, Nathan. "An Artist Unfrozen." *Saturday Review of Literature*, Nov. 4, 1950. Margaret Herrick Library, Academy of Motion Picture Arts and Sciences, Los Angeles.

Rottenberg, Catherine. "Salome of the Tenements, the American Dream and Class Performativity." *American Studies* 45, no. 1 (2004): 65–83.

"Salome of Tenements Big Rialto Feature." *Atlanta Constitution*, Mar. 1, 1925.

"'Salome of the Tenements' Appeals to All Emotions." *Atlanta Constitution*, Feb. 23, 1925.

Sargent, Epes W. "'Salome of the Tenements' Sidney Olcott Makes a Fine Production of an Exotic Story for Paramount." *Moving Picture World*, Mar. 7, 1925.

Sauter, Irene Billeter. *New York City: 'Gilt Cage' or 'Promised Land'? Representations of Urban Space in Edith Wharton and Anzia Yezierska*. Bern, Switzerland: Peter Lang AG, 2011.

Schama, Simon. "Clio Has a Problem." *New York Times Magazine*, Sept. 8, 1991.

Schoen, Carol B. *Anzia Yezierska*. Boston: Twayne Publishers, 1982.

Shapiro, Ann R. "The Ultimate Shaygets and the Fiction of Anzia Yezierska." *MELUS* 21, no. 2 (Summer 1996): 79–89.

Shpayer-Makov, Hanna. "The Reception of Peter Kropotkin in Britain, 1886–1917." *Albion: A Quarterly Journal Concerned with British Studies* 19, no. 3 (Autumn 1987): 373–90.

Sigerman, Harriet Marla. "Daughters of the Book: A Study of Gender and Ethnicity in the Lives of Three American Jewish Women." PhD diss., Univ. of Massachusetts, 1992.

Simkhovich, Mary Kingsbury. *The City Worker's World in America*. New York: Macmillan, 1917.

Slide, Anthony. "Interview with Jetta Goudal." Oral History of the New York Motion Picture Industry collection of the Museum of the Moving Image, New York, 1979.

————. *Silent Players: A Biographical and Autobiographical Study of 100 Silent Film Actors and Actresses.* Lexington: Univ. Press of Kentucky, 2002.

Smith, Adam. *The Theory of Moral Sentiments.* London: printed for A. Millar, in the Strand; and A. Kincaid and J. Bell, in Edinburgh, 1759.

Sollors, Werner. *Beyond Ethnicity: Consent and Descent in American Culture.* New York: Oxford Univ. Press, 1986.

————. *Ethnic Modernism.* Cambridge, UK: Cambridge Univ. Press, 2002; Cambridge, MA: Harvard Univ. Press, 2008.

Squires, Michael. *Living at the Edge: A Biography of D. H. Lawrence and Frieda Von Richtofen.* Madison: Univ. of Wisconsin Press, 2002.

Stanley, Amy Dru. *From Bondage to Contract: Wage Labor, Marriage, and the Market in the Age of Slave Emancipation.* New York: Cambridge Univ. Press, 1998.

Stansell, Christine. *American Moderns: Bohemian New York and the Creation of a New Century.* New York: Henry Holt and Co., 2000.

"Stokes Charges Socialist Wing Is Pro-German." *New York Tribune,* May 4, 1917.

Stokes, Rose Pastor. "A Confession." *Century,* Nov. 1917, 457–59.

————. *I Belong to the Working Class: The Unfinished Autobiography of Rose Pastor Stokes.* Edited by Herbert Shapiro and David L. Sterling. Athens: Univ. of Georgia Press, 1992.

————. Letter to the Editor. *Kansas City Star,* Mar. 19, 1918.

————. Letter to the Editor. *New York Times,* Nov. 1, 1917, 14.

————. "The Second Carnegie Hall Meeting." *Mother Earth,* 1916. Yale Univ. Library, Manuscripts and Archives, Rose Pastor Stokes Papers, MS 573, microfilm, 522–25.

————. Undated note on the unfairness of New York State divorce laws of the 1920s. Yale Univ. Library, Manuscripts and Archives, Rose Pastor Stokes Papers, Ms 573.

————. *The Woman Who Wouldn't.* New York: G. P. Putnam's Sons, 1916.

Stokes, Rose Pastor, and Alice Guy-Blaché. "Shall the Parents Decide?" Rose Pastor Stokes Papers, microfilm, 1917. Tamiment Library and Robert F. Wagner Labor Archives, New York.

Strachey, Lytton. *Eminent Victorians.* London: Chatto and Windus, 1918.

Tamarkin, Stanley Ray. "Rose Pastor Stokes: The Portrait of a Radical Woman, 1905–1919." PhD diss., Yale Univ., Dec. 1983.

Taubenfeld, Aviva F. *Rough Writing: Ethnic Authorship in Theodore Roosevelt's America.* New York: New York Univ. Press, 2008.

Titchener, Edward Bradford. "Introspection and Empathy: History of Mental Concepts, Crossing Dialogues Association." *Dialogues in Philosophy, Mental and Neuro Sciences*, no. 1, 2014, 25–30. http://www.crossingdialogues.com/Ms-E14 -01.pdf 7.

———. *Lectures on the Experimental Psychology of the Thought-Processes*. New York: MacMillan, 1909.

Tolstoi, Leo. *The Journal of Leo Tolstoi*. Translated by Rose Strunsky. New York: A. A. Knopf, 1917.

Tolstoy, Leo. *Anna Karenina*. Translated by Amy Mandelker. New York: Barnes and Noble, 2003. First published in Moscow in 1877.

Trachtenberg, Alan, ed. *Memoirs of Waldo Frank*. Boston: Univ. of Massachusetts Press, 1973.

Trilling, Lionel. *The Liberal Imagination*. New York: Viking Press, 1950.

Twain, Mark. "The Privilege of the Grave." *New Yorker*, Dec. 22, 29, 2008. First published in 1905.

U.S. Department of Labor, Bureau of Labor Statistics. "CPI Inflation Calculator." http://www.Bls.Gov/Data/Inflation_Calculator.htmValentino, Rudolph. *The Intimate Journal of Rudolph Valentino*. New York: William Faro, 1931.

Van Solinge, Hanna, Aart C. Liefbroer, and Frans Van Poppel. "Joden in Nederland." *demos*, Oct.–Nov. 2001. http://www.nidi.knaw.nl/web/html/public /demos/dmo1091.html (Dutch). Netherlands Interdisciplinary Demographic Institute. Last revision Jan. 15, 2002. http://en.wikipedia.org/wiki/History _of_the_Jews_in_the_Netherlands.

Waters, Frank. *Of Time and Change*. Denver, CO: MacMurray and Beck, 1998.

Weiler, Paul C. *Entertainment Media and the Law: Text Cases Problems*. 3rd ed. St. Paul, MN: West Academic Publishing, 2006.

Westbrook, Robert B. *John Dewey and American Democracy*. Ithaca, NY: Cornell Univ. Press, 1991.

———. "On the Private Life of a Public Philosopher: John Dewey in Love." *Teachers College Record* 96, no. 2 (1994): 183–97.

Wharton, Edith. *The House of Mirth*. New York: Penguin Books, 1993. First published by Charles Scribner's Sons, 1905.

"When the Pacifist Comes to the Test." *New York Times*, May 25, 1918.

White, Norval, and Elliot Willensky. *AIA Guide to New York City*. 4th ed. New York: Three Rivers Press, 2000.

Wiebe, Robert H. *The Search for Order, 1877–1920*. New York: Hill and Wang, 1967.

Wieseltier, Leon. "Intellectuals and Their America. Symposium: Part I." *Dissent*, Winter 2010, 40–42.

Wilder, Billy, Charles Bracket, and D. M. Marshman Jr. *Sunset Boulevard*. Directed by Billy Wilder, Produced by Charles Bracket. Los Angeles: Paramount Pictures, 1950.

Wilson, Woodrow. *The New Freedom: A Call for the Emancipation of the Generous Energies of a People*. New York: Doubleday, Page and Co., 1913.

———. "President Woodrow Wilson's War Message to Congress." 65th Cong., 1st Sess. Senate Doc. No. 5, Serial No. 7264, Washington, DC, 1917, 3–8, passim.

Witt, John Fabian. *Patriots and Cosmopolitans: Hidden Histories of American Law*. Cambridge, MA: Harvard Univ. Press, 2007.

"Women's Hotel Opens." *New York Times*, Feb. 4, 1903.

Woolf, Virginia. *A Room of One's Own*. London: Hogarth Press, 1929.

Wuthnow, Robert. *Communities of Discourse: Ideology and Social Structure in the Reformation, the Enlightenment, and European Socialism*. Cambridge, MA: Harvard Univ. Press, 1989.

Yezierska, Anzia. *Arrogant Beggar*. Durham, NC: Duke Univ. Press, 1996. First published in 1927 by Doubleday, Page and Co.

———. *Bread Givers*. Foreword and introduction by Alice Kessler-Harris. New York: Persea Books, 2003. First published in 1925.

———. *How I Found America*. New York: Persea Books, 1991.

———. *Hungry Heart*. New York: Penguin Books, 1997. First published in 1920.

———. *Red Ribbon on a White Horse*. New York: Persea, 1987. First published by Charles Scribner's Sons, 1950.

———. *Salome of the Tenements*. Urbana: Univ. of Illinois Press, 1996. First published by Grosset and Dunlap, 1923.

———. "This Is What $10,000 Did to Me." *Cosmopolitan*, Oct. 1925.

Zangwill, Israel. *The Melting-Pot*. New York: Macmillan, 1909, 1914.

Zipser, Arthur, and Pearl Zipser. *Fire and Grace: The Life of Rose Pastor Stokes*. Athens: Univ. of Georgia Press, 1989.

Index

Italic page number denotes illustration.

Alan Robert Ginsberg (MA, American Studies, Columbia University; JD, Boston University School of Law; BA, English and General Literature, Binghamton University) is a visiting scholar and board member at the Center for American Studies at Columbia University. He has contributed as a freelance writer to periodicals including the *Columbia Journalism Review*, worked as a research analyst in financial institutions in New York, Los Angeles, and London, and served as in-house counsel and program director at a nongovernmental organization at the United Nations promoting women's rights in developing countries.